Individual Rights
in the Corporation

Individual Rights in the Corporation

A Reader on Employee Rights

Edited by Alan F. Westin
and Stephan Salisbury

Pantheon Books, New York

LIBRARY OF CONGRESS CATALOGING IN PUBLICATION DATA
Main entry under title:
Individual rights in the corporation.
   Bibliography: p.
   Includes index.
   1. Labor laws and legislation—United States.
2. Employee rights—United States. I. Westin, Alan F.
II. Salisbury, Stephan.
KF3318.I5   323.4   79–1902
ISBN 0-394-50715-0

Design by Irva Mandelbaum

Manufactured in the United States of America

First Edition

Preface

This volume is the first in a series of books, monographs, and research reports developed by The Educational Fund for Individual Rights, Inc. The Fund is a nonprofit, tax-exempt foundation whose main activity is research, publishing, and educational work on individual rights of employees in business, government, and nonprofit organizations.

This reader about individual rights in the corporate setting was originally developed as a sourcebook for use at the First and Second National Seminars on Individual Rights in the Corporation, held in 1978 and 1979. The First Seminar was co-sponsored by *The Civil Liberties Review* and the Arthur Garfield Hays Civil Liberties Program of New York University Law School. (The *Review* was an independent magazine of analysis and commentary on civil liberties and civil rights issues published between 1973 and 1979 under the auspices of the American Civil Liberties Union Foundation.) The Second Seminar was —and subsequent seminars are—sponsored by The Educational Fund. Each of the seminars featured approximately 100 experts from business, law, government, public-interest groups, labor unions, and the social sciences discussing basic trends and examining concrete experiences of corporations and their employees in the areas of employee privacy, due process, free expression, participation, and corporate self-disclosure. The audiences for those seminars were executives from almost 200 major corporations, as well as representatives from government agencies, industry associations, law firms, unions, specialist groups, and academia.

Our plan is to use this volume for our seminars in 1980–1982 and also for the in-house seminars that the Fund conducts for individual organizations. Readers of this volume who are interested in being put on the mailing list to receive notices of the Fund's seminars and publications are warmly invited to write to the Fund at 475 Riverside Drive, New York, N.Y. 10027. We will be happy to see that you receive regular information about the Fund's work.

Many people aided the editors in the collection and preparation of these materials, and we are happy to acknowledge them here: Luceil

Sullivan, the Fund's Executive Director; Henry I. Kurtz, our Publication Director; Lawrence S. Blumberg, the Fund's Legal Counsel; our student research assistants, Al Feliu, Michael Edelman, Tom Korosec, Deborah McCoy, Neal Milch, Katherine Shields, Mark Thompson, Debra Anne Westin, Angela Sullivan, Anne Karanfilian, Ellen Saideman, and Robert Barad; Barbara Paulsen and Joan Cidron, who helped with manuscript preparation; and Hope Campbell for typing. For their vital help in supporting the creation of the national seminars, we are especially grateful to Norman Dorsen, Ira Glasser, and Aryeh Neier.

The seminars received financial grants from a number of corporations and foundations, and these contributions helped to pay for staff and preparation costs in assembling this collection. Our gratitude goes to:

Aetna Life and Casualty
Allied Chemical Co.
American Telephone and Telegraph
  Company
Avon Products
Bank of America
Cummins Engine Co.
Equifax
Exxon Corporation

Forbes Magazine
Fund for the Future, Inc.
Harcourt Brace Jovanovich
International Business
  Machines Corporation
McGraw-Hill Book Company,
  Inc.
Sentry Insurance
Xerox Corporation

Finally, these acknowledgments would not be complete without expressing our appreciation to the President of Public Interest, Public Relations, Margaret Booth, and her colleagues: Karen Berg, Katherine Gormley, Jim LeMonn, Frank Millspaugh, Siri Reckler, Cindy Rosenthal, and Nancy Stella. Their assistance in the planning and administration of the seminar program and its publications has been invaluable.

A. F. W.
S. S.

Contents

Introduction *by Alan F. Westin* xi

Part I. Liberty and Work: Some General Views of Employee Rights 1

Work in a New America *by Rosabeth Moss Kanter* 3

"Constitutionalizing" the Supercorporation *by Arthur Selwyn Miller* 10

Is an Employee Bill of Rights Needed? *by Donald L. Martin* 15

What Business Thinks about Employee Rights *by David W. Ewing* 21

Part II. Limiting Employer Prerogatives 43

Employment at Will v. Individual Freedom: On Limiting the Abusive Exercise of Employer Power *by Lawrence E. Blades* 45

Unjust Dismissal: Time for a Statute *by Clyde W. Summers* 55

Protection Against Unfair Dismissal *by Jack Stieber* 59

Part III. The Debate Over an Employee Bill of Rights 65

An Employee Bill of Rights—A Proposal *by David W. Ewing* 67

Company Constitutionalism? *by Staughton Lynd* 70

Civil Liberties in the Private Sector *by Ira Glasser* 76

The Myth of the "Oppressive Corporation" *by Max Ways* 79

Part IV. Free Expression on the Job 83

Loyalty—and the Whistle Blower *by Andrew Hacker* 85

Your Employees' Right to Blow the Whistle *by Kenneth D. Walters* 91

Whistle Blower: Dan Gellert, Airline Pilot 106

The Job Was Important, but Ethics Came First *by Lucinda Fleeson* 111

Sexual Harassment: Adrienne Tomkins, Stenographer 117

Unions and Sexual Harassment: AFSCME at Michigan State University *by Lin Farley* 122

vii

"Corporate Malice": *John Pirre* v. *Printing Developments, Inc.* 132

Organization Policy—Making Dissent Respectable and Productive *by Auren Uris* 135

Loyalty, Obedience, and the Role of the Employee *by Phillip I. Blumberg* 140

Speech in the Corporation *by Ralph Nader, Peter Petkas, and Kate Blackwell* 150

Free Speech and Arbitration: Implications for the Future *by David C. Palmer* 156

Part V. Privacy in the Workplace 175

Privacy in the Workplace *by Harriet Gorlin* 177

How Much Does the Boss Need to Know? *by Trudy Hayden* 193

Dilemmas Facing Occupational Health Surveillance *by Alan F. Westin* 200

Health and Privacy *by Anthony Mazzocchi* 203

Privacy in the Workplace Is an Important Benefit *by Robert Ellis Smith* 205

Medical Confidentiality in the Work Environment *by G. H. Collings, Jr., M.D.* 209

IBM's Guidelines to Employee Privacy: An Interview with Frank T. Cary 214

A Profile of Bank of America's Privacy Experience *by Alan F. Westin* 226

The Equitable Life Assurance Society Privacy Principles 244

The Problem of Employee Privacy Still Troubles Management *by Alan F. Westin* 245

State of New York Act to Amend the Labor Law 253

State of Maine Act to Permit an Employee to Review His Personnel File 255

The Privacy Commission Recommendations on Employee Access 257

A Businessman's View of the Privacy Commission's Employment Recommendations *by Allan H. Knautz* 275

Part VI. The Rights of Fair Procedure: Union and Nonunion 279

What Price Employment? Arbitration, the Constitution, and Personal Freedom *by Julius G. Getman* 281

Arbitration and the Constitution *by John E. Dunsford* 286

Arbitrators and Drugs *by Kenneth Jennings*   291

Resolving Personnel Problems in Nonunion Plants *by Maurice S. Trotta and Harry R. Gudenberg*   302

The View from the Ombudsman's Chair *by Frederica H. Dunn*   311

Making Unions Unnecessary: The Open-Door Policy *by Charles L. Hughes*   315

The Grievance Procedure in the Nonunion Setting: Caveat Employer *by Richard L. Epstein*   322

The Antiunion Grievance Ploy (from *Business Week*)   329

Part VII. The Right of Participation   333

Employee Participation in Corporate Decision Making *by Phillip I. Blumberg*   335

Worker Participation and Employee Rights: Some Necessary Links *by Paul Bernstein*   351

Worker Participation: Industrial Democracy or Union Power Enhancement? *by Herbert R. Northrup*   358

What Managers Think of Participative Leadership *by Larry E. Greiner*   365

Labor-Management Cooperation Today *by William L. Batt, Jr. and Edgar Weinberg*   377

The Case for Participatory Management *by Donald K. Conover*   389

Teaching an Old Dog Food New Tricks *by Richard E. Walton*   401

Part VIII. The Right to Information   413

Voluntary Disclosure: Someone Has to Jump into the Icy Water First *by A. W. Clausen*   415

Selections from the BankAmerica Disclosure Code   424

The Bank of America's Rocky Road to Responsibility *by Milton R. Moskowitz*   431

Bibliography   437

The Editors and Contributors   453

Index   459

Introduction

This reader is about a newly emerging issue: the individual rights of people who work in corporate employment, from production and clerical employees to professionals, middle managers, and executives. Basically, it involves the definition and observance of certain new rights to liberty and due process on the job and freedom from reprisals at work for the exercise of individual rights off the job.

While some of these questions began to surface in the corporate world as early as the late 1960s and 1970s, many observers both inside and outside the corporation believe these demands for new individual rights, and the struggle over whether and how to provide them, will reach their mature status in the 1980s. I believe they represent not only a central test for corporate managers in the next decade but also a test of American society's ability to reshape organizational operations in order to produce more liberating and effective settings for people at work in the post-industrial age.

Precisely because these are new and as yet unstructured issues, it is vital to open a reader such as this with some careful attention to definitions and a basic guide to the unfolding debate.

To understand what new rights of corporate employees are involved here, we need first to identify the current legal position of employer and employee in the private sector. Under American law, two clusters of legal principles define this relationship: one set defining employer prerogatives and the other set defining employee protections.

In terms of employer prerogatives, private employers enjoy very broad authority under American law to set personnel policies in their discretion. They are not limited directly by the individual-rights provisions of federal or state constitutions as interpreted by the courts, since those guarantees only apply to government actions. Thus private employers are, in general, entitled to set their own standards for selecting the most qualified employees from pools of available applicants; to require satisfactory work performance as a condition for continued employment; to set reasonable rules for behavior on the job; to assess performance and predict potential in making assignment and promotion decisions; to protect the employer's property from theft or damage by employees; to lay off employees when this is necessary for business reasons; or to fire employees who are found to be violating work rules or committing crimes on the job.

While it may be softened by humane personnel administration or an employer's responsiveness to worker concerns for respect and fair treatment, employment is fundamentally a relationship of superiors to subordinates. This applies from the assembly line or typing pool to the executive suite. The ultimate goal of personnel administration is to select employees and direct their talents and energies efficiently in order to accomplish the employer's goals. Personnel administration is also inescapably judgmental. There are always more candidates for good jobs or higher positions than there are openings, so that some persons must be denied opportunities while others are chosen. Some employees will be selected for bonuses, recognition, and prestige treatment while others will fail to "perform" well enough to win these rewards. Personnel administration must also deal with the fact that some people fit comfortably and happily into the jobs they occupy but others do not —whether because of personal and family problems, lack of fit between job and person, personality clashes with fellow employees or supervisors, or the objective nastiness of the job itself and how it is run.

Reflecting these aspects of private employment in America, the law does not guarantee anyone a right to work or to be retained in a job once hired. The general legal maximum remains that a private employer, unless limited by contract, labor-management agreement, or statute, is free to hire, administer, and fire any employee at will, for any reason or for no reason.

While these are the broad rights of corporate authority over employment, a century of demands and struggle over protection of employees from mistreatment or exploitation has also created a network of statutes that set important limits on these employer prerogatives in particular areas. Labor laws specify minimum wages and maximum hours, and also protect the right of employees to advocate joining and to join unions. Once there is a collective bargaining agreement in a business, a wide range of employee rights and procedural safeguards are usually set by the contract, enforced by grievance machinery and union representation, are subject to impartial arbitration, and can ultimately be enforced by government labor boards or the courts.

In addition, a wide variety of statutes have been enacted that give all employees rights to workmen's compensation, protect occupational safety and health, and safeguard pension rights. Federal and state legislation also forbid discrimination against employees in hiring, advancement, or discharge on the basis of race, nationality, religion, sex, age, and handicap, and in some jurisdictions, on the basis of sexual preference. These employee protection and equality statutes also forbid an employer to take punitive action against employees who complain to government regulatory agencies about alleged violations, or who complain about employer violations of other legal duties, as with statutes requiring employers to follow rules for environmental protection. Finally, courts under the common law can find that the disciplining or firing of an employee violates public policy in some aspect (such as firing an employee for going on jury duty or for testifying to a grand jury about an employer's conduct).

However, American law has stopped well short of those European democracies that mandate worker participation in certain management decisions, or which forbid "unfair" dismissals and create government tribunals to adjudicate the propriety of a contested discharge. Thus, the general situation is that unionized employees have substantial rights and procedural remedies, while both union and nonunion employees in the private sector have legal rights in particular dimensions of their work, such as safety, health, pensions, and equality.

The issues of individual rights for corporate employees and executives begin at just this boundary line. So far, five main topics have been grouped under this topic.

1. RIGHTS OF EXPRESSION AND DISSENT

While private employment has goals, policies and procedures, set by management, and employees are expected to follow those directions in loyal fashion, two countervailing interests are also present: (a) employees are not supposed to have to execute policies that are clearly illegal or unethical, and (b) most managements want to encourage the kinds of employee questioning and criticism that can bring to light important errors or misjudgments in management plans and policies that could otherwise be missed. The subjects of such employee dissent can involve the marketing of dangerous products, creation of safety and health hazards on the job, harming the health of local residents or polluting the environment, violating equality laws, paying bribes and kickbacks, or padding government contracts. Professional employees are particularly involved in conflicts over accounting principles, research standards, or similar conduct that may conflict with codes of professional ethics and responsibility.

What it is proper or improper for an employee to do in voicing dissent is affected by a variety of factors. These involve the level at which the employee is employed (assembly line worker, research chemist, vice president for sales); whether the conduct is clearly illegal or improper or is a matter on which people can differ and where management has the right to decide and bear responsibility for the consequences; whether the employee has used internal channels before raising the question with government agencies or going to the media and the public; and whether the company has provided clear standards of conduct and mechanisms for complaint to deal with such situations. Examples of corporate employees going public as "whistle-blowers" have been increasing significantly in the business world during the past decade, just as they have in government.

2. RIGHTS OF EMPLOYEE PRIVACY

While employers need to collect relevant personal information to make hiring decisions and to compile extensive personnel records to administer the business, recent public concerns over privacy and demands for personal autonomy have raised a new set of issues in the 1970s about employer information practices. Apart from those areas regulated as part of equality protections (e.g., not asking directly about race, religion, etc. or using race-biased personality tests or arrest records), what aspects of a prospective employee's life is it relevant and proper to explore, and through what techniques of data collection? Once an employee is hired, what should go into personnel records and who inside the company should see them? When should employees have the right to examine the information that is put in their files and used to make personnel decisions about them, and what procedures should there be to challenge the accuracy, completeness, or propriety of what is found there? Under what safeguards of notice and consent is personal information about an employee released to third parties outside the company? In addition, what kinds of on-the-job surveillance or interrogation during investigations are proper for employers to use (e.g., closed-circuit TV cameras or lie detectors) and when should an employer take off-the-job activities and associations into account in job-related actions (e.g., arrests for selling drugs from a home, or leadership by a nuclear engineer in anti-nuclear-power demonstrations)?

3. RIGHTS OF FAIR PROCEDURE AND DUE PROCESS

For the three-fourths of corporate employees not covered by the grievance machinery of unionized operations, complaint and appeal systems have traditionally been handled by line managers and the personnel department. Increasing concern has been raised by workers in surveys and by outside critics over the fairness and independence of such mechanisms, including the often-used "open door" concept of top management review. This has led recently to experiments by some companies with ombudsmen, employee advocates, inspectors general systems, and even outside umpires or arbitration to provide a final, disinterested appeal, and the question of just how to provide procedural fairness is now a topic of widespread discussion. Even where employees are covered by a collective bargaining contract, important issues have arisen involving union responsibility for pursuing the individual complaints of employees, and the scope of protection that arbitrators under such contracts should give to the exercise by employees of individual rights.

4. THE RIGHT OF PARTICIPATION

The idea of worker ownership of private enterprises, or even of worker participation in the German and Swedish model of employees on boards of directors, has not drawn wide support in the United States. Yet the problems of alienation and boredom on the job, the presence of inefficient and frustrating work procedures set by top management, and the desire of many employees to feel a sense of participation in the decisions that affect their daily work have given rise in the past decade to a variety of "participative management" and "quality of work life" experiments in the corporate world. Sometimes, these are organized within a particular work unit; sometimes they involve all employees in a plant or installation; and sometimes they may be used in a division or region of a national enterprise. While the types of programs vary (some have unions involved and others do not, some involve major delegations of management power and others do not, etc.), the core of this development is the alteration of decision-making processes so that individual employees at a wide variety of levels are consulted and share in making some corporate decisions.

5. THE RIGHT TO INFORMATION

Disclosure by elected and appointed public officials of what they are doing or planning to do is at the heart of both democratic government and the citizen's right to know in order to exercise the franchise intelligently. In the corporate world, there has long been legal recognition of the rights of boards of directors to know what management is doing or intends, and similar rights have been recognized for stockholders in the company and potential investors. Government regulatory agencies also require considerable disclosure to protect the public interest in the conduct of the industries that are overseen. Where there is a collective bargaining contract, unions have won the right to know certain facts about the conduct of the enterprise, in order to be able to negotiate effectively for workers.

By analogy to these situations, it is now being argued that employees also have a right to know more about the present and future conduct of the company in which they work than has been traditional for American managements to disclose to them. An example is the results of a company's own tests about the effects on exposed workers of various dangerous substances used in production, something that it has not been the practice of managements to disclose unless required to do so by occupational health reporting duties or in lawsuits alleging company liability for harm done by such uses. Several banks have recently developed voluntary "self-disclosure" codes that include employees among the groups that are given rights of access to previously withheld corporate information.

What are the forces and trends that are raising these issues of individual rights in the workplace? There seems to be no single cause or unifying movement, but rather the cumulative effects of more than half a dozen significant social and institutional trends over the past two decades. Here are some of the most important of these:

1. The growing sense among Americans that observance of individual rights and provision of fair procedures are "entitlements" in any large institutional setting, public or private, profit or nonprofit. Rosabeth Kanter of Yale University has noted, based on extensive attitudinal survey research, that there is a rising sense of expectation among American workers, professionals, and executives that more participative decision making and greater protection of individual rights must be built into the job if work is to be satisfying. This is not voiced in an *anti*-management or class warfare framework, but it is an idea that has been gathering coherence and momentum, and poses an immediate challenge for managements that want contented and productive employees.

2. The radiative effects of administering a decade of equal-opportunity and worker protection laws—EEO, federal protection of worker pensions (ERISA), federal health and safety legislation (OSHA), legal protection against sexual harassment by superiors, etc. The provision of rules and procedures to guarantee equitable practice in these areas has created general employee expectations of fair proce-

dure and rational decision making for other personnel practices.

3. The rising incidence of whistle-blowing by corporate employees and heavy legal liability for companies that fail to heed such warnings about unsafe products and illegal or unethical conduct. Juries have been awarding substantial damages in these cases, and judges have begun to enunciate important exceptions to the traditional notion that employees owe unswerving loyalty to management directives.

4. The absence of a meaningful and readily accessible mechanism for raising complaints to top management has been considered recently by courts in deciding whether to hold corporations liable for the acts of company executives, including middle management. As a result, long-dusty complaint procedures have been brought under company scrutiny, and the need for new systems is under wide consideration.

5. In the area of employee privacy, fundamental changes in national attitudes toward life styles, morality, dress, and political ideology have rendered obsolete the "white shirt" and "everyone always speaks for the company" rules that marked the 1950s and early '60s. Relaxation of conformity rules has been paralleled by well-documented concerns of employees and executives over the confidentiality of personnel information maintained by their employers, especially in the new computerized data systems widely used for personnel work, and with growing bodies of sensitive medical and health data, OSHA surveillance data, and similar information in company files. The recommendations of the U.S. Privacy Protection Study Commission in July of 1977, the passage of laws in six states giving private-sector employees the right to inspect their personnel files, and similar outside stimuli have also been important. Many large corporations are now installing new fair employee information practices, in an effort to show by voluntary reforms that federal regulatory laws are not necessary.

6. Responding to surveys showing that both confidence by the general public and corporate employees in business leadership and business ethics have dropped sharply during the past decade (paralleling post-Watergate distrust in government and other private institutions), some companies have developed new policies of corporate self-disclosure. These follow both the rationale and many of the standards used in freedom-of-information laws covering government agencies. Bank of America President A. W. Clausen explained his company's action in this area by saying that the most "powerful deterrent to wrongdoing is a code of disclosure" and "the surest way to invite suspicion is to withhold information from individuals or groups who believe they are seeking it for good reason." Clausen added that letting the company's own employees and executives know more than has been traditional

about company affairs was one strong motive for this new policy.

7. In the unionized sector, covering about a quarter of the corporate work force, labor arbitrators have become much more active during the past five years in examining company discharges to see if there was "just cause," and in applying Bill of Rights concepts of free expression, privacy, and due process to discharge and discipline activities. Serious writing by leaders in the law of arbitration now suggest that it is time for enactment of state and federal statutes to define protected civil liberties also for nonunion workers, and to limit the "employment at will" theory used by the courts where no unions are present.

These are some of the forces that seem to be driving the movement for greater individual rights for corporate employees. However, both in terms of which individual rights might be provided and how corporate managers should respond to the social and legal trends cited, several major ideological positions have been developing that deserve identification and have been represented in this reader.

First are those essentially advocating that American society should "constitutionalize" the basic relationships between employees and managers in corporate enterprise. Because of the size, wealth, and public impact of corporations, it is argued that they are really quasi-governments. As such, they should be held to the same standards of respect for liberty, equality, and due process rights for their employees as government employees are. This would mean that courts or regulatory agencies would apply civil liberties standards to the personnel actions of corporate officials, weighing the justifications of business employers just as is done today in government employment when issues of individual rights such as free speech, privacy, or due process are raised by employees. This "constitutionalizing" position is held by people such as Ralph Nader, Professor Arthur S. Miller, *Harvard Business Review* editor David Ewing, and others represented in this reader. Essentially, the "constitutionalizers" favor enactment of a code of individual rights for corporate employment, and final adjudication by government authorities. In addition, some commentators, such as Staughton Lynd in our reader, argue that only the power of a union representing employees or a pro-worker regulatory agency will translate declarations of employee rights into any kind of reality in the workplace.

At the opposite pole are defenders of current managerial authority against the threats of individual-rights restrictions, especially if incorporated through legal regulatory controls. They argue that there is no evidence of widespread and active employee agitation for these rights, nor is there evidence of major mistreatment of employees in areas such as privacy, dissent, or fair procedure. Creating *legal* rights will only lead to a flood of employee complaints, expensive and lengthy litigation, and further regulatory reporting duties. Since personnel decisions necessarily involve constant judgments about the creativity, talents, effectiveness, and adaptability of people, creating another body of vested rights will invite courts and regulatory agencies to act as super personnel boards, undercutting management authority and further hamstringing the efficiency of private enterprise. Those holding this view see the problems of productivity and responsiveness experienced by many civil service work forces as proof of what happens when managements are not free to manage effectively through use of discipline and discharge. Among those representing such views in this reader are Max Ways of *Fortune,* Professor Donald L. Martin, corporate executive Allen H. Knautz, and Professor Herbert R. Northrup.

The third major position is one that supports the definition and institutionalization of various individual employee rights through voluntary actions by managements, as part of sound human resources policies and good employee-manager communications. Many advocates of this view are executives from large innovative corporations that have pioneered in creating individual rights policies in recent years, or from leading business associations. But there are also academic and legal commentators who share the belief that voluntary action is to be preferred to legal regulation: to avoid further expanding the power of government over the private sector; to keep costs and bureaucracy at a minimum; and to recognize the great diversity of employment settings, occupations, industry conditions, and management styles, which makes general legislation difficult. Expressions of this view in the reader are the 1977 report of the Privacy Protection Study Commission, and selections by editor Auren Uris, IBM chairman Frank Cary, and author Charles L. Hughes.

While these are the three major positions found today on the general question of extending individual employee rights in the corporation, there can be modifications and overlaps depending on the specific individual rights question at issue. This is particularly true because the five topics we have identified are in different stages of ripeness for action, present some dramatically different alternative mechanisms for execution, and involve different degrees of intrusion into current management prerogative. New employee privacy policies, for example, probably have been or are presently being promulgated by a majority of the Fortune 500 corporations, and laws have already been enacted in six states dealing with employee rights of access to and confidentiality rules for personnel records. On the other hand, very few corporations have either ombudsmen or outside review mechanisms for handling nonunion employee complaints, and there is no drive at present to require such procedures by law. Similarly, employee participation mechanisms are still an interest of a minority of American companies, with no legislation on the horizon here. As for problems of dissent and whistle-blowing, the discussion of ways to institutionalize the protection of such expression within the organization is just beginning, though here the possibility of extending to interstate corporations the whistle-blower protections of the 1978 Federal Civil Service Reform Act has surfaced as one legal possibility, along with stricter judicial review of dismissals of employees for adhering to their legal and ethical standards in their jobs.

To return to the theme with which we opened this Introduction, the area of individual rights is still unfolding. Its exact definition, limitations, and mechanisms remain to be developed. Experience with innovative voluntary programs or legislative requirements remains to be assessed. What seems clear, and what this reader has been assembled to show, is that there are going to be central issues for the people who work in and who manage corporations, and for the larger American society that will ultimately have to decide how these issues should be treated.

Alan F. Westin

July 1979

I.

Liberty and Work:
Some General Views
of Employee Rights

Work in a New America

Rosabeth Moss Kanter

Two themes can be said to characterize the ambience of work in America in 1977. One can be called cultural or expressive: the concern for work as a source of self-respect and nonmaterial reward—challenge, growth, personal fulfillment, interesting and meaningful work, the opportunity to advance and accumulate, and the chance to lead a safe, healthy life. The other can be called political: the concern for individual rights and power, for a further extension of principles of equity and justice into the workplace and into the industrial order, for equality and participation both in their general symbolic manifestations and in the form of concrete legal rights. Neither theme denies the extent to which concerns about income and basic material security still dominate the lives of many Americans and propel them into long hours and second jobs. But even in recent years, when unemployment and inflation increased many people's basic economic worries and higher earnings were clearly the major reason job holders looked for another job (34 percent cited this), the themes were present as an undercurrent: 10.6 percent of job seekers wanted better working conditions, 9.8 percent wanted better advancement opportunities, and 9.3 percent wanted a job that would better utilize and develop their skills; no other reasons received as frequent mention.

A more educated work force—as ours has become—is simultaneously a more critical, questioning, and demanding work force, and a potentially more frustrated one if expectations are not met.

The past decades have witnessed an increase in public policy pronouncements directed toward rights at work, as well as in job-holder

Reprinted by permission of *Daedalus* Journal of the American Academy of Arts and Sciences, Boston, Massachusetts 107, no. 1. Winter 1978, *A New America.* Copyright © *Daedalus,* Winter 1978. Footnotes have been deleted.

expectations in this area. On both fronts the issue is the extension of basic civil rights assumed to be guaranteed by a democratic society into organizations which have operated without making all of them explicit —the creation of more "organizational civil rights." The concerns involve equity, on the one hand—fairness, justice, an even chance to obtain the position for which an individual worker is qualified; and discretion, on the other—greater employee control, a larger say in decisions, more power over work conditions.

Equal-employment opportunity and affirmative-action programs are only one instance of a tendency, throughout the twentieth century, for more and more governmental and judicial intervention in the internal practices and policies of employing organizations, on behalf of unorganized as well as unionized employees; and collective-bargaining rights have been extended to important groups of white-collar workers, such as public employees. Since the Civil Rights Act of 1964, and despite the failure of the Equal Rights Amendment to pass in the requisite number of states by the time of this writing, there have been a growing number of state antidiscriminatory statutes and agencies. In 1976, Congress passed a bill dealing with federally funded public works programs that imposed the first criminal penalties for failure to comply with anti-job-bias provisions. Other individual employee rights, such as jury service without employer retaliation, were also guaranteed by new statutes.

Thus, from the perspective of policy makers, the public interest is seen to require a scrutiny of employment practices and an extension of individual rights, because of the centrality of organizations as producers of jobs as well as of products—jobs that have important individual and social consequences. Philip Selznick phrased the legal rationale this way:

> In recent years we have seen a transition from preoccupation with free-dom *of* association to a concern for freedom *in* associations. This renewed awareness stems from a realization that the private organization can be more oppressive than the state. The loss of a job, or the right to pursue a profession, or the opportunity to continue one's education, may be far more hurtful than a term in jail. When these deprivations are inflicted arbitrarily, and there is no recourse, a gap in the legal order exists. We become more sensitive to that gap when the decisions are made by organizations that seem large, powerful, and impersonal, and by men who have the look of officialdom.

In this perspective, then, the women's issue is one example of the pressure for development of appropriate concepts of individual rights inside workplaces as well as structures that maximize the exercise of these rights.

Yankelovich labeled the worker demands that parallel such governmental attention a "psychology of entitlement," which leads to the creation of new social rights as the boundary between the public and private sectors becomes increasingly fuzzy. For example, the college students he studied in 1973 believed, in these proportions, that they were entitled to as a social right: "participation in decisions that affect one's own work" (56 percent), "a secure retirement" (37 percent), "the right to work" (27 percent), "a minimum income" (26 percent), and "an interesting job" (17 percent). Certainly militant women's-rights organizations, such as the coalition of over twenty of them led by the National Women's Political Caucus that lobbied President Carter to offer more jobs for women, are not content with the mere appearance of greater opportunity for women; they expect concrete results—so many people in so many jobs. And, the argument runs, if organizations do not provide both positions and access to opportunity, they should be forced to do so.

Union leaders are also more likely than management to favor an increase in rights—in worker power and control—as a method for improving employee attitudes, although unions have not tended to make these part of their platforms (despite such well-publicized experiments as the job-enrichment innovation at Harman Industries conducted by management and the UAW). However, when asked, some union leaders do support the issues. In much higher proportions than managers, union officials in one recent survey stressed such issues as greater job security, improving working conditions, protecting workers from arbitrary and unfair treatment, better treatment by supervisors, providing greater opportunities for advancement, and giving workers more autonomy on the job. From the other side, some union members would like more of some of these things from the union itself; between 1969 and 1973 complaints about union democracy and leadership on the Institute for Social Research survey doubled.

Among social scientists concerned with work, there is a great deal of interest in the extension of worker rights and justice in the workplace in the form of participation. A rather old idea, which began with "human relations in industry" studies in the late 1920s, is beginning to take new form: the idea that workers are more satisfied (and perhaps, though not necessarily, more productive) if they have a chance to participate in the decisions affecting them. Until recently, unlike the European experience, "participatory democracy" in American organizations tended to be confined both in scope and in the people it affected.

It often meant a human-relations emphasis on more communication from management and more chance for employees to discuss impending changes or tinker with their details; even then it was often restricted to upper white-collar ranks. But "participation" today, as expressed by the National Quality of Work Center in Washington or the Work in America Institute, increasingly means structural support for a larger degree of worker control. And the request implies such major organizational change as flattening the hierarchy, generating self-directed work teams, and providing employees with more job-related information necessary to make decisions.

In short, such proposals (few are as yet implemented in many organizations) encompass a variety of basic "organizational civil rights" —the extension of such legal safeguards as due process, free speech, and open access to information into the workplace. Making such proposals particularly significant is the fact that only about one in five workers in the labor force is a union member, and only about one in nine is covered by a major collective bargaining agreement (those covering one thousand or more workers). Whether collective bargaining will extend further as the major vehicles for power, or whether organizations will ensure more rights on an individual basis (or both), remains to be seen. Access to information is particularly interesting as a right, for a higher managerial or professional monopoly on information is one of the ways workers and even middle managers or paraprofessionals are disenfranchised and disempowered. Thus, the push for equal-employment opportunity on the part of minorities and women may work not only to ensure equity but also to make work systems more transparent. As employment records are subpoenaed and data are collected for court cases, as employment practices are scrutinized for fairness by outside agencies in compliance reviews, then the stage is set for people inside the organization also legitimately to demand and receive more information.

The expectation of more rights in the workplace is given fuel by those social science studies that find the degree of power and control over one's work a major predictor of a range of personal outcomes. These studies are significant for several reasons. First, the evidence has been accumulating with only rare contradictions. Second, and more important, sociologists and psychologists are employed as management consultants and as witnesses in legislative hearings; the 1972 and 1976 Senate Labor Committee hearings called on a large number of social scientists. Third, the control theme is not only a leftist issue; it shows up in studies of job satisfaction, alienation, mental health, political attitudes, and family relations. For example, men low in job autonomy were found to be more severe and hostile toward their sons, confirming a "displacement of frustration" hypothesis. Blue-collar workers in low-control jobs (with limited participation and self-direction) were less democratic in their politics and less creative in their leisure compared with those in similar jobs at the same pay levels but with more control at work. Two of the best predictors of work alienation, in another series of studies, were an organizational setting that provided little discretion in pace and scheduling, and a blocked and chaotic (i.e., out-of-control) career. In still another survey of over three thousand male workers in all occupations, alienation was more directly affected by the degree of occupational self-direction than by ownership or hierarchial position.

My own investigations of work behavior in a large industrial firm lend confirmation to the notion that powerlessness among administrative and managerial personnel (accountability without discretion and with little capacity to independently mobilize resources) was associated with rigid, controlling, rules-minded, and coercive behavior. Indeed, Melvin Seeman, in a major review of research on alienation, pointed out that most reports of increasing self-estrangement at work and desire for meaningful work fail to distinguish between discontent stemming from the absence of intrinsic fulfillment in work and that derived from lack of control at work. He argued that control aspirations seem to be involved in most major outbursts, such as the strikes at Lordstown and at Luton in France.

All such studies provide backup, then, for rights-enhancing policy scrutiny such as the Senate hearings. What they do not do, however, is document the extent of the problem.

Even though it is possible to identify an overarching sense of entitlement and a rights-extension theme, these issues also have complications and problems that are not expressed in the same way, or with equal force, by all segments of the population. First, and most importantly, what happens when rights conflict, or when one group feels its job rights are being violated by another's? The interpretation of antidiscrimination statutes and decisions to involve compensation for past discrimination has come into conflict, in recent years, with other hard-won rights, such as seniority; but a 1977 Supreme Court decision struck a blow against retroactive seniority, perhaps beginning the reversal of a trend toward attempting to remedy the effects of past as well as present sex or race discrimination. Conflict can also center around such special privileges as preference for war veterans in hiring, struck down in Massachusetts in 1976. So even though the rights of some groups have been advancing, other groups have been complaining.

Second, power and participation themes have been expressed most

vociferously by college students, by people in high-prestige occupations, and by educated young workers. But even here it is not clear how
to interpret the data: as indicating a concern for greater job security by
increased "entitlement" in the jobs? for less rules-bound, more flexible
work conditions? for more voice in management and organizational
decisions? or for more autonomy and self-direction? The available evidence points to the first two, at least for the bulk of the working
population, rather than the latter two. In this sense, "rights" might
mean to most people (other than the educated elite) the traditional
bread-and-butter issues of protection from arbitrary job or income loss
for which unions have been fighting since their beginnings.

Autonomy and self-direction, though stressed by many social-science
professionals, have not yet emerged as high on average workers' preference orderings. Studies of occupational prestige, for example, have
found relatively low-autonomy jobs inside organizations accorded more
prestige than jobs with comparable pay that are self-directed but may
also involve risk—for example, office-machine operations and book-
keepers ranking higher than small independent farmers, and assembly-
line workers higher than taxi drivers. This is compatible with the 1969
ISR Survey of Working Conditions, in which advancement opportunity
and loose rather than tightly controlled supervision correlated most
strongly with job satisfaction, whereas autonomy and "enriching" demands ranked seventh and eighth in terms of ability to predict job
satisfaction. Anecdotal, but well-publicized, evidence also comes from
the month-long visit of six American auto workers to the innovative
Saab-Scania plant in Sweden; these workers were indifferent or negative
to the worker participation plan and the self-directed assembly-team
arrangements. Of course, as commentators have pointed out ever since
"participatory democracy" was first suggested as a work option, participation is very time-consuming and unlikely to be appealing to people
who do not see the direct benefits to them or who are not very committed to their jobs in the first place.

Finally, certain organizational innovations with employee rights and
power implications may be opposed by unions if introduced by management, particularly if there is the suspicion that the move is antiunion
or another way to increase productivity without increasing pay. There
is also no clear-cut agreement, even among social scientists promoting
participation or autonomy-enhancing schemes about the best ways to
do this. As for affirmative-action and equal-employment opportunity
programs, there is little consensus about specific steps to take or
changes to make in work conditions other than hiring and promoting
more members of any discriminated-against groups. Thus, the rights

and power issue remains fuzzier and more controversial than matters such as pay, fringe benefits, or flexible work hours.

However, one conclusion that can be drawn is that the political issues of rights and power continue to be involved in American jobs in the 1970s. As rights are extended, contention (such as grievance filing or litigation) also increases. But we are witnessing a predominantly individual phenomenon: a change in job holders' views of what they are entitled to, rather than an increase in strident demands or organized activism.

"Constitutionalizing" the Supercorporation

Arthur Selwyn Miller

If the sovereign state of Delaware is subject to the limitations of the Fourteenth Amendment's due process clause, and thus cannot deprive any person of life, liberty, or property without due process of law, and if it further must adhere to the same amendment's principle that it must give "equal protection of the laws" to all persons within its jurisdiction, then why should not the "corporate state" of DuPont or General Motors or United States Steel be similarly limited? By applying the Constitution to such enterprises—by "constitutionalizing" the super-corporation—might it not be possible to retain some of the benefits flowing from private ownership of business while simultaneously attaining a higher degree of fairness in the social order? A colorable case can be made for such a proposition. Requiring that the supercorporation, which we have defined to include the labor unions, follow due process standards may help maintain a wall of separation between the state and the corporation. Legislation would probably tend to crumble that wall, simply because it has to be broader and more all encompassing. If our hypothesis that the corporate state (with the state as group-person) is being created has validity, the imposition of accountability on the corporations through legislation would further that development, whereas the more limited, narrowly imposed judicial activity would not. More action by the courts might even slow down the seemingly ineluctable movement of events toward American corporativism simply because it could help to preserve the distinction between public and private.

To do so, however, requires a major constitutional leap—the concept

Pages 182 to 187 taken from *The Modern Corporate State* by Arthur Selwyn Miller and used with the permission of the publisher, Greenwood Press, Inc., Westport, Connecticut. Footnotes have been deleted.

10

of "state" or "governmental" action under the Constitution would have to be rewritten (in effect) by the Supreme Court. Not only would the concept of private governance have to be recognized, but a distinction would have to be drawn between official and private government. The first may be easier than the second, for if private governments are made subject to some of the Constitution's provisions, it would be quite difficult to differentiate them in fact from public governance. But the ingenuity of lawyers and judges should be up to the task.

Could the concept of state or governmental action be reinterpreted so as to include the enormous, overmighty economic entities called supercorporations? The short answer is yes; in fact, it already has been in at least two cases (as well as a number of analogous decisions). Since at least 1883, and doubtless before, even though the case was never squarely presented to the Supreme Court, the Constitution has been said to run against governments only. The seminal decision came in the *Civil Rights Cases* (1883), which effectively nullified post–Civil War legislation to enhance the status of Negroes. Said the Court: "It is state action of a particular character that is prohibited. Individual invasion of individual rights is not the subject-matter of the [Fourteenth] Amendment." Therefore, Congress had no power to enact legislation banning racial discrimination by innkeepers and owners of other places serving the public. Since that time the notion of what constitutes "state action" has been progressively broadened. This is not the place to trace the development in detail; however, some highlights may be given.

The *Civil Rights Cases* antedated recognition by the Supreme Court that the corporation is a person within the terms of the Fourteenth Amendment and thus is entitled to its protections. That came in 1886 in what is surely one of the most important decisions in American constitutional history. The essential question, yet to be fully acknowledged by the Court, is whether a "corporate person" that has constitutional protections also has duties to adhere to the norms of the fundamental law. This is not to ask whether the natural person, the human being, has such duties, but whether the Court will recognize the transparency of the fiction that equates General Motors with an individual. That it should is the thrust of the argument here; and that it is can be seen from a series of Court decisions that find it edging ever closer to acceptance of the idea that giant corporations are private governments.

The first breakthrough into the realm of ostensibly private organizations being held to constitutional norms is a series of cases dealing with racial discrimination in voting in Democratic primary elections. After first holding that a political party could not be subjected to the Constitution, the Supreme Court in 1944 held in the landmark case of *Smith* v. *Allwright* that Negroes had a constitutional right to vote in primary elections. Immediately, efforts at systematic and sophisticated evasion of that decree were developed; for example, whites established a small group that designated candidates for the Democratic primary and then permitted Negroes to vote in the primary. But that scheme was negated in 1953 when in *Terry* v. *Adams* the Court held that the Jaybird Party, which had been set up to evade the *Smith* v. *Allwright* decision, could not be foreclosed to Negro voting. Political parties, ostensibly private, had become so public-ized that they were held to be within the ambit of the state action concept. Their function was so fundamental, so basic to the workings of the American governmental system that the law, as Justice Frankfurter once said, would reach sophisticated as well as simple-minded schemes of avoidance. For present purposes, a "private," "voluntary" association has been "constitutionalized."

Of more direct importance is a pair of decisions a generation apart, *Marsh* v. *Alabama* (1946) and *Amalgamated Food Employees Union* v. *Logan Valley Plaza, Inc.* (1968), both of which enforced the Constitution against business corporations. In the *Marsh* case, a member of a religious sect was arrested for trespassing on the private property of the Gulf Shipbuilding Company, which wholly owned the town of Chickasaw, Alabama. Chickasaw, a suburb of Mobile, looked like a typical American town. Mrs. Marsh wished to proselytize for her religion in the residential section of the town. Warned off by officials, she refused to leave, was arrested and convicted for trespass. But she argued that her right to freedom of religion, protected by the First Amendment, was violated by the conviction. Even though private property, she said, Chickasaw should be treated as any other American town; if she could constitutionally prospect for converts elsewhere, then she should be permitted to do so there. A majority of the Court agreed. For the first time in American constitutional history, a corporation had been limited by a specific constitutional provision.

That, of course, is freedom of religion and not due process of law. Nonetheless, the decision rests as a time bomb ticking away in the Court reports ready for use. That that time may be approaching is a possible conclusion from the spate of recent civil-rights decisions relating to sit-ins in restaurants and other places of accommodation. In those cases the Court all but erased the state action concept, this time to find that privately owned places of business were so protected by state law and custom that they should be considered within the broad reach of governmental action. Again, the reasoning was not on "due process of law"; rather, it was first on state action and then on finding an invidious discrimination by businesses holding themselves out to serve the public.

The signal from the Supreme Court helped to trigger so much social pressure that by 1964 Congress passed the Civil Rights Act. It was promptly upheld by the Court. Technically, that act (and the cases validating the public accommodations section) did not reverse the ancient holding in the *Civil Rights Cases* of 1883, for the act applies only to businesses within the reach of the power of Congress to regulate interstate commerce. But what businesses are in interstate commerce has been so broadly and loosely interpreted by the Supreme Court that almost any organization—restaurant, motel, hotel, etc.—that serves the public and that has even a tenuous tie with commerce (by way of customers, food served, etc.) is within the reach of the act. In effect, then, if not in theory, the *Civil Rights Cases* of 1883 have been overruled; by a combination of political action and judicial approbation, the Constitution now applies to private businesses—at least insofar as Negro rights are concerned. Accountability—in law, although perhaps not in societal acceptance—had come to the corporation.

Other provisions of the Civil Rights Act apply to employment by businesses in interstate commerce, and the nondiscrimination clause has been a part of federal contracts for almost four decades. Here again political action is forcing constitutional norms on private businesses. "State action," long considered to be a barrier, was neatly sidestepped by using congressional power to regulate in commercial affairs.

Finally, the 1968 decision in the *Logan Valley Plaza* case held once again that a private company was subject to the First Amendment— this time the freedom of speech provision was at issue. Members of a labor union were arrested for picketing on the property of a shopping center. Their conviction for trespass was reversed by the Supreme Court, with the majority of justices relying on the 1946 decision in *Marsh* v. *Alabama*. The *Marsh* time bomb had exploded—not entirely, to be sure, but enough to indicate that the 1946 decision was no mere one-shot aberration.

Some other judicial decisions exist, but none that call the corporation sufficiently like a government to bring the Constitution into play. In a few state courts, notably Kansas and California, labor unions at times have been held subject to constitutional limitations when they had closed-shop agreements. And there are scattered statements in some Supreme Court decisions to the same effect. Perhaps the other outstanding decision was one in which that Court assumed that the Constitution would apply to a private company (in this instance, a streetcar line), but held on the merits that it had not violated rights of riders who had complained about music, news, and commercials being piped through the streetcars to "captive" audiences.

It should not be inferred that corporate "constitutionalization" has gone very far or has even been recognized as valid by many commentators. But the concept is far from dead, as the foregoing discussion reveals, even though it has more potential than actuality. However, it is an idea whose time has come, and one need not be thought overly rash to predict that this—and surely the next—generation of constitutional lawyers will increasingly be concerned with private governments. Corporate due process, within a broadly defined corporate community, will be central to that concern. Individuals directly involved with the supercorporation and who are subjected to some type of corporate sanction—loss of a franchise, failure to be accorded fair treatment in personnel policies, arbitrary action of any type—will, it seems likely, seek to invoke constitutional precepts. Possibly some plaintiff will even get a court to agree that he has a right to a decent environment—to be free from pollution—and get relief from what has become the newest American commonplace: the rapid "deprovement" of the planet.

The trend toward constitutionalization of the corporation has, however, been halted, at least temporarily, by some more recent Supreme Court decisions. Although these decisions do not overrule *Marsh* and *Logan Valley,* nevertheless they have not expanded the application of the Constitution to corporations. In fact, in the most recent, *Jackson* v. *Metropolitan Edison Co.,* the Court expressly held that a public utility was not within the ambit of the state-action concept and hence could not be held amenable to due process standards. The case involved termination of a utility's service to a customer without notice and without a hearing. The lower courts had held that a hearing ("procedural due process") was required, but the Supreme Court reversed. Some other recent decisions are of the same tenor.

Nevertheless, there are no solid reasons for not making the supercorporations amenable to the Constitution. Certainly their power overshadows even (public) government itself in many instances. Nothing quite like the corporate giant has been known in human history. The growth of the living Constitution could—in my mind, should—be in that direction. That document should reach *all* instruments of American governance, not merely those historically recognized. Eventually even the Supreme Court will perceive that need.

Is an Employee Bill of Rights Needed?

Donald L. Martin

The perception of the corporation as an industrial form of government in which management plays the role of the governor and labor the role of the governed has been particularly popular since the end of World War II. "Industrial democracy" has been the slogan of the labor movement in the industrial relations community. This analogy has recently given rise to demands for an "Employee Bill of Rights." Such a bill would guarantee the worker the same *due process* that the Constitution guarantees the citizen. It would protect the worker from the arbitrary and inequitable exercise of managerial discretion.

WHERE THE INDUSTRIAL DEMOCRACY ANALOGY FALTERS

But the industrial democracy analogy surely must be false. Two important considerations obviate it. First, a crucial distinction between government at any level and private economic organization, corporate or otherwise, is the right entrusted to government to exercise legitimate and reasonable force in its relations with its citizens. Second, the cost to a citizen of switching affiliation between governments is far greater than the cost to an employee of switching affiliations between firms. Since governments will surely violate public trust through their police powers, and since the costs to citizens of changing leaders or residences are relatively high, citizens will seek institutions to insulate themselves

From *The Attack on Corporate America,* edited by M. Bruce Johnson. Copyright © 1978 by the Law & Economics Center, University of Miami School of Law. Used with permission of McGraw-Hill Book Co.

from the arbitrary and exploitative use of such powers by their elected and appointed representatives. These institutions include the first ten amendments to the United States Constitution (the Bill of Rights) and the Fourteenth Amendment (guaranteeing due process).

THE PROBLEM OF THE MONOPSONISTIC LABOR MARKET

Something close to an analogous use of exploitative power in the private sector occurs in the world of monopsonistic labor markets. In those labor markets, would-be employees have few, if any, alternative job opportunities, either because of an absence of immediate competitive employers or because of the presence of relatively high costs of moving to available job alternatives in other markets. With few or no job alternatives, workers are more likely to be the unwilling subjects of employer prejudice, oppression, and personal discretion than if labor market competition prevails.

No one would claim that the American economy is completely free of monopsony power. There is not a shred of evidence, on the other hand, that such power exists in the large American corporation of today. Indeed, there is impressive evidence to suggest that monopsony is not likely to be found in large, private corporations. Robert Bunting's examination of labor market concentration throughout the United States among large firms, for example, finds that employment concentration (measured by the fraction of total employees in a geographic area who are employed by the largest reporting firm in that area) is related inversely to labor market size, while firm size is correlated positively with labor market size.

It is well known that monopsonistic powers reside in the collusive owners of professional sports teams, precisely because these powers are exempt from antitrust laws in the United States. Professional sports firms, however, do not number among the large corporations at which "Employee Bill of Rights" proposals are directed.

Interestingly, monopsonistic power in the labor market may be a significant factor at the local government level. Evidence of monopsony exists in such fields as public education, fire and police protection, and nursing.

THE NATURE OF EMPLOYER-EMPLOYEE AGREEMENTS

The Constitution of the United States does not extend the Bill of Rights and the due process clause of the Fourteenth Amendment to the private sector unless agents of the latter are performing public functions (*Marsh* v. *State of Alabama,* 66 S. Ct. 276 [1946]). Instead of interpreting this limitation as an oversight of the founding fathers, the preceding discussion suggests that the distinctive treatment accorded governments reflects the conscious belief that market processes, more than political processes, yield a degree of protection to their participants that is closer to levels that those participants actually desire. It also suggests that this inherent difference justifies the institutionalization of civil liberties in one form of activity (political) and not in the other form (market).

This interpretation is consistent with the repeated refusal of the United States Supreme Court to interfere with the rights of employers and employees (corporate or otherwise) to make mutually agreeable arrangements concerning the exercise of civil liberties (otherwise protected under the Constitution) on the job or in connection with job-related activities. (The obvious legislative exceptions to this generalization are the Wagner Act of 1935 and the Taft-Hartley Act of 1947. These acts proscribe the free speech rights of employers with regard to their possible influence over union elections on their own property, while allowing labor to use that same property for similar purposes.)

In the absence of monopsonistic power, the substantive content of an employer-employee relationship is the result of explicit and implicit bargaining that leaves both parties better off than they would be if they had not entered into the relationship. That both are better off follows because each is free to end the employment relationship at will—unless, of course, contractual relationships specify otherwise. Americans have demonstrated at an impressive rate a willingness to leave current employment for better pecuniary and nonpecuniary alternatives. During nonrecessionary periods, employee resignations contribute significantly to turnover statistics. In an uncertain world, the workers who resign generate valuable information about all terms and conditions under which firms and would-be employees can reach agreement.

THE COSTS OF WORKPLACE CIVIL LIBERTIES

If information about each party to employment and information about potential and actual performance are costly, both firms *and* employees seek ways to economize. Indeed, the functions of a firm, from the viewpoint of employees, are to screen job applicants and to monitor on-the-job activities. A firm's final output is often a result of the joint efforts of workers rather than a result of the sum of the workers' separate efforts. This jointness of production makes individual effort difficult to measure, and on-the-job shirking becomes relatively inexpensive for any given employee. The reason is precisely that all employees must share the cost of one employee's "goldbricking." As a consequence, shirking, if done excessively, threatens the earning opportunities of other workers. Other white-collar crimes, such as pilfering finished products or raw materials, have similar consequences.

To protect themselves from these threats, workers use the firm as a monitoring agent, implicitly authorizing it to direct work, manage tools, observe work practices and other on-the-job employee activities, and discipline transgressors. If employers function efficiently, the earnings of workers will be higher than if the monitoring function were not provided.

Efficient *employer* activities, however, may appear to others, including some employees, to be flagrant violations of personal privacy from the perspective of the First, Fourth, Fifth, and Ninth Amendments to the Constitution. These employer activities, on the contrary, are the result of implied agreements between employers and employees, consummated by demand and supply forces in the labor market. The reduction in personal liberty that workers sustain in a firm has a smaller value for them, at the margin, than the increase in earning power that results. Thus, limitations on personal liberty in a firm, unlike such limitations in governments, are not manifestations of tyranny; they are, instead, the product of a mutually preferred arrangement.

It should not be surprising that higher-paying firms and firms entrusting more valuable decision-making responsibility to some employees would invest relatively more resources than would other firms in gathering potentially revealing information about the qualifications of prospective employees and about the actions of existing employees. Since the larger a firm is, by asset size or by employee number, the more likely it is to be a corporation, it should also not be surprising that corporations are among the firms that devote relatively large amounts of resources to gathering information of a personal nature about employees.

Prohibiting the gathering of such information by superimposing an "Employee Bill of Rights" on the employment relationship has the effect of penalizing a specific group of employees. This group is composed of those persons who cannot otherwise compete successfully for positions of responsibility, trust, or loyalty because the high cost of information makes it unprofitable for them to distinguish themselves from other workers without desirable job characteristics. Thus, federal protection of the civil liberties of employees in the marketplace may actually harm those who wish to waive such rights as a less expensive way of competing.

Under an "Employee Bill of Rights" the process of searching for new employees and the process of managing existing employees are relatively more costly for an employer. This greater cost will be reflected not only in personnel policy but also in the cost of producing final outputs and in the prices consumers pay for them. An effect of an "Employee Bill of Rights" would be limited dimensions on which employees may compete with each other. Although there are precedents for such limitations (for example, federal minimum wage laws), it is important to recognize that this kind of protection may have unintended effects on the welfare of large numbers of employees. The anticompetitive effects of institutionalizing due process and civil liberties have long been recognized by trade unions. These effects constitute an important reason for the interest unions have in formalizing the procedures employers use in hiring, firing, promoting, demoting, rewarding, and penalizing union employees. It is false to argue, nevertheless, that an absence of formal procedures and rules in nonunionized firms is evidence that workers are at the mercy of unfettered employers, or that workers are more likely to be exploited if they are located in corporations rather than in noncorporate forms of organization.

Even the most powerful corporations must go to an effectively competitive labor market for their personnel. Prospective employees see arbitrary and oppressive personnel policies as relatively unattractive working conditions requiring compensation of pecuniary and nonpecuniary differentials over and above what they would receive from alternative employments. Those workers who want more certainty in the exercise of civil liberties pay for that certainty by forgoing these compensating differentials. This reasoning suggests that the degree of desired democracy in the labor market is amenable to the same forces that determine wages and working conditions. There is neither evidence nor persuasive arguments that suggest that workers in large corporations somehow have been excluded from the process that determines the degree of democracy they want.

What Business Thinks about Employee Rights

David W. Ewing

Of all the disturbing trends and ideas of the past fifteen years, none has caused more concern to businessmen than a recent challenge to management prerogatives. Here and there, judges and attorneys as well as managers and other employees have been questioning the oldest management tradition: that an employee owes unquestioning loyalty and obedience to his or her employer.

Earlier in this century management prerogatives were questioned and curbed by the rise of unions and collective bargaining. But the new thinking goes further than the union challenge. That is why it agitates so many management people, especially senior executives. The proposition advanced now is that any employee, whether a union member or not, whether a manager or a worker paid by the hour, can exercise certain freedoms from management control without risking his or her job, security, and chances for advancement. Although the freedoms are not listed in any official agenda or legislative proposal, they are generally considered to range from "whistle blowing" and privacy to freedom of choice of outside activities and conscientious objection to unethical orders.

The traditional rule, reiterated many times by the courts, has been that an employee can object to a company policy at any time but can also be fired for doing so. In other words, he has no "right to a job." This rule is rooted in centuries of custom and Western legal precedent concerning the master-servant relationship.

In a *Harvard Business Review* survey of subscribers' attitudes toward the emerging philosophy made in 1971, respondents supported it with surprising strength. However, that survey took place before a series of traumatic events—a worldwide recession, climbing unemployment, serious financial reverses for many corporations, the end of the Vietnam war, Watergate, and the corporate payoff scandals. After this period of upheaval the mood of the country generally became more conservative, and even on college campuses a reaction against activism seemed to settle in. It appeared to many people that such changes would put an end to talk about "constitutionalism," or established basic rights for employees, in business.

This article reports on a new survey of business people's attitudes toward employee rights. In February 1977 the *Harvard Business Review* mailed lengthy questionnaires to a random sample of about 7,000 of its subscribers. Usable responses came from nearly 2,000 of them, a return of 28 percent (see Exhibit I). The highlights of the findings, which will be reported in detail later in this article, are:

• Throughout industry there seems to be a steady broadening of support for methods of assuring "due process" to employees who feel they have been wronged by management.

• Among both top executives and lower management people there is increasing willingness to hear employees speak out on controversial issues.

• Strong majorities of subscribers favor advances in the right of privacy for employees.

• A majority of *Harvard Business Review* subscribers are well ahead of the courts in favoring protection for dissident employees, including "whistle blowers."

• While corporate constitutionalism draws businessmen with its heat, it frightens them with its flames. Respondents fear that it can be costly to customers and, to a lesser extent, stockholders. Moreover, in the long run they worry more about threats to the social and economic order than about the supression of individualism.

Exhibit I: Profile of Respondents (7,000 questionnaires mailed; 1,958 returned. Response: 28%)

Management level

Top executive (director, owner, chief executive, president; partner, vice president, etc.)	36%
Middle management (division head, department manager, functional director, assistant to the president, etc.)	36
Lower management (assistant department manager, supervisor, salesman, accountant, etc.)	20

Nonmanagement (lawyers, teachers, government officials,
retired executives, etc.)   7%

Age

Under 30	12%
30–39	38
40–49	28
50–59	17
60 or over	4

Region

New England	11%
Middle Atlantic	19
Midwest	28
Southeast	11
South Central	10
Mountain	5
Far West	15

Function

Accounting	6%
Engineering, R&D	7
Finance	9
General management	40
Marketing	13
Personal or labor relations	7
Production	4
Public relations	1
Other	12

Company
Kind of business

Manufacturing consumer goods	14%
Manufacturing industrial goods	23
Advertising, media publishing	4
Banking, investment, insurance	10
Construction, mining, oil	5
Defense or space industry	2
Education, social services	7
Government	7
Management consulting	6

Exhibit I - *Continued*

Retail or wholesale trade	6%
Personal consumer service	3
Transportation, public utility	5
Other	6

Size by number of employees

1–49	13%
50–99	5
100–249	9
250–499	8
500–999	9
1,000–4,999	20
5,000–9,999	8
10,000–19,999	6
20,000 or more	21

Size compared to other companies in industry

One of the largest	42%
Larger than most	24
About average	20
Smaller than most	11
One of the smallest	3

Many people who favor more rights and freedoms for employees have problems with the question of enforcement. How can the person who exercises such a right be protected against retaliation from arbitrary and unethical bosses? For example, the *Harvard Business Review* questionnaire invites comment on the case of an employee who criticizes a company policy. One respondent, a management information systems director, favors a policy of openness to such criticism but adds: "I see no way to legally prevent the man's firing if that is what his boss wants. If one charge is not legal ground for termination, another will be concocted."

The situation is a familiar one. It was dramatized a few years ago by the case of A. Ernest Fitzgerald, an outspoken Pentagon official who revealed the Air Force's attempt to cover up cost overruns on the C5A, a giant cargo plane being built at the time. When Fitzgerald's seniors saw they could not dismiss him outright, for political and legal reasons, they endeavored to force him to resign. They subjected him, said Senator William Proxmire, "to a campaign of abuse and harassment that boggles the mind." In fact, with trumped-up charges and embarrassing assignments, they managed to perforate his ego more than Bonnie and Clyde in the final frame.

Because of the possibility of such retaliation, methods of due process take on great importance. They are the means by which an employee can seek relief when he is punished for exercising a right. The abusive boss may be reprimanded or fired, the employee may be allowed to transfer to another department, or other measures of restitution can be used.

In both the 1971 and 1977 *Harvard Business Review* questionnaires, respondents were asked to report what kinds of grievance procedures, if any, were operating in their organizations. The question in the recent survey is worded as it was in the earlier survey to permit comparison. Respondents were asked which, if any, of six types of procedures were in force.

Exhibit II: "Due Process," 1971–1977

Mechanism	Percent of companies	
	1971	1977
Management grievance committee.	9%	14%
Corporate "ombudsman" or "ombudswoman."	8	11
Hearing procedure that allows employee to be represented by attorney or other person, and with a neutral company executive deciding on the evidence.	6	11
Assistant to the president or vice president who investigates grievances and reports to top management.	14	11
Personnel executive who investigates grievances and reports to top management.	43	42
Senior executive whose "door is always open" to employees who think they have been wronged.	68	63

The three top procedures (as illustrated in Exhibit II) are "tougher" than the others, because, given competent personnel and top management support, they work more predictably and focus more attention on problems of injustice. The other three procedures *may* be effective, and sometimes are very much so, but they are more informal. Frequently, they imply less top management commitment, at least, to employee rights of the kind considered here. The personnel investigator, the presidential assistant, and the senior official whose "door is always open" have many other tasks to do. Cases of subtle harassment, discrimination, and retaliation may be less important to them than larger issues of morale and productivity. The unhappy employee who goes to them may learn, as Zorba the Greek put it, that "you can knock forever on a deaf man's door."

As Exhibit II shows, the three stronger procedures have gained in popularity since 1971. While only a minority of companies have them, their number is growing more substantial. In contrast, the three weaker procedures have declined in popularity. (Conceivably, the changes shown could be due in part to differences in the 1971 and 1977 samples of business people, but this seems unlikely. The samples show great comparability in many other respects.)

Support for dissenters: "In the past the man has been first," said Frederick Winslow Taylor, pioneer in management methods. "In the future the system must be first." Do businessmen agree? Judging from what *Harvard Business Review* respondents say, the answer is no. Other comparisons of the 1977 and 1971 surveys show growing support for individuals who question, dissent from, or seek to participate in decision making:

• When asked about an accountant who finds something extra in her pay envelope—a pink slip—after refusing to falsify some earnings figures, an extremely high percentage of subscribers in 1971 took her side against the boss and voted to restore her to her job. Today, the percentage favoring reinstatement is greater still. Also, an even larger percentage think the accountant would in fact be reinstated if the incident were to take place somewhere in their companies (see Part A of Exhibit III).

Exhibit III: Growing Support for Employee Rights, 1971–1977

A. Reinstatement of a conscientious objector

An accountant is asked by her boss to falsify the company's profit-and-loss statement in order to show a small profit. Without the changes requested, a small loss would be shown. The accountant refuses on the ground that the requested action is dishonest. The boss then explains that the P&L is going to be shown to a bank, and that if a profit is not shown, the bank will surely turn down the company's application for a loan. The accountant still refuses to make the change. The boss fires her for insubordination. The accountant appeals for reinstatement to a senior executive.

Percent answering **yes**	1971	1977

---

1. Assuming the accountant's work record is satisfactory in other respects, do you think the company

should feel obligated to put her back on the payroll, either in her former job or in an equally good one?	94%	96%
2. If an incident like the foregoing one happened in your company (or in your part of the company if it has many divisions or subsidiaries), is it likely, in your opinion, that the accountant would be reinstated?	76	78

B. Voting

Should employees be asked to vote on decisions and policies traditionally reserved to top management? Please consider the following case, reported in *The New York Times,* and then give us your reactions to the questions that follow: When the Thermon Manufacturing Company of Houston found that increasing demand for its heat-transfer products would require larger plant facilities, Richard Burdick, its president, consulted his 80 employees about moving the plant. More than 70% voted to move to San Marcos, a small town in Texas. The *Times* article went on to indicate that the company planned to relocate as voted.

Percent answering **yes**	1971	1977
If your company were considering moving one of its offices or plants to another location, do you think the employees in the offices or plant involved should be asked to vote on the sites being considered by management?	36%	48%

Turning now to U.S. industry at large, do you think it would be desirable for employees in a typical company to be able to express their preference, by some suitable voting means, on various policies followed by the company? Please check any of the following questions on which voting *would* be appropriate, in your opinion. Assume management is *not* bound by the outcome of the vote.

	1971	1977
1. Whether all employees in the company should be subject to relocation by management as new plants and offices are opened, regardless of their desire to move.	29%	43%
2. Whether retirement should be mandatory for all company employees at age 65 or some other age.	29	44
3. Whether the company should continue working on certain controversial contracts for the Defense Department (e.g., chemical warfare, armaments for African countries), or phase out of such work as soon as possible.	16	23

• When given the case of some dissident managers who want their company to take stricter measures to control its pollution of air and water, numerous subscribers urge a course of action that was not mentioned in 1971: The managers should go to the board itself with their case if they cannot interest the company president. Suggests the chief executive of a Florida concern: "The board of directors should provide access to its audit committee, and the committee should hear the dissidents' case. This should work if the audit committee members are independent outside directors."

• Today, many more business executives would favor letting employees vote on such questions as relocating a plant, mandatory retirement at age 65, whether to continue controversial defense contracts, and ordering an employee to move to another plant or office regardless of his personal wishes.

To be sure, a majority still worry about asking rank-and-file employees to consider such issues, perhaps because of a feeling that the problems will only trouble them. As Mr. Micawber, in *David Copperfield*, complains about an affair of state that became public, "The mistake was made of putting some of the trouble out of King Charles's head into my head." But the majority who feel this way is growing slim. Consistent growth of support for voting shows up in Part B of Exhibit III.

Clime and punishment: Although the responses from subscribers in different regions, industries, and other classifications are remarkably consistent on most issues, regional differences occasionally are conspicuous.

For instance, on the question whether to punish or encourage the dissident managers who challenge their company's efforts at pollution control, the least support for the group comes from subscribers in the Southeast, South Central region, and Midwest. Whereas less than a third of the respondents from any of these regions would encourage the dissidents to "press their case until they get a fair hearing from top management," about 40 percent of respondents in the Middle Atlantic states and the Northeast would.

Again, whereas only about one subscriber in eight from companies employing five hundred or more people would tell the dissidents to get out of the organization, about one subscriber in six from smaller companies would. This hard-nosed line also is taken more often by top executives than by lower-level managers (18 percent as against 11 percent), and by executives over the age of 40 than by managers under 30 (17 percent as against 9 percent).

PRIVACY AND PREJUDICE

In Studs Terkel's study *Working,* many employees, in describing their feelings about their jobs, criticize their bosses for snooping and trying to find out too much. If managers show this tendency, it is no wonder, for the law has encouraged them. Authorities agree that the constitutional concept of a right to privacy has had little influence on personnel relations. Employee complaints about invasions of privacy have tended to fall into the crack between two legal causes of action, the right to privacy of a private citizen and defamation of character.

In recent years there have been signs that this situation may change. IBM has taken a strong, vigorous, and well-implemented stand in favor of privacy of employees' personal information. And in Washington, the government's Privacy Protection Study Commission wants to extend the principles of the Privacy Act of 1974 (for federal government employees) to the private sector.

What do *Harvard Business Review* subscribers feel about strengthening an employee's right to privacy? Do they agree with Moses Herzog in Saul Bellow's novel that "man's life is not a business"? To answer this question, the *Review* asked the nearly two thousand respondents to indicate their agreement or disagreement with four guidelines for private protection (see Exhibit IV). Although these principles are incorporated in IBM's policy, they go beyond the recommendations of the Privacy Protection Study Commission and the measures of the Privacy Act for federal employees. Presumably, therefore, they are controversial.

The results may surprise many people. By whopping majorities, as Exhibit IV shows, those sampled favor all four principles. What makes these returns all the more impressive is that they come from all groups of the *Review*'s subscribers, however classified. Executives in construction, mining, and oil are a little more inclined than the average to protect privacy; so are businessmen from the Southeast, lower-level managers, and young managers. But the rousing vote of approval goes across the board, and between the lowest and highest groups there are insignificant differences.

Among the comments written on the questionnaires, the following suggest the interest of many subscribers in stretching the bounds of privacy further: "Lie detector equipment should go, too" (treasurer, large West Coast company). "Another question is company-run insurance programs that require the employee to submit claim forms with diagnosis to the company. We've had a lot of employee concern here about invasion of privacy in this area. Some who should be making claims are not submitting them" (vice president, small New York company).

The employee's new clothes: One conspicuous exception to the tendency to support privacy and related rights is in regard to clothing and grooming. Asked to comment on the case of a young manager who

Exhibit IV: Support for Privacy

During recent years the subject of employee privacy, especially with regard to personal information, has been discussed by many businessmen and attorneys. We are interested in your opinion on the following policies. Please check as many as you wish that you agree with; assume you are answering for your current or most recent employer company.

Percent **in favor**

Information in an employee's folder should never be given to outside credit officials, landlords, journalists, and prospective employers except with the employee's permission.	94%
Management should permit no recordings of employees' conversation in or outside the organization unless they are given advance notice.	90
Every employee should be able at any time to see the information in his or her personnel file and challenge any data considered inaccurate, with the exception only of confidential opinions on qualifications for promotion, on likely future salary increases, and on grievance cases the employee may be involved in.	87
Information about an employee's home mortgage, company loans, legal problems, and nonjob-related medical problems should be available for inspection only by personnel department officials and not by his or her work supervisor.	61

Note: The privacy policies did not appear in this order on the questionnaire.

appears for work in gaudy shirts and youth-styled slacks, and also grows a beard and long sideburns, subscribers render as harsh a judgment as they did in 1971 (see Part A of Exhibit V).

A communications company executive who explains her position probably speaks for the majority. "The reality of our world today," she says, "is that appearance can affect performance. For example, if an individual's job is to provide services to clients face-to-face, and the clients are negatively affected by his or her appearance, performance may suffer. Management has to measure and manage performance."

As might be expected, the respondents under the age of 30 judge this case more leniently. The percentage who say that "what the kid wears and how he looks is his own business" is almost three times larger than for respondents over 60 (25 percent versus 9 percent). Also, there is much more sympathy for the young manager among businessmen who (in another part of the questionnaire) report that their greatest societal concern is with obstacles to individualism. But

Exhibit V: Questionable Rights

A. Appearance

A capable young manager in a financial service company returns from a month's vacation with a beard and long sideburns started. He also begins appearing frequently in gaudy sport shirts and youth-styled slacks. The company is one in which all managers traditionally have dressed conservatively in business suits. During his years of service in the company prior to the recent vacation, the young man had conformed to the usual standard appearance. Following his vacation, he resumed working with his accustomed vigor and sincerity. Other executives in the company have wide-ranging reactions to the young man. Please check the view in the following list that most nearly expresses your own opinion.

Percent	1971	1977
"His supervisor should sit down with him, tell him that some people object to his appearance, and that we'd like to have him stay with us but not if he looks like a hippy."	52%	49%
"What the kid wears and how he looks is his own business."	18%	19%
"How he looks is his own business unless it irritates people, in which case I would tell him either to change his ways or begin hunting for another job."	30%	31%
"He should be dismissed outright. He's worked with us long enough to know better."	0.1%	1%

B. Outside Activities

Several top executives of a company in a large city are disturbed by community activist organizations that are protesting the treatment of minority groups. The executives feel that the activists, while abstaining from violence, are doing more harm than good to the schools, urban renewal programs, public transportation, and retail business. The chief executive himself has articulated his fears about the activists at local business meetings. However, a young official in the personnel department thinks that the activists are on the right track. He goes to work for the leading activist organization, spending many evening and weekend hours doing unpaid volunteer tasks. Occasionally he is quoted in the newspaper and identified with the employer company.

The personnel director of the company comes under pressure from several senior executives. They urge him to warn the young official either to stop working for the activists or resign. How should he answer them? If you were the personnel director, which of the following possible responses would come closest to the answer you would make?

	1977
"This is a question for the chief executive to decide, not you or me."	5%

Exhibit V - *Continued*

"People in this company and especially this department should be free to express their opinions on public problems. I'll go to bat for the young man as a matter of principle."	19%
"As long as this person keeps doing a good job for the company, I shall not interfere."	6%
"I agree it's bad business for the chief executive to be saying one thing and a lesser official to be saying just the opposite. I'll tell the young man he's got to stop."	8%
"As long as this person keeps doing a good job, and until there is some concrete factual evidence that the company's public image is being hurt by his association with the activists, I shall not interfere."	62%

even this group votes by more than three to one against permitting nonconformity in appearance.

The guy who went out in the cold: Even outside the company, an employee may not be free to "do his own thing" under certain circumstances. Asked to judge the case of an earnest young manager who works nights and weekends for a community activist organization that top executives of the company do not approve of, and who is occasionally identified with the company in newspaper reports about the organization, only a fourth of the *Review*'s respondents said they would not interfere as a matter of principle (see Part B of Exhibit V). Three-fifths would not interfere with the young manager until it appeared his activities were tarnishing the company image, but that condition is a big one, for "company image" is an elastic concept that can be stretched to fit top executives' preconceptions.

These reactions typify the concerns of the managerial mind. When protection of privacy and other rights associated with constitutionalism are seen as a threat to corporate well-being, their stock falls on the managerial Dow-Jones index. After all, businessmen reason, if a company fails to turn a profit, it cannot be even a poor employer.

SECOND-GUESSING THE JUDGES

In novels, television dramas, and the press, business executives usually come across as arch-conservatives: If they could take the law into their own hands, they would run the world in a reactionary way. When humanitarian advances such as equal-employment opportunity and collective bargaining are made, writers indicate, the credit goes to activist judges and legislators. The *Harvard Business Review* survey suggests that this popular image is a myth, at least as far as civil liberties are concerned. In the questionnaire, subscribers are asked to consider three situations where employees are put down for lack of "loyalty" to management. Unbeknown to most respondents, each situation parallels a court case decided in recent years (for the sake of brevity and disguise, many details are omitted or changed). In each case, the *Review*'s subscribers turn out to be more "liberal" than the judges were.

Even allowing for any inclination on their part to be more generous in the questionnaire than they would be in actual practice, the results show a strong civil liberties consciousness among the *Review*'s subscribers—considerably stronger than that of the courts.

Case of the immoral instruction: The first case describes a secretary of a service company who is instructed to record outside telephone conversations without the outsiders' knowledge. Her protests are bootless: She is directed to do as she was told (see Part A of Exhibit VI).

The situation resembles that of Shirley Zinman, who resigned from a Philadelphia employment agency rather than surreptitiously monitor telephone conversations with prospective clients "for training purposes." When she sought unemployment compensation, the state board turned down her application on the ground that she didn't have a "strong and compelling" reason to resign; that is, in the agency's view she was supposed to behave loyally even if this meant being immoral and possibly illegal. With the help of the American Civil Liberties Union, she appealed to the Pennsylvania Commonwealth Court. In 1973, in a decision hailed as precedential by civil liberties advocates, the court reversed the state board, holding that she should receive unemployment pay.

When asked how they would handle the situation described in the questionnaire, only 6 percent of the respondents said they would back up the secretary's boss. The great majority would have the vice president rescind the order, as Exhibit VI shows. What the computer tabulation does not show, but readily apparent from the large number of written-in comments, is that numerous subscribers would not only rescind the order but would also fire the executive who gave it.

Thus the *Harvard Business Review* executives take a bolder position than the court did, for, while the judges were willing to depart from tradition and award unemployment compensation to Zinman, they did not indicate that she deserved her job back. Indeed, as of this writing there appear to be no court decisions that go this far. As Lawrence E. Blades, dean of the Iowa University Law School, points out, the law has adhered to the age-old rule that, with few exceptions, employers "may dismiss their employees at will . . . for good cause, for no cause,

Exhibit VI: Judgments on Three Dissidents

A. Case of the immoral instruction

A secretary of a service firm is instructed by her boss, a vice president, to record telephone conversations with outside people who call to inquire about the range and cost of services offered. "Under no circumstances are you to let on to them that you're recording the conversation," the boss instructs her. "This is confidential data for use in sales." She protests that the action is unethical and possibly illegal but is assured, "We know what we're doing. Now just do as you are told." Visibly upset, the secretary goes to the owner of the firm. "I've worked hard and well for 2½ years and I would like to keep my job," she pleads with him. "But I would rather resign than do something immoral."

Speaking just for yourself now, which of the following actions would you be most likely to take if you were the owner:

Percent	
Back up the vice president and let him handle it in his own way.	6%
Tell the vice president to compromise by rescinding the order to the secretary and finding someone in another office who will cooperate in recording outside calls.	8
Tell the vice president to rescind the order.	61
Other.	25

B. Case of the solicitous salesman

A 13-year sales veteran of a large metals company becomes disturbed about the safety of a new product to be marketed. Although approved by management, the tests raised serious safety questions in the minds of various engineers. The salesman himself is convinced, on the basis of his experience with users, that the product is likely to cause serious accidents. First he mentions his fears to his field sales manager. Told to "relax and forget it," he goes to the district manager, next to the regional head. "It's not your worry," they say. "Just go out and do the good selling job you've been doing." Finally he goes to the vice president of marketing at corporate headquarters. Incensed that the salesman did not follow the advice of the sales managers, the vice president fires him. "I'm aware you went through channels and didn't upset the other salesmen," the vice president tells him, "but you're a nuisance just the same."

1. Speaking just for yourself now, might you have taken the same action?	3% yes	96% no
2. Suppose you were the chief executive of this company. Would you back up the vice president after you hear about the case? (Assume no		

press publicity or employee group protest.)	11%	yes	87%	no

3. On the basis of what you know about business practice in general in your industry, how typical do you consider the vice president's action?	7% 26%	very typical typical	33% 31%	unusual very unusual

Exhibit VI: Judgments on three dissidents (continued)

C. Case of the nettlesome novelist

Ben Brown, a chemical engineer, has been employed by his company for more than a dozen years. Although known to be critical of many company policies, Brown is fairly well liked by associates, his work has been good, and he has earned regular increases in salary. To everyone's surprise, he and his wife coauthor a novel published by a small publishing firm. While the story takes place in a fictional setting with fictional characters and events, the novel is clearly a lampoon of the company. It represents management as greedy, inflexible, and obtuse to scientific progress. Although the book is not likely to sell many copies, many company managers are incensed.

If you were the department head to whom Brown reports, which of the following actions would you be most likely to take? (Assume no employment contract and no union.)

Percent	
Do nothing, fend off people who want Brown disciplined.	41%
Call Brown in, warn him that nothing will happen this time but he'd better give you a chance to say "No" in advance of any future publication that satirizes the company.	39
Fire Brown.	12
Keep Brown on the payroll but assign him to tasks he won't like, cut any future raises, and hope he will resign after finding a job elsewhere.	7

or even for cause morally wrong, without being thereby guilty of legal wrong."

Case of the solicitous salesman: Harvard Business Review subscribers also have little sympathy with the rash handling of a veteran salesman who is worried about the safety of a new product. When told by local managers to relax and forget his qualms, he goes to the marketing vice president, who is so incensed by the man's behavior that he fires him.

As Part B of Exhibit VI shows, only a few respondents said they would have done the same thing; only a tenth would back up the vice president; and only about a third consider the handling of the case more typical than atypical. These results are fairly consistent across age, job level, geographical, functional, and other classifications.

In 1974 the Supreme Court of Pennsylvania decided a similar case, involving a thirteen-year veteran of a large steel corporation who believed that a new tubular casing had been inadequately tested and was potentially dangerous for users. After voicing his misgivings to superiors, who told him to "stop shoveling smoke," he went to the sales vice president, who summarily discharged him. According to the court record, the salesman had been doing his job and had not upset other employees with his questioning. By a four-to-three vote, the court clung to tradition and decided in favor of the company.[1]

In commenting on the questionnaire case, many subscribers criticize the vice president for failing to look into the product tests and to reason with the salesman. "The vice president used poor judgment," says the vice president of a large restaurant chain in California. "I cannot back him up. Better communication might have solved this problem."

Of course, *Harvard Business Review* subscribers are looking at the case from an administrative standpoint rather than from the strictly legal view taken by the Pennsylvania Supreme Court. Withal, the difference in philosophy seems sharp and clean. The businessmen see no reason that the salesman must go around with his head below the grass —at least, not if he is competent and genuinely concerned. Judging from their responses, they view loyalty as a two-way concern, not a one-way street, as the law since Hammurabi has seen it. "The VP works for the company too," explains a director of a large financial institution.

Case of the nettlesome novelist: Another of the cases given to subscribers concerned a veteran chemical engineer who, with his wife, wrote a novel about a fictitious company staffed with pecksniffian top executives who took an obtuse attitude toward scientific progress. Seeing obvious parallels in the novel with their actual organization, some managers got hot under the collar. Does freedom of the press apply, or has the engineer violated a duty of loyalty?

As Part C of Exhibit VI shows, respondents are ambivalent on this question. Four out of five would not penalize the chemist *this* time. However, two of these four would make it clear to him that *next* time they expect to be consulted in advance and given a chance to say no.

In the real-life version of this case, Louis V. McIntire, a chemical engineer who had worked for a large chemical company for thirteen years, was not so lucky. Soon after his superiors looked at a copy of the novel by McIntire and his wife, they sacked him. In 1974 McIntire sued the company, claiming that his discharge was unconstitutional, but the district court applied the common-law rule of employer prerogatives and decided against him. The rule applied by the judges, it would seem, is that "you cannot run with the hare and hunt with the hounds, at least, not in this business." McIntire's case now is being appealed.[2]

Clearly, this case makes many business people in the *Review*'s audience uncomfortable. Less than a majority want the chemist to be free to write as he pleases (assuming the novel is not libelous). At the other extreme, only 19 percent would fire him or put pressure on him to resign. In between there is a gray area where about two in five would like an option to decide on the case later on. However you look at it, though, respondents are more sympathetic to the chemist than the court was.

FOR WHOM THE WHISTLE BLOWS

For more than a decade whistle blowers have been attracting national attention. Like the early Christians, they usually have been thrown to the lions; on the other hand, some of them have had the satisfaction of being lionized in the media. Examples of the latter are Henry Durham at Lockheed, Ronald H. Secrist at Equity Funding, Thomas M. Howard at Cenco, Robert Mallozzi of the Connecticut State Labor Department, and A. Ernest Fitzgerald (mentioned earlier).

According to the stereotype, the executive of a corporation or public agency despises whistle blowers. "If they don't like this company, they should find another place." His or her advice to a would-be critic might be Frank Tyger's suggestion, "You can only improve on saying nothing by saying nothing often."

The findings of this survey run head-on into the stereotype. When offered eight contrasting attitudes toward whistle blowers, the majority indicate agreement with the more tolerant views. For instance, 61 percent agree that if the whistle blower "believes sincerely he is acting in the best interests of customers, stockholders, or the community, he should be respected and not penalized." More than 40 percent agree that "it's a free country, and if we're free to criticize government we should be free to criticize business." After all, some businessmen reason, the company is the beneficiary if the whistle blower is right. To paraphrase John Donne, "Never send to know for whom the whistle blows; it blows for thee." And if the whistle blower is wrong, management can demonstrate that fact (43 percent agree with this view).

In contrast, only a third say that if the whistle blower doesn't like the company, he should leave it. Less than a tenth think he or she should be penalized if there is "factual evidence that the whistle blowing is hurting sales or customer relations." About one-fifth want to discourage criticism because it "is bound to upset morale."

Fear of failing: One subscriber, now chief executive of a Pennsylvania company, gives an example of why protection and encouragement should be afforded to whistle blowing. Some time ago, he worked for a large corporation in the *Fortune* "500." He and other managers in one division knew that their division head, by manipulating the computer invoice system, had defrauded the company of a small yacht. But who wanted to blow the whistle on him? Among the junior managers (of whom our subscriber was one) there was terrific competition for promotion. A small thing could make or break one's chances of staying in the running, and much angst was suffered for fear of incurring the top man's disfavor.

Dissidence was unthinkable. In fact, only the *Harvard Business Review* subscriber ever mentioned the fraud to the division head, and that was when the subscriber planned to leave the company and needed to protect his interest in a company savings plan—the division head threatened to block him from getting his money out. Later on, the division head was apprehended—but by a sales tax official, not by the company. The culprit had forgotten to pay a state sales tax on the bogus transaction that he entered in the division's accounts.

It may be realities like these, which surely are common in sizable corporations, that lead so many subscribers to give whistle blowers the benefit of the doubt. Even among those over the age of 50, who presumably are the most conservative, nearly 60 percent believe that whistle blowers, if sincerely motivated, should be protected and not penalized for attempting, in Senator Proxmire's phrase, to "commit the truth."

Postscripts: Subscribers nevertheless feel uneasy about whistle blowers as individuals. Of about 1,500 of the nearly 2,000 respondents who commented on the statement that most whistle blowing "is done for personal gain, glory seeking, or possibly revenge," 56 percent agreed with the statement. In addition, many executives fear pragmatically that whistle blowing, if legitimized, could be exploited by the least responsible and poorest informed elements of the work force. As Shakespeare said, "Beggars mounted run their horse to death," and it could be that a right to criticism would be worked to death, too.

Suppose the whistle blower works not for a commercial organization but for a public agency, such as an urban bus company? Nearly nine in ten subscribers disown the boss who retaliates against a bus driver who speaks out on a safety violation. But a majority (57 percent) feel that such suppression is more typical than not in public agencies. This dim view of public sector management may reflect the impact on public opinion of Watergate, the Arizona state crime scandals, and other such revelations.

ECONOMIC TAR BABY?

Although *Harvard Business Review* subscribers appear to be taking an increasingly sanguine view of employee rights, they feel that the movement is costly. About three-fourths of the respondents believe that grievance procedures, privacy, equal employment opportunity, and other gains in constitutionalism are increasing the price tags of products and services. Only 5 percent feel that customers are paying less because of the gains; 20 percent feel product and service costs are about the same. But customers may not be the only ones footing the bill. In the opinion of 43 percent of respondents, stockholders are receiving less return on their investments as a result of the expansion of rights. Only one respondent in ten feels that stockholders actually may be receiving more return (presumably because rights are believed to improve the health and morale of an organization).

How can these findings be reconciled with respondents' sympathy for employee rights? One possible explanation is that in 1977, as in 1971, the majority of those responding believed that a corporation should serve not just the owners alone, nor should it even give priority to the interests of stockholders over certain other interests. Rather, they agreed with the questionnaire statement that it should "serve as fairly and equitably as it can the interests of four sometimes competing groups —owners, employees, customers, and the public." If management is as concerned with serving employees and the public as it is with serving stockholders and customers, it makes sense to support privacy, due process, conscience, and open inquiry even though they add something to costs.

A second explanation might be that businessmen don't know how much constitutionalism costs. Who does? Obviously, employee rights may be a drain on the time and energy of top management. But how much of a drain? Obviously, too, procedures like IBM's "open door" system for handling grievances and Donnelly Mirror's joint work committees impose some overhead cost.

On the other hand, constitutionalism may have a salubrious effect on morale. Also, in some cases it may directly reduce costs for customers and shareholders. For instance, if the whistle had blown earlier on some of the embezzlement, payoff, and other illicit schemes reported in the past decade, many millions of dollars in legal fees, public relations expenses, and operating costs could have been avoided. An investigation into the costs of forms of constitutionalism as practiced in a few corporations should be rewarding.

MORE IMPORTANT THAN RIGHTS

There may be still another reason for business executives' ambivalence about rights and their costs. As Exhibit VII shows, executives worry more about social instability than about drags on individualism.[3] While they may sympathize with the need for this man's privacy and that woman's right to equity, they do this against a brooding concern with perceived tremors in the societal landscape. Numerous comments added to the returned questionnaires amplify this concern. A great many respondents indicate that they regard lessening respect for law and order, authority, discipline, and hard work as a kind of San Andreas fault under the corporate community. They find it hard to concentrate on threats to individualism in view of the more general portents. Also, they are impatient with the clamor for more freedom because they feel that their own freedom of expression as managers is being curbed by "big government." Managers' perceptions of the effects of employee rights reflect these basic concerns. For instance:

• Of the respondents most worried about social instability, 76 percent fear that customers are paying more because of employee rights, but only 63 percent of respondents concerned most with threats to individualism hold that opinion.

• Of the first group, 46 percent suspect that stockholders are getting less return, compared with 33 percent in the second group.

• Also, of the first group, 63 percent see whistle blowers as motivated by "personal gain, glory seeking, or possibly revenge," compared with 37 percent in the second group.

Will business leaders support future advances in employee rights? The answer depends on three conditions:

1. *Perceived merits of constitutionalism.* Thus far, business experience with employee rights has been good. However, it has been limited. If more companies find that a "bill of rights" is workable, practical, and possibly even salubrious, the news is likely to spread quickly. Particularly important will be experience with methods of due process, for those methods can make it possible to pursue equity in a systematic, predictable, and workaday manner.

Exhibit VII: Problems of Greatest Future Concern

The economic, political, and social turbulence in the United States during recent years has been the subject of endless editorials, books, and TV programs. We are interested in knowing what broad problems most concern HBR subscribers as they look ahead into the next ten years. As best you can, given our space limitations, please rank the following in terms of how much they concern you, with "1" for the problem that concerns you the most, "2" for the problem of next greatest concern, etc.

Percent	1	2
Social instability, including confusion about sexual standards, treatment of criminals, attitudes toward drugs and alcohol, respect for the family and authority, breakdown of law and order, disintegration of the work ethic.	46%	31%
Economic insecurity, including the possibilities of job loss for you or your children, financial sacrifices, cutting back of opportunity for advancement, inability to keep up with inflation.	35	39
Obstacles to individualism, including difficulties in the path of people who seek unusual career goals, wish to pursue "different" life styles, want to question the value of traditional institutions, desire to define success in original ways.	16	24
Other	3	6

2. *National attitudes.* Ambient feelings about privacy, conscientious objection, freedom of criticism, due process, and other rights naturally will color business people's thinking. President Jimmy Carter's aggressive stand for human rights could be a factor here, influencing the image of American rights at home as well as abroad. Study groups like the Privacy Protection Study Commission also are important.

3. *Social and economic stability.* If business leaders become much more alarmed over breakdowns in law and order, declining respect for authority, financial upheaval, and other trends mentioned in Exhibit VII, they may react by turning against all advances in employee participation. Employee rights as well as job enrichment, joint work councils, and other innovations would be casualties. Indeed, the action of the socioeconomic seismograph could have a more important bearing on this subject than anything else.

Notes

1. *Geary* v. *U.S. Steel Corporation,* 319 A.2d 174 (1974).

2. *McIntire* v. *E.I. DuPont de Nemours & Co.,* 165th Judicial District Court, Harris Court, Harris County, Texas, No. 954,904.

3. This question was based on an idea from Daniel Yankelovich, "The Status of *Ressentiment* in America," *Social Research,* Winter 1975, p. 760.

II.
Limiting Employer Prerogatives

Employment at Will v. Individual Freedom: On Limiting the Abusive Exercise of Employer Power

Lawrence E. Blades

The existing sources of protection for the employee [against unjust discharge] are patently inadequate. The question arises whether any other kind of sanction might be used. An appropriate legal response would be to confer on the afflicted employee a personal remedy for any damage he suffers when discharged as a result of resisting his employer's attempt to intimidate or coerce him in a way that bears no reasonable relationship to the employment. For convenience, a discharge so motivated might be termed an "abusive" discharge.

The employee faced with the prospect of losing his job can ordinarily anticipate the expenses of searching for new employment, losing earnings in the meanwhile, and perhaps being forced ultimately to settle for less remunerative employment at some distant place. Beyond these economic losses, he may also fear the stigma and mental anguish that normally accompany being fired.[1] It has been pointed out that "white-collar employees, unlike their brothers in blue collars, are psychologically unprepared for the loss of security and status following on unemployment."[2] That is, the fear of discharge, and thus the vulnerability to employer coercion, is especially acute among professional and other white-collar employees—the very ones whose numbers are increasing and whose jobs are least likely to be protected by collective bargaining agreements.

If the employee had some assurance that he would not have to bear such losses, he would be in a far better position to withstand oppression

Excerpted from the *Columbia Law Review* 67 (1967). Copyright © 1967. Reprinted with permission.

at the hands of his employer. Such assurance could be provided by arming the employee with a damage action where his discharge is caused by a refusal to submit to the employer's improper or overreaching demands. It should be emphasized that so to limit the employer's right of discharge would not give blanket protection to the employee's interest in job security. There is a distinction between the right to employment and the right of the employee not to be obliged to his employer in ways bearing no legitimate connection to the employment.[3]

Recognition of such a cause of action would of course tend to deter an employer from discharging an employee for an abusive reason. Further, employers would face the danger that a subsequent discharge, even though for good cause, might be associated with a prior attempt of the employer to interfere with the employee's individuality. Thus the fear of lawsuits would have the salutary effect of discouraging improper attempts to interfere with the employee's freedom or integrity, even when the employer does not intend to discharge the employee for refusing to submit to his desires. But beyond the more immediate effects, and perhaps more important, legal protection for the abusively discharged employee would inevitably develop a keener awareness of and greater respect for the individuality of the employee. Indeed, it is conceivable that this consciousness of employee individuality would do much toward solving the dilemma of the organization man, the employee in middle management whom William H. Whyte saw as too prone to identify with his employer and especially subject to the power of his employing organization.[4]

The remedy suggested here for the abusively discharged employee is not without parallel. The National Labor Relations Board is empowered to grant damages (in the form of "back pay"), and reinstatement as well, to an employee whose discharge is found to have stemmed from his involvement in certain labor union activities. Similar remedies are granted by the various Civil Rights and Fair Employment Practices Commissions which have been given the responsibility of protecting against discriminatory practices in both hiring and firing. And judicial and quasi-judicial remedies are available to wrongfully discharged employees in a number of continental European countries.

The Federal Automobile Dealer Franchise Act of 1956 also provides a precedent, in the damage remedy it gives to wrongfully disenfranchised dealers, and in its economic background.[5] The expendability of the automobile dealer introduced an imbalance in bargaining power into his relationship with the manufacturer. As with the employer's power over the employee, the real source of the manufacturer's ability to take unfair advantage of the dealer resided in its power to terminate the relationship.[6] The courts failed to respond to the dealer's need for protection,[7] but the dealer's strong lobby brought about a congressional investigation which uncovered a number of abusive uses of the manufacturer's power. The upshot was the 1956 act with its explicitly stated purpose "to guarantee the one party freedom from coercion, intimidation, or threats of coercion from the other party"—a goal identical with that toward which this entire discussion is directed. . . .

If a damage remedy were to be extended to abusively discharged employees, it would protect personality interests of the employee— interests which by definition have no legitimate connection with the employment relationship or "contract." If the employer invades legally protected rights of the employee, for instance by the infliction of bodily injury or by defamation, the existence of the employment "contract" does not stand in the way of determining the employee's rights under the law of torts.[9] Since analogous interests of the employee are at stake when the employer unreasonably attempts to interfere with his personal freedom, it seems reasonable to bypass the law of contracts and its unyielding requirement of consideration by turning to the more elastic principles of tort law for a suitable basis upon which to predicate the discharged employee's action for damages. Such a basis may exist in the various types of tort liability that have evolved in connection with the exercise of a right for an improper, ulterior purpose.

Legal recognition that one can be held liable solely on account of wrongful motives is more or less a twentieth century development. Earlier, the law's general attitude toward bad motives found expression in the oft-stated maxim that "malicious motives make a bad act worse, but they cannot make that wrong which in its own essence is lawful."[10] This maxim, however, has come to be recognized as mere question begging,[11] and there are now many instances of tort liability based largely on the defendant's bad motives. Numerous, for example, are cases in which motive has resulted in liability for building spite fences,[12] for drilling wells to cut off the plaintiff's underground water,[13] for promoting numerous other nuisances designed only to harass the plaintiff,[14] or for unwarranted interference with favorable contractual relationships.[15] Many of the cases of tort liability based on the defendant's bad motives have been grouped under the rubric of "prima facie tort," which found expression in the classic statement:

> Now intentionally to do that which is calculated in the ordinary course of events to damage, and which does, in fact, damage another in that other person's property or trade, is actionable if done without just cause or excuse.[16]

It has been pointed out that this is "no more than a form of words emphasizing the importance of motive."[17] But regardless of whether this notion is stated in terms of prima facie tort or bad motives, it lends general support to the proposition that tort liability ought to attach in cases of abusive discharge.

An analogy that seems particularly suited to the case of a discharge caused by improper motives is the tort action designed to prevent the perversion of legal procedures to ulterior purposes—abuse of process. Essential to recovery for abuse of process is the defendant's intent to exercise a right, lawful and valuable in itself, for a purpose other than that for which it was designed. Unlike the related tort of malicious prosecution, the action for abuse of process does not depend on the absence of probable cause—the gist of the action is exercise of a right for an ulterior purpose regardless of whether it can or cannot be otherwise justified. This emphasis on state of mind makes the doctrinal framework of abuse of legal procedures especially suitable for an approach to the problem of abusive dismissals. To elaborate: In *Grainger* v. *Hill*,[18] the landmark case on abuse of process, the defendants were held liable chiefly because, in the words of one of the judges, "The process was enforced for an ulterior purpose; to obtain property by duress to which the Defendants had no right." Liability should similarly be visited upon the employer who uses his power of discharge for an ulterior purpose and as a means of duress. It can be said that discharge of the at-will employee, like resort to legal procedures, is in its essence lawful. It can also be said, as with the right to invoke the processes of the law, that the employer's right of discharge is too valuable a right to be encumbered with unnecessary limitations. But, as with any individual's right to bring legal action, the law should not allow the employer to exercise his right of discharge in order to effectuate a purpose ulterior to that for which the right was designed.[19] Just as the use of legal processes as a means of extortion gives rise to a damage remedy, so too should the oppressive use of the right of discharge.

While cases dealing with abuse of process provide the most suitable analogy, further support for the employee's action can be derived from the growing body of cases in which interference by a third party with the employee's interest in the at-will employment relationship has given rise to recovery in tort.[20] *United States Fidelity & Guarantee Co.* v. *Millonas*[21] is illustrative. The plaintiff-employee filed a claim with the defendant, the employer's insurer, for compensation for an injury he had suffered in the course of his employment. The defendant told the plaintiff that he would lose his job if he persisted in his claim. Then, by threatening cancellation of the employer's policy, the defendant procured the plaintiff's discharge. The defendant argued that no cause of action could arise from its threatening to do what it had a legal right to do—to cancel the employer's policy. The court rejected this argument with the statement that the plaintiff's discharge was not procured as "the consequence of the exercise of a lawful right, but of the unlawful use of that lawful right by the defendant."[22]

This decision and others like it go beyond merely exemplifying further the role of wrongful motives in tort liability. They find liability not only when the defendant acts from ulterior motives, but also when he acts "without justification." Thus, a defendant may be held liable though he lacks the state of mind that makes the employer's discharge "abusive" in the definition urged here. But despite the imperfection of the analogy, the interference cases demonstrate that an employee's interest in an at-will employment relationship is considered deserving of legal protection. And if the interest is protectable, it is difficult to see why it should matter whether the employee's discharge is procured by the abuse of a "lawful right" by a third party or by the employer.

Many of the cases involving interference by a third party with the at-will employment relationship concern protection of the employer's valuable interest in keeping his employee.[23] So, it might be argued, if the employee's interest in the relationship is to be protected from interference by the employer as well as by third parties, the employer's interest in preserving the same relationship should be similarly protected from employees. The answer to this argument is that an equation of the rights of the employer with the rights of the employee is inconsistent with the basic inequality in the positions of the two. Moreover, the freedom of the individual not to work for a particular employer has come to be regarded as a more valuable right than the freedom of the employer to select his employees. The employer's freedom has been limited by our child labor laws, the legally protected status of labor unions, and the growing body of laws prohibiting discrimination in hiring. And while the employer's right to select his employees has been thus limited, the freedom of the individual to refuse to work has, perhaps because of our abhorrence of slavery, become virtually inviolable. As one court put it in holding a third party liable for procuring the discharge of an employee:

> The right to dispose of one's labor as he will . . . is incident to the freedom of the individual, which lies at the foundation of the government in all countries that maintain principles of civil liberty.[24]

In short, the employee's right to work for whom he chooses is too valuable to be circumscribed or limited to prevent abuse of the almost negligible coercive power of an employee's threat to quit his job. The situation of the employer differs drastically from that of the employee.[25] There is nothing more than the appeal of symmetry and a harkening back to hollow notions of mutuality to uphold any suggestion that the rights of employers must correspond to the rights of employees.

The cases involving interference with an employment relationship by a third party also provide a suitable basis for measuring damages in cases of abusive discharge. Generally speaking, the most significant item of damages in such cases has been the amount the employee would have earned but for the defendant's wrongful act.[26] While it may not be sound to presume that the employment would have endured for the remainder of the employee's working life, the courts have deemed such a presumption fair because the defendant himself has made impossible any meaningful inquiry into what would have happened but for his wrongful act.

In cases of wrongful procurement the plaintiff is generally held not entitled to any damages that may have been or might yet be avoided by reasonably diligent efforts to obtain other employment. Application of this principle in cases where the employee has been abusively discharged would be especially fitting, since the employee who is likely to suffer the least damage is also the one least affected by employer coercion. In other words, the employee who has enough mobility to avoid the consequences of his discharge will also have enough mobility to make him an unlikely target for oppression by the employer. But where the employee's experience is of special value only in his present employment or where his advanced age makes it doubtful that he can readily obtain comparable employment, he is more susceptible to improper exertion of the employer's power and less likely to succeed in mitigating damages.

There is, however, some authority to the effect that the employee is under no duty to avoid the consequences of his discharge by seeking other employment where the defendant has wrongfully procured his discharge.[27] This approach is punitive. If punishment is the objective of the remedy, explicitly punitive damages should be awarded.

The assessment of punitive damages in cases of abusive firings would be fitting and desirable. They are typically awarded where the plaintiff's loss is caused by the defendant's "malicious, oppressive, willful, wanton, or reckless" behavior,[28] and the usual objective is deterrence.[29] Deterrence should also be a prime objective of the remedy for abusive discharge. The possibility of furthering this objective by the assessment of punitive damages provides an additional argument for a tort rather than a contract remedy. While punitive damages have been awarded in a number of cases involving tortious interference with the employment relationship by a third party, they have generally not been recoverable against an employer in an action for breach of the employment contract, regardless of how evil the employer's motive in breaching.

Notes

1. In Comerford v. International Harvester Co., 235 Ala. 376, 377, 178 So. 894, 895 (1938), for example, the plaintiff-employee alleged that as consequence of his wrongful discharge he "was greatly humiliated and embarrassed, and was caused to suffer great mental anguish and was caused to lose a lucrative and profitable position, and was put to great trouble, expense, annoyance and inconvenience in and about obtaining new employment, and was caused to be without employment for a long period of time, and to lose a large sum of money for salary he otherwise would have received. . . ."

2. Andrew Hacker, "Introduction: Corporate America," in Andrew Hacker, ed., *The Corporation Takeover* (New York: Harper & Row, 1964), p. 9.

3. Compare the distinction drawn with respect to public employment in Dotson, "The Emerging Doctrine of Privilege in Public Employment," *Public Administration Review* 15 (1955): 77, 87: "Even if it were granted that no constitutional right to employment could be established, this concession would not imply that, by virtue of public employment, an individual might be deprived of his *other* constitutional rights" (emphasis in original).

4. William H. Whyte, *The Organization Man* (New York: Simon & Schuster, 1956). Judicial sanctions could not, however, cure this problem to the extent that it stems not from the coercive power of the employer but from the employee's own psychological need to identify his own goals with those of his employer.

5. See generally Kessler, "Automobile Dealer Franchises: Vertical Integration by Contract," *Yale Law Journal* 66 (1957): 1135; Brown and Conwill, "Automobile Manufacturer-Dealer Legislation," *Columbia Law Review* 57 (1957): 219.

6. Brown and Conwill, *supra* note 5, pp. 222–23: "The manufacturer is . . . in a position to cause serious financial loss to the dealer through use of its power to terminate the relationship. By threatening to terminate the relationship the manufacturer can force the dealer to make unwanted purchases or to take other disadvantageous steps in the conduct of his business." Strand and French, "The Automobile Dealer Franchise Act: Another Experiment in Federal Class Legislation," *George Washington Law Review* 25 (1957): 667, 668: "The real source of the manufacturer's power over the dealer lies in the

termination provisions of the franchise agreements."

7. The usual ground given by the courts in refusing to enforce the automobile dealer franchise agreements was a lack of "mutuality." See, e.g., Ford Motor Co. v. Kirkmeyer Motor Co., 65 F.2d 1001 (4th Cir. 1933); Oakland Motor Car Co. v. Indiana Auto. Co., 201 F. 499 (7th Cir. 1912); Superior Motor Co. v. Chevrolet Motor Co., 112 Kan. 522, 212 P. 100 (1923).

8. 15 U.S.C. § 1221(e)(1964). The fact that there have been few reported cases brought under this act in which dealers have prevailed has caused a number of commentators to leap to the conclusion that the legislation has been ineffective. See, e.g., Freed, "A Study of Dealers' Suits Under the Automobile Dealers' Franchise Act," *University of Detroit Law Journal* 41 (1964): 245, 256–61; Comment, "The Automobile Dealer Franchise Act of 1956—An Evaluation," *Cornell Law Quarterly* 48 (1963): 711, 741–42. But in the most thoroughgoing study ever made of this legislation and its effects it has been pointed out that these commentators overlook the benefit that the legislation has produced in acting as a spur to the creation of private machinery for the settlement of manufacturer-dealer termination disputes.

9. See, e.g., Imre v. Riegel Paper Corp., 24 N.J. 438, 132 A.2d 505 (1957), where the employee recovered medical expenses and loss of wages incurred as a result of the negligence of his employer. The employer's liability for negligence has, of course, been largely superseded by the workmen's compensation acts.

10. See Jenkins v. Fowler, 24 Pa. 308, 310 (1855). The statement was endorsed in T. Cooley, *A Treatise on the Law of Torts* (1st ed. 1879), p. 497.

11. William L. Prosser, *Handbook of the Law of Torts,* 3d ed. (St. Paul, Minn.: West Publishing Co., 1964), p. 24: "This of course merely begs the question, since unless motive is to be eliminated altogether, it must be taken into account in determining whether the act is 'in its essence lawful' in the first place."

12. E.g., Larkin v. Tsavaris, 85 So.2d 731 (Florida 1956); Hornsley v. Smith, 191 Ga. 491, 13 S.E.2d 20 (1941); Flaherty v. Moran, 81 Mich. 52, 45 N.W. 381 (1890); Hibbard v. Halliday, 58 Okla. 244, 158 P. 1158 (1916); Racich v. Mastiovich, 65 S.D. 321, 273 N.W. 660 (1937); Erickson v. Hudson, 70 Wyo. 317, 249 P.2d 523 (1952).

13. E.g., Katz v. Walkinshaw, 141 Cal. 116, 74 P. 766 (1903); Gagnon v. French Lick Springs Hotel Co., 163 Ind. 687, 72 N.E. 849 (1904); Barclay v. Abraham, 121 Iowa 619, 96 N.W. 1080 (1903); Chesley v. King, 74 Me. 164 (1882); Stillwater Water Co. v. Farmer, 89 Minn. 58, 93 N.W. 907 (1903).

14. See generally Ames, "How Far an Act May Be a Tort Because of Wrongful Motive of the Actor," *Harvard Law Review* 18 (1905): 411; Fridman, "Motive in the English Law of Nuisance," *Virginia Law Review* 40 (1954): 583.

15. See generally Carpenter, "Interference with Contract Relations," *Harvard Law Review* 41 (1928): 728; Green, "Relational Interests," *Illinois Law Review* 29 (1935): 1041; Sayre, "Inducing Breach of Contract," *Harvard Law Review* 36 (1923): 663; Harper, "Interference with Contractual Relations," *Northwest-*

ern University Law Review 47 (1953): 873; Prosser, *Handbook, supra* note 11, at § 123.

16. Lord Bowen in Mogul Steamship Co. v. McGregor, Gow & Co., 23 Q.B.D. 598, 613 (C.A. 1889). For general discussions of the prima facie tort concept, see Holmes, "Privilege, Malice and Intent," *Harvard Law Review* 8 (1894): 1; Brown, "The Rise and Threatened Demise of the Prima Facie Tort Principle," *Northwestern University Law Review* 54 (1959): 563; Note, "The Prima Facie Tort Doctrine," *Columbia Law Review* 52 (1952): 503.

17. Prosser, *Handbook, supra* note 11, at § 26.

18. 4 Bing., N.C. 212, 132 Eng. Rep. 769 (C.P. 1838). In *Grainger,* the plaintiff mortgaged his vessel to the defendants under terms giving the plaintiff the right to retain possession. Thereafter, however, the defendants demanded that the plaintiff give up the register to the vessel, without which he could not go to sea. Upon plaintiff's refusal, the defendants obtained his arrest and imprisonment under a writ of capias–in order to compel him to give up something to which the defendants were not entitled under the terms of the mortgage.

19. The sort of emphasis our common law has placed on the defendant's bad motives in certain instances may also be found in the civil law concept of liability for "abusive use of a right" or abus de droit. This concept is based on the notion that rights are limited not only in their extent, but also in their exercise, and that there is therefore an abuse of the right if it is exercised with the intent of injuring another. French law has long employed this reasoning in cases where legal processes are used for ulterior purposes and in cases of discharge from employment without just cause.

20. See, e.g., Canuel v. Oskoian, 184 F.Supp. 70 (D.R.I. 1960); London Guarantee & Accident Co. v. Horn, 206 Ill. 493, 69 N.E. 526 (1903); DeMinico v. Craig, 207 Mass. 593, 94 N.E. 317 (1911); Carneso v. St. Paul Union Stockyards Co., 164 Minn. 457, 205 N.W. 630 (1925); Warschauser v. Brooklyn Furniture Co., 159 App. Div. 81, 144 N.Y.Supp. 257 (2d Dep't 1913); Jones v. Leslie, 61 Wash. 107, 112 P. 81 (1910); Mendelson v. Blatz Brewing Co., 9 Wis. 2d 487, 101 N.W.2d 805 (1960); Giblan v. National Amalgamated Labourers' Union, [1903] 2 K.B. 600 (C.A.). The source of common law protection of the employment relationship appears to be the Ordinance and Statute of Labourers, 23 Edw. III, St. 1 (1349) and 25 Edw. III, St. 1 (1350), which were enacted after the Black Death had reduced the labor force in England by almost one-half. W. Holdsworth, *A History of English Law* (3d ed. 1923) 2:459–60. It was the employer's interest that these fourteenth-century statutes sought to protect. The connection between these ancient provisions and modern-day protection of the employment relationship, and indeed of all contractual relations, is shown in the landmark decision of Lumley v. Gye, 2 E. & B. 216, 118 Eng. Rep. 749 (Q.B. 1853). In holding the defendant liable for enticing a famous opera singer from the employ of the plaintiff, the court reasoned that even though the relationship of the opera singer and the plaintiff was not of the sort defined in the Statute of Labourers, the injury suffered by

the plaintiff was so closely analogous to that encompassed by the statute that an extension of its underlying principle was warranted.

21. 206 Ala. 147, 89 So. 732 (1921). A case similar to *Millonas* is American Surety Co. v. Schottenbauer, 257 F.2d 6 (8th Cir. 1958).

22. 206 Ala. at 151, 89 So. at 735.

23. It was the employer's interest in the employment relationship that the law first sought to protect. See note 20 *supra.*

24. Berry v. Donovan, 188 Mass. 353, 355–56, 74 N.E. 603, 604, *appeal dismissed,* 199 U.S. 612 (1905). See also Rape v. Mobile & O. R.R., 136 Miss. 38, 100 So. 585 (1924), where the court, in finding a contract for "permanent" employment to be terminable at will, expressed a concern for unwary parties who might tie themselves up in perpetual contracts.

25. McClelland v. N. I. Gen. Health Services Bd., [1957] 1 W.L.R. 594, 612: "As a matter of practical common sense, the situations of the employer . . . and that of one of its servants are very different. The loss or damage to the [employer] occasioned by the departure of one of its servants would, save in very exceptional circumstances, be negligible. To a servant . . . the security of employment . . . is of immense value."

26. See, e.g., Hill Grocery Co. v. Carroll, 223 Ala. 376, 136 So. 789 (1931); Sullivan v. Barrows, 303 Mass. 197, 21 N.E.2d 275 (1939).

27. Carmen v. Fox Film Corp., 204 App. Div. 776, 198 N.Y.S. 766 (1923).

28. Sebastian v. Wood, 246 Iowa 94, 101, 66 N.W.2d 841, 845 (1954).

29. 246 Iowa at 100, 66 N.W.2d at 844: "The award of such damages constitutes an effective deterrent to such offenders, and a salutary protection to society and the public in general."

Unjust Dismissal:
Time for a Statute

Clyde W. Summers

First, it is time, and past time, for us to provide all employees general legal protection against unjust discipline. Through numerous statutes and through collective bargaining we have long ago repudiated the legal rule that an employer may discharge an employee for any reason or no reason at all. In the face of these statutes and collective agreements, no one can seriously contend that this outmoded rule is either necessary or appropriate to the efficient and orderly functioning of our society. More than a third of our employed work force is now given general protection against unjust dismissal under collective agreements, civil service systems, or tenure rules. That protection has earned acceptance as an essential element of a tolerable and humane employment relation, and it expresses an increasing recognition that employees have valuable rights in their jobs that society ought to protect against arbitrary action. Few employers would seriously propose to remove "just cause" clauses from their collective agreements, and no union could seriously consider such a proposal. Yet, more than half of our employed work force are still without such protection and hold their jobs subject to the whim, arbitrariness, or vindictiveness of their employers. In the words of Justice Roberts in the *Geary* case, "The time has surely come to afford unorganized employees an opportunity to prove in court a claim for arbitrary and retaliatory discharge." This country is among the last to leave workers unprotected against such employer action.

It is naïve or disingenuous to assert, as some do, that employees need no legal protection because most employers do not abuse their power —that employees are seldom unjustly discharged. The number of arbitration cases under collective agreements in which discharged employees win reinstatement demonstrates that even when employers know their actions will be reviewed, and know from past experiences that a wrongful discharge can be costly, their decision-making processes still go astray. How many employees not protected by collective agreements are victims of abusive disciplinary action cannot be determined, for unorganized individuals deprived of adequate legal recourse cannot make known the injustices they must silently suffer. It would be a modest assumption, however, that those without protection are more often arbitrarily dismissed than those who have recourse to arbitration or other protection. We know that the dangers of injustice are enough to cause unions to insist that collective agreements include "just cause" clauses and to establish procedures ending in arbitration to protect employees against unjust dismissal.

Second, any realistic hope for increased legal protection of employees must look for fulfillment to legislation, for the courts have thus far shown an unwillingness to break through their self-created crust of legal doctrine. Legal theories rooted in torts, contracts, and property law are readily available. The judges' self-doubt that they would be able to develop the standards to be applied should have been allayed by the cases under the Selective Service Act and by the availability of standards that can be borrowed from the law of arbitration. The "uncharted territory" has long since been mapped in considerable detail by arbitrators. A few bolder judges have pointed the way, but the great majority have lacked the courage or desire to follow.

Third, legal protection against unjust dismissal can best be built upon the standards and procedures of our existing arbitration system. The term "just cause" provides a workable standard because it has already been given content by thousands of arbitration decisions that have worked out both substantive and procedural principles and submitted them to the test of continued criticism and experience. Unlike other countries that have used equally flexible phrases as statutory standards, we have a large body of precedent and general understanding as to what "just cause" means. Perhaps more importantly, our arbitration system has developed a substantial cadre of individuals who are experienced in hearing discipline cases and applying the "just cause" standard. No other country, when it enacted its unjust-dismissal statute, had available such a trained judiciary. Finally, the customary arbitration procedure provides the flexibility and informality most suitable for the handling of these cases.

Given these three general propositions, the general outlines of the solution are readily apparent: statutorily articulate the right of employees not to be disciplined except for "just cause" and channel the adjudication of cases arising under the statute into the arbitration process. The structural problem would not be difficult if legislation were at the state level, as it should be to maintain its simplicity and provide more accessible forums, and to permit variety and experimentation.

The statute need not, indeed ought not, attempt to define "just cause," for the existing body of precedent has given it a workably defined content while preserving its flexibility to accommodate special circumstances and changed conditions. Having created the right not to be disciplined without just cause, the statute would provide that claims arising under it should be submitted to arbitration. If the parties were unable to agree upon an arbitrator, then the arbitrator would be selected from a panel maintained for that purpose by the state mediation service or some other state agency. The adjudication would thereby be channeled into the arbitration system and governed by arbitration procedures.

In a number of states, state mediation services already maintain panels of arbitrators from which parties with a labor dispute can select an arbitrator, or from which the mediation service may assign one. In Connecticut, for example, standing panels of union, employer, and neutral arbitrators are maintained by the Board of Mediation and Arbitration. When the parties agree to arbitration through the board, a tripartite panel is selected and provided without cost to the parties, the board paying the arbitrators a statutory rate from state funds. The New York State mediation board has long had two panels of neutrals —"staff" arbitrators who are provided by the board without cost to the parties, and "panel" arbitrators who are provided by the board but are paid by the parties. In North Carolina the commissioner of labor maintains a list of arbitrators from which he selects one when the parties are otherwise unable to agree. The costs are paid by the parties unless the commissioner determines that it is in the public interest that the costs be paid by the state. Such panels could be used to provide arbitrators for deciding cases arising under an unjust dismissal statute.[1]

A statute so structured would give employees not covered by collective agreements substantially the same protection as that now enjoyed by employees covered by collective agreements. They would have access to the same arbitration procedure, would have their cases heard by some of the same arbitrators, and would be judged by essentially the same standards.[2] This could be accomplished with a minimum of administrative machinery, for all that would be required would be maintaining a panel of arbitrators and naming arbitrators from that panel to hear cases as they were filed. In most states these functions could be added to existing mediation and arbitration agencies.

The proposed structure is similar in principle to one used for many years in Pennsylvania for adjudicating smaller civil suits. Under the so-called Compulsory Arbitration Act the courts of common pleas in each county may adopt rules requiring all civil actions except those involving real estate to be submitted to arbitration by a panel of three lawyers. The lawyers are selected from a list maintained by the court and generally assigned in alphabetical order, and are paid a statutory stipend. More than six thousand cases a year are disposed of in Philadelphia alone through this procedure, which is administered by a clerk with a small staff.

Notes

1. The mediation agency could perform the function of attempting to conciliate the case before assigning an arbitrator. This function would be particularly important because in many of the cases there may have been no meaningful previous discussion between the parties.

2. The standards would differ in that, in the absence of a union, there would be no list of offenses either negotiated with or acquiesced in by the union, nor would there be any precedents established by prior grievance settlements. Thus, the only disciplinary rules and practices would be those unilaterally established by the employer. These, however, would not be binding on the arbitrator, and at most would have presumptive validity. The arbitrator would have to judge the fairness and appropriateness of the employer's rules and practices just as he must in cases in which the union has not agreed to the employer's posted rules and contests the fairness of those rules either generally or as applied in a particular case. The protection given unorganized employees would diminish to the extent that the arbitrator gave deference to employer rules that were harsher than they would be if a union were present. However, arbitrators may be less deferential to rules that have been unilaterally established by the employer without being subject to union challenge.

Protection Against Unfair Dismissal

Jack Stieber

Employers who operate under collective bargaining agreements in the United States realize that in order to discipline or discharge an employee they must be able to persuade a union and, if necessary, an impartial arbitrator that they had "just cause" for such action. Public employers and school systems, whether or not they are subject to collective bargaining, operate under similar constraints due to civil service rules or tenure system procedures provided by law. In total, about one-third of all employees are protected against unilateral disciplinary action by their employers.

How about the remaining two-thirds who are not represented by a union and are not protected by civil service or tenure rules? Except for protection against discriminatory treatment for union activity provided by federal or state statutes, or by other laws prohibiting employment discrimination because of race, creed, nationality, sex, or age, these employees are subject to the common law that, absent some explicit contract provision, "an employee can be discharged for good cause, for bad cause, or for no cause at all."

BRITISH LAW ON DISMISSAL

This distinction between different groups of employees, while taken for granted in the United States, is found in few other industrial nations. Most countries provide some degree of legal protection, at least against unjust dismissal, for all employees. This spring while on sabbatical leave in England, I had an opportunity to examine the experience under the unfair dismissal provisions of the Employment Protection Act of Great

Reprinted from Michigan State University, School of Labor and Industrial Relations *Newsletter,* Fall Quarter, 1978.

Britain. The British experience, in addition to its significance for employers and employees in that country, may also have important implications for the United States.

The British law recognizes that every employee who has been employed for at least six months has the right not to be unfairly dismissed by his employer. The burden of proof is on the employer to satisfy a tripartite industrial tribunal that he acted "reasonably." The tripartite composition of the tribunal is designed to bring to bear on each case the industrial experience of the employer and trade union members as well as the legal background of the chairman.

COMPLAINT PROCEDURES

The emphasis in unfair dismissal cases is on accessibility, speed, and informality. The average time for a case to be heard by a tribunal is ten weeks from the date the complaint is presented. Decisions are usually rendered within a few weeks by tribunals which conduct hearings in various cities. Industrial tribunals are not bound by strict rules of evidence which apply in ordinary courts. Parties bear the cost if they engage legal representatives.

In practice, most workers are represented by a trade union official or someone else of their choice, or they present their own cases. (I observed one hearing in which the employee was represented by her brother and another in which an elected town councilor represented the employee.) Employers are usually represented by their personnel officer or legal counsel. Legal costs are awarded only against a party who acts frivolously or vexatiously or who causes unnecessary postponements. Tribunal decisions may be appealed to a tripartite Employment Appeal Tribunal and, on questions of law, to the courts. Although there are important differences, the function of industrial tribunals in unfair dismissal cases is similar to that of labor arbitrators in the United States.

REINSTATEMENT RARE

Complaints alleging unfair dismissal are first sent to the Advisory, Conciliation and Arbitration Service (ACAS), where a conciliation officer tries to help the parties resolve their dispute without the need for a hearing by an industrial tribunal. During conciliation, applicants often withdraw their complaints or the parties agree to a settlement providing compensation to the employee or reinstatement. If the complaint is not withdrawn and there is no settlement through conciliation, the case is referred to an industrial tribunal for hearing. In 1977, over 35,000 unfair dismissal cases were resolved, of which somewhat less than two-thirds were withdrawn or settled by ACAS and about one-third were decided by industrial tribunals.

The remedy in most cases settled by ACAS involved the payment of compensation to the complainant by the employer. The median compensation agreed upon in conciliated cases was less than $300. Reinstatement of the employee to his former position or to some other job was agreed to by the employer in less than 3 percent of the cases.

Of some 12,800 cases decided by tribunals in 1977, about 70 percent were won by employers and 30 percent were decided in favor of the complainant. As with conciliated cases, the remedy in cases where "unfair dismissal" was found was almost always to award compensation to the employee. Reinstatement was ordered for only 180 of the employees—0.5 percent of all cases decided by tribunals. More than half the compensation awards made by industrial tribunals were less than $800, and less than 2 percent came to more than $6,000. Thus the average compensation awarded by tribunals to complainants was more than twice as large as in cases settled during conciliation. This is not surprising, since it is reasonable to assume that complainants who think they have a strong case will hold out for larger settlements and take their chances with a tribunal, if the employer is not prepared to meet their terms.

American industrial relations specialists may wonder at the extremely small number of cases in which complainants found to have been dismissed unfairly were reinstated to their former positions. This is contrary to experience in the United States where arbitrators will almost always reinstate employees found to have been discharged without just cause, often awarding back pay as well. The explanation for this difference in remedies lies in the reluctance of the British to compel an employer to reemploy an unwanted employee. There is a strong belief that such forced reinstatement will not work out in practice. Therefore, although tribunals may order reinstatement, they have no authority to enforce such an order. However, if an order of reinstatement is not complied with, the tribunal must make an additional award of compensation to the employee.

TWO CASES IN POINT

The unfair dismissal law applies to all employees including professionals and those employed in a management capacity. Two cases which received considerable press coverage in Great Britain illustrate the diversity of cases heard by industrial tribunals. One case involved Claridge's, one of the most famous and most expensive hotels in London. Richard Elvidge, a 19-year-old trainee chef, charged that he had been unfairly dismissed for union organizing, but the hotel said Elvidge was discharged for ruining a serving of *ratatouille*—a spicy vegetable dish. After several days of hearings, the parties reached a settlement under which Claridge's gave the trainee chef $1,810 in compensation and $1,170 to "assist him to continue his professional career in cooking" but not at Claridge's. "It would not be in anybody's interest for Mr. Elvidge to return to the hotel after so much publicity," said the hotel management.

At the other extreme is the case of Mr. C. Gordon Tether who for twenty-one years wrote the *Financial Times*'s "Lombard" column. His longevity earned him an entry in the *Guinness Book of Records.* But in 1976 he was dismissed, and he appealed to the Industrial Tribunal. Hearings in Tether's case began in May 1977 and were still in process more than a year later when I left the country.

CRITICISMS OF THE LAW

The unfair dismissal law has been subjected to considerable criticism, particularly by employers:

1. The Engineering Employers' Federation found that more than half of its members responding to a survey said the law had been a "significant inhibiting factor" in restricting hiring.

2. The law reverses the usual "innocent until proved guilty" principle because a dismissed employee does not have to show even a *prima facie* case in order to summon his employer before a tribunal. The employer then has the burden of proving the dismissal was fair.

3. It costs at least $6,000 to employers, applicants, and public funds to make an average award of about $1,000 to a successful applicant.

4. Unions claim that the proceedings are too "legalistic."

5. The law is particularly burdensome to small employers who do not

have formal personnel procedures and therefore have difficulty proving to tribunals that they acted reasonably in dismissing an employee.

A 1978 study of employers in manufacturing industries made by the Policy Studies Institute (PSI) of Great Britain found most of the above criticisms to be unjustified. The study indicated that the chief effect of the unfair dismissal law has been to encourage the reform or formalization of procedures in disciplinary action and dismissals. Employers said they now exercised greater care in selecting new employees and in appraising employee performance. There was also evidence that unfair dismissal measures have reduced rates of dismissal, particularly in the establishments where levels were relatively high prior to the legislation, which was instituted in 1971 by the Conservative Government and retained with some modifications by the Labour Government. The study found little evidence to support the view that the unfair dismissal law hit hardest small employers who were previously unconstrained in their manpower policies and procedures.

IMPLICATIONS FOR THE UNITED STATES

There are too many important differences in the industrial relations systems of Great Britain and the United States to draw definitive conclusions for the United States from the British experience. For example: approximately 50 percent of Britain's workers belong to unions as compared with about 25 percent in the United States; the highly developed grievance and arbitration procedures provided by almost all collective bargaining agreements in the United States do not exist in Great Britain; the industrial relations function is more professionalized in American companies than among employers in Great Britain.

Nonetheless, the British experience does provide interesting and useful information on how that country's effort to protect *all* employees against unfair dismissal has worked. The need for legislation with the same broad objective would appear to be even more necessary in the United States, because of the much lower extent of union organization in this country. Employees working under collective agreements in the United States probably have better protection against unjust discipline and dismissal than in any other country. On the other hand, unorganized employees, comprising the overwhelming proportion of our labor force, lack the protection against unjust dismissal which is accorded workers in most other countries. There is no rational basis for this distinction.

The failure of the United States to provide protection against unfair dismissal for unorganized workers has received little attention from legislators, scholars, and industrial relations practitioners. The time is long past due for this country to address itself to this issue.

III.

The Debate Over an Employee Bill of Rights

An Employee Bill of Rights—
A Proposal

David W. Ewing

Obviously, the philosophy of unlimited employer access into an employee's life does not jibe with current notions of privacy, yet the law reflects the no-privacy-is-good-policy tradition. What is needed here, as in cases involving infringements upon freedoms of speech, press, and political and personal association, is a set of guidelines—a bill of rights for employees—which will balance the legitimate needs of management with the legitimate needs of employees. The bill of rights that follows is one person's proposal, a set of working ideas for discussion:

• No organization or manager shall discharge, demote, or in other ways discriminate against any employee who criticizes, in speech or press, the ethics, legality, or social responsibility of management actions.

• No employee shall be penalized for engaging in outside activities of his or her choice after working hours, whether political, economic, civic, or cultural; nor for buying products of his or her choice for personal use; nor for expressing or encouraging views contrary to top management's on political, economic, and social issues. This provision does not authorize an employee to come to work beat in the morning because of moonlighting. If on-the-job performance suffers, the usual penalties may have to be paid.

• No organization or manager shall penalize an employee for refusing to carry out a directive that violates common norms of morality.

• No organization shall allow audio or visual recordings of an employee's conversations or actions to be made without his or her prior knowledge and consent. Nor may an organization require an employee or applicant to take personality tests, polygraph examinations, or other tests, which constitute, in his opinion, an invasion of privacy.

• No employee's desk, files, or locker may be examined in his or her absence by anyone but a senior manager who has sound reason to believe that the files contain information needed for a management decision that must be made in the employee's absence.

• No employer organization may collect and keep on file information about an employee that is not relevant and necessary for efficient management. Every employee shall have the right to inspect his or her personnel file and challenge the accuracy, relevance, or necessity of data in it, except for personal evaluations and comments by other employees which could not reasonably be obtained if confidentiality were not promised. Access to an employee's file by outside individuals and organizations shall be limited to inquiries about the essential facts of employment.

• No manager may communicate to prospective employers of an employee who is about to be or has been discharged gratuitous opinions that might hamper the individual in obtaining a new position. The intent of this right is to stop blacklisting. The courts have already given some support for it.

• An employee who is discharged, demoted, or transferred to a less desirable job is entitled to a written statement from management of its reasons for the penalty. The aim of this provision is to encourage a manager to give the same reasons in a hearing, arbitration, or court trial that he or she gives the employee when the cutdown happens.

• Every employee who feels that he or she has been penalized for asserting any right described in this bill shall be entitled to a fair hearing before an impartial official, board, or arbitrator. The findings and conclusions of the hearing shall be delivered in writing to the employee and management. This very important right is the organizational equivalent of due process of law as we know it in political and community life. Without due process in a company or agency, the rights in this bill would all have to be enforced by outside courts and tribunals, which is expensive for society as well as time-consuming for the employees who are required to appear as complainants and witnesses.

With judicial, governmental, and even managerial opinion shifting toward the establishment and protection of basic employee rights, consideration must be given to the possibility of a constitutional amendment. This is the most ambitious proposal. In one giant step, rights could be created for employees of all private and public organizations. This was the course the country took in extending the Bill of Rights to blacks after the Civil War and suffrage to women after World War I. Employee rights would be a particularly fitting subject for a constitutional amendment since they represent a fresh extension of principles in the Bill of Rights.

If a constitutional amendment is proposed, it should be fairly general and flexible so that the courts can interpret, modify, and expand it in response to changing times, as they have done with other amendments. For instance, a constitutional amendment might read as simply as this:

> No public or private organization shall discriminate against an employee for criticizing the ethical, moral, or legal policies and practices of the organization; nor shall any organization discriminate against an employee for engaging in outside activities of his or her choice, or for objecting to a directive that violates common norms of morality.
>
> No organization shall deprive an employee of the enjoyment of reasonable privacy in his or her place of work, and no personal information about employees shall be collected or kept other than that necessary to manage the organization efficiently and to meet legal requirements.
>
> No employee of a public or private organization who alleges in good faith that his or her rights have been violated shall be discharged or penalized without a fair hearing in the employer organization.

Because the constitutional road is so direct and visible, it is likely to catalyze opposition more than any other approach would. But it is also the fairest way to achieve employee rights, and in the end it may prove the most satisfactory.

Company Constitutionalism?

Staughton Lynd

Mr. Ewing's bill of rights has some important omissions. In seeking to protect speech that criticizes the ethics, legality, or social responsibility of management actions, Mr. Ewing's concern is for speech about corporate action damaging to the *public*. Mr. Ewing eulogizes employees who sought to keep their companies from polluting and who tried to bring to public attention the defective condition of the buses they drove. He praises workers who refused to record conversations with prospective clients or to dump toxic materials into the Cuyahoga River, as well as those who took affirmative action and "blew the whistle" on improper practices of their governmental employers or who published an article critical of the company in a community newspaper. In short, Mr. Ewing defends employees who have acted like Ralph Nader at the risk of losing their jobs.

Mr. Ewing is much less interested when workers criticize their *own* exploitation. Indeed, he is inclined to fire them when they do.

> Protection does not extend to employees who make nuisances of themselves or who balk, argue, or contest managerial decisions on normal operating and planning matters. . . . Nor does the protection extend to individuals who malign the organization. We don't protect individuals who go around ruining other people's reputations, and neither should we protect those who vindictively impugn their employers.

The analogy of speech critical of a corporation to libel of an individual is especially unfortunate. With regard to speech outside the workplace, the nation has painfully come to the conclusion that penalizing criticism of individual governmental officials—the crime of seditious libel—has no place in the law of the First Amendment. Criticism of the

Reprinted by permission of The Yale Law Journal Co. and Fred B. Rothman & Co. from *Yale Law Journal* 87, no. 4, March 1978. Copyright © 1978 by The Yale Law Journal Co., Inc. Most footnotes have been deleted.

boss is the seditious libel of the workplace. For Mr. Ewing it remains a crime, justifying discharge—industry's form of capital punishment.

In other ways, too, Mr. Ewing's concept of free speech in the workplace is significantly less protective than that already sanctioned by the Supreme Court. Outside the workplace, as previously indicated, Mr. Ewing would permit an employee to speak and associate freely unless the activity caused "palpable harm to the organization." Inside the workplace, Mr. Ewing would restrain speech considered by management to constitute railing, vindictive impugning, balking, and other nebulously defined misdeeds without requiring the employer to show that the speech, however irritating, also caused palpable harm. The Supreme Court, on the other hand, has found speech in both the private and public workplaces to be protected unless it causes tangible disruption. Moreover, Mr. Ewing proposes a constitutional amendment to create free speech rights in the workplace without mentioning that the Supreme Court has already held that, within the jurisdiction of the National Labor Relations Board, an employee's right to free speech is inalienable in the sense that a union cannot bargain it away.

Similarly, Mr. Ewing's notion of conscientious objection predates development of this concept in Selective Service cases growing out of the Vietnam war. He would require "that the conscientious objector . . . hold to a view that has some public acceptance. Fad moralities— messages from flying saucers, mores of occult religious sects, and so on —do not justify refusal to carry out an order." By contrast, since *United States* v. *Seeger,* a conscientious objector to military service has been required to show only that "a given belief that is sincere and meaningful occupies a place in the life of its possessor parallel to that filled by the orthodox belief in God of one who clearly qualifies for the exemption."

The limitations of Mr. Ewing's approach become especially apparent when one turns to enforcement of procedural rights. Mr. Ewing has a tendency to equate "senior managers" with impartial magistrates. Thus he considers it the functional equivalent of a magistrate's search warrant if a "senior manager . . . has sound reason to believe that the [absent employee's] files contain information needed for a management decision." The hearing Mr. Ewing has in mind would ordinarily be a hearing "in the employer organization" presided over by officers of the very company that initiated the discipline at issue. Wherever the hearing is held, moreover, in Mr. Ewing's view it should lack certain rights considered integral to due process outside the workplace.

The employee is guilty until proven innocent. "The burden should be on him or her to offer clear and convincing evidence. It should *not* be up to the employer to prove that the discharge was for incompetence, laziness, or economic reasons. If the burden of proof is on the employer, managers will be inhibited from building the most able and efficient staffs they can."

There is no right to judgment by a jury of one's peers. The closest Mr. Ewing comes to the Sixth Amendment is to praise a procedure in one company where the employee appears before "five non-management employees, chosen at random," who in turn report their findings of fact to the company president, who "renders a decision."

There is no equality before the "law of the workplace." Nothing in Mr. Ewing's book begins to suggest that a "senior manager" who vindictively impugned an employee would be subject to the same summary discharge as an employee who rails against a boss, or that a supervisor starting a fight would be evenhandedly disciplined under the shop rule prohibiting fighting by hourly workers.

Mr. Ewing, then, sacrifices workplace civil liberties when they threaten to cut too sharply into managerial efficiency. He also fails to recognize that the arguments that underlie extending such liberties to industrial relations at all—the predominant role of the job in each worker's life and the fundamental human need for self-development and independence—also support establishment of a more democratic structure for all decisions made in the workplace. The logical conclusion of his reasoning is not, as Mr. Ewing contends, autocratic management limited by specific rights. Rather, it is some form of workplace democracy where the employees themselves decide not only what civil liberties should be protected but also how leisure should be balanced against income, whether better working conditions are worth some loss of profits, and how the work itself should be done.

Part of Mr. Ewing's unwillingness to push his thesis farther seems to be based on a foreshortened sense of history. Repeatedly he insists that lack of democracy in the workplace has become a concern "only in recent years"; that prior to the 1950s "employee constitutionalism was hypothetical"; that in the nineteenth century "perhaps the most important source of support of employer prerogatives was the attitude of *employees.* Poorly educated, poorly trained, and poorly motivated, as a rule, they were content to let wisdom and insight reside in the heads of organizations."

This picture of the past overlooks, first, the Jeffersonian sentiment that there can be no democracy unless every man is his own boss and that factory labor is a form of slavery. Early in the industrial revolution, American workers responded to the factory system with demands for more freedom at work. More immediately pertinent, Mr. Ewing's notion that efforts to bring constitutional liberties to the workplace began in the 1950s distorts history. By far the strongest thrust in recent years toward both workplace democracy and employee civil liberties coincided with the CIO insurgency in the years 1935–1947. The 1950s represented the quiescence of this movement, not its birth.

During the New Deal years, labor won a wide variety of employee liberties. Under Section 7 of the National Labor Relations Act, workers attained the right to associate for mutual aid or protection, a workplace analogue of the First Amendment right, and the right to be represented by agents of their own choosing, an equivalent for the Sixth Amendment right to counsel. In a series of dramatic Supreme Court cases, employees won the First Amendment right to free speech in and near the workplace.[1]

Any doubt about whether the congressional mandate and these court decisions reflected a desire to extend constitutional rights to the workplace is settled by examining the NLRB briefs in such cases as *Republic Aviation.* Drawing on First Amendment ideas just then gaining currency from the Supreme Court decisions concerning the Jehovah's Witnesses, the board successfully argued to the Court that Section 7 should be read to incorporate the concepts of overbreadth, of chilling effect, and of the irrelevance of alternative speech opportunities. Furthermore, Section 7 would require a showing of substantial and material disruption—the workplace equivalent of clear and present danger —before speech might be restrained. The same concepts have subsequently been elaborated in public employee speech cases, such as *Pickering* v. *Board of Education,* which upheld the right of a teacher to criticize school board policy. But, contrary to Mr. Ewing's view of history, the Court in that case adopted ideas already well established in the private sphere more than twenty years earlier.

Mr. Ewing's disregard for the union movement and its judicial achievements suggests a disturbing thought. Perhaps Mr. Ewing's constitutionalism-without-unions is a resurrection of the movement for "industrial democracy," more aptly characterized as company unionism, that flourished in the 1920s. Perhaps what Mr. Ewing is advocating is a way for companies to head off unionism among their

1. These decisions included *Hague* v. *CIO,* 307 U.S. 496 (1939) (municipal streets and parks are public forums subject to First Amendment easement); *Marsh* v. *Alabama,* 326 U.S. 501 (1946) (First Amendment also extends to similar areas in privately owned company town); *Thomas* v. *Collins,* 323 U.S. 516 (1945) (state may not impose prior restraint on First Amendment activity by requiring union organizers to be licensed); *Thornhill* v. *Alabama,* 310 U.S. 88, 94 (1940) (pickets who "appear to have been on company property" were engaged in protected speech because "in the circumstances of our times the dissemination of information concerning the facts of a labor dispute must be regarded as within that area of free discussion that is guaranteed by the Constitution"); and *Republic Aviation Corp.* v. *NLRB,* 324 U.S. 793 (1945) (employee speech on employer's property is presumptively protected if it occurs during nonworking time).

employees by creating from above a facsimile of the rights unionism would provide.

Let us consider, in fairness, the rebuttals that Mr. Ewing might offer to this hypothesis. If the creation of unions were strictly limited and if most workers were obligated to remain unorganized, there might be cause for focusing on the implementation of specific rights to the exclusion of unionization. Mr. Ewing rightly points out that fifty million employees in the private sector do not belong to unions. He also observes correctly that in its recent *Bell Aerospace* decision, the Supreme Court held that managerial employees are not covered by the National Labor Relations Act. But the bulk of nonunionized employees in the private sector *are* covered by the National Labor Relations Act and their obvious first step toward civil liberties in the workplace would be to seek collective bargaining recognition.

Again rightly, Mr. Ewing indicates that many unions "seem to be as despotic and corrupt as the worst corporate management teams" and that union organizations "are subject to the same managerial diseases as other types of organizations." These are reasons to wage a vigorous struggle for internal union democracy. They are not reasons for preferring a company-initiated grievance plan to a union as a means of protecting employee rights against management.

In addition, the civil liberties Mr. Ewing is most concerned to protect are not necessarily protected by Section 7 of the National Labor Relations Act, because Section 7 protects protest only when it is related to wages, hours, and working conditions and is the concerted action of more than one person. Hence the single person seeking to prevent a company from marketing an unsafe product may get no help from the board. Mr. Ewing performs a service in highlighting the plight of such individuals. Surely, however, protection should be extended to persons thus situated in addition to the more prosaic safeguards provided by unions, rather than as an alternative to unionism.

Mr. Ewing's strongest rebuttal to the charge of antiunionism is a passage in which he advocates that unions bargain collectively for civil liberties.

> Is there any reason that employee unions or associations cannot write civil liberties into the contract? Apparently this step has not yet been taken. Judging from the general trend in collective bargaining, however, there seems to be no reason that it cannot be done—and the movement is unmistakably in this direction. For example, unions have been going outside the conventional scope of work conditions and dealing with problems of sexism in the office. . . . Also, unions are becoming ever more conscious of the rights of minorities, as spelled out in the Fourteenth and

Fifteenth Amendments to the Constitution. If union officials consider
rights like these important, surely they can add others to the list.

This is a most creative suggestion and, whatever may be Mr. Ewing's
overall views about unions, it deserves to be pursued. In my judgment,
Mr. Ewing is quite right to believe that bargaining for civil liberties is
at the edge of the possible. In the recent contest for president of the
United Steelworkers of America, both candidates espoused the idea
that an employee should be innocent until proven guilty: that is, the
employee should remain at his or her job, at regular pay, until any
discipline sought by management has been finally adjudicated.

Perhaps the best way to sum up the sense in which Mr. Ewing is
antiunion is to clarify the degree to which he is promanagement. The
parameters of this book were established by polls and surveys addressed
by Mr. Ewing to corporate executives; its audience, clearly, is management. Mr. Ewing believes that rights can be established for individual
employees without changing the fundamental allocation of power between management and labor. Inevitably, then, he must persuade himself that power will yield without a demand: that the corporate
hierarchy, guided by enlightened self-interest, will itself set in motion
the changes needed to make the work environment more decent and
humane. This is paternalism. Even if feasible, Mr. Ewing's program
would be humiliating to workers in a way that Mr. Ewing does not seem
to perceive. And implementation of the program is not possible, because, on Mr. Ewing's logic, decency must give way when it conflicts
with profit.

In short, Mr. Ewing's constitutionalism is constitutional monarchy.
Mr. Ewing expressly rejects the idea that individual rights must be
protected by democratic self-government: the idea, in the words of the
Declaration of Independence, that "to secure these rights, governments
are instituted among men, deriving their just powers from the consent
of the governed."

Civil Liberties in the Private Sector

Ira Glasser

Ewing's book is not an exhaustive, scholarly documentation of the problem [of extending constitutional rights into organizational life]. Nor does it adequately identify, much less attempt to resolve, some of the very complex analytic dilemmas involved. For example, if it becomes illegal for a private employer to discriminate on the basis of political belief, would that mean that an organization like the NAACP would no longer have the discretion to refuse to hire a lawyer who believed in racial segregation? Would a Catholic parochial school no longer be able to refuse to hire non-Catholic teachers? Would a newspaper no longer be free to hire editorial writers and columnists who agreed with the publisher's point of view? If such organizations were permitted such discretion when they hired lawyers, teachers, or editorial writers, should they be permitted the same discretion when they hire secretaries, telephone switchboard operators, or janitors? Those are not easy questions to resolve. Even assuming a resolution, it is very difficult to write laws that would embrace such distinctions, limiting discretion in certain situations but not others.

Ewing does not adequately deal with such problems. He believes, as I do, that "whistle-blowers" should be protected. That is, he would like to see people who publicly reveal certain company secrets protected against recrimination by the company. He cites as one example a research manager in a large company who publicly criticized the company's efforts, which he regarded as superficial, to comply with newly enacted anti-pollution laws, and who was harassed and punished on the job in a variety of ways until he finally was forced to leave. But what

Excerpted from *Social Policy*, March-April 1978, copyright © 1978 by Social Policy Corporation, New York, New York 10036.

about the research manager who reveals trade secrets to a rival company? Should the employer be able to prevent that sort of revelation? And how should a law be written to distinguish the two? The problem is not unlike the one presented by the Daniel Ellsberg case. Were the Pentagon Papers properly part of public policy debate or did they contain national security secrets? Did their revelation further the ends of the First Amendment, or was what Ellsberg did treasonous? All that depends, of course, on how the laws are written, and on how the rules governing the classification of information are written. These are complicated problems, and Ewing does not deal with them in sufficient detail.

Ewing's attempt to reduce his principles to specific language is also inadequate. For example, the first principle of his proposed bill of rights for employees in private organizations would prohibit the employer from firing, demoting, or punishing any employee who criticizes "the ethics, legality, or social responsibility of management actions." Any employee? What about the company accountant? As everyone who has ever hired an accountant knows, the tax law is a flexible instrument, subject to many interpretations. What is legal or illegal is not always so clear. What you want an accountant to do is to stretch the law as far as possible to your advantage and, when the government questions certain items, to argue in your behalf. You might lose that argument, but you have hired the accountant to make it for you as effectively as possible. Suppose now, in the midst of a legal dispute, the accountant publicly attacks the position you have hired him to defend. Can you fire him and hire another accountant?

Similarly, what about the company lawyer? Again, as everyone knows each legal dispute has at least two sides. Your lawyer is employed to argue your side. Can you fire her when she publicly criticizes your legal position? I should hope so. Not even Richard Nixon should be forced to retain a lawyer who publicly denounces his legal position. Could we have a different standard for Exxon?

However, if a cafeteria worker in the company lunchroom writes a letter to the editor of a newspaper publicly criticizing the company's position in an antitrust suit, certainly that employee should be protected from recrimination. Without resolving the problem, I think it is clear that a legal principle that applies to "any employee" may be insufficient.

Finally, I do not understand why an employee's right to speak out ought to be limited to matters of "ethics, legality, or social responsibility." I do not see why a worker on a General Motors assembly line should not be able to publicly come out for the abolition of gasoline engines, or urge people to buy Fords. If he can own a Ford, why can't he recommend it to others? If he can refuse to own a car, why can't he lead a campaign, after working hours and on weekends, to replace autos with mass transit?

But having raised certain problems with Ewing's formulations, I must decline to quibble. Ewing has not attempted to write a treatise or a model code. Rather, he has tried to start an argument that is long overdue, and he is to be unambiguously commended for the effort. He is calling attention to a huge problem and urging that we adopt a stance toward it.

Free speech is not the only aspect of the problem. Privacy in the workplace is also not guaranteed. For example, labor unions have reported to me the increasing use of remote-controlled video surveillance of workers as well as other, more traditional devices such as open bathroom doors so that management can see if an employee is in the bathroom for legitimate purposes or just to take a smoke.

Compulsory submission to lie detectors, under penalty of dismissal or as a condition of hiring, is also widespread, and impossible to resist legally. Management searches of employees' lockers, desks, files, or other belongings is also without legal limit. Not even the Army has such unfettered discretion over buck privates!

Such intrusions are difficult, and often impossible to remedy. Most unions can do nothing about such intrusions unless they are specifically prohibited by contract, which is not usually the case. And where there are not unions, there is no protection whatsoever.

Fair procedures when disputes arise or charges are made are also missing from many private workplaces. In unionized workplaces, there are grievance procedures, although even those are not always adequate and often cannot be invoked by the employee unless the union agrees. Sometimes the employee finds himself aligned against both the union and the employer, and thus without recourse. But many workplaces are not unionized and their employees have no legal rights to fair procedures at all, other than what may be voluntarily granted by the employer. But such voluntary grants are hardly rights, since they may also be voluntarily taken away. Ewing quotes former Attorney General Ramsey Clark effectively on this point: "A right is not what someone gives you; it's what no one can take from you." As Ewing then remarks, not too many employees have rights by that definition.

The Myth of the "Oppressive Corporation"

Max Ways

If enough voices declare that the pace of change in the workplace is "too slow," and that this should be blamed on concentrated corporate power, then, obviously, somebody is going to limit the power of the corporate Leviathan.

Proposals along this line are set forth in *Freedom Inside the Organization* by David W. Ewing, an editor of the *Harvard Business Review.* Subtitled *Bringing Civil Liberties to the Workplace,* the book falls into a familiar pattern: generalizations about existing conditions are drawn from atrocity stories and selected opinions of employees. In the dark picture of corporate oppression that results, the author sees an urgent need for drastic legal remedies.

"For nearly two centuries," Ewing begins, "Americans have enjoyed freedom of press, speech, and assembly, due process of law, privacy, freedom of conscience, and other important rights—in their homes, churches, political forums, and social and cultural life. But Americans have not enjoyed these civil liberties in most companies, government agencies, and other organizations where they work. Once a U.S. citizen steps through the plant or office door at 9:00 A.M., he or she is nearly rightless until 5:00 P.M., Monday through Friday."

Ewing has in this opening passage disclosed a fundamental misconception about the nature of our cherished rights. A few pages later, this mistake leads him into a shocking distortion.

"For all practical purposes," he writes, "employees are required to be as obedient to their superiors, regardless of ethical and legal considerations, as are workers in totalitarian countries."

A writer so insensitive that he can equate U.S. corporate practices, even at their worst, with the system that produced the Gulag Archipelago is hardly qualified to lecture businessmen on their lack of concern for human rights.

The historic rights enjoyed by Americans protect them against the abuse of government police power, not against all unpleasant consequences that may follow from their speech or action. Free speech, for instance, means that Americans cannot be fined or imprisoned for what they say; the exceptions are a small and shrinking number. It does not mean that they cannot be sued for slander. It does not mean that what they say may not deprive them of the respect of their children, the affection of their parents or spouses, the company of their friends. If an American's speech is rude enough, or malicious enough, or silly enough he may find that people don't listen to him and he may even be ostracized. Cases where such penalties are "unjust" do occur. But these instances are not violations of our right of free speech.

The human damage that can be done by words is so great and so plain that (most) children learn early to watch what they say. These inhibitions can be psychologically or socially hurtful, but civilized life would be impossible without them and the person-to-person sanctions by which they are maintained.

Most corporations today allow employees great latitude in their personal behavior, including speech. But corporations, like individuals, retain the power to employ all private sanctions that are not illegal in themselves (e.g., assault and battery) to express disapproval of an individual's speech. They can argue, remonstrate, and warn. The most extreme penalty at their disposal is to dissolve their association with the speaker by firing him. This can be, indeed, a serious penalty—but not necessarily more serious than divorce, which is frequently provoked by speech.

Reciting a number of instances where corporations have fired employees for what they said, Ewing deems many, though not all, of these to be "unjust." He points out that some companies invoke penalties only after a scrupulously enforced "due process." He cites an IBM policy that guarantees many freedoms to employees and establishes internal procedures to review penalties imposed by managers. More and more companies have moved in this direction.

Ewing's argument is that if some corporations choose to behave in this way then all corporations should be required by law to do likewise. The legal reasoning is reminiscent of that which produced the Eighteenth Amendment. First, the human damage done by alcohol was exaggerated, then "the power of the liquor interest" was blown up out of all proportion to reality, then attention was called to the fact that many Americans—perhaps half the adult population—hardly ever used alcohol. Ergo, let's have a law requiring everyone to conform to the best practice.

Sure enough, Ewing, too, wants an amendment to the Constitution of the United States. His draft starts, "No public or private organization shall discriminate against an employee for criticizing the ethical, moral, or legal policies and practices of the organization. . . ."

In addition to protecting individual employees, Ewing frankly desires to encourage "whistle blowing" in cases of corporate wrongdoing. That might accomplish some desirable changes in corporate behavior. But this hypothesized advantage has to be weighed against some foreseeable disadvantages. Who is to distinguish between whistle blowing and spiteful accusation? Speech now is protected from government penalty, in most cases, even if the utterance is proved untrue. Would Ewing's amendment continue this broad protection? Or would courts have to sift evidence to discover whether the employee's charge against the corporation was true? In the first case an organization might be required to keep on its payroll an employee who continually lied about it. In the second case, courts, which are not winning much public applause for the way they discharge their present responsibilities, would have to take on a huge new burden of deciding not only whether charges were true or false, but whether ethical norms had or had not been violated by the defendant organization.

The incidence of these cases could become such a nuisance to companies that all employees might wind up having, in effect, life tenure in their jobs, like the Civil Service or the tenured faculty of universities. Neither of these examples is necessarily reassuring.

It's true, of course, that a company's right to fire has long been limited by the National Labor Relations Act, which has worked rather well in forbidding firing for union activity. In this narrow class of cases it is relatively easy to determine whether the forbidden practice has occurred. In a much larger group of cases under equal-opportunity acts, corporations are forbidden to discriminate in respect to race or sex. Enforcement here has been less effective and has caused more confusion. Ewing's amendment is so much broader than the equal-opportunity laws, and its criteria so much vaguer, that the imagination boggles at the legal chaos that might ensue.

Such practical objections Ewing brushes aside with a quote from Judge Learned Hand: "To keep our democracy, there must be one commandment: Thou shalt not ration justice." The distinguished jurist said many wise things, but this was not one of them. In any society justice must always be less than perfect. A free society recognizes that its government should not pretend to dispense total justice. In that sense justice in a democracy must always be "rationed."

Much injustice that occurs among citizens is beyond the reach of courts or of any government instrument. The state in which that limitation is not recognized, the state that believes itself empowered to set all norms of conduct and to deal with every incident of ethical transgression, is the absolute state, Leviathan.

IV.

Free Expression on the Job

Loyalty—and the Whistle Blower

Andrew Hacker

"Ethics, Loyalty, and Dissent." I am particularly taken by the center-piece of that trinity. The very word "loyalty" has an antediluvian ring. Particularly in its implication that one should be loyal to one's employer. Even alluding to the idea raises eyebrows in many circles. But let's hear the case for loyalty. From the top person in one of our nation's largest organizations:

> Some critics [he said] are now busy eroding another support of free enterprise—the loyalty of a management team, with its unifying values of cooperative work. Some of the enemies of business now encourage an employee to be disloyal to the enterprise.
>
> They want to create suspicion and disharmony, and pry into the proprietary interests of the business.
>
> However this is labeled—industrial espionage, whistle blowing, or professional responsibility—it is another tactic for spreading disunity and creating conflict.

Well, what is your reaction to those remarks—made, by the way, by the most recent chairman but one of General Motors. Does the phrase "loyalty to the management team" fill your breast with pride? Or do you see it as a slogan for sycophants?

Let's go back almost a quarter of a century. In 1956 a young editor of *Fortune* named William H. Whyte, Jr., published a book entitled *The Organization Man.* It became an immediate best-seller, not least because it was bought by the very people it was about. Whyte offered both an analysis and a response to the outlook of the Eisenhower Era. As a prelude to that period, millions of young men had returned from

Reprinted with permission from the Conference Board. Originally appeared in *Across the Board* in November 1978.

World War II looking forward to postwar life. Many attended college on the GI bill, and of those, a considerable percentage entered corporate careers.

They were grateful for the opportunities they saw lying ahead. Most came from modest backgrounds. To become part of management would fulfill their American Dream. Moreover, companies were pleased to take them in. The economy was expanding and had lots of room for beginners. All that was asked was that you work hard and be a good organization man.

(No apologies tendered here for the word "man." In those days, women married soon after high school or college, and proceeded to have 3.2 children almost as a conditioned response. Those organization wives deserve a dissertation of their own. If they were a lost or wasted generation, their plight foreshadowed the revolution yet to come.)

Why was that generation so loyal? As I have intimated, gratitude was clearly a factor. Another is that many came from a tradition of small towns and urban neighborhoods, where one deferred to figures of authority. Teachers and parents, priests and ministers were accorded habitual respect. That earlier parochial America had more of a class structure than we care to remember. People tended to know their place. You did the bidding of your betters if you knew where your bread was buttered.

On top of all this, corporate employers promised a payoff for loyalty. Work hard, be constant to the company, and a place at the top will be found for you. Of course, no promises were made. Still, why should a young man put in sixty hours a week, tolerate frequent transfers, indeed, make over his personality, if there wasn't an open road ahead?

A further element should be mentioned. The typical employee of those days saw himself as a businessman. He may have accepted an organizational ethic, but it was a business ethic nonetheless. The ideology of professionalism had yet to take hold. The Eisenhower Era was the last echo of an age when the business of the nation was business. A cabinet officer could assert that the best interests of the country coincided with those of its largest corporation. And while some people smirked, no one really had a rebuttal.

Loyalty was not merely the order of the day. Employees were ready, willing, and eager to render themselves faithful to the organizations which employed them. I am speaking here not simply of how people thought but of how history shaped their character. Interestingly, the Depression never really disillusioned us about capitalism. What we wanted were places in that system. World War II and the years that followed provided those opportunities.

All this has changed, of course. Many, perhaps most, people today may want corporate careers or their equivalent. But the history of the last generation has wrought some basic changes in our character. Not least is an incapacity for the kind of loyalty that prevailed in an earlier era. Am I suggesting that there are disloyal people on corporate payrolls today? Well, I suppose I am implying just that. The reasons for this development deserve at least passing mention. To begin with, gratitude is gone. Today, individuals expect challenging, well-paid employment as a matter of personal right. (They certainly complain loudly enough when they don't get it. Read the Op-Ed columns of the *Times.*) This comes, in some measure, from our having been so indiscriminate about telling everyone what fine people they are. They tend to believe all that flattery, and think they deserve nothing but the best.

In addition, deference to authority has all but disappeared—and for many of the same reasons. Individuals may sign up for a job, but that does not mean they will regard their employer as especially deserving of fealty. This is an age when we have no idols: Everyone is fair game to be sniped at. We may complain that our nation lacks leaders, yet let one such candidate come along, and we chop him off at the knees. Recall what the Democrats did to George McGovern even before his campaign got under way. And how many Republicans can you find willing to confess they voted for Nixon? The same holds for employment. People talk much more freely about the shortcomings of their bosses. And not just in the company washroom.

Moreover, I feel constrained to add that in one sense the Eisenhower Era betrayed those who so loyally served it. The young men taken on in the 1950s had been told that allegiance would not go unnoticed. Yet as it turned out, the vast majority never got anywhere near the top. There just isn't enough room for everyone. In fact, it is amazing how many people with impressive titles never reach a salary of $50,000. A Marxist with some surplus compassion might argue that even executives can be exploited. Imagine, after long hours and endless travel, plus fragmenting your family life, seeing your corporate career peak at 38 as someone younger becomes your superior.

Today's employees understand all this. In consequence, many acknowledge at the outset that they will settle for middling success. They leave promptly at 5:00 P.M.; turn down transfers they find uncongenial; and manage to spend most weekends without a bulging briefcase.

Indeed, an increasing number of corporate employees do not think of themselves as businessmen. I do not mean they are oblivious to the bottom line. They know their company wishes to maximize its earnings, and they are expected to contribute to that end. Even so, a growing proportion of people on business payrolls conceive of themselves as "professionals."

Ours has become a generation where status comes more from providing services than fervidly pursuing profits. Here the experience of the 1960s has been imprinted more than we realize. Business lost much of its historic legitimacy during that curious decade. But not so much because of things it did or did not do. Business was not really blamed for Vietnam; nor was it held culpable for violations of civil rights, or opportunities denied to women. What happened, rather, was that during the 1960s our entire conception of what comprises a worthwhile life began undergoing revision. In particular, fewer people accepted the tenet that you could make the most of your years here on earth by committing your career to business.

The ideology of professionalism thus meets a deeply felt need. Through it you can see yourself being true to objective, ethical standards. You find your peers in your fellow professionals; a nationwide guild devoted to truth, progress, quality. Your touchstone is service to society rather than profits or special interests. In a sense, professionalism serves as America's variant of socialism, but within a capitalist context. People want esteemed status, comfortable incomes, and what we generally think of as the good life. But they also wish to believe they are advancing justice, benefiting society, and remaining true to their conscience. But being a professional means you are less than completely loyal to the organization for which you work.

J. Edgar Hoover handed down an Iron Law to his subordinates: Never Embarrass the Bureau. Most corporations feel much the same way. It is not simply that embarrassments can lower public confidence in a company, with an accompanying decline in sales. For those at the top, the firm is much like a temple to which they pledged their careers. To defile its name, especially outside the precincts, approaches a profane act.

Who has so acted? The list contains members of middle management, professionals with impressive credentials, and persons in lesser but still responsible positions. Their common experience is that they "embarrassed" their employers by protesting practices they considered wrong. Moreover, in each of these instances they first tried company channels. Only after those avenues failed did they move to a public forum. Here are a half-dozen cases where "loyalty" became an issue:

• A medical director for a well-known pharmaceutical firm objected to promotional techniques that, in his judgment, used hard-sell tactics and misleading testimonials. When his company refused to mend its methods, he testified before a Senate committee investigating the drug industry.

• A veteran pilot found what he considered a fatal defect in equipment installed in his company's planes. When the airline derided his doubts, he took his case to the National Transportation Safety Board.

• Two auditors with a leading retail chain questioned company construction expenditures, including unreported renovations in executives' homes. Fired for their persistence, they brought suit against their employer, detailing their charges in open court.

• An automobile safety inspector discovered that exhausts from one of his company's models leaked into the passenger compartments. When his superiors suppressed his findings, he turned them over to Ralph Nader, who used them in several speeches.

• An engineer for a construction company operating in Latin America refused to falsify financial reports so as to recoup unanticipated costs. When his company persisted in this practice, he appealed to the General Accounting Office.

• A supervisor at another firm engaged in construction felt that the welding at a nuclear power plant was not sufficiently strong to restrain radioactive materials. When his company refused to acknowledge this danger, he sent his data to the Atomic Energy Commission.

Having examined these and other cases, I am convinced that the employees involved are neither neurotics nor misfits nor malcontents. Indeed, most are middle Americans, with no intrinsic animus toward capitalism or records of political radicalism. They are people who found themselves troubled over some things their employers were doing. One put the matter very simply: "I reached a point where I could no longer live with myself." We have always claimed we are creatures of conscience. Here are individuals who acted on that principle.

I want to mention one other trait they all possessed in common. None had lofty executive ambitions. In none of these cases did the employee seek to rise much higher than the level at which he stood. Individuals who aspire to a corner office must calculate how their words or actions may affect their upward climb. After all, promotion to higher management goes to those with a record of company commitment. As I said earlier, it used to be that many people shared that dream. Now the ranks of those so committed are considerably thinner than before.

Will the diluted loyalties of employees have long-term economic effects? Here it is too easy to argue a priori. One can contend that subverting the "proprietary interests of the business" (James Roche's felicitous phrase) will undermine sales, endanger earnings, even cripple capital investment. But we don't really know. The same arguments were made when reformers sought to install guards over lethal machinery. But this time the admonishers could be correct. For involved are not only costs but the basic legitimacy of business pursuits.

It may well be that free expression, justice, and public service can only be had at an economic price. They are vital human principles, but they carry an eventual cost. Are we willing to contemplate declining efficiency in production, with a lower material standard of life? After all, expanding the rights of individuals means the machinery will have to slow down to accommodate individual cases. Those willing to take that risk should say so explicitly. To protest that we can have the best of all possible worlds has been an American weakness since the start of our Republic. However, recent experience, both at home and abroad, should have cured us of that indulgence.

Your Employees' Right to Blow the Whistle

Kenneth D. Walters

A recent manifestation of the perpetual tug-of-war between employees and employers is the new phenomenon known as whistle blowing. A whistle blower has been called a "muckraker from within, who exposes what he considers the unconscionable practices of his own organization."[1] Having decided at some point that the actions of the organization are immoral, illegal, or inefficient, he or she acts on that belief by informing legal authorities or others outside the organization. Such a public denunciation of policies or practices that an employee deems intolerable has been characterized as a deed of "courage and anguish that attend[s] the exercise of professional and personal responsibility."[2]

Organizations have always had to contend with outside muckrakers and critics, but the current movement emphasizes the responsibility of inside critics to uncover and report organizational misconduct. Within the last three years several books that emphasize the importance and frequency of employee whistle blowing have been written.

The first published and still the best general treatment is the report, *Whistle Blowing*, edited by Ralph Nader, Peter J. Petkas, and Kate Blackwell. This report describes the dilemmas faced by employees in deciding to tell the public about their companies' defective products, concealed hazards, pollution, corruption, or law breaking. Nader insists that "loyalties do not end at the boundaries of an organization."[3] The defense of "just following orders" was rejected at Nuremberg, he argues. In addition to spelling out the rationale underlying the whistle-blowing ethic, the report also contains a series of cases in which employees have blown the whistle. According to a reviewer in the *Wall*

Reprinted from *Harvard Business Review* 53, no. 4. Copyright © 1975 by the President and Fellows of Harvard College.

Street Journal, this report "probably deserves far wider readership at all levels of the corporate ladder than it is likely to get."[4]

A. Ernest Fitzgerald, the Pentagon cost specialist who revealed cost overruns in the production of C-5A transport planes and whose job was therefore abolished, wrote *The High Priests of Waste.*[5] He recounts numerous official attempts to hush up what he calls bureaucratic bungling, chiseling, waste, collusion, and fraud on the part of defense contractors. As a result of taking legal action, he has been reinstated to his position.

In *Blowing the Whistle: Dissent in the Public Interest,* Charles Peters and Taylor Branch present several case studies of government employees who have revealed organizational abuses or deceptions.[6] Peters and Branch, editors of *Washington Monthly,* see whistle blowing as a notable new development in the history of American reform movements.

Louis McIntire, who worked as a chemical engineer for Du Pont, claims he was fired for writing *Scientists and Engineers: The Professionals Who Are Not,*[7] a fictional account of a chemical corporation's attitude toward its professional employees.

In *Advise and Dissent: Scientists in the Political Arena,* Joel Primack and Frank von Hippel urge scientists to assume a wide variety of professional and ethical responsibilities, including whistle blowing.[8]

THE WHISTLE BLOWER: JUDAS ISCARIOT OR MARTIN LUTHER?

Reflecting a radical departure from long-held organizational beliefs, the basic assumption behind this new genre of literature is that employees who disagree with organizational policy on grounds of conscience are obliged not to quit their jobs but to remain in their organizations and act as forces for change from within. This stance is very different from the traditional role of the employee whose "preeminent virtue is loyalty" and whose "principle is 'your organization, love it or leave it.' "[9] Some businessmen hold to this traditional view and strongly oppose any effort to dilute the undivided loyalty expected from employees. In 1971, James Roche, then chairman of the board of General Motors Corporation, warned against what he considered to be the insidious effects of whistle blowing:

> Some critics are now busy eroding another support of free enterprise—
> the loyalty of a management team, with its unifying values of cooperative

work. Some of the enemies of business now encourage an employee to be disloyal to the enterprise. They want to create suspicion and disharmony, and pry into the proprietary interests of the business. However this is labelled—industrial espionage, whistle blowing, or professional responsibility—it is another tactic for spreading disunity and creating conflict.[10]

Roche's views reflect the fact that from the time we are children we are taught the value of "playing on the team." Learning to get along by showing loyalty to others is a vital social lesson, especially in a society where more and more earn their livelihood in an organizational environment. This institutional loyalty, coupled with a general loathing for traitors and tattletales, casts the whistle blower more in the role of Judas Iscariot than in that of Martin Luther. Peters and Branch have remarked that "in fact, whistle blowing is severely hampered by the image of its most famous historical model, Judas Iscariot. Martin Luther seems to be about the only figure of note to make much headway with public opinion after doing an inside job on a corrupt organization."

Some organization theorists seem to agree that employees should have undivided loyalty to their employers. Paul R. Lawrence says, "Ideally, we would want one sentiment to be dominant in all employees from top to bottom, namely a complete loyalty to the organizational purpose."[11] Harold J. Leavitt comments that Likert's ideal organization has loyal employees who see no conflicts between personal goals and organizational purposes.[12] In his critique of organization theory, Robert Presthus appears to regret but to admit that "organizational logic . . . has been essentially authoritarian."[13]

Other theorists stress the idea that employees in a free society should not be obligated to restrict their loyalty to only one institution or cause. Clark Kerr advocates allowing plural loyalties as a necessary guarantee against totalitarianism: "A pluralistic system assumes a 'pluralistic person,' that is, one who is willing to work with divided loyalties and set his own pattern of activities, rather than have it set for him by a single external institution."[14] Kerr's fears have proved to be well-founded. We have recently been reminded of the consequences of following a Nixonesque pattern of demanding complete loyalty from subordinates. It is one thing to expect employees to commit themselves to pursuing broad organizational objectives; it is quite another to see the contract of employment as a Faustian bargain in which employees suspend all critical judgment to serve their superiors.

THE INFORMER IN PUBLIC ORGANIZATIONS

Advocates of whistle blowing point out the need for legal protection of critics within an organization. In "Whistle Blowing and the Law," Arthur S. Miller, a specialist in constitutional law, notes that the present legal system offers little protection to such informers.[15] While it is true that most employees undertake to blow the whistle at their own risk, a fact that has received little notice is that employees in public organizations do have substantial legal protection in this regard. It arises from the First Amendment's provision that government may not deny citizens freedom of speech. Although current legal protection for whistle blowers extends mainly to employees in government organizations, managers in private organizations as well should be aware of these new legal trends. Whistle blowers in private organizations are steadily gaining legal support and may someday enjoy essentially the same rights as employees in government organizations.

In *Pickering* v. *Board of Education* in 1968, the U.S. Supreme Court established legal protection for certain kinds of whistle blowing by public employees. In a letter to the editor of a local newspaper, Pickering, an Illinois high school teacher, criticized the school board for its policies, particularly for its allocation of funds to athletic programs. Pickering was fired for this act of disloyalty, which the school board found "detrimental to the efficient operation and administration of the schools of the district." Pickering sued, alleging a right to free speech. The U.S. Supreme Court found that Pickering's "right to speak on issues of public importance may not furnish the basis for his dismissal from public employment." The right to raise such an issue publicly is protected by the First Amendment:

> The question whether a school system requires additional funds is a matter of legitimate public concern on which the judgment of the school administration, including the School Board, cannot, in a society that leaves such questions to popular vote, be taken as conclusive. On such a question free and open debate is vital to informed decision making by the electorate.

The Court went on to say that teachers like Pickering have special competence and interest in speaking out on issues that affect the organizations for which they work:

Teachers are, as a class, the members of a community most likely to have informed and definite opinions as to how funds allotted to the operation of the schools should be spent. Accordingly, it is essential that they be able to speak out freely on such questions without fear of retaliatory dismissal.[16]

A survey of cases involving public employees since the *Pickering* case shows that nearly all whistle blowers who have been punished for their outspoken views do win their cases when they challenge such punishment in court.[17] The courts appear to be agreeing with an assessment that Peters and Branch have made, which is that the "strength on which whistle blowers have relied is basically that they have been judged *right* by most of the people who have studied the conflicts from outside the battle area." Such a consensus seems rather ironic if we contrast it with the specter of treachery that shadows whistle blowers. The nearly unanimous conclusion that they "did the right thing" perhaps testifies to the morality of the positions they have taken.

DISLOYALTY OR LEGITIMATE DISSENT?

As Peters and Branch point out, not all organizational loyalty is bad, and not all whistle blowing is good. What factors, then, should determine whether an employee who protests company practices should be protected against sanctions that are imposed by the organization? Perhaps the best way to answer this question is to look at the legal cases that have arisen from public employees' criticizing their bosses. The courts have outlined some general guidelines that are helpful in distinguishing between whistle blowing that deserves protection and that which does not. It should be stressed that these rules currently apply only to whistle blowers in government and public organizations, but some legal scholars believe that similar rules will soon be applied to organizations in the private sector, a matter I will examine later in this article.

Motive: The employee's motive for blowing the whistle has been an important factor used by the courts in determining whether or not the employee's freedom of speech should be protected. Uusually an informer attempts to publicly expose misconduct, illegality, or inefficiency in an organization. Several cases fit this pattern. In *Rafferty* v. *Philadelphia Psychiatric Center,* for instance, Mrs. Rafferty, a psychiatric nurse, was fired following the publication of a news article in which she was quoted as being critical of patient care and medical staff behavior at the state mental hospital where she was employed. Her comments caused great controversy at the hospital, and the staff appeared to resent her statements. The court concluded, however, that Mrs. Rafferty "was engaging in precisely the sort of free and vigorous expression that the First Amendment was designed to protect."[18]

In *Muller* v. *Conlisk,* a policeman discovered that other policemen had taken stolen property they had recovered in the course of their duties into their own use. He reported this fact to his superiors, waited, and saw no indication that they were investigating the charge. Finally, he appeared on a television news program and suggested that the fact he had reported was being covered up. He was fired for making "derogatory comments reflecting on the image or reputation of the Chicago Police Department." The court ordered him reinstated on the ground that the rule prohibiting derogatory comments was "unconstitutionally overbroad," and that the First Amendment protects "some speech by policemen which could be considered 'derogatory to the department.' "[19]

Sometimes the issues addressed may seem so trivial that they can hardly be characterized as whistle blowing. Nevertheless, superiors who are the objects of even mild criticism sometimes react (or overreact) defensively, and then the courts are forced to step in and protect the employee's freedom of speech.

For example, in *Downs* v. *Conway School District,* an elementary school teacher with over twenty-five years of experience publicly voiced concern over the use of an open incinerator on the playground during school hours. She also assisted students in composing a letter to the school cafeteria director that requested that raw instead of cooked carrots be served occasionally. For these and other similarly innocuous activities, the superintendent decided not to recommend Mrs. Downs for renewal of her teaching contract. The court found that "the superintendent demanded blind obedience to any directive he gave, whether illegal, unconstitutional, arbitrary or capricious." It ruled that Mrs. Downs's activities were constitutionally protected by the First Amendment:

> When a School Board acts, as it did here, to punish a teacher who seeks to protect the health and safety of herself and her pupils, the resulting intimidation can only cause a severe chilling, if not freezing, effect on the free discussion of more controversial subjects.[20]

Internal channels: Does it make a difference if whistle blowing takes place inside or outside an organization? Perhaps the employee owes his or her employer enough loyalty to try to work first within the organization to attempt to effect change. This is a sound general rule to follow, but the Supreme Court in the *Pickering* case did not sanction organizational rules requiring that employees always resort first to internal grievance procedures:

> There is likewise no occasion furnished by this case for consideration of the extent to which teachers can be required by narrowly drawn grievance procedures to submit complaints about the operation of the schools to their superiors for action thereon prior to bringing the complaints before the public.

In fact, employees usually do seek change within the organization first. Perhaps this is an indication that most employees appreciate the harm that could be done to the organization if every problem were aired publicly before attempts to solve it inside were made.

The organization's internal environment for free speech should be a key consideration in deciding whether employees must exhaust internal channels of communication before they seek outside help. In general, employees will probably tend to go through organizational channels before going public if they have not had too much trouble with bureaucratic red tape in the past, if their superiors have demonstrated some empathy with them for legitimate grievances in the past, and if the employees perceive their superiors to be more or less colleagues. Whistle blowers are most likely to go directly to the public when their earnest criticisms are met with bureaucratic runarounds, deaf ears, or hostility.

The subject matter of the grievance may also determine whether it is reasonable to expect employees to resort to internal grievance channels before going public.

In *Tepedino* v. *Dumpson,* social investigators in the New York City Department of Welfare wrote a letter to an HEW official in Washington. In it, they criticized existing procedures and asked for information they had been unable to receive from superiors. The suspended employees' superior argued before the New York Court of Appeals that the social investigators had violated the grievance procedure mandated by the department. The court held that in many cases it is reasonable that employees be required to follow grievance procedures, but that the nature of some grievances are such that they need not be raised through established procedures: "The subject matter of the letter, critical though it may have been of the Welfare Department's operations, could not be appropriately raised or dealt with through its grievance machinery." The court distinguished between "individual problems of employees" and "broad issues" and ruled that the latter need not be carried through grievance procedures.[21]

One can also foresee cases in which whistle blowers should not be required to go through internal channels when time is important. They may be warning against an imminent danger, and, by the time they have gone through a complex and time-consuming bureaucratic maze, the harm of which they warn may have already occurred.

Another problem is that the requirement that all employees go through organizational channels before speaking in the forum of their choice conflicts with the constitutional principle that prior restraints on speech are "impermissible with but the narrowest of exceptions."[22]

One can see that it is impossible to lay down a simple yet fair rule on the issue of whether employees must exhaust internal remedies before making public allegations. Each case must be examined on its own merits. This matter will be clarified further as the courts look at a wider variety of cases raising the issue.

Organizational friction: One of the major concerns of the courts in adjudicating whistle-blowing cases has been the question of harm done to personal relationships in an organization because of such actions. Aside from the aspect of possibly damaged public relations, the organization must often deal with upset working relationships between the informer and his or her co-workers and superior.

The Supreme Court in *Pickering* noted that the public statements were "in no way directed towards any person with whom appellant would normally be in contact in the course of his daily work as a teacher" and "thus no question of maintaining either discipline by immediate superiors or harmony among co-workers [was] presented." Pickering's relationships with the school board and the superintendent were "not the kind of close working relationships for which it can persuasively be claimed that personal loyalty and confidence are necessary to their proper functioning." The Court therefore held Pickering's speech to be protected but warned that "significantly different considerations" could apply if "the relationship between superior and subordinate is of such a personal and intimate nature that certain forms of public criticism of the superior by the subordinate would seriously undermine the effectiveness of the working relationship between them."

The problem that must be squarely faced in deciding whether speech that disrupts personal relationships should be protected is that, in virtually all whistle-blowing cases, these relationships are already upset to one degree or another. The very nature of whistle blowing implies the presence of conflict or disagreement. A comment by the California Supreme Court in *Adcock* v. *Board of Education* recognizes this fact and points out that all organizational conflict is not necessarily dysfunctional:

Disharmony and friction are the healthy but natural results of a society which cherishes the right to speak freely on a subject and the resultant by-products should never prevent an individual from speaking or cause that individual to be penalized for such speech.[23]

Because of this unavoidable friction in relationships, the real task of the courts is to balance the benefits from the employee's freedom of speech (which are often quite substantial in whistle-blowing cases) with the costs or harm from the speech. Only after this careful weighing of the employee's and the employer's interests do the courts reach a decision.

In both the *Downs* and the *Rafferty* cases, the courts obviously felt that the whistle blowers had not harmed their organizations seriously but had performed a public service. In *Rafferty,* one of the alleged reasons for the nurse's discharge was the "staff anxiety" created by her public criticism of hospital conditions. The court found this anxiety to have been overstated by the employees and not an acceptable reason for firing Mrs. Rafferty. And in *Downs,* although the superintendent and the school board were upset by what they regarded as Mrs. Downs's impertinence, the court felt that for her not to have warned of the open incinerator on the school grounds "would be violative of her moral, if not legal, duty to protect the health and safety of her students."

Courts have sometimes ruled that the employer's assertion that working relationships have been seriously harmed have simply not been proved from the facts. In *Dendor* v. *Board of Fire and Police Commissioners,* a fireman said that the village's fire marshal did not know how to manage the fire department and predicted that his lack of direction would "end in disaster." The employer discharged Dendor because his continued presence "would be seriously detrimental to the discipline, morale, and efficiency of the Fire Department." But the court said that the employer "has the burden of proving that the forbidden speech rendered the speaker unfit for public service or so adversely affected the public service involved that it justifies impairment of free speech." The employer, the court said, "did not find, and describe by such finding, the kind of harm inflicted on the village fire department by Dendor's derogatory statements."[24]

Other courts have concluded that the disharmony resulting from an employee's speaking out is the result of "oversensitivity to criticism" on the part of the superior or "bureaucratic paranoia."[25]

Discretion: There are other factors that courts will obviously have to consider as new whistle-blowing cases arise. Whether the allegations are true or false is certainly relevant, as is the degree of care exercised in gathering the data on which the charges are based. A negligent dissenter who harms an organization by recklessly making serious charges that are false does not deserve to be protected.

A further factor to consider is confidentiality. On the one hand, unauthorized disclosures of confidential information obviously cannot be permitted every time an employee personally feels the public would benefit from having such information. On the other hand, organizations should not be allowed to hide a multitude of sins under the guise that the matters are proprietary or confidential. Individual cases will have to determine the delicate balance between revealing misconduct and maintaining legitimate requirements of confidentiality.

WHEN WHISTLE BLOWERS LOSE

We have already suggested that a whistle blower who seriously damages personal relationships in an organization by saying things that have no countervailing benefit to the organization or to society would probably not be given legal protection. We also saw that some situations may require that a critic exhaust internal remedies before going outside the organization. No court, however, has actually held that a whistle blower's freedom of speech would be unprotected in such situations.

In only two cases have the courts held that the public employee's criticisms were not protected by the First Amendment. In *Kelly* v. *Florida Judicial Qualifications Commission,* the Florida Supreme Court split four to three over whether a Florida district court judge could be disciplined for criticizing his fellow judges in public for their alleged failure to establish procedural reforms in judicial administration. Saying that he was motivated by personal vanity and political ambition rather than by genuine concern for the public interest, the majority upheld the censure of Judge Kelly. In essence, the majority seemed to feel that Judge Kelly lacked the true whistle-blowing ethic—a desire to improve the performance and quality of public service. The dissenting judges disagreed with the majority's finding that Judge Kelly was motivated by self-interest.[26] The *Kelly* case illustrates that determining an employee's motive can be a difficult but critical task, since it differentiates the true whistle blower from the employee whose real object is harassment or blackmail.

In *Watts* v. *Seward School Board,* a teacher publicly criticized the school administration in an open letter to the school board and as a result was not rehired.[27] The case is interesting in that its facts are quite similar to the landmark *Pickering* case, decided by the U.S. Supreme Court. The Supreme Court of Alaska distinguished Watts's case from Pickering's (unpersuasively, a dissenting judge said) when it noted that the teacher's letter in *Watts* was not met with "massive apathy and total disbelief" by the general public as in *Pickering* but became a very disruptive force in this small Alaskan community.

WHISTLE BLOWING IN PRIVATE ORGANIZATIONS

As we have seen, employees in public organizations can generally engage in open dissent within certain reasonable limits. The issue remaining is: What will be the future for whistle blowers who work for private organizations? Speculation on future trends and laws is risky, but certain forces that could greatly expand the legal rights of whistle blowers are already at work.

Professor Thomas I. Emerson, perhaps the nation's foremost First Amendment scholar, has made the following observation:

A system of freedom of expression that allowed private bureaucracies to throttle all internal discussion of their affairs would be seriously deficient. There seems to be general agreement that at some points the government must step in. In any event the law is moving steadily in that direction.[28]

Another legal scholar, Phillip I. Blumberg, has explored in detail the current law on the employee's duty of loyalty to the employer. Blumberg predicts that whistle blowing "will become an area of dynamic change in the corporate organization and in time will produce significant change in established legal concepts."[29]

A complete discussion of the legal trends to which Professors Emerson and Blumberg refer is impossible here, but I can briefly cite three of them:

1. *Collective action:* First, if unionism spreads to new employee groups, one can expect that legal protection for whistle blowers will include these groups. Union contracts generally specify that employees may only be discharged for just cause or good cause. Whistle blowing is not usually considered to be just cause for firing. Edward A. Gregory, a perennial thorn in General Motors' flesh for his whistle blowing on auto design safety, credits his union with protecting him from attempted disciplinary actions by General Motors.[30]

A second but related development involving collective employee action is the banding together of employee groups who refuse to work for organizations that condition employment on the sacrifice of basic rights. This appears to be a course of action appealing particularly to professional and scientific employees. For example, the American Chemical Society is proposing to set up a legal aid fund for members who are punished for criticizing their organizations' policies and to institute sanctions against offending employers.[31] The Federation of American Scientists has a similar program and goal.[32]

2. *Rights of employment:* Another trend that in the long run may produce more fundamental changes in employee rights is the movement of courts away from the time-honored rule that an employee who has no formal contractual rights to employment may be fired for any reason or for no reason, within the limits of statutory law (for example, civil rights laws). This rule has been uniformly applied in all states and has been described by Lawrence E. Blades as "what most tends to make [the employee] a docile follower of his employer's every wish."[33]

But in *Petermann* v. *International Brotherhood of Teamsters* an employee fired for testifying against his employer (a labor union) at a legislative hearing was found to have been unlawfully discharged. The court ruled that the firing was "against public policy" even though there was no formal contract of employment.[34] And in 1974 the New Hampshire Supreme Court in *Monge* v. *Beebe Rubber Co.* ruled that a married employee with three children could recover damages when she claimed she was fired because she refused to go out on a date with her foreman. The court declared:

> We hold that a termination by the employer of a contract of employment at will which is motivated by bad faith or malice or based on retaliation is not in the best interest of the economic system or the public good and constitutes a breach of the employment contract.[35]

The decisions in the *Petermann* and the *Monge* cases do not seem revolutionary given the facts involved, but the basic rationale underlying the decisions reveals the willingness of some courts to examine the circumstances surrounding discharges of nonunion employees, an inquiry that the courts previously have studiously avoided in all cases. *Petermann* and *Monge* may be harbingers of future employee claims that whistle blowing is not a ground for discharge and that discharge of a whistle blower can be "against public policy."

3. *Regulatory provisions:* A final legal development is the appearance of specific statutory provisions that prohibit employers from discharging or disciplining an employee who discloses conduct that the statute forbids. An example of this kind of provision is Section 110(b) of the Coal Mine Safety Act:

No person shall discharge or in any other way discriminate against or cause to be discharged or discriminated against any miner or any authorized representative of miners by reason of the fact that such miner or representative (a) has notified the Secretary of his authorized representative of any alleged violation or danger, (b) has filed, instituted, or caused to be filed or instituted any proceeding under this Act, or (c) has testified or is about to testify in any proceeding resulting from the administration or enforcement of the provisions of this Act.[36]

MAKING WHISTLE BLOWING UNNECESSARY

How can an organization work with its employees to reduce their need to blow the whistle? Here are five procedures that might be kept in mind:

• First, managers should assure employees that the organization will not interfere with basic political freedoms. Management theorists have increasingly stressed that organizations should encourage an open environment in which employees freely express their often controversial views.

• Second, the organization's own grievance procedures should be streamlined so that employees can get a direct and sympathetic hearing for issues on which they are likely to blow the whistle if their complaints are not heard quickly and fairly. Much whistle blowing occurs only because the organization is unresponsive to early warnings from its employees. A sincere commitment to an "open door" policy makes much whistle blowing unnecessary.

• Third, the organization should take a look at its concept of social responsibility. Too often social responsibility is seen as being limited to corporate gifts to charity parceled out by top management and the board of directors. But the organization's interface with society is far more complex than this, and employees at all levels have a stake in the organization's social performance. Keeping the internal channels of communication open, not only on personal issues affecting employees but also on these larger questions of corporate social policy, decreases external whistle blowing.

• Fourth, organizations should formally recognize and communicate to employees a respect for the individual consciences of employees. Jay W. Forrester has proposed that the modern enterprise "should develop around a 'constitution' that establishes the rights of the individual and the limitation of the power of the organization over him."[37]

• Fifth, the organization should recognize that dealing harshly with a whistle-blowing employee could result in adverse public reaction and publicity. Respecting an employee's right to differ with organizational policy on some matters, even if the law does not currently require it, may be in the best interests of the organization in the long run.

Notes

1. Charles Peters and Taylor Branch, *Blowing the Whistle: Dissent in the Public Interest* (New York: Praeger, 1972), p. 4.

2. Ralph Nader, Peter J. Petkas, and Kate Blackwell, eds., *Whistle Blowing, The Report of the Conference on Professional Responsibility* (New York: Grossman, 1972), p. 10.

3. Ibid.

4. Richard Martin, "Why People Inform on Their Bosses," *Wall Street Journal,* October 17, 1972.

5. A. Ernest Fitzgerald, *The High Priests of Waste* (New York: Norton, 1972).

6. Peters and Branch.

7. Louis V. McIntire and M.B. McIntire, *Scientists and Engineers: The Professionals Who Are Not* (Lafayette, La.: Arcola Communications, 1971).

8. Joel Primack and Frank von Hippel, *Advise and Dissent: Scientists in the Political Arena* (New York: Basic Books, 1972).

9. Nader et al., p. 26.

10. James M. Roche, "The Competitive System, To Work, To Preserve, and To Protect," *Vital Speeches of the Day,* May 1, 1971, p. 445.

11. Paul Roger Lawrence, *The Changing of Organizational Behavior Patterns: A Case Study of Decentralization* (Boston: Division of Research, Harvard Business School, 1958), p. 208.

12. Harold J. Leavitt, "Applied Organizational Change in Industry," in *Handbook of Organizations,* ed. James G. March (Chicago: Rand McNally, 1965), p. 1156.

13. Robert Presthus, *The Organizational Society* (New York: Vintage Books, 1962), p. 321.

14. Clark Kerr, *Labor and Management in Industrial Society* (Garden City, N.Y.: Anchor Books, 1964), p. 17.

15. Arthur S. Miller, "Whistle Blowing and the Law," in *Whistle Blowing,* ed. Nader et al., p. 25.

16. Pickering v. Board of Education, 391 U.S. 563 (1968).

17. Tepedino v. Dumpson, 249 N.E.2d 751 (1969); Muller v. Conlisk, 429 F.2d 901 (1970); Brukiewa v. Police Commissioner of Baltimore, 263 A.2d 210

(1970); Downs v. Conway School District, 328 F.Supp. 338 (1975); Donahue v. Staunton, 471 F.2d 475 (1972), *cert. den.* 93 S.Ct. 1419 (1973); Turbeville v. Abernathy, 367 F.Supp. 1081 (1973); Dendor v. Board of Fire and Police Commissioners, 297 N.E.2d 316 (1973); Rafferty v. Philadelphia Psychiatric Center, 356 F.Supp. 500 (1973); Adcock v. Board of Education, 513 P.2d 900 (1973). The current United States Supreme Court has also recently upheld the whistle-blowing concept in Perry v. Sindermann, 408 U.S. 593 (1972), where a college professor alleged that his termination was the result of testimony he gave before the state legislature and other public criticism of the school administration.

18. Rafferty v. Philadelphia Psychiatric Center, 356 F.Supp. 500 (1973).

19. Muller v. Conlisk, 429 F.2d 900 (1970).

20. Downs v. Conway School, 328 F.Supp. 338 (1971).

21. Tepedino v. Dumpson, 249 N.E.2d 751 (1969).

22. Board of Education v. West Hempstead, 311 N.Y.S.2d 708, 710 (1970).

23. Adcock v. Board of Education, 513 P.2d 900 (1973).

24. Dendor v. Board of Fire and Police Commissioners, 297 N.E.2d 316 (1973).

25. Roberts v. Lake Central School Corporation, 317 F.Supp. 63 (1970); Murray v. Vaughn, 300 F.Supp. 688, 705 (1969).

26. Kelly v. Florida Judicial Qualifications Commission, 238 So.2d 565 (1970).

27. Watts v. Seward School Board, 454 P.2d 732 (1969).

28. Thomas I. Emerson, *The System of Freedom of Expression* (New York: Vintage Books, 1970), p. 677.

29. Phillip I. Blumberg, "Corporate Responsibility and the Employee's Duty of Loyalty and Obedience," *Oklahoma Law Review,* August 1971, p. 279.

30. "Lonely Causes: For Edward Gregory, General Motors Corp. Is Employer and Target as Assemblyline Inspector, He Publicly Raises Issues About Standards, Defects," *Wall Street Journal,* December 31, 1973.

31. Nicholas Wade, "Protection Sought for Satirists and Whistle Blowers," *Science,* December 7, 1973, p. 1002.

32. "New Ethical Problems Raised by Data Suppression," *Federation of American Scientists Professional Bulletin,* November 1974, p. 1.

33. Lawrence E. Blades, "Employment at Will vs. Individual Freedom: On Limiting the Abusive Exercise of Employer Power," *Columbia Law Review,* December 1967, p. 1405.

34. Petermann v. International Brotherhood of Teamsters, 344 P.2d 25 (1959).

35. Monge v. Beebe Rubber Co., 316 A.2d 549 (1974).

36. Coal Mine Safety Act, §110(b), Public Law 91-173.

37. Jay W. Forrester, "A New Corporate Design," *Industrial Management Review,* Fall 1965, p. 14.

Whistle Blower: Dan Gellert, Airline Pilot

I had been a pilot for over twenty-five years, the last ten of them with Eastern Airlines, when in 1972 I blew the whistle on a serious defect in the new Lockheed 1011 aircraft. At the time I was in middle management, involved in flight training and engineering safety. Eastern had sent me to the Air Force Safety School, the Army Crash Survival Investigators Course, and Aerospace Systems Safety, a training course given at the University of Southern California. You might say that they created their own monster because, through my safety training, I was able to spot a serious design problem in their 1011 aircraft, first coming into service at that time. But my warnings were ignored and the design problem resulted in a crash killing 103 people. Now, five years, two lawsuits, and a $1,600,000 judgment later, I am still with Eastern and still effecting flight safety.

It all started in the summer of 1972 when I was going through flight training school for the 1011. My roommate was in a simulator when the auto pilot and flight engineer instrumentation disengaged, crashing the flight simulator on a practice landing approach. Even though you don't get hurt when a simulator crashes, he reported this to Eastern's flight operations people. They ignored him.

When Lockheed designed and manufactured the 1011, they failed to recognize a serious safety hazard in the auto-pilot mechanism. The problem was much more insidious than an engine fire or a wing coming off, which most people recognize as a safety hazard. Instead, the defect involved the complex interaction between the crew and the auto pilot and related instrumentation which they relied upon to conduct a safe approach to a runway when landing the aircraft. About ninety seconds before reaching ground level—or about two thousand feet above the ground—the auto pilot would disengage without any warning. In es-

Reprinted from *The Civil Liberties Review,* September–October 1978. Copyright © 1978 by *The Civil Liberties Review.*

sence, the instruments would lie to the pilot at the critical part of the approach, telling him that he was maintaining elevation when, in fact, he was not. If the weather was bad or there were other visual obstructions to ground level, or there was some other distraction, the crew could easily fail to recognize their situation and a crash could result.

In September of 1972 I was flying a 1011 and I noticed that the auto pilot tripped off a number of times without any warning or triggering an alert light on the instrumentation panel. I made a verbal report to a management official who said, "We'll look into it." I replied, "You'd better before we kill a bunch of people." And that's exactly what happened barely four months later.

On December 29, 1972, an Eastern Airlines 1011 crashed, killing 103 people. After learning of the accident, I immediately wrote to the top three people in the company—Frank Borman, vice president of operations; Floyd Hall, chairman of the board; and Samuel Higgenbottom, president of operations—sending them a two-page evaluation of the 1011 auto-pilot system. Then I just sat back and waited. It wasn't until February that Borman replied with a letter, pointing out that it was pure folly to say that any one safety procedure could prevent all accidents. I realized that I had to do something else.

I then sent my two-page evaluation to the Airline Pilots Association and to the National Transportation Safety Board (NTSB) which was about to conduct a hearing into the crash. At this point my main concern was not the crash, but the horrors that potentially lay in store for Eastern Airlines: more crashes, deaths, destruction of property, and punitive damages assessed against the company.

Immediately after receiving my letter the NTSB called me to discuss the situation. They agreed that the auto pilot was a cause of concern, and they sent me a subpoena. A number of "friends" at Eastern suggested I ignore the subpoena and not testify. Instead, I ignored my so-called friends.

At the NTSB hearing, I stressed the problem with the auto pilot. All the other witnesses, however, blamed the crash on pilot error; after all it's the pilot's responsibility to monitor the flight instruments. Nevertheless, since the time available for the crew to catch the malfunction was minimal—especially during any sort of stress situation—a safe landing under the circumstances would be difficult, at best. In June 1973 the NTSB released their "probable cause" results—pilot error. This, of course, took the pressure off Eastern and Lockheed. Instead of having to pay punitive damages to the relatives of the people killed in the December crash, they only had to pay compensatory damages.

Through all these months I had little idea of the collusion between

Eastern and NTSB, a government agency, in their attempts to cover up the real cause of the crash and the fact that Eastern had been warned of it in time to have prevented a disaster. The day after the crash in December, the head of 1011 flight training, Thad Royall (who was promoted to a management position after he had caused a fiery crash of two airliners on a runway while serving as a pilot), and Mr. Turner of the NTSB went into the flight simulator and flew the same flight pattern as the crashed aircraft. They did exactly what the original crew did and crashed the simulator at almost exactly the same spot where the aircraft actually crashed. Royall, who was later removed from flight training and put into another management position, was one of the people I had notified when I first recognized the problem with the auto pilot. He and Turner decided to keep the incident quiet. Then in March 1973 there was a meeting attended by Borman, Royall, and other Eastern executives, where Borman decided not to change the design of the 1011 because "the FAA had approved it." It wasn't until July, after the NTSB released its findings, that they decided to quietly modify the auto-pilot design.

After the NTSB findings, I tried to just forget the whole incident. But in December 1973, I was flying in a 1011 when the auto pilot tripped off twice. The second time it happened the plane broke out of the clouds about 200 feet over houses, when our instruments said we should have been at 500 feet. The crew had to put on take-off power in order to make the runway. I knew it was time to take action.

I wrote a twelve-page petition to the NTSB explaining the situation (I didn't know that the design was being modified at this time) and requesting modification of the "probable cause" findings. I sent a copy of this petition to Borman. I still considered myself a loyal Eastern employee and thought it was possible that Borman just wasn't fully informed of the situation. I realized that I might be getting myself into trouble, but I just didn't see any other way I could deal with the situation in good conscience; after all, lives were at stake.

The next thing I knew, Eastern demoted me to co-pilot. Twice a year pilots bid on a base, a position, or a particular airline. Eastern, in a letter addressed to "Dear Occupant," said that I returned a blank bid sheet so they had no choice but to give me a co-pilot slot. Since I had not returned a blank bid sheet at all, I soon realized that I was being penalized for my petition to the NTSB. I then wrote a letter of protest to Borman.

Before receiving Borman's reply, I decided that perhaps I should leave Eastern for a while, if not for good (I was permitted to take a three-year leave of absence). The FBI was recruiting agents at that time who had a knowledge of Eastern Europe. Since I had grown up in Hungary, I decided to apply. I had passed the interview and was all set to work for them when I received Borman's reply to my letter—I was grounded.

In grounding me, Eastern sent me an astonishing letter that questioned my ability to fly an aircraft since, they said, I had written so many letters concerning safety. In my quarter of a century as a pilot, I had never had a passenger complaint or a crew complaint. I had never so much as blown a tire. Not only was I furious, but I started wondering what Eastern was going to do to me next. Rather than leave Eastern and join the FBI—which I felt would make it appear that Borman had justification for grounding me—I decided to remain with Eastern and salvage my reputation. I decided the only way to protect myself from further action was to file suit against them.

It took seven months of going through grievance procedures before I was allowed to fly again in the second half of 1974. In 1975 my attorney filed suit against Eastern charging them with "intentional affliction of mental stress." Then on May 27, 1977, four months before my case was finally tried, I was grounded again. Apparently, Eastern thought that by grounding me they would prove to the Florida jury that I was incompetent. But this attempt at influencing the jury backfired on them and, in fact, helped me to win the case when it reached the courts in September. I had asked for $1,500,000 in damages, but the judge awarded me $1,600,000—the extra $100,000 was just to show Eastern how really angry the judge was at Eastern's blatant attempt to discredit me.

After the ruling Eastern grounded me once again in an effort to "starve me out." They knew that I couldn't find work at any other airline because they had blackballed me. (They told me that not only would they not recommend me, but they wouldn't even answer letters of reference that were sent to them by prospective employers.) They wanted me to sign a letter that they had written which said that I relieved them of any liability involved with the case. In other words, in exchange for my job, I would not make them pay me the $1,600,000. I realized that my only alternative was to file a second suit.

In June 1978 I filed a $12 million lawsuit charging Frank Borman, Tim Buttion, vice president of flight operations, and Bill Bell, Eastern's attorney, with "civil conspiracy to force me out of employment." I expect the case to reach the courts by spring of 1979, if it gets that far. After losing the first case (which they are appealing now), Eastern has no defense; I expect them to try to settle with me out of court. Since June when I filed the second suit I have been put back on salary, although I'm still not flying. I do hope to be flying by this September though.

As the events of the past five years seem to be drawing to some sort of conclusion, I find it odd to note the change in my "image." I began as a conservative Republican, firmly entrenched in the middle management echelon of big business. And now I am labeled a "whistle blower." The whole nightmare of these years is that I never wanted to be a whistle blower, but my professional ideals and my conscience would allow me to be nothing else. We airline captains have a responsibility to our passengers, our fellow crew members, and our aircraft that supersedes the balance sheets or the income statements of our corporations. And if more of us would speak up instead of protecting our jobs by remaining silent about safety hazards like the one in the 1011, who knows how many accidents could be averted and lives saved.

The Job Was Important, But Ethics Came First

Lucinda Fleeson

Rarely do any of us face such a clear choice: Submit to an order or make an ethical stand that may exact a harsh price. That was the situation faced by Dr. A. Grace Pierce, a research doctor for Ortho Pharmaceutical Corporation, when she opposed the testing on children of a drug with an unusually high saccharin content.

After her refusal, Dr. Pierce's research projects were taken away and, she says, she was demoted and told she was irresponsible and unpromotable. Believing she was being forced out as punishment for her stand, she resigned. Dr. Pierce sued the giant Raritan-based drug manufacturer, charging that her professional reputation had been damaged. Ortho insists it did not demote Dr. Pierce and says that any problems it had with her work had nothing to do with her refusal to test the disputed drug. Beyond that, the company refuses to comment on the case.

Last month, an appeals court granted Dr. Pierce a full trial. If she wins, her case may become a landmark for professional ethics in New Jersey. Her case also offers a glimpse into what can happen in the corporate drug world when experts clash over whether a drug is safe.

For Dr. Pierce, a 58-year-old specialist in obstetrics and gynecology, the price of making her ethical stand has been high. She says she has been effectively blackballed from the drug research industry, which she considered to be her life's work. She now scurries around the western part of the state as a part-time physician at day and night clinics, earning about half the $46,000 salary she was paid at Ortho.

This wasn't the first time Dr. Pierce has given up a job because she felt her medical ethics were being compromised. Fourteen years ago she

Reprinted with permission from the *Bergen Record,* March 29, 1979.

resigned from the Food and Drug Administration because she believed the federal government was stalling on issuing warnings about the risks of taking birth control pills.

Dressed for a recent interview in a baggy raincoat and no-nonsense polyester pantsuit, and with a fierce brush of graying reddish hair, Grace Pierce presents a nondescript appearance. Yet on second examination one notices the strong hands, the sturdy glasses, and the businesslike way she puffs at a low-tar cigarette. But her eyes, guileless and self-confident, are the real clues that this is a woman who feels in command and who is not often torn by self-doubt.

Dr. Pierce was medical director in charge of therapeutic drugs at Ortho in early 1975 when she was assigned to a team researching a new prescription drug. Loperamide, a liquid formula for treatment of diarrhea, was to be used by infants, children, and old people who could not take solid medicine.

SWEET FORMULA

The team was concerned almost immediately; to make the formula sweet, twelve ounces of the medicine contained a large amount of saccharin—forty-four times the amount permitted in a can of diet soda by the FDA. The team toxicologist reported that no other known drug contained such high levels of saccharin.

Ortho contended then—and contends now—that the loperamide formula was safe. According to the company, although a full bottle of the medicine had high amounts of saccharin, the amount of the sweetener actually prescribed for a 24-hour period was less than in one can of diet soda.

Saccharin's safety is still highly disputed. The FDA proposed banning saccharin from foods in 1977, because the substance had been shown to cause cancer in animals, but Congress delayed the ban until this May. No standards have ever been adopted regulating saccharin in drugs.

The loperamide project team met March 6, 1975, and agreed unanimously, according to court documents and the team's own memos, that although the drug was marketed in Europe, it was unsuitable for use in the United States. The team decided that using high amounts of saccharin was a needless risk, especially for old people and infants and children who suffered from chronic diarrhea and might use the formula daily for years.

Preliminary research indicated that an alternative formula using sugar or low amounts of saccharin could be developed in three months.

Throughout March 1975 the team sent unanimous memos to company executives reporting that the loperamide formula was unsuitable.

ROUTINE DECISION?

"I didn't think there would be any problem, as reformulation would be an improvement on the product. It was a routine decision," recalls Dr. Pierce.

But it proved not to be so routine. Loperamide was manufactured by a Belgian firm, Janssen, which, like Ortho, is a subsidiary of Johnson & Johnson. Ortho, well-established as a producer of contraceptives, was then in a big push to enter the therapeutic drug market. A Janssen doctor visited Ortho. Shortly thereafter, the team was ordered to proceed with human testing of the formula.

Dr. Pierce says she still doesn't know why management decided to proceed. She says she thinks that the company had decided on a product and a deadline and didn't want to deviate. "The marketing people can go off half-cocked sometimes," she says. "They think millions of dollars are waiting to fall in their laps, promotions are to be had, careers to be made."

At first the team objected to the order. Then, according to court documents, the team apparently acceded to pressure from management, despite private pleadings from Dr. Pierce. "The others supported me to a point, but then it became politically inadvisable to go against the order," she says. "I'm not very good at politics."

Dr. Pierce, the team's only physician, was responsible for designing the human testing of the drug and supervising doctors who would dispense it to test subjects. "I was the only one who had to meet face to face with the doctors and tell them what was in it," she says.

REVIEW SOUGHT

Dr. Pierce asked her superior, Dr. Sam Pasquale, Ortho's medical director, to consider compromises. She asked that the drug be reviewed by an impartial committee of outside experts, or be sent to the FDA for discussion. She says both proposals were rejected. "I could not ethically take it out and give it to the children," she says. "The others were prepared to follow an order. But I don't think that excuses anyone. In this world you make your own decisions. I made mine."

When Dr. Pierce arrived at the Ortho headquarters in Raritan in 1973, most of the decisions in her life had already been made, and made in a way that centered on her work. "I'm not married, and I don't have any children, so most of my time and energy is given to my job," she says.

She had at first wanted to be a nurse, but when she was graduated from high school at 17, she was too young for admission to nursing school. At Allegheny College in her hometown of Meadville, Pennsylvania, she chose premed, going on to Temple University Medical School.

She applied for a surgical residency in 1945, but choice hospital posts were filled by homecoming war veterans. She was offered only a residency in obstetrics and gynecology, and she took it.

For eleven years she had her own practice in Canton, Ohio. Worn out by delivering babies at all hours of the night, she went to Washington, D.C., as a medical director for the FDA.

There she met her first test of personal ethics. She had reviewed research showing that oral contraceptives had potentially dangerous side effects, and for a year argued with her superior's delay in changing warning labels. Finally, she resigned over the issue in 1965.

She turned to private industry, first at Hoffmann-La Roche Inc., then moving to a better job at Ortho.

She found she loved the work. "In drug research you get results in a very short time. You can tell whether a drug has no value, or is worthwhile, and once in a while you hit on something that really works."

Former colleagues say she was considered a good scientist who believed in what she was doing at Ortho.

"I thought of her as a fine scientist. She was levelheaded and not the emotional type," recalls one colleague. She lived with her mother and her work was interrupted only by gardening and golf.

How, then, did such an apparently calm and confident doctor run into an unresolvable conflict with her superiors?

The company acted swiftly after Dr. Pierce informed it in early May 1975 that she could not in good conscience follow the order to proceed with human testing. "I really did not anticipate the punishment," she says now. "I thought they would take me off the project and I would continue my other work."

She was relieved of the loperamide project within a week of her decision. She recounts how a few days later Dr. Pasquale called her into his office and told her she would be demoted, that she was irresponsible, had unacceptable productivity, and was unable to work with the marketing people. He told Dr. Pierce that top Ortho executives considered her unpromotable.

Other criticisms she found even more bewildering. Ordered to attend a medical conference in Texas, she was now criticized for staying a day too long. She was reprimanded for taking a research associate along on a field trip to Alaska, although she says that taking a second person was a routine procedure that had been approved by the company's vice-president. By the end of the session with Dr. Pasquale, she was in tears. "I really didn't believe it. It's the first time in industry that I've cried," she says. Ortho offered her a choice of other projects, but she says she felt that the offer was not genuine. She resigned.

Ortho offers a different version of events. The company denies that Dr. Pierce was demoted. It says she was given another assignment in her field at no salary reduction. Although the company won't elaborate, it says that her resignation was accepted because of "certain ongoing employment problems totally unrelated to loperamide, and her personal dissatisfaction at not having received a promotion long before the loperamide issue."

Six weeks after her resignation, Dr. Pierce decided to sue. "Financially it was a very great loss to me, but there was more to it. I wasn't exactly bitter, but I was sorely disappointed. I think it was unjust."

She had interviews with other companies, but says she was never made a good offer. "I have to think the Ortho problem has something to do with it. I don't think the fact that you've sued your former employer is a plus on your curriculum vitae."

Her suit seeks damages resulting from the termination of employment, claiming that because of Ortho's actions, her career was interrupted, her professional reputation damaged, and salary, retirement, and seniority benefits were lost.

The liquid loperamide formula was never tested by humans and never marketed. A spokesman says that after Dr. Pierce left the company, Ortho decided that the liquid form was inconvenient to patients. A syrup formula was substituted.

Grace Pierce lost her first court decision. A Somerset County judge ruled after an abbreviated hearing that under New Jersey common law, an employer is free to fire an employee at will, unless the employee is hired under a contract. Dr. Pierce had no contract. But on appeal, the Appellate Division of Superior Court last month ordered a full trial, saying that now may be the time for New Jersey to review the "at will" relationship when professional ethics are at stake.

Courts in twelve states have in recent years carved out narrow exceptions to this "at will" rule, but only in cases where a clear public policy had been violated—for example, where an employee was fired in retaliation for exercising statutory obligations such as serving on a jury. Dr. Pierce is arguing that a professional should not be penalized for following ethical standards. No trial date has been set.

In the meantime, she is building a new home in Somerset that will include a small doctor's office. She hopes to give up the peripatetic clinical work she has been doing since she left Ortho and open a private practice. She says, "I know my decision not to give the drug to anyone was the right thing. I sleep well at night."

Then, for only a moment, even she has some doubts. She wonders aloud whether her idealism has perhaps been too costly. "Sometimes, I think I'm a jerk," she says.

Sexual Harassment: Adrienne Tomkins, Stenographer

Five years ago, I was the victim of sexual harassment on the job. Unlike most women who suffer similar abuse, I did not give in, and I refused to leave my job voluntarily. As a result, I paid a high price in terms of my health and my financial well-being. Last November, though, I finally had the satisfaction of hearing a federal appeals court judge rule that the sort of harassment I suffered—which previously was considered outside the protection of the law—was, in fact, a form of sex discrimination and a violation of Title VII of the Civil Rights Act of 1964. This is the story of how I won my victory.

I began work at Public Service Electric and Gas Company in New Jersey in April 1971. In August of 1973, I started working as the private secretary—my title was "stenographer"—to a new supervisor. On October 30 my supervisor informed me he wanted to discuss my promotion, over lunch, which surprised me since I had only been working for him for a short time.

It was during this luncheon, at a nearby hotel restaurant, that the incident occurred: He said he "wanted to lay me" that he "couldn't walk around the office with a hard-on all the time," and that "it was the only way we could have a working relationship." When I tried to leave the restaurant, he restrained me physically, and angrily declared that I wasn't going anywhere except with him to the executive suite on the thirteenth floor of the hotel. When I protested again, he advised me not to seek help, that since he had "something" on everyone in the company, including top management, no one would venture forth to help me. This made sense to me since he was a brilliant man and in a key position in the company.

I was frightened. I didn't know what would happen if I resisted him,

Reprinted from *The Civil Liberties Review*, September–October 1978. Copyright © 1978 by *The Civil Liberties Review*.

but I felt I had to find a way to maneuver out of it. I recalled being told he had been very close to his late mother, so I mentioned my mother and her recent operation, telling him that she needed me at home and that I was, in fact, already late for my appointment with her. This apparently moved him enough to allow me to leave, but not before he forceably held and kissed me.

I initially felt I had no alternative but to leave the company. However, at the time I was supporting myself and my mother and was paying off a large car loan—I could not take unemployment lightly. I sought advice at my unemployment office and was told that it was possible to collect benefits, but an investigation would have to be held first. Another possibility, they said, would be to request a transfer through the personnel department, which is what I did.

My supervisor's superior then contacted me and listened to my story. He seemed genuinely concerned, advised me to stay home, and said he would look into the matter. When he called the next day, however, his attitude had changed completely. He spoke of "a big misunderstanding," and advised me to return to work to my supervisor. I angrily told him that under no circumstances would I return and that my unemployment office had informed me that I could file a complaint. He then readjusted his position and said a comparable position would be found for me elsewhere in the company. With this new possibility, I decided to return to work at Public Service Electric and Gas. I was very trusting at that time.

The "comparable" position turned out to be a lower-level one, but I was assured it would be only temporary. I was advised not to speak about the matter. My duties in this new position were almost nonexistent; I felt as though I were just occupying space. When I noticed and then inquired why stenographers were being hired from outside the company, I was told I would be interviewed shortly.

The interview I was eventually granted, however, was not for a comparable position. I was asked my reasons for requesting a transfer, and I tactfully said there had been a problem with my former supervisor. Yet when I returned to my department, I was berated for saying too much, was told I was lucky I wasn't being sued for slander, and that I should have been fired long ago!

I began to realize that, not only would I not be transferred, but that the company was going to make things as difficult as possible for me. This suspicion was confirmed when, following my interview, I was informed that no one wanted me because of my absences, I was not capable of performing my duties, I shouldn't be receiving my salary, and my title should be changed. The charges of frequent absences and poor job performance were all fabrications. My absences were not excessive: I had not even used up my paid sick days. As to job performance, since I began work at the utility, my salary and responsibilities had increased with each move I had made, which is hardly what happens to an employee not capable of performing her duties. I challenged all their accusations with a presentation of these facts.

I again contacted my unemployment office where I was told that I could resign and file charges that the company had failed to reinstate me as promised as well as the initial charge against my supervisor. When I told the utility that I intended to do this unless transferred as promised, they granted a transfer which, again, was not comparable to my previous job but, needing to work, I took it—still with some hope.

The secretary from my former department, which served as the personnel office for that division, told me some weeks later that a large amount of written material about me was coming in from other departments where I had worked at the utility. Each report said that because of poor job performance I had been transferred out. Looking back, I can only guess that because of my threat to press charges unless appropriately transferred, the company, trying to protect itself, began to amass "evidence" on their behalf and so had "ordered" departments to forward statements as to my "poor performance." It finally became crystal clear to me that nothing had really changed for me at the utility, nor would it, and that my days there were numbered.

I began to get physically ill, suffering a variety of anxiety symptoms such as nausea, palpitations, extremity pain, even passing out. My absences were closely monitored and pay subtracted from my salary. If notes from my doctor did not meet what seemed to be arbitrary and fluctuating specifications, I again had pay subtracted.

When it became so unbearable that I could not bring myself to go to work, I contacted my doctor asking him to recommend a psychotherapist to help me. When I returned to work, after a three-day absence, I was informed that since verbal counseling about absences had done no good, I was to receive a disciplinary layoff of one week without pay. I had never received any "verbal counseling" about absences.

Despite such treatment, I remained at my job, although the harassment continued, and my absences became more frequent. With support from my therapist I filed charges with the Equal Employment Opportunity Commission (EEOC), even though they advised me that there were no laws governing sexual harassment. I continued to file additional charges, as incidents occurred, hoping a favorable decision would be made while I was still employed. I received a second disciplinary layoff —this time two weeks without pay.

I was fired, finally, in January 1975. The EEOC investigated the company's charge of excessive absence and no cause was found for my charges. The commission did issue me a Notice of Right-to-Sue.

Some people may feel that I could have saved myself a lot of anguish had I just left my job, but I had earned my employment and I wasn't going to let it be taken from me. Others may feel I did all I could, and maybe I did, but it wasn't enough to protect my job. I did not know my rights—or even that I had any in this situation. I lacked a vehicle to deal effectively with my problem. I had been trusting, had followed procedures, and was powerless, given the company's intransigence and duplicity, to get a fair hearing for my charges of harassment.

Disillusioned, I took my Right-to-Sue Notice and filed an affidavit with the federal district court in Newark, asking them to appoint an attorney for me. They put me in touch with the Women's Rights Litigation Clinic at Rutgers Law School in Newark, New Jersey. They agreed to represent me, and my case was presented before the United States District Court for the District of New Jersey in 1976. The court upheld my charge against the company but dismissed my charge against my supervisor. The judge, in his decision, characterized my experience as a "physical attack motivated by sexual desire on the part of a supervisor and which happened to occur in a corporate corridor rather than a back alley." In other words, the utility had no responsibility for the actions of my supervisor since it was considered a personal matter.

However, when I appealed my case to the United States Court of Appeals for the Third Circuit, the court noted that the district court's characterizing my supervisor's acts as an abuse of authority for personal purposes overlooked the crucial issue: that my employer, the utility, by knowing about the incident and not taking immediate and appropriate remedial action, had acquiesced in my supervisor's sexual demands, making them a necessary condition to continuing in my job. The setting of the incident—a luncheon to which my supervisor invited me for the sole purpose of discussing my promotion—was strong evidence of a job-related condition, the court said. More importantly, my supervisor's saying "it's the only way we could have a working relationship" was a clear indication to the court that my employment depended on acceding to his sexual demands. Because my job status depended on agreeing to his demands, my claim fell within the jurisdiction of Title VII, and the court reversed the dismissal of my complaint and remanded the case to the district court for final determination.

In having pursued this law suit, I believe I will help deter other companies from turning a blind eye to overt sexual harassment on the job which countless employees suffer daily. I think what is of utmost importance is ensuring that the type of treatment I experienced will not occur again. If the courts cannot guarantee women freedom against abuse, then, hopefully, legislation will be enacted to accomplish this end.

But perhaps court-ordered protections will be enough. Remanded to district court, my case was finally settled out of court. Public Service Electric and Gas will pay me $20,000 for having suffered physical and emotional damages, plus my attorney's fees and court costs. More importantly, under other terms of the settlement, the company has notified every nonunion employee in writing—approximately 13,000— of their rights under Title VII. Secondly, a review panel has been set up to hear all grievances regarding sexual harassment, discharge for cause, or any grievance entailing position or salary discrimination under Title VII. All review panel meetings are to be recorded on tape for documentation purposes, and the panel's decisions and reasons for their decisions are to be put in writing to the employee. The panel is to consist of an employee of the complainant's choice, an employee at the same job level as that of the complainant, any witnesses, the employee relations manager, the EEOC manager, and the industrial relations manager. Third, a film has been produced that will be shown on an ongoing basis to all employees at the utility. It illustrates the different types of discrimination covered by Title VII, what protection is available, and what resources are available to an employee who wants to take action. Fourth, a pamphlet entitled "Employee Relations Review Procedure" documenting the steps in processing a complaint is being distributed to every employee and will become part of the company's administrative procedure booklet. Finally, my own personnel file will be reinstated to what it was prior to the initial incident. Any information released to prospective employers will be limited to only the fact that I was employed there and the dates of my employment. If the company violates any of the conditions, it will be held in contempt of court and the case can be reopened.

Unions and Sexual Harassment: AFSCME at Michigan State University

Lin Farley

The American Federation of State, County and Municipal Employees has executed a survey of all its state councils and locals to determine the number of women active in union affairs. This survey was also meant to serve as a subtle pressure on local leadership [to begin to act on women's issues]. Indicative of what unions could accomplish if they had the will, this effort accidently sparked an amazing fight by one of the locals against the sexual harassment by foremen of female employees.

AFSCME Local 1585 represents all the nonexempt employees at Michigan State University—approximately 1,100 service and non-skilled maintenance workers, about half of whom are women. In 1976 a new chief steward began investigating persistent rumors of sexual harassment of female employees in the custodial department. Two female janitors subsequently agreed to sign statements about the sexual demands one foreman had made on them. A survey of all the female janitors was then executed; this resulted in a carefully researched report of serious, extended sexual abuse within the department as a whole. The union decided to act. It went directly to the university's campus labor relations board, where it presented both the signed statements and the report with a demand for reform that included the removal from any position of authority of one foreman in particular.

The AFSCME local never intended to take on such a crusade. The rumors about sexual harassment in the custodial department had been around for a long time; only a series of apparently unrelated events appears to have made its involvement possible. These events included, as a result of the national survey, the formation of a minorities committee, which only women attended; an incident of severe harassment; the election of an idealistic chief steward; and, finally, the hiring of an outside feminist to write up the sexual harassment questionnaire. The people brought together by each of these events didn't necessarily like or even trust one another, but they nonetheless combined to force this seemingly unexceptional local to face up to the real needs of half its members.

The local's office in Lansing, Michigan, is squeezed into three small rooms. There are folding chairs, an American flag, and an enormous bulletin board which is virtually empty save for a few giant glossies advertising Red Wing safety shoes. The chief steward, Roy Barr, is a huge man with an air of perpetual worry. He welcomed me with a handshake. Richard Kennedy, the president, looked on. Both men are in their forties; their pants have cuffs and their hair is short; they are obviously ill-at-ease. Kennedy, who started out as an animal caretaker, has worked his way up over a long history with the local. Barr is relatively new, although he is a veteran of many other unions including the Hod Carriers, the Teamsters, and the UAW, where he was a shop steward.

When the rumors first surfaced at what Kennedy calls the antidiscrimination committee, he said, "I wasn't too concerned. I just didn't think it was that big a deal. Employees get upset a lot. I thought we had more rumor than substance." After the investigation by Barr, however, Kennedy recalled, "I found out I was wrong. We do have a serious problem. It's especially serious because the people who are having these problems probably won't come to you. They are suffering in silence. If you've got rumors, you've got to take a look at it."

Barr's investigation began with getting names from the committee and talking to the women janitors firsthand. He said, "I could see right away what was happening was not right. However, I could also see it was highly sensitive. I talked to a lawyer, who said we should get signed statements. We still can't get more than two. It's there but the women won't sign. They just don't want any more hassle and they're frightened of repercussions. They don't want their names associated with sexual acts. They don't want their husbands to know because they're afraid they'll try to hurt the supervisors. One woman who has signed is very influenced by her husband and he's constantly telling her she's going to get fired or sued or something. Many of these women can't read or write too well; they are afraid if they try it will just backfire on them."

Barr is also quite clear that his own sex was an obstacle in gaining the women's confidence. "They didn't come to us; remember, we had to go to them and then that we were men, it was really difficult. They just didn't trust us." It was partly for this reason that Barr was inclined to include a woman at a later stage of the investigation. This stage developed as the two men began to look for a way the union could correct the foremen's abusive treatment of the female janitors. Their plan eventually involved bypassing the regular grievance procedure. Barr explained, "There are five different steps in our regular grievance procedure, and that would have meant a lot of people would know the identities of the people involved. It seemed like that would be bad for the women and bad for the union. In a case like this discretion is important." Kennedy added, "I didn't know what our liability would be if we had to use names."

The two men consequently decided to go directly to the university campus labor relations board, but before taking this step they wanted better documentation of the problem among the female janitors. Barr explained, "In this particular department there are transfers for all kinds of reasons. Women say they want to be closer to a bus line or one wants a building with an elevator or reasons such as that, and it was difficult to pin down who had left for sexual advances." This is how they hit on the idea of a questionnaire to help determine the extent of the problem, and Barr enlisted the aid of a local feminist who compiled it.

Kennedy said, "The results of that made it absolutely without question. There are at least three of the seven supervisors in that department who are clearly doing things that they shouldn't, but there is one guy who is really, really a problem. He is the one we are focusing on. Barr added, "We don't want to destroy the guy, we just don't want him supervising our people."

Roy Barr, who has been the prime mover behind the union's stand, has two regrets:

"I think you've got to have a woman in an official capacity in on this kind of thing from the beginning. The women's committee also wasn't too helpful. There was one woman who had made a statement about sexual harassment in 1974, that long ago, but the committee didn't do anything. The problem was one woman on that committee wanted to be Queen of the May. She was jealous of her position. She had the group go to personnel and pursued it there; of course they didn't get anywhere. I don't know why they didn't try and use the union."

Mary Walker is head of the Women's Committee. Originally from Chicago, where she worked as a packer with Jergen's Lotion, she has worked for the MSU custodial department at various jobs and for the last five years has been a swimming pool operator. Her small house sits in an area of Lansing that resembles a bombed-out battlefield, strewn with craters from the last flood. Walker greeted me at the back door and then settled us down with a pack of doughnuts and some instant coffee for a thorough briefing:

About the discrimination committee:

I always had a lot of mouth and I always enjoy meetin' different peoples. I called womens on the telephone. I was always slippin' around places, talkin' to the womens, gettin' them to come to a meetin' because they was refusin' to give the womens to the jobs they was qualified for. If you was a brown-nose you got the job. Always givin' it to the hometown boys. If we got enough people to look into things, the things might change.

About the rumors:

We always go to the union. At the time there was twenty-four womens was supposed to have met. In 1973 we had one lady out there who was workin' for one foreman who any girl wears a dress turns him on and if she don't give in to him she works so many days and then she's fired. This girl didn't tell me, but she told someone else and the other party told me. I thought it was lousy. I went and talked to the steward and he said to find out how long she worked and when she left and where she lives. The steward say, "There's not very much we can do about a situation like this." I thought it was his place to find out the information he wanted. I can't pull her file but he could. He make me very mad. I went to a friend at personnel but she say to go back, to take it to the president of the union. The president was very busy and had no time. So then I went to the day steward, Roy Barr. He said he'd try to pressure the union to do somethin' about it.

About the problem:

In some cases men have been sayin' if you love me I get you a better job. Of course, if it's seniority job and you only been there six months you shouldn't have the job. Husbands are goin' to know somethin' is wrong. We have about three foremen out there that has been confronted by the husbands. We had to try and force the foremens to give one women a foreman's job. They didn't want her 'cause she is older and not so pretty and didn't play along.

If you don't play along they say you a surly type person. They don't really go for that. There's one guy who likes girls to be nice to him and if they aren't he put the lie on them. He'll report them to foreman about their job. If you don't know to call the union you can get fired. I believe a lot of the womens goes along with things 'cause they think they should.

One time one white guy go into the office to complain about favoritism. He'd seen what was goin' on, that some girls is havin' it really easy because they been nice to the foreman. The foreman got real nasty. He say if he didn't shut his mouth and mind his own business the nigger gonna get his job. He had gone in to complain about treatment of a black girl he worked with. Afterward he turned really cruel and mean. He got scared they'd get rid of him and he just changed. The foreman he complained to is now a general foreman.

About the acceptance of sexual harassment:

I was always under the impression when I first got hired if you didn't play with the mens, if you didn't go out with them, you didn't get a good job. That's what I was told.

This is the way I found out what was goin' on. A maid asked me if I knew any peoples who was goin' out. She started namin' names of ladies, then she say do I know such-and-such a foreman. I say, "Wow." She say you should learn the score around this place. You will learn if you go with a foreman you okay but if you don't you gonna get fired. Then another lady tell me the same story. I was transferred to another department and they tell me the same things. Then I say, "Wow," what you all do if you is married already? So then they tell me about a foreman who was confronted with two womens' husbands, the same year. One night one husband was lookin' for him and they didn't even let him go on his route.

About her own struggle against it:

There was one time this one woman was goin' along with a foreman. She was young and childish but she got thirteen kids. He was really nasty to all of us. She started flirtin' around with him, thinkin' she'd get it easier on the job. We filed a grievance on him for liftin' weight. She got mad and say, "Why did you go to union office on him, you wreckin' overtime and you only bumpin' me. I wanna do the job." They try to get me to drop the grievance. I say as long as I stay black I'm gonna do the grievance. She really couldn't do the job either, but because she was smilin' all the time she was gonna get help.

About her escape:

I didn't want no one messin' with me. Real quick I got a relationship with the union steward. That wasn't all of it, but I did go with him a little bit for job reasons. Now that's over ain't no one gonna bother me 'cause they know I go to the union. I want more womens to use it. The union don't help so good all the time. Sometimes I don't even see notice of meetin's. You got to talk to people. You got to make it work. Me and my committee is helpin'. Now womens feel they got a place to go to. Most people now is takin' it into consideration.

About the abuse:

I think this sexual harassment is rotten. I think it's one of the worst things on earth that a person would have to do. I think it's terrible you have to make love or put out or screw just to keep a low-down dirty job. You workin' for yourself. I can do without work if I had some other way of livin', you know, but myself if I had to feel up to some guy I might wind up on welfare. I mean, how many times you wanna have to do that?

The questionnaire distributed by the union defined sexual harassment in categories ranging from "leering, suggestive looks, insults, and innuendos" to "subtle or out-and-out threats to a job or working conditions if one didn't cooperate with sexual demands." It was distributed to seventy-seven (80 percent) of the ninety-six female custodians. The questionnaires were unsigned and no names were requested, but respondents were asked to specify their shift and building so that names of the seven foremen could be readily identified. When the results were compiled, 73 percent of the women reported sexual harassment to be a problem that should be remedied and four foremen were identified as engaging in harassment. Of these four there was one who had harassed nine separate women, several to the point of outright physical force. The other three foremen had respectively intimidated three, two, and one women, for a grand total of fifteen victims who could be traced to specific foremen. There were four more reports of harassment, but three failed to identify their building and shift while one reported harassment from an earlier foreman whom she didn't name. In all, then, a full one-quarter of the custodial women were being harassed by at least half or more of their foremen.

Joan Nelson of Lansing is a woman's counselor on rape, a teacher of self-defense for women, and a recent social science graduate of Michigan State University. It is largely by her efforts that the twenty-five-page report on sexual harassment (which corresponds totally with all previous studies) came into being. This was only accomplished by many long hours of meeting with groups of the female janitors.

Nelson explained:

I asked them to meet me at the union office because a significant number of women in that department can't read because of being Latino or poor black and white women with little education. Twenty-six women out of the ninety-six total actually met with me. We then talked to women at work on their breaks, at lunch, whenever we could. We continued to do this for about three weeks and that brought the total of interviews to seventy-seven women. Some women did it on their own. Some I helped to understand the questions. The nineteen women we didn't contact were on various kinds of leave: sick, maternity, and military. The twenty-six women who came the first time was a tremendous turnout. It seemed indicative that the women felt strongly about sexual harassment, because even five or six at a meeting is really phenomenal. Apathy is really high in the union. It also seemed to indicate that the women's committee had probably been supportive. The majority of that first group was black.

In Nelson's experience almost all the women were surprised the union was taking an interest and they believed nothing would come of it. She also observed that because she expressed a receptive attitude they would eventually feel free to express both anger and frustration. "They were never really punitive. By far the largest category of options they would choose was to remove the man from a supervisor's position but not go beyond that." Nelson also found the women as a group to be anxiety-ridden: "They were really frightened. Most of them feared talking at all because it could result in a scandal for the university and they thought they would be the ones to pay. That they'd be transferred or fired. I just can't say how many women also feared they'd be blamed. An amazing number were also terrified of what their husbands would do, not only to the men but to them. Often they were deathly afraid of their husbands."

Hilly (a pseudonym) is a slender, soft-spoken young woman in her twenties who is married and has one child whom she adores. Five years ago she began working in the custodial department; this experience had led to her signing one of the two written statements despite both her husband's and mother-in-law's vigorous protests—they think she is "acting like a fool." At her house in the suburbs a few hours before she was due at work, she was tense, unsmiling. "My husband doesn't know I let you come out here. He'd be furious. I know he cares about me. He just feels nothing will be done. I guess I've just got to take a chance."

Hilly had worked in the custodial department for three years without a problem until she was transferred. One week later her new foreman requested she leave her regular building and drive with him over to another building, where he locked the two of them inside. Subsequently escorting her into a basement room with a couch he invited her to relax and have intercourse. This request occurred about 10 P.M.; her shift lasted until 1 A.M.; throughout most of that time the foreman pursued her around the floors of the empty building. Repeated requests that he stop were ignored, until finally at 12:30 A.M. he agreed to unlock the doors and drive her back to work.

Hilly talked to no one about what had happened. Two days later she was in the museum with another female janitor when the foreman showed up and told the second woman to go home sick. "I got her alone and I begged her not to go 'cause I knew what he was up to. She said she wasn't sick but she thought she should go. When she left she said she was sorry." The foreman returned later and forced himself physically. "I was real scared but I got free of him and I took off running. I could hear him walking around in the building trying to find me." Eventually Hilly thought she heard him leave and she stopped hiding, but he quickly reappeared, lunging at her. "I screamed, then I hollered I'd report him." Running away again, she darted into the telephone office. "The supervisor there asked me what was wrong and I told her. She said it didn't surprise her because she knew of his reputation. I talked to her the rest of the night. She said I could come in there and hide if he kept it up."

The foreman showed up again a week later. He told Hilly she was a sad case, that he just wanted to help her, then he left. After this Hilly arranged to come to work with her fifteen-year-old brother; the foreman would see her brother and leave. This continued until one night the two of them were playing cards on her break when the brother left to use the john. The foreman immediately slipped into the room and closed the door. "He was really upset. I got mad and I found my brother and I found Dolores [a pseudonym], the lady I work with. I said I just had to get away from that foreman. Dolores said she'd go tell my old foreman, because he had once said if I ever had any trouble to get in touch with him."

Hilly's former supervisor showed up immediately. When she told him the problem, however, he thought it was funny. He also encouraged her to keep quiet. "He told me to call the general supervisor, who transfers people, and tell him I was afraid of the snakes up on the third floor of the museum." Following the foreman's advice, she was promised a transfer but only in one or two weeks. The foreman renewed his attacks and Hilly finally told the general supervisor the real reason. She was immediately transferred. This was not the end of her trouble. The transfer placed her under the supervision of one of the man's friends, who continuously complained about her work; this culminated in an attempt to have her fired. Hilly kept her job, but only as the result of a third transfer at the request of the union.

Throughout most of the trauma Hilly could hardly think beyond the fact she needed her job. Her daughter has a disease that requires a doctor's care monthly. Her husband works as a utility man. "I just have to keep my job. We're barely keeping our heads above water now. So all I could think was that if I talked I'd get fired for being a troublemaker. I also couldn't tell my husband because I knew he'd try and kill the foreman. I just didn't know where to turn. I didn't trust the union. My girlfriend was all I had and all we could think of was trying to get witnesses."

After the reaction of her former foreman when she finally did talk, Hilly also felt all her fears had been well-founded. "He made me feel so little. He acted like it was all my fault. I got scared all over again. I was really desperate when I finally told the general supervisor the truth. Of course, afterward, I realized by the way he didn't ask any questions that he must have already known about him." After the first transfer Hilly felt she could no longer keep the situation from her husband. Once more her worst fears were confirmed. "He told me he'd take care of it. He said he'd kill him. I had a terrible time convincing him not to do something like that."

Hilly's attitude about the union is a mixture of amazement and cynicism. Her only previous experience with the union was a complete bust. After a fall on company property that soon required that her tailbone be removed, the company refused to pay for the operation and the union never pressed her claim. Hilly hired her own lawyer. "I won, but it was no thanks to the union. That's why I was shocked when they got involved. Roy Barr is wonderful; I just wish there were more union officials like him. I'm glad the union's involved, of course, but I can't help thinking they might not follow it through."

Seeing it through and standing up for her rights has not been easy for Hilly. After bucking the opposition of both her husband and her mother-in-law, who feel she is uselessly jeopardizing her job, she has been sorely disappointed by a lack of support from other women. "It's so hard. Many of the women have gone all the way with that foreman. They are completely compromised. They didn't want to, but now they won't do anything. I don't want to jeopardize my job either, but I do want to stop that man. There was one woman who even went on the ten-o'clock shift to get away from him. I'd like to feel like I had some power behind me. It's just me and my girlfriend."

According to union sources, the Michigan State University Campus Labor Relations Board turned the sexual harassment report over to the general supervisor, who called a meeting of all the foremen involved. What happened at that meeting is not known. About two weeks later the CLRB informed the union president, Richard Kennedy, by letter that there was "not enough evidence" to take any action. They advised that any future course follow the regular grievance procedures. Kennedy sent a letter to a reputedly liberal member of the university's board of trustees to which there has to date been no response. On December 1, 1976, Roy Barr resigned his post. A short time later Guy

Munger, one of the foremen in the custodial department, committed suicide. He left a note for the general supervisor, but the contents have never been made public. As of this writing Hilly is in grievance about her harassment.

"Corporate Malice": John Pirre v. Printing Developments, Inc.

Plaintiff had since 1947 been employed as an engineering aide by the defendants. He had performed his services with outstanding success and was highly regarded by all of P.D.I.'s employees as well as by the outside contractors with whom he had worked. In 1970 there occurred a change in management and Brian M. Chapman became plaintiff's superior. New management—especially Mr. Chapman—started innovating new policies. Plaintiff, having the benefit of years of experience, could see that these new policies would be disastrous. In loyal discharge of his obligations to the corporation, he so advised Mr. Chapman. Disregarding plaintiff's advice, Mr. Chapman proceeded to implement the new policies. As plaintiff had forecast, disaster followed.

Not unpredictably this turn of events caused Mr. Chapman to hate plaintiff, and he determined to get rid of him. Since plaintiff had no contract of employment but was working "at will," Mr. Chapman could have fired him out-of-hand, giving no reason. However, apparently fearing that such action would disgrace himself and the corporation in the eyes of plaintiff's fellow employees and of those outside contractors who had over the years developed respect for plaintiff, Mr. Chapman together with other members of management decided to make a "paper record" to justify the firing. This paper record consisted of a series of memoranda to plaintiff, each containing accusations of disloyalty known to be false, and each containing a hypocritical and self-serving declaration of good will and esteem for plaintiff.

Not content with causing these memoranda to be written, Mr. Chapman saw to it that their contents were widely disseminated among plaintiff's fellow employees and among those of P.D.I.'s contractors as

This article is a case write-up by Alan F. Westin and Stephan Salisbury.

had previously held plaintiff in high esteem. The obvious and intended consequence of this conduct was to cause plaintiff to be held in obloquy and shunned by his former friends, and to cause him untold and predictable emotional stress and pain, and financial loss.

Upon the foregoing facts, plaintiff seeks to recover damages from the corporation for wrongful discharge and for defamation. We conclude that summary judgment dismissing the former claim is appropriate but that issues of fact remain as to the latter.

With respect to his action for wrongful discharge, the plaintiff is met with the insuperable obstacle that his employment was at will and that as a result he could be discharged for any reason or for no reason.

With respect to plaintiff's claim for libel and slander, defendants argue that because he is not suing Mr. Chapman and the other supervisors who defamed him but the corporate employer, his complaint has no legal basis. According to the defendants, either Mr. Chapman and the others were actuated by personal malice and spite or by a desire to protect the interests of the corporation (or by both). If (or to the extent which) the former was the motivation, Mr. Chapman (and the others) were off on frolics of their own, and the corporation is not responsible under the doctrine of respondeat superior. If (or to the extent which) the latter was their motivation, the corporation is fully protected by the qualified privilege for communications in which the participants have an interest described in *Stillman* v. *Ford* (1968). In that case the former president of a foundation claimed that individual officials of the organization defamed him when they criticized his position on certain questions of policy and his performance as executive. The Court of Appeals ruled:

> The parties herein were engaged in a dispute about the policy of an institution in which they were all deeply interested. In defending their respective positions, each faction accused the other of misrepresenting its views in order to win support. Whether or not, in the final analysis, any of these accusations were true or false is hardly relevant. As long as the statements were motivated not by ill will or personal spite but by a sincerely held desire to protect the institution, they are not actionable.

Thus, defendants urge, in order to overcome the privilege plaintiff must show that the defendants he is suing acted with malice or exceeded the scope of the privilege. Since plaintiff has selected corporations rather than individuals as defendants and since an individual's malice cannot be imputed to his employer, defendants further urge, plaintiff must prove that there was a corporate purpose to act with malice towards himself. Defendants conclude that because plaintiff has offered no evidence to suggest such a purpose the complaint must be dismissed.

Although we found defendants' argument initially appealing we must reject it. It is clear that the qualified privilege on which defendants rely can be overcome by a showing of recklessness as well as of malice (*Stillman* v. *Ford,* supra). Plaintiff has cited several cases where employers were held liable on the theory of respondeat superior for other privileged defamations by their employees: *Levesque* v. *Kings County Lafayette Trust Co.* (E.D.N.Y.1968) 293 F.Supp. 1010; *Chambers* v. *National Battery Co.* (W.D.Mo.1940) 34 F.Supp. 834; *Sias* v. *General Motors Corp.* (1964) 372 Mich. 542, 127 N.W.2d 357; *Brown* v. *Great Atlantic & Pacific Tea Co.* (1st Dept. 1949), 275 App.Div. 304, 89 N.Y.S.2d 247. In each of those cases the corporate defendant could have had no corporate purpose in being malicious and the necessary finding of malice sufficient to defeat the privilege must have been imputed. Although none of the opinions is explicit in its reasoning, malice must have been imputed on the theory that the corporation was reckless in not preventing the malicious acts of its employees. See *DeRonde* v. *Gaytime Shops Inc.* (2d Cir.1956), 239 F.2d 735, which expressly applied that reasoning. Such a theory is certainly open here where it is alleged that Chapman's alleged misconduct continued unchecked over a period of several months. Accordingly, summary judgment dismissing plaintiff's defamation claims cannot be granted.

May 6, 1977; U.S. District Court, Southern District of New York.

Organization Policy—
Making Dissent Respectable
and Productive

Auren Uris

An organization may be kindly disposed toward dissent, and want to seek its benefits. But there is a common problem that may have to be acknowledged and coped with before the organization can reap any advantages. The fact is, dissent is most productive when the organization takes cognizance of it and adopts policies that promote the process. But this must not be taken to mean that dissent is to be encouraged, in the sense that it becomes an approved, smiled-upon function. This approach would pervert the nature and usefulness of disagreement.

Dissent, as the dictionary points out, is a "nonconcurrence with a decision of a majority," and "a difference of opinion." The values and ideas represented by dissent hold potential benefits for management in the very fact that they are in opposition to the prevailing view.

Dissent has value because it poses an alternative to the establishment way. To institutionalize it to the point where it is invited would destroy its cutting edge. Dissent improves matters through the heat that results from intelligent people opposing one another. Management, then, must be careful not to weaken with overacceptance the counterthrust to the status quo that dissent represents.

Designing a policy that nurtures dissent is not simple. In ordinary situations, say, when management wants to boost output, the options available are easily identified: add capacity, improve equipment, further train the employees, and so on. But the rewards of dissent cannot be gained by such direct or quantifiable measures. Urging people to dissent is useless—at the very least the enriching hybridization is less likely to take place. A policy and a procedure that seek to foster dissent cannot, therefore, be developed naively. An effective policy must encompass the dilemma: what you want you can't ask for. If there is any "asking" at all, it is by indirection, by creating a facilitating climate.

When incorporated into organizational life at the policy-making level, the following elements can help along the dissent process.

Building receptivity. There are few organizations in which policies on handling dissent are put in writing, and yet every organization reflects in its attitudes and traditions unique ways of viewing dissent. In addition to the "organization way," the feelings of individual officials is a major factor. A generally enlightened organization may have authoritarian executives who try to discourage protest. Similarly, relatively authoritarian organizations may have enlightened executives who go out of their way to treat dissenters constructively.

Notwithstanding the variations that result from individual executives' attitudes, every organization should have, if not a policy, at least a general awareness of dissent and the need for guidance on the part of those who must deal with it. A favorable attitude at the top induces similar feelings in the lower echelons. Positive and negative reinforcement—praise for dissent well handled, criticism for that mishandled—further establishes management's commitment to the process of dissent.

The psychic benefits of dissent. Interviews with managers who chafe at dissent, who resent it as an intrusion on management's prerogatives, usually reveal some ignorance of its indirect benefits.

In his book *The Concept of the Corporation* (New York: John Day, 1972), Peter Drucker has pointed out that to employees at all levels "the problem of dignity and fulfillment—of status and function—is real. . . . The problem cannot be solved alone by more or better opportunities for advancement or greater economic rewards." The human need that Drucker describes is at least partially satisfied by dissent, which is essentially an act of self-assertion, a statement of individuality. It is for this reason that the act of dissent should be received favorably even if the substance of the protest is rejected. What managers must learn to appreciate is that dissent reinforces the integrity and freedom of the employee.

Compensate for inexperience. The danger in over-encouraging protest has already been mentioned. Yet it can be helpful, particularly for the inexperienced manager and for those whose personalities make dealing with disagreement difficult, to outline criteria for a productive and systematic approach. Most mature managers know what to do. But in instances where individual managers have difficulty grasping the spirit and practice of your policy, the rudiments of an acceptable procedure should be taught, perhaps using a handbook put out by Personnel.

Blend with the organization's communications system. It is undesirable to handle dissent as though it were taking place in a vacuum. Dealing with dissent should involve all the usual communications pathways. Every organization has its own patterns of communication: weekly management meetings, periodic reports to employees, special councils of managers and subordinates, junior boards of directors, and so on. The workaday world of management should not deviate much in the face of dissent. The presentation of and response to protest should receive a fair amount of exposure so that everybody directly involved or merely interested can know what happened.

Remember the hazards. For management, two potentially difficult situations may be triggered by dissent. The first involves legal repercussions, the other a snowballing of employee hostility. The *Wall Street Journal* reported the case of an auto company supervisor who was coming along well in his career, having started as an assembly-line worker, and rising to a management-level job in testing and product development. Unexpectedly, his department was eliminated, and the manager, Richard M., then 53 years old, was demoted to a position of engineer.

Indignant and upset, and feeling that he wasn't getting any satisfaction from his immediate superiors, Richard M. fired off a letter to the chairman of the company. Eventually he got a call from the personnel department saying his claims of unfairness weren't valid. He then decided to sue for reinstatement to his former position.

In court, the company argued that Richard M. was demoted without having to take a cut in pay at a time when "thousands of employees were being released outright" due to a recession. Richard M. countered that in his department there was actually a 15 percent net gain in personnel during that same period. And, although his salary wasn't cut (he was earning about $45,000), he says he "lost prestige, a private office, a secretary, and any right to a bonus." He declared, "I didn't have any illusions that I could go much higher than one more notch, but the demotion put me further back in the pack for any future advancement."

The *Wall Street Journal* describes the Richard M. case as one of an increasing number in which middle managers go to court over what they feel is unfair treatment. Discrimination on the basis of age is common among these suits. Federal law prohibits discrimination based on race, religion, or national origin, and any time these factors underlie a protest, there is the possibility of a suit. Of course, discrimination is not the only thing that leads to legal action. For instance, suits are frequently filed for breach of an employment contract.

The "snowball" situation can be exceedingly hard to handle. Usually the protest begins with an individual's complaint. If he is treated particularly unfairly, others may rally around him. The organization is then confronted with a situation of larger and more serious dimension. This usually happens in one of two ways. First, a protester's peers may side with him, even though they have no direct interest in the organization's capitulating to the dissident. Nevertheless, perhaps because of his leadership qualities or his popularity, others line up behind him.

Second, the dissent may focus on an issue of direct interest to all employees. Whenever a large number of employees stand to benefit personally from one person's supplication, you can bet that many will go to bat for him. . . . The best way to minimize the problem, if not eliminate it, is to treat protesting employees fairly. And management should train its representatives to recognize the possibilities of legal action or group protest, and to learn how to contain such dissent at an early stage.

Tailor the policy. There is one cardinal quality your policy must have: It must be of a piece with the climate of your organization, particularly in its degree of authoritarianism. There should be congruence between the organization's character and its philosophy concerning protest.

For example, Company A is a small organization with a tightly knit group of top people who share a vision and strategy for achieving its objectives. This company, with its strong central authority, is unproductive soil for contrary views. Rather than try to graft on to the organization a policy toward dissent that is out of character with its basic outlook, it would be more appropriate to openly discourage dissent. This does not mean total repression, but that disagreement should be kept within well-defined limits. There is no pretense that management "is always interested in hearing what people really think."

Company B, on the other hand, is idea hungry, and relishes the heat that can be created in rubbing two opposing ideas together. It welcomes dissent, doing almost everything but put up posters to get its managers to speak their minds. In such a company it would be foolish, even damaging, to adopt a conservative policy toward dissent.

One last point: A policy should also reflect what managers down the line will not only accept but support.

Review and assessment. Dissent is the sort of activity that goes on virtually constantly, and yet large numbers of executives are unaware of it because it doesn't touch them personally. The average top executive would understandably have difficulty answering questions like the following:

1. How would you rate your organization in terms of how effectively it handles dissent?

2. Is dissent a lively, active process?

3. Too lively?

4. Do your managers think dissent yields benefits?

5. Do they know what the benefits are?

6. Do they know how to make sure that these gains are actually derived?

7. Do the managers know *your* attitude toward protest?

8. Do your managers themselves dissent from time to time?

9. If not, why not?

If you find your answers to be rather negative or vague, it is likely that you have come upon a top-priority agenda item for the next few management meetings. How far top executives should go in briefing managers on the benefits from dissent will vary from individual to individual. But in cases where a review suggests that conformity is devitalizing the organization, clearing the way for lively intelligent dissent is an obvious antidote.

Loyalty, Obedience, and the Role of the Employee

Phillip I. Blumberg

In the balance of the conflicting rights of the government employee as citizen and the objective of government for efficient administration, the courts have placed a lesser value on the traditional duties of loyalty and obedience and have subordinated these duties to the employee's right of free speech in order to enable the employee to play a role as a citizen in matters of public controversy. Similarly, one may inquire whether, in time, erosion of the traditional employer-employee relation and the traditional concepts of loyalty and obedience will not also occur within the major American corporation.

The basic problem goes to the employer's right of discharge of an employee who is publicly acting contrary to the interests of the employer: the Polaroid worker picketing in protest of Polaroid's alleged involvement with apartheid; the Eastern Airlines pilot disobeying standard operating procedures for dumping excess kerosene in the atmosphere instead of draining it on the ground; the automobile worker who protests the shipment of allegedly unsafe cars from his employer's factory; or the employee who "leaks" non-public information in accordance with the "public interest disclosure" proposal.

At common law, the employer's freedom to discharge was absolute. Over the years, this right of discharge has been increasingly restricted by statute and by collective bargaining agreements, but the basic principle of the employer's legal right to discharge, although challenged on the theoretical level, is still unimpaired.

In *NLRB* v. *Local Union No. 1229,* [1] the Supreme Court held that the discharge of striking employees of a television station because of their

Excerpted from the *Oklahoma Law Review* 24, no. 3. Copyright © 1971 by the *Oklahoma Law Review*. Reprinted with permission. Most footnotes have been deleted.

attack on the station for poor programming and service did not constitute an "unfair labor practice" under the National Labor Relations Act.
The employees' effort to discredit the employer's business, as distinct
from his labor practices, was held "such detrimental disloyalty" as to
constitute "just cause" for discharge.

Accepting without discussion the employer's absolute right of discharge, except as limited by statute, the Court emphasized "the importance of enforcing individual plant discipline and of maintaining
loyalty." Insofar as the limited purposes of the National Labor Relations Act were concerned,[2] the Court stated: "There is no more elemen-
tal cause for discharge of an employee than disloyalty to his employer,"
and upheld the employer's right to discharge for "insubordination,
disobedience, or disloyalty."

Discharge of employees for causes not related to unionization has
been upheld under the National Labor Relations Act, including such
"offenses" as being a member of sympathizer of the Communist Party
or invoking the protection of the Fifth Amendment at a congressional
hearing or refusing to complete a defense agency security questionnaire.
Discharge for testifying under subpoena against the employer in a
criminal proceeding has also been upheld. On the other hand, a review
of arbitration awards in this area has concluded that these activities
were not normally regarded as constituting "just cause" under collective agreements and that some "resulting adverse effect upon the employment relationship which makes the retention of the employee a
detriment to the company" was required.

In an illuminating article, Dean Blades has re-examined the traditional concept of employment at will and the employer's traditional
power to discharge the employee at any time for any reason (or indeed
for no reason) and has suggested that in time the doctrine—already
hedged in by statute and collective bargaining agreements—will be
modified, possibly by the legislatures, perhaps by the courts, to protect
the employee against discharge for exercise of those personal rights
which have no legitimate connection with the employment relationship.

It is noteworthy that even Dean Blades, who has ventured boldly to
foresee limitations on the employer's right of discharge, has restricted
himself to two areas: the protection of the employee against improper
employer influence over those areas of the employee's life unrelated to
the employer; and safeguards to enable the employee as a practical
matter to insist on those rights already theoretically granted him under
agency law not to be an unwilling participant in immoral, unlawful, or
unprofessional activity. Dean Blades further recognizes that "there
may even be occasions when an employee's public utterances on contro-

versial subjects can be considered incompatible with his professional position and the duty of loyalty he owes to his employer."

Thus, even this proposed transformation of employee status from its traditional role of employment at will would only restrict the employer from "overreaching domination" which is "clearly not justified by the employer's legitimate concerns." It would not protect the Polaroid employee, or the Eastern Airlines pilot, or the employee of the giant automobile corporation making unauthorized disclosure to a "public interest clearing house."

Professor Blumrosen has similarly suggested that the employer's unrestricted right of discharge has been changed so drastically by a "complex network of contract and statutory provisions" and the "restraints on that freedom are now so extensive that the principle itself is in question, and the United States's legal system may be moving toward a general requirement of just cause and fair dealing between employer and employee." He can offer no authority, however, to support this conclusion insofar as it relates to employees not protected by collective agreements or by statute.

Where a collective agreement covers the employee, the requirement of "just cause" for discharge and other provisions has been construed in the rough and tumble of the labor arbitration process to afford significantly greater protection to the employee than indicated by the traditional statements in the older legal authorities. The living law has progressed beyond the law in the books. This, no doubt, underlies Professor Blumrosen's conclusion as to the movement of the law in this area. A new view of the corporation and of the role of the employee will also undoubtedly result in further modification of the concept of "just cause" under collective agreements.

In a changing society with changing values, long-prevailing views on social relationships will inevitably change as well. Thus, the suggestion that the employee of the major corporation has certain rights and duties as a citizen which transcend his traditional obligations as an employee may find increasing support, although the suggestion conflicts with long-accepted legal doctrines.

If the public school teacher can be protected against discharge for public criticism including allegedly false statements concerning the school board and the school superintendent, is it too much to suggest that a similar protection may develop in time for the employee of one of America's giant corporations who publicly challenges the conduct of his employer in a sphere of public interest? In the absence of constitutional protection for the corporate employee, unlike the governmental employee, the question is whether new law—whether created by statute, judicial decision, arbitration award, or collective agreement—will develop in the future to reach a similar result.

In any such analysis, the nature of the employee's conduct is fundamental.

Participation in public controversy involving the employer through the exercise of free speech presents the most appealing case for extension of employee rights. In the light of the balance of interests expressed in the *Pickering* case on the constitutional level, should the Polaroid employee be free, without fear of retaliation, to urge publicly that American corporations, including Polaroid, cease doing business in the Union of South Africa or Greece or the Soviet Union, if he so chooses? Should his duty of loyalty and obedience be so construed as to deprive him of his right to speak out on public issues? Although courts may not uphold such a position at the present time, will not changing social values likely produce such a conclusion in the law of the future? On the other hand, is there justification for the Polaroid employee joining in a concerted campaign to injure his employer through an organized boycott of its products? Does this involve free speech or economic warfare?

The Eastern Airlines case rests on the reasonableness of the employer's instructions in the light of the intense public concern with environmental abuse. Even today, one might inquire whether in arbitration under a labor agreement permitting discharge only for "just cause," an arbitrator would hold that such conduct, however disobedient, justified discharge, or whether some lesser penalty such as reinstatement without back pay might not be deemed appropriate.

In view of the absence of theoretical support for any right of unauthorized disclosure on the governmental level or of any relationship between such conduct and the employee's right to conduct himself like any other citizen, it is hard to visualize the development of a legal right of unauthorized disclosure for the corporate employee. Further, there is the additional hurdle of the decisions under the National Labor Relations Act that the use or disclosure of confidential information is just cause for discharge for the limited purposes of the statute, even when related to unionization activities.

As one moves from the theoretical level to the practical level, one may inquire whether the employer's right of discharge has not already been impaired at least in those cases where public sympathy is squarely behind the employee, as in the case of the Eastern Airlines pilot who placed his concern with air pollution above obedience to company regulations. The rules of law may condemn such activity as a clear breach of the duty of loyalty and obedience. The corporation may be tempted to exercise its right of discharge, but its freedom of action (without regard to obligations under any union contract) will be severely restricted by the climate of public opinion which may well have been significantly influenced by the publicity attending the affair.

In the arena of public opinion, the issue will involve the merits of the conduct of the employee, not whether the conduct was contrary to instructions. In the Eastern Airlines case, the intentional violation of regulations and the impracticability of allowing each of the 3,700 Eastern Airlines pilots to "make his own rules" were not the issues before the public. The subject of the public debate was the impact of the Eastern Airlines practice on air pollution. Unless the corporation can prevail in the battle for public opinion on the merits of the conduct in issue, it must yield to public clamor or face the consequences of unfavorable public reaction. Moreover, if the employer is unionized, it is unlikely that the union efforts on behalf of the employee will be limited to the legal question of whether the conduct constitutes "just cause" for discharge under the collective agreement.

At this stage, whatever the traditional legal doctrines, the corporation's right of discharge may be illusory. The major corporation must recognize that it has become a public institution and must respond to the public climate of opinion. Thus, whether or not the major corporation, in the law of the future, comes to be regarded as a quasi-governmental body for some purpose, it operates today as a political as well as economic institution, subject to political behavior by those affected by it and to public debate over those of its actions that attain public visibility.

The pervasive public concern with corporate social responsibility will unquestionably lead to employee response to an appeal for disclosures of confidential information tending to show corporate participation in the creation of social or environmental problems. It is only realistic, therefore, to anticipate the appearance of the government-type "leak" in the major corporation. Whether or not it violates traditional agency concepts, a "public interest clearing house" may be expected to transact considerable business. Aggrieved employers are hardly going to feel free to resort to theoretically available legal or equitable remedies for redress so long as the unauthorized disclosures relate to "antisocial" conduct and do not reflect economic motivation. The corporation that is guilty of environmental abuse reported to the "clearing house" will not be well advised to compound its conduct by instituting action against the "clearing house" or the employee (if it can identify him) and thereby assure even greater adverse publicity with respect to its objectionable environmental activities.

The "corporate leak" will join the "government leak" and serve the same political purposes. Whatever the incidental cost, business will survive, as has government, and indeed wrongful though it may be, the possibility of such a "leak" may serve a useful therapeutic or preventative function. Nevertheless, it may be well to review some of the inevitable aspects of the "public-interest disclosure" proposal. An official of the Federal Highway Safety Bureau commented in the *New York Times,* "Many a night I've spent late at the office trying to 'Nader-proof' a regulation. The pipelines this guy has into this agency are unbelievable."

Fortune similarly reports:

> Both reporters and professional politicians find him [Mr. Nader] extremely useful. "Nader has become the fifth branch of government if you count the press as fourth," says a Senate aide who has worked with Nader often in drafting legislation. "He knows all the newspaper deadlines and how to get in touch with anybody anytime. By his own hard work he has developed a network of sources in every arm of government. And believe me, no Senator turns down those calls from Ralph. He will say he's got some stuff and it's good, and the Senator can take the credit."

Once the duty of loyalty yields to the primacy of what the individual in question regards as the "public interest," the door is open to widespread abuse.

In a society accustomed to governmental "leaks"—deliberately instigated by an administration as trial balloons as well as by bureaucrats dissatisfied with administrative decision—extension of the conduct described above to the corporate area will be merely more of the same, part of a tolerated pattern in a political world, embracing the major corporation as well as government. At the same time, it sharply poses the question of the desirability of encouraging the spread of such patterns of violation of the concepts of loyalty and obedience from government to major business. The proposal for disclosure to private groups —however disinterested their objective or public-spirited their purpose —seems an excessive and dangerous response[3] to the problem of subordinating to social controls the tremendous economic and social power of the major public corporations.

The problem of unauthorized disclosure inevitably has political overtones. The significance of the erosion of the employee's traditional duties of loyalty, obedience, and confidentiality may be better appreciated if the problem is viewed in a setting that does not involve issues of social and environmental responsibility that are currently matters of such deep national concern. Such a setting may be found in the case of the university communities which are increasingly troubled by reports that the Federal Bureau of Investigation, the military, or the local police has been maintaining surveillance over campus activities. In some cases, university staff personnel, such as security officers and switchboard operators, apparently on an individual basis, have been supplying information about faculty, students, and campus activities. These university employees have made apparently unauthorized disclosure of non-public information in response to the appeals of government officials for information to enable them to discharge their concept of their public law-enforcement responsibilities. No doubt, these employees were responding to their personal views of their social responsibility to cooperate with the "authorities." This problem has created deep concern at many institutions. Thus, at Swarthmore College, President Robert D. Cross responded by warning faculty, students, and staff that "those who divulged confidential information not demanded by law or college policy risked dismissal."

In brief, unauthorized disclosure of confidential information presents serious problems for any organization; the matter can hardly be allowed to rest on each individual employee's decision as to the nature of his responsibilities to society and to his employer.

Other alternatives to reach the same objective without the same corrosive effect on personnel and the same potential for private abuse are available. These involve the use of governmental machinery with governmental safeguards with respect to the use of information received.

1. Traditional doctrines of agency law recognize the privilege of employees to report violations of law to proper governmental authorities. Private vigilante efforts should not be essential to achieve effective administration. "Public interest" groups would seem better advised to continue to concentrate their attention on improving the efficiency and effectiveness of the regulatory processes.

2. Another alternative is to extend further the growing statutory and administrative requirements of disclosure of conduct in areas of social responsibility. Examples include the Employer Information Report EEO-1 on minority employment practices filed with the Federal Equal Employment Opportunity Commission, the Affirmative Action Compliance Program filed with the Office of Federal Contract Compliance, the water pollution data filed under the Federal Water Pollution Con-

trol Act, and the reports on work-related deaths, injuries, and illnesses under the Federal Occupational Safety and Health Act. Enforcement of such matters by public agencies under public standards and with public personnel and safeguards would serve the basic object without the serious disadvantages involved in the "public-interest disclosure" proposal.

3. Still another alternative is the development of the so-called social audit or a systematic quantitative (and possibly qualitative) review of a corporation's activities in the area of social responsibility. This proposal, suggested almost twenty years ago, has been gathering increasing attention and strength with a number of institutions and corporations endeavoring to develop a satisfactory methodology. Such disclosure and evaluation seem an inevitable product of the forces making for greater corporate participation in the solution of social and environmental problems. Development will obviously take some time. In the meanwhile, "public interest" groups and others have proposed resolutions calling for wider disclosure in this area for consideration at the annual meetings of such corporations as General Motors Corporation, Honeywell, Inc., American Metal Climax, Inc., Kennecott Copper Corporation, Phelps Dodge Corporation, and Gulf Oil Corporation.

Another aspect of the proposal for a "public interest clearing house" has considerable merit. This is the objective to provide protection through exposure to public opinion for corporate employees discharged for refusal to participate in illegal, immoral, or unprofessional acts. Involving no breach of confidentiality, this is a laudable effort to translate into reality the theoretical legal rights of the employee recognized at common law and in the *Restatement of Agency* in the face of the grave economic inequality between the individual employee and the giant corporate employer. Such an effort should receive the support of all interested in raising the standards of industrial morality.

The related objective of assuring employee rights to participate in the public discussion of corporate conduct, including that of their employer, may also be achieved through extension of employee protection in collective bargaining agreements. As public concern over the social implications of corporate conduct continues to increase, and as more employees feel an individual sense of responsibility by reason of their identification with their employer and its activities, it is not unlikely that protection of employee freedom of speech and even of unauthorized disclosure to advance the "public interest" will increasingly become topics both at the collective bargaining table and in arbitration proceedings over the meaning of "just cause."

An example of the power of the trade union is provided by Mr. Nader:

> For example, the Fisher Body inspector who, five years ago, turned over information to me about defective welding of Chevrolet bodies, after the plant manager and all his other bosses told him to forget it, is still on the job. Why? Because he is a union member. Had he been an engineer, or a scientist, or a lawyer, or any nonunion person, G.M. could have showed him the door at 5 P.M. and he would have had no rights.

Statutory relief is another possible method to achieve appropriate protection for the rights of employees covering unionized and nonunionized employees alike. Anti-discrimination employment statutes already prohibit discrimination on the basis of "race, color, religion, sex, or national origin," age, or union membership. They might well be extended to make unlawful discrimination for political, social, or economic views,[4] even when publicly expressed in opposition to an employer's policy. Similarly, statutory prohibition of discharge for refusal to participate in acts that are illegal or contrary to established canons of professional ethics, or for cooperation with governmental law-enforcement, legislative, or executive agencies,[5] deserves serious consideration.

The duties of loyalty and obedience are essential in the conduct of any enterprise—public or private. Yet they do not serve as a basis to deprive government employees of their rights as citizens to participate in public debate and criticism of their governmental employer and should not be utilized to deprive corporate employees of similar rights.

As employee attitudes and actions reflect the increased public concern with social and environmental problems and the proper role of the corporation in participating in their solution, traditional doctrines of the employee's duties of loyalty and obedience and the employer's right of discharge will undergo increasing change. The pressure of "public interest" stockholder groups for increased corporate social responsibility will also be reflected by employees. At some point in the process, disagreement with management policies is inevitable. When the employees persist in their disagreement and the disagreement becomes public, an erosion of the traditional view of the duties of loyalty and obedience will have occurred. Yet this hardly seems a fundamental problem for the corporation or undesirable from the point of view of the larger society. The real question is to establish civilized parameters of permissible conduct that will not keep employees from expressing themselves on the public implications of their employers' activities in the social and environmental arena and at the same time will not introduce elements of breach of confidentiality and impairment of loyalty that will materially impair the functioning of the corporation itself. A balancing of interests, not a blind reiteration of traditional doctrines, is required. It is hoped that this preliminary review will suggest some possible solutions to the problem.

Notes

1. 346 U.S., 464, 74 S.Ct. 172, 98 L.Ed. 195 (1953).

2. The Act expressly provides: "No order of the Board shall require . . . reinstatement . . . if such individual was suspended or discharged for cause." 29 U.S.C. § 160(c) (1964).

3. The possible disclosure of what the employer may regard as trade secrets further aggravates the problem.

4. Mr. Nader has recommended: "Congress should enact legislation providing for safeguards against arbitrary treatment by corporations against employees who exercise their constitutional rights in a lawful manner." This statement assumes that employees have "constitutional rights," and thus misses the point. The problem is that at the present stage of the law, the constitutional safeguards protecting government employees against governmental action are inapplicable to corporate conduct, so that corporate employees do not have constitutionally protected rights as employees. This is the very factor that makes statutory protection essential. Further, the reference to "a lawful manner" constitutes an odd contrast to Mr. Nader's proposal for disclosure, which is of dubious validity under traditional legal doctrines.

5. In today's world, it would be difficult to defend the right of an employer to be free to discharge an employee for testifying under subpoena for the government in a criminal case against the employer. *Cf.* Odell v. Humble Oil & Refining Co., 201 F.2d 123 (10th Cir. 1953), *cert. denied,* 345 U.S. 941, 73 S.Ct. 833, 97 L.Ed. 1367 (1953). An anti-pollution bill being drafted by a subcommittee of the Senate Public Works Committee would prohibit the discharge of an employee who filed a complaint or who testified against his employer during investigation of an alleged violation. *Wall Street Journal,* July 19, 1971.

Speech in the Corporation

Ralph Nader, Peter Petkas, and Kate Blackwell

The corporation and organizations of employees that represent or purport to represent corporate employees—professional societies and labor unions—are in the best position to respond to the challenge of citizen-employees. Each organization should freely experiment with different approaches consistent with its own needs and the needs of its members. Since professional societies frequently compete among themselves and with labor unions for members, and since corporations frequently compete with each other for the best talent, it is to the interest of each to develop wise and beneficial approaches. Finally, professional societies, unions, and corporations, if we are to believe their leaders and apologists, should be sufficiently flexible to make the kinds of changes necessary to accommodate this new type of citizen-employee.

Professional societies should reformulate their codes of ethics to make them relevant to the employment relationship as well as to the client-professional relationship. The Code of Professional Responsibility of the American Bar Association, for example, does not directly deal with the lawyer who is employed on a full-time basis by a corporation. The explanatory notes to the code do suggest that when he gives business advice, the lawyer who is "house counsel" is subject to different obligations. But it does not explain how business advice differs from legal advice, nor does it suggest what the lawyer's obligations are when business and legal advice are inextricably mixed together. And the two

From *Whistle Blowing* by Ralph Nader, Peter Petkas, and Kate Blackwell. Copyright © 1972 by Ralph Nader. Reprinted by permission of Viking Penguin Inc.

are often indivisible. The distinction is critical to the internal logic of the code, since *all* lawyers, whether serving one employer-client or a number of clients, are required to "exercise independent judgment." One resolution to this dilemma would be to impose duties on *employers* as well as on employed lawyers. The American Association of University Professors (AAUP) does precisely that to preserve academic tenure for its members. Institutions that do not provide procedures to protect or do not in fact protect the academic independence of faculty members are subject to censure. AAUP can in turn significantly limit the ability of the institution to recruit the teachers it wants. Professional societies could establish similar mechanisms to censure employers that ignore the ethical obligations of society members.

Professional societies should establish independent appeal procedures for corporately employed members who have exhausted whatever procedures are available in the corporation. Similarly, they could offer to arbitrate disputes when the corporation is unable or unwilling to provide any internal mechanism for dealing fairly with dissent. If a firm refuses arbitration, the society should nevertheless proceed to make a determination and to make its decision public. Independent appeals procedures could complement the type of internal due process that enlightened corporate managers should establish. Unfortunately, too many of these societies are either so subservient to industry or so involved in defining their own identity that it is unlikely that these changes will occur in the absence of vigorous efforts by individual members.

Societies should also intervene on behalf of members involved in controversies over the application of their professional ethics. Charles Pettis reports that the American Society of Civil Engineers, through its executive director, has attempted to clear his name with potential employers. When a professional's dispute becomes a matter of public concern, the society should intervene, whether or not it is requested to do so, at least to the extent of offering its services as a reasonably disinterested but expert referee. And societies should actively seek employment for members fired for behaving ethically.

Few societies have become involved in legislative controversies unless broad "pocketbook" interests of members are at stake. Of the major engineering societies, only the National Society of Professional Engineers engages in any extensive lobbying effort. The other societies could, if they chose, organize separate lobbying arms and still preserve their own preferred tax status. They could promote legislation to protect members from employer retaliation for obedience to the law. A scientist who refuses to file a false report with a federal regulatory agency should not be forced to pay for his employer's attempted misconduct by involuntarily giving up his livelihood. Likewise, an engineer who reports an employer's illegal conduct to "appropriate authorities," as he must under the NSPE code of ethics when that conduct threatens public health or safety, ought to be protected from retaliatory firing, demotion, or transfer. The government agency authorized to prevent the illegal conduct can also be given the power to penalize a vindictive employer and to order compensation for the employee. But agencies will not be given additional authority unless groups that purport to represent the interests of engineers and other professionals demand that legislatures grant it.

Societies could contribute to other legislative efforts as well. For example, those with members employed by large corporations ought to be leading the fight to require that pensions "vest" early and that pension rights be transferable from one employer to another. The fear of losing a pension is one of the invisible chains that limit an employee's freedom to speak out or refuse to do work that might wantonly imperil others. The American Chemical Society (ACS) has been trying to organize a central pension fund for members much like the one that college teachers enjoy. They have met stiff opposition from large corporations that employ chemists and from the pension fund industry. Since employer participation (voluntary or not) is essential to the success of such a fund, the society could alternatively compel by statute the same result. At this writing the ACS has given no serious consideration to throwing down the gauntlet with such verve. If ACS continues to hesitate, older chemists, except those fortunate enough to be college teachers, will continue to be the indentured servants of their corporate masters, unable to dissent and unable to blow the whistle without fear of losing far more than current income.

Typical of the corporation's power to influence more than the salaries of its employees is its power to sever pension rights even after retirement. DuPont's pension plan, for example, allows the company to cancel a retired employee's rights to receive benefits if he has involved himself in "any activity harmful to the interest of the company." Such vague language cannot help but have a chilling effect on many forms of employee dissent and dissent by retired employees.

Finally, professional societies, especially those that have paid lip service to professional responsibility in the past, ought to investigate the extent of dissent and whistle blowing among their members. The American Society of Planning Officials (ASPO) recently published a study by staff member Earl Finkler entitled *Dissent and Independent Initiative in Planning Offices.* Finkler surveyed planning office directors as well as staff members to come up with the first comprehensive inquiry into dissent in his profession. He explored attitudes, put together five case studies based on real controversies, and developed tentative guidelines for dissent for both employers and employees. ASPO is to be commended for sponsoring such a study. But its executive director, Israel Stollman, apparently tried to dissociate the society from Finkler's effort. In an unprecedented "dissent" to the report, he wrote, "The normal path of internal review for each PAS [Planning Advisory Service] report that we issue produces staff agreement on its content. The report remains an individual statement of the author but falls within a broad range of ASPO policies and views. This report by Earl Finkler does not entirely fall within this broad range." Whether ASPO uses the Finkler study as the basis for further inquiry and action is highly problematical. If it does not, it will have missed an opportunity that few other societies have had for concrete action to protect dissenters.

Labor unions are sometimes cited as the ideal alternative to new legal protections for whistle blowers and to internal channels for free employee expression. In theory the union may, through the collective bargaining process, demand both substantive rights to protest work that threatens the public and procedural devices for a fair hearing when those rights are asserted. In practice, this potential has been neglected. First, according to union spokesmen, collective bargaining agreements today simply do not prohibit discharge and other forms of retaliation for protests directed against company policies and practices other than those traditionally associated with pay scales, work rules, retirement benefits, and job classification. Article 14, Section 1 of the United Auto Workers contract with Ford, for example, specifically reserves all "designing" and "engineering" questions to management.

Second, grievance procedures have not been considered appropriate forums for challenging the work product as well as working conditions. UAW officials, for example, agreed with Edward Gregory on the carbon monoxide leakage problem, but took action only on the issue of whether or not his transfer was authorized under the collective bargaining agreement. The *real* reason for his transfer, his persistent complaints about safety defects in the automobiles he was assigned to inspect, were considered by the union beyond its authority.

Third, unions traditionally have been mesmerized by bread-and-butter issues to the exclusion of others. Some of the professional unions affiliated with the AFL-CIO, however, have recently expressed an interest in pursuing noneconomic concerns of professional employees. They have a significant self-interested motivation, of course, since professionals have resisted collective bargaining as a threat to their status as professionals. If professional societies continue to avoid the issue of professional independence for their employed members, unions will have a growing appeal, especially to younger professional employees. Several professional unions have successfully organized new bargaining units by convincing potential members that collective bargaining is the only effective means to make ethical norms and professional autonomy integral elements of the employment relationship. Representatives of the American Federation of State, County and Municipal Employees told the authors that younger professionals in government service have been amazingly responsive to this approach.

Until the trade union movement rejects management's tendency to view employees—professional as well as nonprofessional—as obedient cogs and moral neuters rather than as responsible citizens, workers will be unable, for example, to object publicly to unsafe products, environmental hazards, and fraudulent sales practices without fear of retaliation. The experience of steelworker Gilbert Pugliese demonstrates that in the absence of strong pressures from the membership, unions, or at least their local leaders, are not likely to come to the immediate aid of a single embattled member. On June 5, 1969, Pugliese refused to pump any more oil into the Cuyahoga River from the Cleveland plant of the Jones and Laughlin Steel Corporation. The Cuyahoga River, one of the most polluted rivers in America, has been officially described by the city of Cleveland as a "fire hazard." Jones and Laughlin was under pressure from pollution abatement officials at the time and declined to make an issue of Pugliese's refusal. He did not receive a similar order until July 14, 1971. Pugliese, fifty-nine years old with eighteen-year seniority and six years away from pensioned retirement, adamantly refused. The only union official nearby, the assistant chief grievance official, tried to persuade him to follow orders and file a protest later. But Pugliese refused and was suspended for five days for breach of discipline with the strong likelihood that he would be fired at the end of that period.

Pugliese then called everyone he could think of to get action, but he got no response from the pollution agencies or from the local media. Finally, a former news reporter put in a few calls on his behalf. By the end of the next day he had become a *cause célèbre* in Cleveland and beyond. He was told by a fellow worker, "This puts the union on the spot and they've got to do something now after all the publicity." On the next day other workers were threatening a wildcat strike unless Pugliese received his job back. The union's chief grievance official immediately returned from Washington—he was attending the second week of industry-wide negotiations with the steel companies—and Pugliese's grievance began moving through regular channels. By the afternoon of the second day, Pugliese had been reinstated with pay. When he returned to work on Saturday, July 17, the company was installing drums and pumps to dispose of the oil. Ironically, this was precisely the method he had recommended when he first refused to pour the oil into the river in June 1969.

Free Speech and Arbitration: Implications for the Future

David C. Palmer

Fifteen years have passed since the United States Supreme Court handed down the decisions in the *Steelworkers* Trilogy,[1] substantially limiting the scope of judicial review in the private process of labor arbitration. For all intents and purposes, the courts have followed strictly the standards set out by the Trilogy to handle suits concerning the enforceability of arbitration awards.

It can thus be said that the role of the Court, the eternal overseer of public policy, in the arbitral process is well established. The antithesis is not at all true. The role that the arbitrator and the private forum that he or she oversees has in regard to public policy is a question that has been debated among the arbitration family for years. The discussion centers around the essential question of how often and to what extent arbitration should concern itself with issues outside of the contract, but admittedly of public concern.

On one side of the fence is the group advocating that the arbitrator be oblivious to everything except the terms and conditions of the collective agreement in question.[2] Another faction adheres to the view that if he or she is competent, the arbitrator should make every effort to deal with public policy questions when they are entangled with the arbitrable issue.[3] Numerous other opinions fall within these two extremes.

The Supreme Court has provided some guidelines for the arbitrator to follow in the areas of equal employment protection[4] and health and safety issues.[5] The NLRB has established deferral policies with the *Spielberg*[6] and *Collyer*[7] doctrines in cases involving the contract and the national labor laws. The guidance provided has not been totally effec-

Reprinted from *Labor Law Journal,* May, 1976. Published and copyrighted © 1976 by Commerce Clearing House, Inc., Chicago, Illinois 60646.

tive, as problems and conflicts remain in these and other areas.

One such conflict that has arisen of late is the question of the constitutional rights of the individual in an employment relationship. While this question has been well settled in the public sector, constitutional issues are fairly novel and far from settled in the private sector. A recent appellate court decision, *Holodnak* v. *Avco Corporation and UAW Local 1010,*[8] extended the protection of substantive constitutional rights to the private sector. In particular, it granted First Amendment rights to individuals in a private employment relationship. The implications of this case for arbitration, as a system of industrial jurisprudence, are far-reaching.

THE PARQUETRY

Mike Holodnak was an employee of the Avco-Lycoming Division of the Avco Corporation, a defense contractor mainly in the business of manufacturing gas turbine engines used in army helicopters. In 1969, he authored an article which appeared in a small, biweekly newsletter, castigating the company, the UAW as the bargaining representative, and the grievance process prescribed under the collective agreement.

The article accused the incumbent union leadership of "alienating and frustrating the membership to no end," and charged the management of Avco with "union busting" despite the fact that it was "stupid, incompetent, and irresponsible." Holodnak also deemed the grievance process of no consequence in rectifying these injustices since the arbitrators were biased and company-owned.[9] The article concluded by advocating a replacement by referendum of the present union hierarchy with a more responsive group and the use of wildcat strikes, if necessary, for the workers to obtain the rights due them as employees of Avco.

The company subsequently discharged Holodnak for violating plant rule 19, included in the agreement between Avco and the UAW, which authorized suspension or discharge for "making false, vicious, or malicious statements concerning any employee or which affect the employee's relationship to his job, his supervisors, or the company's products, property, reputation, or good will in the community."

Holodnak filed a grievance contesting the discharge which was ultimately taken to arbitration by the union. No claim was made at the hearing by the union attorney representing the grievant that a First Amendment questioned was involved, even though the arbitrator questioned the counsel concerning this issue. During the hearing, the arbitrator took part in questioning the grievant about his past political activities outside the plant and tried to impress upon him that the bargaining representative at Avco was a "very militant and zealous union that seeks the protection of the rights of the membership." The arbitrator sustained the discharge without a written decision.

Holodnak brought suit in the U.S. District Court in Connecticut against the union and the company. The court reversed the arbitrator's decision on grounds of "evident partiality" of the arbitrator and the failure by the union to fairly represent the grievant. Judge Lumbard refused to reinstate Holodnak because he had shown no desire to seek employment during the period his suit was pending. Back pay and punitive damages were awarded. Upon appeal, the Second Circuit modified the decision only to the extent of refusing to award punitive damages. It agreed with the lower court in regard to all other aspects of the decision. Consequently, the decision of the district court will be the base for the discussion throughout this article.

In its decision, the district court stated that one of the reasons the union violated its duty of fair representation was that it did not properly emphasize the free speech considerations existing in the case. The court also inferred that the grievance should have been dealt with on First Amendment grounds at the arbitration hearings. The implications of considering a constitutional question at the arbitration hearing is the subject of the next sections. We will first look at why, in this situation, the court granted Holodnak his rights under the Constitution, then look at how arbitrators have handled cases involving employee speech and loyalty. Lastly, a few provocative arguments for granting individuals their constitutional rights in a private employment relationship will be examined.

THE "STATE ACTION" PROBLEM

The issue of free expression is controlled in the public sector by the Supreme Court decision in *Pickering* v. *Board of Education.*[10] The Court held that a teacher may not be required to relinquish the First Amendment rights that would otherwise be his or hers as a citizen. "The teacher's interest," the Court stated, "as a citizen in making public comment must be balanced against the State's interest in promoting the efficiency of its employees' public services."[11]

In deciding upon the amount of protection granted the teacher as a public employee, the Court applied the same standards it laid down in *New York Times* v. *Sullivan*[12] in saying, "absent proof that those false statements were knowingly or recklessly made by him, a teacher's exercise of his right to speak on issues of public importance may not furnish the basis of his dismissal from public employment."[13]

Thus, in a suit involving unjust dismissal in the public sector on First Amendment grounds, the courts are required to canvass the facts of each case separately. Though the protection is not absolute,[14] stringent protection of an individual's free speech rights has nevertheless been granted. Such protection is totally absent in the private sector. Nearly three decades ago, the courts held that free speech protection under the First Amendment does not exist in a private employer-employee relationship.[15] In light of *Avco,* this supposed clear principle becomes a bit muddled.

In order for the Constitution to apply in the private sector, sufficient government involvement, or "state action," must be found. The task is not an easy one since no definitive standards have been set. As the Supreme Court noted, the business of finding "state action" is one of "sifting facts and weighing circumstances."[16] Noting that Avco was a major defense contractor and its buildings were on property owned by the federal government, the district court concluded that this was sufficient to find "state action" on the authority of *Burton* v. *Wilmington Parking Authority.* The Second Circuit agreed, finding a "symbiotic relationship"[17] between the government and the corporation sufficient to render the government as a "joint participant" in Avco's activities.[18]

Whether the standards used by the district and appellate courts were meritorious are of no consequence. The important point is that one of the main reasons that requisite government involvement was found was the existence of substantial contracts between the government and Avco. The implications of this can be readily seen in that, with ever-expanding government budgets over the past several decades at the federal, state, and local levels, the number and dollar value of government contracts secured by the private sector has risen to huge amounts.[19] This could conceivably lead to a finding of "state action" in increasing numbers of cases. The effect would be to grant greater numbers of employees protection against unjust dismissal that would go far beyond the collective agreement.

How will such an occurrence affect the arbitration process? To put it in the terms of the facts of *Avco,* if the union representative had challenged Holodnak's dismissal on First Amendment grounds, what would have been the proper role of the arbitrator? It would seem that the arbitrator would have had three choices in such a situation: deal with the claim himself; refuse to deal with the claim and write the decision with the proviso that it may be altered upon the finding in other forums of a First Amendment violation, thus opening the door for the courts to review an award on the merits; or postpone the hearing, pending decision by the courts on the constitutional question.

If the arbitrator had opted for adjudicating the question, procedural problems would have arisen over whether the ability to deal with such an issue is within the scope of the arbitrator's authority under the standard arbitration clause. In deciding whether substantial government involvement exists, the court examines financial records and questions company officials concerning the company's relations with the state. Could the arbitrator subpoena the information and witnesses necessary to conduct such an investigation? Beyond that, does he have the expertise needed to examine financial records and extract the relevant facts?

Problems would also present themselves if the arbitrator had followed a policy of deferral. If he had continued the hearing and noted in his award that it might be altered upon the finding that the Constitution applies in this case, an argument can be made that the individual could not have been given a fair hearing since the constitutional question had been ignored. Choosing the option of postponement and deferral to the courts would have hardly made the arbitration process, in this case, an expedited or final procedure.

It is probable that an arbitrator would defer to the courts rather than attempt to handle the First Amendment claim. However, sound legal arguments exist that would require the arbitrator to deal with such an issue. These will be discussed later in the article. The arbitration hearing will also be left for the moment. The discussion will now turn to the role of the courts in a deferral situation, by examining the issue of whether requisite state involvement must be proven in order that an individual may be guaranteed any free speech rights in an industrial setting.

The district court in *Avco,* discussing an individual's free speech rights in industry, used the oft-quoted Supreme Court statement, "Free discussion concerning the conditions in industry and the causes of labor disputes appears to us indispensable to the effective and intelligent use of the process of popular government to shape the destiny of modern industrial society."[20]

The question therefore presents itself as to whether there are other cloaks besides the Constitution which protect an individual's right to speak freely in a private employment relationship, namely, our national labor laws.

FREE SPEECH AND SECTION 7

Bypassing the state-involvement question, the district court noted that Holodnak's actions may have been protected by our national labor laws since an employee's right to speak out on matters concerning labor relations is protected by Section 7 of the National Labor Relations Act.[21] It cites the recent Supreme Court decision in *NLRB* v. *Magnavox Co.,*[22] as an example. Here the Court upheld the NLRB finding of an unfair labor practice where a company rule forbade the distribution of pro- or anti-union literature within the plant. Of greater importance to the individual, it was also held that the union, acting alone, could not waive the right to distribute such literature in the collective bargaining agreement.[23]

To what extent is an individual's speech, which in a situation involving the government would be protected by the First Amendment of the Constitution, protected by the NLRA? We are now speaking of a situation such as *Avco,* where the speech involved more than just the union, for this is admittedly protected by Title I of the Labor-Management Reporting and Disclosure Act.[24] But what about the individual who lambastes the collective bargaining situation or, even further, strikes out against the employer's product or public policies. Does such an action warrant Section 7 protection?

The extent to which an individual's speech is protected by the NLRA depends upon how broadly the "concerted activities" protected by Section 7 are defined. The courts have consistently held that protected activities are not limited to those where the employees are acting through a union.[25] As long as the activity is legal and involves a number of employees acting together for mutual aid or protection, it would probably be held as within the employee's Section 7 rights.

When the activity involves the actions of a group acting in conflict or without the approval of the majority involved, the courts employ a much more prohibitive stance in granting Section 7 protection. While the Seventh Circuit, in *NLRB* v. *Kearney and Trecker Corp.,*[26] noted that "concerted activities" are not limited to union activities, it added that the right to engage in such an activity is not unlimited. The court went on to say that when a minority group attempts to control the actions of a majority, the protection of such action is extremely limited and can be protected only after a careful scrutiny of the facts involved.

An individual is granted extreme latitude in regard to his or her activities if they have been supported by the union or a majority of employees in a bargaining unit. In *NLRB* v. *Peter Callier Kohler Swiss Chocolate Co., Inc.,* [27] the Second Circuit upheld an NLRB order reinstating a local union president discharged for making public statements against the company. The individual authored an article published in the town newspaper protesting the employer's participation, along with a cooperative dairy farmers' association, in an effort to raise the price of milk. The Board and the court held that the published article was a protected activity because it was a union resolution, voted on by the membership.

In discussing the form such activities may take, Judge Hand stated: "Such activities may be highly prejudiced to the employer; his customers may refuse to deal with him, he may incur the enmity of many in the community whose disfavor will bear hard upon him; but the statute forbids him by a discharge to rid himself of those who lay such burdens upon him."

LONE SPEAKER

In sharp contrast to the protection of speech under Section 7 granted to the individual representing the union viewpoint, the protection given to the employee speaking out alone is virtually nonexistent. The district court in *Avco* cites the Third Circuit decision, *NLRB* v. *Nu-Car Carriers,* [28] as justification that the NLRB might have held Holodnak's actions as protected under the NLRA. There the court ruled that attempts by a union member to bring about change in the union membership's attitude toward the collective bargaining relationship was a protected activity. But the activity in question involved oral discussions with fellow employees at the workplace.

It is hard to accept the inference by the court that the activity by the individual in *Nu-Car* was similar to Holodnak's public scourging of the company, the union, and the grievance process. The district court also ignored a more recent Tenth Circuit decision that goes against the Third Circuit by holding action similar to that of the individual in *Nu-Car* as not protected by Section 7.[29]

Perhaps the clearest statement concerning the extent that individual activities are protected under the NLRA can be found in the Third Circuit holding in *Mushroom Transportation Company* v. *NLRB.* [30] There the Court held that a conversation among employees is not protected as a concerted activity merely because it relates to employee interest. It must at least have the object of initiating, inducing, or preparing for group action in the interest of the employees.

From these cases and others looked at by the author the conclusion can be drawn that the protection of the individual's right to speak out under Section 7 of the NLRA is, at best, minimal. If the speech is with fellow employees and deals only with the collective bargaining relationship, it could arguably come under the protection of our national labor laws. But where the speech is public and contains material that is allegedly slanderous or deals with areas other than the collective bargaining relationship, as in Holodnak's case, it is doubtful whether such activity would be protected.

The reason for the lack of individual protection under the NLRA is that the purpose behind the passage of the act was to legalize majority rights in the industrial sector. Section 9(a) of the act,[31] giving exclusive representation to the certified union, establishes this regime of majority rule. Though the purpose is tempered to some degree by safeguards for the protection of individual interests, especially employment discrimination, Congress nevertheless sought to secure to all members of the designated bargaining unit their strength as a whole, fully aware that the rights of some individuals might be subordinated to the majority interest.[32]

It is appropriate now to return to the arbitration process and examine how the action of an individual speaking out to the public on aspects of the employment relationship or other matters concerning the company and/or the union have been handled in different cases. The issue to be examined throughout the next section is how the case was dealt with. Did the arbitrator look at the effect of an individual's speech or examine it only on its face? Also, were the individuals' past employment record or outside activities a factor?

REPORTED CASES

The issue of free speech in employment whittles down to the question put forth by arbitrator McCoy in a 1972 case, "Can you bite the hand that feeds you and insist on staying for future banquets?"[33] Arbitrators have usually answered the question with a flat no. The overriding reason seems to revolve around employee loyalty. Other considerations do come into play, for example, the audience to which the individual is speaking and the effect the speech has on the audience.

In *Four Wheel Drive Auto Co.*,[34] the arbitrator refused to uphold the company's decision to discharge an employee for slandering the wife of a member of the company's board of directors. The arbitrator did not deal with the issue of whether the remarks were themselves slanderous, only with the effect of the statements. The arbitrator stated that the company has the right to protect its reputation and, in line with this right, properly may discipline an employee damaging that reputation. But the effect of the remarks was not to damage the company's reputation because they were made to fellow employees, not the general public.

Thus, in examining the effect of an individual's speech, a distinction is drawn between an employee's rights within the employment structure and those in public. This distinction is further drawn out in *Carl Fischer Inc.*[35] There the arbitrator upheld the discharge of an employee for sending to the company president a letter in which he threatened to complain to the Better Business Bureau. The threat was based upon the employer's refusal to refund the purchase price for a malfunctioning TV set that he had previously purchased from his employer's shop.

The arbitrator found that the employee's threatened act was essentially incompatible with the employment relationship and was an act of disloyalty toward the employer. He recognized the fact that the employer could have done nothing if the threatened complaint had come from a customer with no employment ties. But because the employee was given a substantial discount as a result of his employment, his customer relationship was "inextricably connected" with his employment relationship. His rights as a customer were therefore limited to the extent that he did not have the right to make such a threat without suffering the consequences of a loss of a job.

A perplexing question concerning this case would come up if the employee had not been given a discount and paid the list price for the television set. Would the arbitrator still have been able to find a sufficient connection between the individual's status as an employee and status as a customer to warrant the restriction of his rights as a customer?

Some light can be shed on this question upon examining two later cases. In *Pepsi Cola Bottling Co., Inc. of Chattanooga,*[36] it was held that the employer improperly discharged an employee for alleged "disrespect towards the company." The case involved a laid-off driver-salesman who told five of his approximately two hundred customers that he had been laid off because of union activity. The arbitrator did find that the statements were erroneous and showed bad judgment. This, in the view of the arbitrator, was of no consequence. The discharge was improper because the remarks made were not disparaging or malicious toward the company, its officials, or its product, and the effect of the statements was minimal.

In another case, a discharge was upheld by the arbitrator for "indisputable disloyalty."[37] The discharged employee doubled as the local union business agent and editor of the local union paper. He was immediately dismissed after writing and publishing an article that appeared in the union paper stating that the employer was "insisting on bad parts" on production of military orders. The arbitrator found that the effect of the article was to disparage the employer's products and reputation. The case is novel in that it is the only one the author found where the arbitrator looked into the intent of the speech as well as the effect. It was decided that malicious intent existed, further justifying the discharge. Because of the effect and the intent, the arbitrator also rejected the claim that the action constituted privileged action by a union officer or the use of the labor relations technique of fighting fire with fire.

EFFECT ON REPUTATION

It seems that the dominant consideration guiding the arbitrator in deciding whether individual speech on issues connected with his or her employment justifies discharge is the effect the speech has on the employer's product and reputation. Effect depends on who the audience is. Thus it is logical that an employee has greater rights to speak to a group of fellow employees or a small audience. Though there are instances where such things as the employee's past employment record[38] or intent of the speech may be taken into account, they are of minor importance in this type of case.

As a final example, the *Forest City Publishing Co.*[39] decision should be mentioned because its facts most closely relate to those in *Avco.* Here the employee, a newspaper writer, wrote an article in a magazine of much larger circulation than the newsletter in which Holodnak's article appeared. The article criticized the employer for aiding in the national media's disguising of the My Lai massacre. The newspaper summarily suspended and then discharged the writer, saying that the article undermined the employee's working relationship with his employer. The union claimed that the writer's action was justified because of the public's right to know.

The arbitrator upheld the discharge. In his view, the article not only damaged the employer's reputation, but also, as the publisher had claimed, undermined the employment relationship. In his words, the writer could not be reinstated because, "Neither case law, nor arbitral precedent, would support such a decision, and the serious breach that is in evidence, between the grievant and his employer, would strongly suggest an impossible relationship."

The above quotation summarizes quite well the train of thought followed by the majority of arbitrators in weighing an employee's free speech. The loyalty that an employee owes to his or her employer, whether written into the contract or implied because of the existence of an employment relationship, seems to have been held as implicit in the cases examined.

If one sits back and ponders why arbitrators have, for the most part, refused to grant any free speech protection, a few answers come to mind. The major reason is not a lack of legal or arbitral precedent. Arbitrators are required to fashion awards with only the agreement as a guiding light. I believe it goes beyond lack of precedent. The major reasons revolve around the issue presented at the outset of this article, the extent to which arbitration has placed itself in the realm of public policy.

This initial answer is based on the assumption that the arbitrator, to use a cliché, stays within the four corners of the contract. Though the contract spells out the terms and conditions of employment for the employees, the parties to that contract are the employer and union, not the employees.[40] It would therefore be odd indeed for the employer to jeopardize his reputation by giving the employee a chance to speak, in an agreement to which he was a party. It would likewise be odd for the union, already hindered by the reporting requirements and member guarantees of the LMRDA, to hinder in any way its status as exclusive bargaining representative in an agreement in which it was a party by granting to the individual rights of free speech. On the contrary, it is much more logical and common for the contract to contain some form of loyalty pledge that applies to individual employees. If the arbitrator stays only within the bounds of this contract in deciding a grievance, he or she will be stopped from granting any type of free speech to the individual.

Other plausible answers as to why there has been this extreme restriction on individual rights of free speech are based on the assumption that the arbitrator does take public policy questions into consideration. The initial problem in this situation lies in the fact that the one area of public policy with which it has been accepted that arbitrators should deal, the national labor laws, provides no concrete rights protecting an individual's free speech.

To go further, even if the arbitrator feels that justification exists to grant the individual First Amendment protection, it was shown earlier that it would be inconceivable to apply the Constitution without a court mandate. Thus all the arbitrator could do would be to attach a proviso to the award that it may be altered upon a finding of "state action."

In the future, the awards of the arbitrator in this area could change. For the whole problem of a showing of requisite government involvement in order for the Constitution to apply could be cast aside in regard to the arbitration hearing. The reasons for this will be discussed next.

BEYOND "STATE ACTION"

As stated earlier, the *Avco* case muddled the supposedly clear principle of law that constitutional rights did not apply in a private employment relationship. But the apparent novelty of the district and appellate court decisions that sufficient government involvement existed to grant the employees at Avco constitutional protection may be of no consequence in a few years. For it is conceivable that the question of "state action" may be of no concern to the arbitrator. In its decision, the district court alludes to two related arguments that would give employees in the private sector constitutional rights and require the arbitrator to enforce those rights. Because the arbitrator's decision in *Avco* was overturned for partiality and the union's breach of its duty of fair representation, the court felt it unnecessary to consider the arguments.[41] Nevertheless, they will be discussed here because of the potential effects they have on the arbitration process.

Ever since the landmark 1957 decision in the *Textile Workers* v. *Lincoln Mills,*[42] arbitration has been held to be an arm of national labor policy. Judicial deference to arbitration was clearly established in the *Steelworkers* Trilogy[43] and has been emphasized numerous times since.[44] Thus, since an arbitrator is an instrument of national labor policy, he is not merely a "private person," but rather one acting on behalf of the government. Because he is acting on behalf of the government, it logically follows that the arbitrator should be required to deal with the First Amendment and other questions involving constitutional rights when they arise in the industrial sector, the sector he or she is overseeing as an arm of the government. Following this logic, substantial government involvement need not be proven. By the mere existence of a clause establishing arbitration at the pinnacle of industrial jurisprudence in a collective agreement, an individual is guaranteed the protection of the Constitution in the employment relationship.

This is the line of thought that the first argument follows. It is based upon the Second Circuit case of *Buckley* v. *American Federation of Radio Artists.* [45] In this case, the AFTRA contended that congressional authorization of the union shop under Section 8(a) (3) of the NLRA makes the existence of a union shop provision in a collective agreement between private parties "state action."

In support of this contention, the AFTRA relied on *Railway Employees Department* v. *Hanson.* [46] The Supreme Court in that case held that the union shop provisions contained in the Railway Labor Act transmutes otherwise private union shop agreements into "governmental action." While this principle seemed clear, one problem remains. While the RLA explicitly provides that union shops are permissible despite any state law that would otherwise prohibit them, Section 14 of the NLRA, on the other hand, declared that a state "right to work" law forbidding union shops will not be superseded by Section 8(a) (3).

The union in the *Buckley* case got around this issue by relying on the First Circuit decision in *Linscott* v. *Miller Falls Co.,* [47] which ascribed little significance to any differences between the RLA and the NLRA. The appellate court felt that *Hanson* did apply to the NLRA and therefore a union shop agreement under the auspices of that act constituted sufficient government interest. In the court's words: "If federal support attaches to the union shop, if and when the parties agree to it, it is the same support, once it attaches, even though the consent of a third party, the state, is a precondition."[48]

The court's rationale for its conclusion was the same as that used by the Supreme Court in *Hanson:* "The federal statute is the source of the power and authority by which any private rights are lost or sacrificed."[49]

The second argument follows closely along the lines of the first. Its major premise is that the labor laws express a public policy encouraging free association and communication among individuals in an employment relationship. Because of this, the courts are free to review or vacate an arbitration award that conflicts with this policy. The justification for this belief can be drawn from the Supreme Court holding in *Hurd* v. *Hodge.* [50] Here the Court held that it is no less true in suits brought under Section 301 of the NLRA to enforce arbitration than it is true in other lawsuits that the "power of the federal courts to enforce the terms of private agreements is at all times subject to the restrictions and limitations of the public policy of the United States."

The relevant public policy in a case involving an employee's right of expression would, for the most part, be our national labor laws. Since these laws encourage the right of free association, and since communication and arbitration have been viewed as an avenue for the enforcement of these laws, shouldn't arbitrators be required to encourage what the national labor policy encourages?

CONCLUSION

The implications of the *Avco* decision for arbitration lie not in the decisions of the district and appellate courts. Though the finding of the requisite government involvement needed to grant the protections of the Constitution to the employees at Avco may be novel, it will have little effect on arbitration as an institution. The fact that the award of the arbitrator was overturned because of the presence of partiality at the hearing may require arbitrators to take better heed of their actions at a hearing. But this is a procedural issue, reflecting a trend that is leading arbitration in the direction of a more formalized, court-like procedure.

In terms of substantive issues, it is improbable, in light of the present position of the courts, that the arbitrator would ever be required to deal with a First Amendment claim by first rendering a judgment on sufficient government involvement. The only reasonable action of the arbitrator if such a claim arises in the private sector would be deferral to the courts.

For arbitration today remains too deeply submerged in the sea of contract to be able to stick its head far enough above water to deal with the Constitution and its relation to private employment.

The real implications of *Avco* lie in its role as a predictor. It may have provided us with a preview, in the area of dismissals at least, of what arbitration could be in the future. The institution of arbitration need not bat an eyelash if the courts continue to require a showing of "state action" for the Constitution to apply in a private sector situation. For even if such involvement is found in increasing numbers of cases, the change will circumnavigate the process of arbitration, not affect it internally. But if either one, or both, of the arguments mentioned in the previous section are accepted by courts, and individuals are granted constitutional rights in employment because of the existence of arbitration, change would be certain. Procedurally, arbitration would evolve into a court.[51] It would also open yet another door for the courts to review an arbitration award on its merits.

The author now turns to speculation. Realistically, would the courts ever hold arbitration in the light it is presented in the previous section, and thus require the arbitrator to deal with an issue of constitutional violation? In *Alexander* v. *Gardner-Denver,* [52] the Supreme Court held that arbitration was an inappropriate forum for final resolution of the rights guaranteed under Title VII of the Civil Rights Act. Any award that deals with a Title VII question, the Court stated, would require "de novo determinations" by the courts, in order for the award to be enforced by the courts.

The rationale behind the Court's decision was that the characteristics of arbitration do not allow the arbitrator equitably to adjudicate as high a matter of public policy as employment discrimination. Would it not logically follow that the Court would take a similar view in a situation where an arbitrator dealt with a constitutional question? If Title VII issues were guaranteed de novo consideration because of their importance as a public policy, it would seem that the highest-ranking public policy of all, the Constitution, would be given at least an equal guarantee.

Therefore, it is unlikely indeed that the right of final consideration of constitutional questions in dismissal cases would be given to the arbitrator. As the Court stated in *Gardner-Denver,* "The resolution of statutory or constitutional issues is a primary responsibility of the courts."

The amputation of a limb never renders the individual helpless. Thus, the realization that arbitration will never have status to deal with constitutional issues greater than that which it has been granted in dealing with Title VII cases does not smother the sound argument that, because the arbitrator is acting on behalf of the government to enforce the national labor laws, the employees should be granted constitutional protection. The question arises of how employees in the private sector can be granted the free speech guarantees of the Constitution without having to deal with the Constitution itself.

One feasible solution to the problem may be in passing a statute guaranteeing to the individual free speech in an employment relationship similar to the protection Title I of the LMRDA gives the union member in speaking out on internal union affairs. The statute could be incorporated into our national labor laws, allowing the NLRB, the courts, and the arbitrator to enforce it. The standards for protection could follow along the same lines as the guarantees an employee has in the public sector, discussed earlier. [53]

Does the individual have the right to speak out against his or her employer? If so, in what areas? It all boils down to the argument brought out by the courts and arbitrator: employee loyalty. In any industrial setting there must be a balancing of management's right to direct an employee's behavior with the employee's right to retain control over his or her behavior.

It is granted by the author that an individual's rights are modified, to some degree, when he or she accepts voluntarily those responsibilities that accompany the entering into an employment relationship. The federal courts have stated that, even in situations involving the First Amendment, "minor infringements" are allowable to promote stability in an employment situation.[54] But, on the other hand, a contractual right to discharge for just cause does not equip the employer with an absolute right to direct the employee to do or not to do anything the employer feels will promote the goals of the enterprise. It is because a jungle of ambiguity exists in trying to balance, in the private sector, an employer's right to loyalty versus an employee's right to speak that statutory guidance is needed.

Notes

1. Steelworkers v. American Mfr. Co., 363 U.S. 564 (S. Ct. 1960) 40 LC ¶ 66,628; Steelworkers v. Warrior and Gulf Navigation Co., 363 U.S. 574 (S.Ct. 1960) 40 LC ¶ 66,629; and Steelworkers v. Enterprise Wheel and Car Corp., 363 U.S. 593 (S.Ct. 1960) 40 LC ¶ 66,630.

2. Notably, B. Meltzer, "Ruminations about Ideology, Law, and Labor Arbitration," in Dallas L. Jones, ed., *The Arbitrator, the NIRB, and the Courts,* Proceedings of the 20th Annual Meeting, National Academy of Arbitrators (Washington, D.C.: BNA, 1967), p. 1.

3. See Edwin R. Teple, "Deferral to Arbitration: Implications of NLRB Policy," *The Arbitration Journal,* (June 1974), pp. 65–97.

4. Alexander v. Gardner-Denver Co., 519 F.2d 503 (CA-10, 1975) 10 EPD ¶ 10,254.

5. Gateway Coal Co. v. United Mine Workers, 94 S.Ct. 629 (U.S. 1974) 72 LC ¶ 14,192.

6. Spielburg Mfr. Co., 112 NLRB 1080 (1955).

7. Collyer Insulated Wire, 192 NLRB 837, 1971 CCH NLRB ¶ 23,385.

8. 514 F.2d 285 (CA-2, 1975) 76 LC ¶ 10,676.

9. The article, "Why the UAW Local at Avco is Floundering: Building a Union Local," is reprinted in the appendix of the district court decision, ibid., pp. 2350–51.

10. 391 U.S. 563 (S. Ct. 1968).

11. Ibid., p. 578. For a more extensive and articulate discussion of constitu-

tional rights in the public sector see Benjamin Aaron, "Constitutional Protections against Unjust Dismissals from Employment: Some Reflections," keynote address, 2nd Annual Convention of the Society for Professionals of Industrial Dispute Resolution. Chicago, Nov. 13, 1974.

12. 376 U.S. 254 (S.Ct. 1964).

13. Pickering, cited at note 10.

14. As no free speech under the First Amendment is. See New York Times v. Sullivan, cited at note 12, Chaplinski v. New Hampshire, 315 U.S. 568 (1942), and Time, Inc. v. Hill, 385 U.S. 374 (1967).

15. NLRB v. Edward Budd Mfr. Co., 169 F.2d 571 (CA-6, 1948) 15 LC ¶ 64,703.

16. Burton v. Wilmington Parking Authority, 365 U.S. 715 (1961) at 722. Cited in Avco, at note 8, at 2345.

17. 88 LRRM 2951 (1974), at 2953.

18. The appellate court, in its affirmation, relied on both Burton, supra, at note 17, and Jackson v. Metropolitan Edison Co., 43 LW 4110 (1974), which stated that when the state becomes a joint venturer with the private party in the enterprise, the inference of state responsibility can be more easily drawn.

19. For example, in 1972 the Department of Defense alone spent $35 billion in new negotiated contracts involving "millions of different goods and services." This does not include longer-term contracts which were still in effect in that year. Source: Report of the U.S. General Accounting Office, "Ways for the Department of Defense to Reduce its Administrative Costs of Awarding Negotiated Contracts," (U.S. Government Publication No. 05414) May 1974.

20. Thornhill v. Alabama, 310 U.S. 88 at 103 (S.Ct. 1940) 2 LC ¶ 17,059, cited in Avco, cited at note 8, at 2348.

21. 29 U.S.C. Sect. 157, Section 7 provides that "employees shall have the right to self-organization, to form, join, or assist labor organizations, to bargain collectively through representatives of their own choosing, and to engage in other concerted activities for the purpose of collective bargaining or other mutual aid or protection, and shall also have the right to refrain from any or all of such activities except to the extent that such right may be affected by an agreement requiring membership in a labor organization as a condition of employment as authorized in Sect. 8(a) (3)."

22. 415 U.S. 322 (S.Ct. 1974) 73 LC ¶ 14,332. Cited in Avco, cited at note 8, at 2347.

23. The district court, while granting that Holodnak's dismissal could arguably have been an unfair labor practice, refused to state definitively whether Sect. 7 protected Holodnak since it was a matter within the NLRB's jurisdiction. See Avco, cited at note 8, footnote 9 and 10 at 2344.

24. Supra at note 21, Sect. 411.

25. For example, Southern Oxygen Co., Inc. v. NLRB, 213 F.2d 738 (CA-4,

1954) 26 LC ¶ 68,512; and NLRB v. Kearney and Trecker Corp., 237 F.2d 416 (CA-7, 1956) 31 LC ¶ 70,257.

26. Ibid. Also, see The Emporium Capwell Co. v. Western Addition Community Organization, 95 S.Ct. 977 (U.S. 1975) 76 LC ¶ 10,657, where it was held that the NLRA does not protect concerted activity by minority employees to bargain with their employer over issues of discrimination in employment, thus bypassing their exclusive bargaining representative.

27. 130 F.2d 503 (CA-2, 1942) 6 LC ¶ 61,187.

28. 189 F.2d 756 (CA-3, 1951) 20 LC ¶ 66,379; cited in footnote 9 of Avco.

29. NLRB v. Meinholdt Mfr., Inc. 451 F.2d 731 (CA-10, 1971) 66 LC ¶ 12,231. The court held as unprotected by the NLRA an individual discussing ways of raising wages and bettering conditions with other employees. Some of the ways advocated by the individual involved dealing with management directly.

30. 330 F.2d 683 (CA-3, 1964) 49 LC ¶ 18,921.

31. See note 21.

32. See Emporium, cited at note 26, for a further discussion of the purpose of our national labor laws and its conflict with the rights of the individual.

33. Forest City Publishing Company, 58 LA 773 (1972).

34. 20 LA 823 (1953).

35. 24 LA 674 (1955).

36. 38 LA 467 (1962).

37. General Electric Co., 40 LA 1127 (1963).

38. See Tkokol Chemical Co., 52 LA 1254 1969–2 CCH ARB ¶ 7805. Here an employee was held to be discharged for just cause because for many years he had harassed his employer with groundless complaints and made false and defamatory statements to outsiders against the employer which damaged the company's reputation. Besides the effect of the employee's action which led to his discharge, the arbitrator relied upon the fact that the employee was a malcontent with a long history of such activity. See also Thompson Bros. Boat Mfr. Co., 56 LA 973 (1971). Where the fact that the grievant was a known troublemaker was a factor in the arbitrator's decision to uphold a discharge.

39. Cited at note 33.

40. For the sake of argument, the author grants that, legally, the employees are parties to the contract since the union is the agent acting in their behalf. This argument is based upon the author's belief that the union is more than a separate entity, with separate concerns for continued existence and such, than an agent.

41. Avco, cited at note 8. See footnote 12 at 2347.

42. 353 U.S. 448 (CA-5, 1957) 32 LC ¶ 70,733.

43. Cited at note 1.

44. For example, see Boys Markets, Inc. v. Retail Clerks Union, Local 770,

398 U.S. 235 (1970) 62 LC ¶ 10,902, in which the right of a federal court to enjoin a strike in violation of a no-strike clause in a collective agreement where the issue was arbitrable was upheld. Most recently, Gateway Coal Co. v. United Mine Workers, cited at note 5, where the Court ruled that a broad arbitration clause covered disputes over safety conditions, and a strike over the issue of safety was enjoinable.

45. 496 F.2d 305 (CA-2, 1974) 73 LC ¶ 14,506, the case involved a different issue, whether a union shop provision in a collective agreement mandating the payment of dues as a condition of employment was an infringement on the First Amendment. The only aspect of the case relevant here is that the Court held the collective agreement as evidence of "state action."

46. 351 U.S. 225 (1956) 30 LC ¶ 69,961, cited in Buckley, ibid., pp. 309–10.

47. 440 F.2d 14 (CA-1, 1971) 65 LC ¶ 11,624.

48. Ibid., p. 16. This holding must be qualified with the obvious caveat that it is only a circuit court decision. The Tenth Circuit disagrees. In Reid v. McDonnell Douglas Corp., 443 F.2d 408 (CA-10, 1971) 65 LC ¶ 11,798, it held that Sect. 8(a) (3) does not render union shop agreements "government action."

49. Hanson, cited at note 46, p. 718. Cited in Linscott, ibid., p. 16.

50. 334 U.S. 24 (1948).

51. Not only would First Amendment rights be guaranteed to employees, but also other constitutional guarantees, especially due process. There is an obvious difference between due process rights established under a collective agreement, or even court principle, and the guarantee of due process under the Constitution.

52. 94 S.Ct. 1011 (U.S. 1974) 7 EPD ¶ 9148.

53. The idea is by no means novel. A similar conclusion has been reached by another author in a related area. See Benjamin Aaron, "The Impact of Public Employment Grievance Settlement on the Labor Arbitration Process," a paper presented to the American Arbitration Association Conference at Wingspread, Wisconsin. November 14–15, 1975.

54. See Hanson, cited at note 46, Gray v. Gulf, Mobile and Ohio R. R., 429 F.2d 1064 (CA-5, 1970) 63 LC ¶ 11,022, and Yolt v. North American Rockwell, 501 F.2d 398 (1974).

V.
Privacy in the Workplace

Privacy in the Workplace

Harriet Gorlin

The collection, maintenance, and protection of personal information by private-sector organizations is now under investigation by a federal study group and is the subject of proposed legislation in Congress. Employers, already operating under a threatening cloud of substantial penalties for the failure to protect employees' rights to safety and equal employment, may be required both to justify the legitimacy of their need for any information about the people in their employ and to guarantee its confidentiality.

Clearly, the issue of employee privacy is in the air—and in the press. Articles on privacy, like crocuses in spring, have been cropping up in every type of magazine, conveying a sense of urgency:

> The odds are 50-50 that your privacy will be invaded before the year is out.[1]
>
> The regulations are coming, and now is the time to . . . plan.[2]
>
> The personnel administrator should take active steps to influence the course of legislative activities.[3]

Literally hundreds of privacy bills were introduced in Congress and various state legislatures in the past two years, and legislative controls for the private sector appear to be imminent.

Yet, there are no militant citizen or employee groups clamoring for "file protection," nor is there a newsworthy clash of interests among obvious opponents. The rush of employees demanding access to their own personnel files in those states where the law provides such access has produced little more than a faint breeze. Employee records have not emerged as a burning issue in recent collective bargaining talks. Chief among the supporters for employee privacy rights and for a code on

Reprinted with permission from the *Information Bulletin No. 27,* September 1977. Copyright © 1977 by The Conference Board, Inc.

corporate information practices are the very companies whose computers have enhanced the efficiency of data collection as well as data abuse (IBM, for example). Moreover, the most frequent offenses against the privacy of individuals in society are said to be committed by government agencies; in this area, legislation already exists to regulate any indiscriminate demands and unauthorized disclosures of personal information about individuals.

What or who, then, is the driving force behind this burgeoning concern? Computers? Self-serving legislators? Watergate revelations? These and many other factors may have added some special momentum; historically, however, the trend toward the protection of personal information entrusted to employers has been a predictable development.

Certainly, the advent of the computer—with its ability to reduce the facts of a life into binary bits that are compacted into dossiers and displayed on terminal screens—has fueled a worship-distrust relationship with "big" business and "big" government that is characteristically American. The American people's finely honed sense of individuality is one of those concepts that, like Hamlet's custom, is more "honour'd in the breach than in the observance." David Linowes, chairman of the Federal Privacy Protection Study Commission, said: "The psychological dimension of privacy is as important as the actual dimension. Even if individuals do not use provisions which allow them to control the flow of information, they will feel more secure knowing that the controls exist."

WHAT IS EMPLOYEE PRIVACY?

What is at stake are the data of a confidential or personal nature generally found in, but not limited to, an organization's personnel files —résumés, application forms, benefits documents, letters of reference, wage garnishments, compensation levels, performance appraisals, medical evaluations, credit checks, and so forth. The potential for harm to the data subject in the unauthorized or abusive use of such information is considerable enough when the information is accurate and is of untold magnitude when it is in error. Senator Sam Ervin, in support of the Federal Privacy Act of 1974, was quoted in *Financial Executive* of June 1976, making the point in very plain language: "Once data is collected, it is out of the individual's control and can be bought, sold, stolen or altered without the individual's knowledge."

EMPLOYEE RIGHT-TO-KNOW

Knowledge is the linchpin in the protection of the employee's privacy. The employee's awareness of the particular data collected and of the very existence of such files is now termed the employee's "right to know." To satisfy the right to know, an employer must grant access to the data in some manner—computer printouts, copies of all documents held, or direct examination of the original files. And with the right to know as the fulcrum, the employee's control must also depend on some form of "file grievance"—the ability to dispute the data and to correct, erase, or amend it. Then, all that remains for the employee to be in full control of his or her "privacy" is the right to determine the use and dissemination of the information—other than the purpose for which it was originally collected. This original purpose, it is presumed, was explained to the employee, along with consequences for not providing the information, when it was originally requested.

The vanguard of employers—those with voluntary privacy policies —feel these measures contribute to good employee relations, but the existence of employee privacy policies in industry is by no means general. Significantly, where companies have adopted privacy codes, it was not in response to employee demand but was entirely management-initiated.

THE RIGHT TO PRIVACY IN COMMON LAW

The evolvement of the right to privacy in the United States took its lead from the Bill of Rights with the protection of life, property, and papers against deprivation and search without due process of law. The common-law judgments handed down through the years in civil suits for slander and libel extended the definition of personal property to include reputation and community standing. But the right to privacy in its present context may be said to have originated in 1890 with an article in the *Harvard Law Review* by two young lawyers, Warren and Brandeis.[4]

The "right to life" was extended by them to mean "the right to enjoy life" and to be let alone. Private property was defined "to comprise every form of possession—intangible as well as tangible," including "an inviolate personality." Warren and Brandeis pleaded for protection against the "blighting influence" of gossip. They championed the right of the individual to control dissemination of one's "thoughts, sentiments, and emotions," even when expressed to another on paper. In effect, this gave "privacy" a new and significant dimension in the face of rapidly developing communications systems.

Still, these ideas, however eloquent and irrefutable, did not carry the force of law. A precedent had yet to be established. The Supreme Court of Georgia, in a case regarding the unauthorized use of a photograph, gave the right to privacy its first legal toehold in 1905 by acknowledging the concept of privacy and awarding damages to the victim. The court held that while the actual negative belonged to the photographer, the subject should retain full control over the use of the image.

Since then, petitions to the courts to remedy invasions of privacy have been accorded a fairly standard interpretation of the law from state to state; but litigation for slander or libel is often far beyond the means of the aggrieved person and, in cases involving employee records, almost impossible to prove without employee access to those records and further aid from the law.

Warren and Brandeis felt that the right to privacy was already established by judicial legislation and common law and that "further protection would be merely another application of an existing rule." Nevertheless, additional laws have been passed, especially in the last decade, as the public perceived new aspects of its privacy and new threats to it.

PRIVACY IN LEGISLATION

Dr. Alan F. Westin, a professor of public law and government at Columbia University and a noted authority on privacy, reduced the concern for the privacy of information to three key elements: "what should be collected, with whom it should be shared, and what rights the individual should have to know and challenge the accuracy and use of the data."[5] With this as a guide, the trend in modern legislation bearing on privacy issues can be traced more easily.

From Articles IV and V of the Bill of Rights to the Privacy Act of 1974, legislators have left signposts pointing the way to H.R.1984, the current proposal in the House by Representatives Edward Koch and Barry Goldwater, Jr. (The number was deliberately chosen by the authors to recall George Orwell's prophetic novel of repression.)

• Early concern for the collection of certain personal information about employees and job applicants by employers was brought to public attention by the Equal Employment Opportunity Commission, the administering agency of Title VII of the Civil Rights Act of 1964, in their guidelines for personnel records.[6]

• Protection against the inadvertent disclosure by government agencies of personal and medical data is supposed to be assured by the exemptions to the Freedom of Information Act of 1966.

• The Fair Credit Reporting Act of 1971 begins to suggest the shape of things to come; it provides the first direct means by which employees in the private sector may have some control over information about themselves, especially in cases where employment is denied on the basis of a credit report containing inaccurate information.

• The Buckley Amendment to the General Education Provisions Act of 1974 provides complete control over the dissemination of information for students in regard to their school records, thereby limiting a prime source of reference for employers about their employees and job applicants.

However, there has been a history of problems and horror stories dogging each new law. The court calendars are clogged with cases of "information victims" seeking redress under these laws. But the problems of computer errors, incorrect data, and the trafficking in personal information persist—in fact, increase. Controls over information practices in government and industry would eventually be required.

The Privacy Act of 1974—the first comprehensive federal legislation based on the Department of Health, Education and Welfare's (HEW) principles of fair information practices—is an amendment to the Freedom of Information Act and covers information about individuals, including employees, in federal agency files only. H.R.1984 proposes to extend the controls delineated in the Privacy Act to information systems in the private sector and in state and local governments.

The HEW principles of fair information practices are to be expanded to ten guidelines. These add the considerations of a clearly established need as a basis for collecting data; the fair and honest means of such collection; direct access to, and information about the dissemination of, the records by the data subject; and a special restriction on government agencies to collect personal information only as expressly authorized by law. Furthermore, the use of the social security number as a universal identifier in information systems is to be prohibited, except where specifically required by federal law or in the administration of the social security program. A Federal Privacy Board, consisting of five members, is to be established to assure compliance, conduct public hearings, and publish an annual data base directory.

H.R.1984, cited as the "Comprehensive Right to Privacy Act," is likely to undergo many changes, but passage in some form is assured in the near future according to privacy "followers." Representative Koch's first privacy bill—H.R.667, which was also comprehensive in its scope, covering all sectors and all manner of data subjects—weathered five years of amending and rewriting to become the Privacy Act of 1974.

STATE REGULATION

Legislative activity on the state level is intense; about thirty-six states have passed or are considering some form of privacy bill. At present, California and Maine are the only two states that have enacted laws affecting private-sector personnel files. The Roberti Bill of California, passed in September 1975 and effective January 1976, directs *all* employers to provide employee access to files "which are used or have been used to determine that employee's qualifications for employment, promotion, additional compensation, or termination or other disciplinary action." It is widely interpreted by personnel officers in California to preclude information that would jeopardize another person's privacy, medical data, files pertaining to litigation, and management-generated human resource plans and notes. The law explicitly exempts records relating to criminal investigations and letters of reference.

The Maine statute, effective June 29, 1976, gives employees and former employees, upon written request, the right to review their personnel files which "shall include, but not be limited to, any formal or informal employee evaluations and reports relating to the employee's character, credit, work habits, compensation and benefits which the employer has in his possession." Exemptions of the kind currently claimed in California would be more difficult to justify in Maine. Although neither state explicitly provides for anything more than the opportunity to review the files, challenges to the data by the employee may be implicit in the exercise of the right.

Experience in either state is still too limited to evaluate. According to Robert Olesen, personnel director at Rockwell International, in his testimony at the Privacy Commission hearings last December, very few Californians have availed themselves of their newly gained right. At one Rockwell division only 13 out of 3,600 employees have requested to see their files in all of 1976—and only one man disputed the information in his file. But the company has not notified employees of their file-access right, and it may be that people in either state are unaware of the new laws.

HEARINGS AND STUDY GROUPS

It is unlikely that any action will be taken on H.R.1984 before the recommendations of the Federal Privacy Protection Study Commission will be released in the summer of 1977. This group, empowered by Congress under the Privacy Act of 1974, was ordered to conduct an eighteen-month inquiry to determine the feasibility of extending the requirements and principles of the Privacy Act to the private sector and to state and local governments.

Other study groups have recently issued reports contributing to the public awareness of the privacy issue and to the vast compilation of abuses. Significant among these is the state of Indiana's Governor's Commission on Individual Privacy, which released its report in 1976 after an eighteen-month study. The commission recommended seeking a balance between the individual's need for privacy and the informational needs of society. It supported the development and adoption of a voluntary code of fair information practices in the private sector. This reflects the philosophy held by many in industry that individual privacy is not an absolute right, and that legislation should be a last resort to be used only if voluntary programs fail.

The Domestic Council Committee on the Right of Privacy, appointed in February 1974 by President Nixon with Vice President Ford as its head, and later under the direction of Vice President Rockefeller, submitted its report to President Ford in the last month of his administration. The report identifies the major problems facing the control of information on a national scale and recommends that the policy-making machinery of a coordinated national information policy be entrusted to the Executive Office of the President, a view not too attractive since Watergate.

PRIVATE-SECTOR VIEWS

Corporate opinion on codes of information practices and expanding privacy legislation is understandably strong, especially where employee demand is absent. The prospect of legislative controls on internal management procedures and the imposition of costly conversion and compliance programs will naturally be challenged by industry. A Conference Board survey of opinion on the privacy issue among thirty-four selected senior executives with personnel responsibilities and an examination of some of the corporate testimony presented to the Federal Privacy Protection Study Commission indicate the active role industry is willing to assume in influencing the legislators. Also apparent is a sincere desire on the part of some companies to meet and maintain high standards of privacy protection for their employees.

In testimony before the Privacy Commission, IBM acknowledged its special responsibility as an information-handling business, not only in general matters of data security but also in the more sensitive areas of personal information management. Furthermore, Frank Cary, chairman of the board and chief executive of IBM, has publicly committed his company to a tireless effort toward a satisfactory solution of the problems. In an interview for the September-October *Harvard Business Review* last year, he said: "When I became chairman, it seemed to me that this subject was going to become an issue for us, as auto safety has become a major issue for Ford and General Motors. Privacy is not a passing fad." He emphasized the need for IBM to take leadership; to that end, IBM has financed and participated in studies of privacy by leading academic and legal authorities to the tune of $40 million since 1972. It has also developed and publicized a model "employee privacy" policy.

Reactions by the corporate community to H.R.1984 and the stepped-up state legislative activity generally fell into three patterns: (1) attempting to influence legislation by the voluntary submission of testimony to official hearings and through the pressure of private interest groups like the Business Roundtable; (2) the forming of a task force to study the feasibility of compliance with anticipated privacy controls; and (3) doing nothing until the dust settles on specific legislation.

Leading the corporate contingent to Washington to inform the Privacy Commission were the following: Equitable Life Assurance, General Electric, IBM, Inland Steel, J.C. Penney, Ford Motor, Manufacturers Hanover Trust, Exxon, DuPont, Rockwell International, Aetna, ALCOA, Atlantic Richfield, Nabisco, Cummins Engine, Honeywell, Caterpillar Tractor, Koppers, General Motors, Mobil Oil, and AT&T. Eleven of these companies also participated in The Conference Board's survey of executive opinion.

The preliminary findings of a Koch-Goldwater privacy questionnaire sent to the five hundred largest industrial firms indicate that industry is concerned with several aspects in particular: (1) high conversion costs; (2) deletion of social security numbers; (3) employee access to performance appraisals and other evaluative material; (4) the possibility of penalties for noncompliance levied on the employees handling records; (5) the requirement of employee permission before transferring records out of the country; and (6) the problem of multibranch operations in complying with varying state privacy laws. But these early indications also imply that the private sector is resigned to legislated restrictions on its information practices. The points of insistence made by the responding executives in The Conference Board inquiry suggest no such resignation and go well beyond those considerations.

There was general agreement with the five HEW principles. In fact, several of the companies have already adopted a code of employee information practices based on the HEW recommendations. GM's statement to the commission typifies this philosophy: "General Motors' implementation of these five information practices is based upon its belief that protecting the integrity of personal employee data is not only in the best interest of its employees but also is a matter of sound business."

The majority of the responding executives avowed a respect for the "employee's right to be free from unreasonable invasions of personal privacy," as a senior vice president of a large oil company put it. An appreciable number of them also felt that their companies' present posture was not insensitive to their employees' right to privacy. They generally concurred that there appeared to be no published evidence of wide-scale abuse of personnel data in the private sector. Many of them protested the territorial sweep of H.R.1984, both in their company testimony before the Privacy Commission and in response to The Conference Board survey. A vice president of human resources at an industrial chemicals firm voiced this concern in answer to a survey question:

> What I deplore is the tendency for the members of Congress to make sweeping accusations that damn industrial concerns along with everyone else. You cannot lump a corporate personnel-records-keeping system into the same category as a bank credit system, an insurance claim system, or the records-keeping system of a law enforcement agency. All companies are not blameless in this area, but I emphasize the absolute necessity of drawing distinctions between the broad types of systems and their purposes, and insist that each area be investigated before any "omnibus" legislation is created.

The Privacy Commission is thinking along these lines as well. David Linowes, chairman of the commission, also suggested in a recent interview that areas of heavy abuse in data collection and disclosure are found mainly in government agencies, credit agencies, insurance companies, and banks. Furthermore, he stated that he would not like to see the creation of more superstructures; he recommended that insurance companies, which are regulated on a state basis already, be further monitored for "privacy" by state insurance commissioners with the Federal Trade Commission providing final review, but he did not rule out new federal legislation.

Almost all the survey participants argued that the case has not been made for federal controls in the private sector. They urged that voluntary correction should be encouraged if sufficient evidence of abuse were to be found. Only if that failed should federal legislation, applying solely to the specific abuse, be considered as a last resort—or if states adopted incompatible laws. The inexplicable rush to the enactment of privacy bills on the state level may actually force the private sector to support preemptive federal legislation, ad hoc or otherwise, for the sake of uniform requirements in multistate operations.

EXEMPT DATA

Perhaps the hub of controversy regarding employee access is the definition of a personnel file. Every survey respondent claimed the need to exempt some types of data. Top priority went to sensitive material of a tentative or speculative nature involving human resource planning—succession lists, replacement charts, in fact, the whole range of salary and promotion recommendations. It was argued in one task-force report that access to future career potential assessments and plans would reduce the incentives of the "crown princes" and destroy the morale of everyone else. One suggestion for handling such material was to make it available to top management only and to destroy it as soon as a decision was made or an objective statement could be entered into the "accessible" file. There was general agreement in the survey group, however, that company confidential material should be honored as such.

Additionally, companies insisted on the right to privacy for supervisors' thumbnail records and notes on the performance of current staff members. These should not be open for review, but should not constitute a "secret" file. A vice president of human resources of a major publishing concern, a company with a fairly liberal right-to-know policy, supported the need for such closely held, temporary records and felt that their necessity in decision making outweighed the problems that might arise.

Executive opinion, as evidenced in this inquiry, was in agreement that the degree to which an organization can allow employee participation in planning for the future depends on the management style and the sophistication of staff relationships. A director of personnel development of a manufacturer of communications and building materials expressed his personal view that he could "easily visualize circumstances where letting employees know what future plans the company might have for them becomes the natural way of doing business. In the spirit of open adult-adult relations I would consider this to be a desirable goal to pursue. But we are a long way from that kind of sharing."

References from previous employers, whether written or oral, were high on the exempt list. Personnel officers felt that such an exchange must be protected to insure the frankness of the reference. One executive in management development and compensation, who preferred to respond to the survey over the telephone, believed that, in any case, "written references from former employers are not worth the paper they are written on." A manager of compensation research for a maker of photocopying equipment, in replying to the survey questions, described the situation concerning any third-party evaluations as a dilemma for personnel people: "There are times when an organization needs information of a personal nature which is uncontaminated by any bias introduced when the writer knows it may become 'public.' On the other hand, it would personally upset me to know that such information was inaccurate and the basis of decisions."

Along with management plans and letters of reference, medical data were also cited as "delicate" records. Except for two companies that are now considering opening up medical files for the inspection of employees, survey participants were equally divided between those who would offer qualified access only through the employee's physician and those who would not grant access at all. Such files, usually restricted to the company medical department, contain preemployment physical exams, records of illness, safety considerations, environmental exposure data, incident history, reports on clinic visits, and psychiatric evaluations. They are particularly vulnerable to abuse and have generated almost as much furor, to judge by the press, as the whole subject of employee privacy.

Even the narrow exchange afforded other company confidential material may be viewed as a gross violation of individual privacy when medical information is involved. While all the survey companies indicated that medical data were held closely by their medical personnel, a two-year study on health records and computers (by Dr. Alan F. Westin under the sponsorship of the National Bureau of Standards) concluded that personal data about individuals from hospitals' and doctors' medical files were disclosed to companies too often and then carelessly handled in personnel departments to the detriment of data subjects. The matter is very much under a cloud and is of special concern to the Privacy Commission.

DISCLOSURE PROCEDURE

The requirements regarding disclosure of file data to third parties were another area of contention for personnel people. They objected to the idea of a required disclosure log or "audit trail" for every incident of file access. The consensus among the survey executives is for the following:

1. Unrestricted internal routine file use, including overseas transfer of records, where necessary, by authorized personnel on a need-to-know-only basis

2. Disclosure to a third party without prior consent of the employee to consist only of work location, term of employment, and last position held

3. Employee notification of disclosure of subpoenaed records, or where required by law

4. All other requests only with prior employee consent

In fact, these practices were reported to be fairly common procedure in the companies surveyed, even where there was no formal privacy policy. Nevertheless, the commission hearings in December 1976 revealed some evidence of companies that routinely notify local credit bureaus of hires and terminations and make other disclosures without the awareness of their employees.

CONVERSION AND COMPLIANCE COSTS

Costs figured strongly in the thinking of these officers. There would probably be very little difference in philosophical posture between privacy proponents and resistant companies were it not for the high costs of converting present information systems to meet anticipated requirements and to maintain compliance. A number of executives said they would welcome the excuse to review personnel files and purge obsolete and irrelevant material. The opportunity to study data collection in their companies and establish need-to-know standards for personal information would be beneficial to them and could be combined with a review for Equal Employment Opportunity compliance as well. But costs must be considered.

Programming the system to handle new requirements is expected to account for one-third of the total conversion costs, depending on the degree of centralization of existing records. Of course, companies with fairly comprehensive privacy policies in force, or human-resource information systems that can be adapted to privacy needs, will suffer little immediate budgetary strain. However, the adequate training of operators and users and the required additional physical security—which account for two-thirds of the conversion costs—may not have been fully realized in the voluntary situation. Upkeep costs—those entailed in the maintenance of accurate and timely records, notification, and grievance procedures—would apply equally to all. Cummins Engine described such a situation before the Privacy Commission:

> Our costs have been in the development of the Human Resource Information System (HRIS). Our concern for privacy has influenced some of the decisions we have made, but not the costs of HRIS. Privacy costs would have been much higher if this was not done in the course of our work to overhaul our employee data processes generally.
>
> However, the overall process requires both knowledge and company and conceptual flexibility. We have to think "privacy" every step of the way. It also requires lots of time and attention and things cannot be changed overnight.

Cummins Engine, whose president, Henry Schacht, was appointed to the Privacy Commission of the state of Indiana in April 1975, has been actively concerned with employee privacy since 1974. The company has shared its studies and experiences with the corporate world through the Privacy Workshop at the 1976 Conference of Human Resource Systems Users and through its Privacy Case Study (to be used by the Harvard Business School in its MBA program).

To return to the matter of costs, unit estimates, which are more convenient for comparison, have been offered by a variety of sources. Robert C. Goldstein and Richard L. Nolan, in a *Harvard Business Review* article of March–April 1975, developed a cost calculation model of six systems, including a corporate personnel file. According to their model, such a system with 10,000 subjects and 50,000 transactions a year would cost $142,000 for privacy conversion and $40,000 a year for compliance. This boils down to $4.00 per subject per year and 80¢ per transaction. Another set of annual operating figures was estimated by the Association for Computer Machinery in 1975. These figures ran from 57¢ to $6.96 per data subject, and from 15¢ to $3.93 per transaction. A life insurance company in The Conference Board survey estimated that total conversion would cost between $10,000 and $14,000 per file, $2,000 of which would go to provide a printout with an easily understood format.

Some companies offered overall figures. General Electric testified before the Privacy Commission that it would cost them $35 million for the installation of a system to meet the anticipated privacy requirements and $15 million a year to operate. The results of a task force on privacy at another life insurance company estimated an initial conversion cost of $2.9 million and at least $4.7 million annually for compliance, based on the Goldstein-Nolan model. (Such high figures, however, may be relative to an insurance company system only and would include data subjects other than employees.)

UNIVERSAL IDENTIFIERS

Held to be the single most costly provision of proposed privacy legislation, the removal of social security numbers as universal identifiers in systems containing personal information prompted several of the survey companies to submit special statements to the Privacy Commission regarding their objection to this requirement. While most of the companies feel this demand to be an inconveniecne, by itself it would not create an impossible burden, after the initial deletion, were social security numbers still not required by many government agencies—such as Internal Revenue Service, Occupational Safety and Health Administration, and the Social Security Administration itself. Inland Steel, in its testimony before the Privacy Commission, claimed it would cost about $250,000 to remove social security numbers from all its internal record systems if, and only if, all the federal, state, and local reporting requirements also withdrew their social security number requirement. On the contrary, recent federal legislation has called for an increased use of this identifier in company records.

The argument that the use of the social security number alone hastens the snowballing of information about individuals from one system to another and increases the harm of unverified, misleading, and obsolete data was challenged by many companies. Caterpillar Tractor, in its observations to the Privacy Commission on the continued use of the social security number, suggested that legislation

> should be directed at the real source of possible harm. Records of data about individuals should not be combined *externally* between independent companies. We feel that therein lies the concern, and the real objective of privacy legislation should be to protect individuals from "created" dossiers containing possibly untrue and erroneous information. The proposed legislation should be directed toward prohibiting inappropriate record linkage or unwarranted data interchange *externally* between agencies or companies (either by social security number, or any other number as "a key").

SURVEY RESULTS

A brief line-up of the positions of the thirty-four survey participants reveals nine companies with operational privacy policies or privacy-related procedures in force; five companies in the process of developing a formal policy; fourteen preparing in some way to meet anticipated requirements; and six companies that will make no changes until legislative constraints are clear.

An analysis of the descriptions of employee-accessed systems yields a list of common elements that would probably satisfy anticipated privacy requirements:

1. Centrally controlled files
2. Access authorization of personnel on a need-to-know basis only
3. External disclosure through employee release only, except where required by law or subpoenaed
4. Employee access without need to state reason
5. File grievance procedure for correction, deletion, or appendage of employee statement
6. Qualified disclosure for medical records
7. Retention schedule to assure regular purging of unnecessary data
8. Formal procedures for safeguarding files, including positive identification of individuals requesting access or information
9. Employee identifier not a social security number

Notes

1. "Protecting Your Privacy." *Business Week*, April 4, 1977.

2. Harold C. Ruff, Jr. and Kenneth L. Gottschall, "Legislative Controls Over Data Files: Now is the Time to Plan," *Financial Executive*, June 1976.

3. Virginia E. Schein, "Privacy and Personnel: A Time for Action," *Personnel Journal*, December 1976.

4. Samuel D. Warren and Louis D. Brandeis, "The Right to Privacy," *Harvard Law Review*, December 15, 1890.

5. In *Senior Management and the Data Processing Function*, edited by Stanley J. PoKempner and Rochelle O'Connor, The Conference Board, Report No. 636, p. 114, 1974.

6. For a fuller treatment of the impact of Title VII on personnel data collection see *Nondiscrimination in Employment: Changing Perspectives, 1963–1972* by Ruth G. Shaeffer, The Conference Board, Report No. 589, 1973.

How Much Does the Boss Need to Know?

Trudy Hayden

Most job applicants must fill out lengthy questionnaires, submit to interviews, undergo tests to demonstrate their skills, and provide the names of earlier employers who can testify to their proficiency, honesty, and other professional and personal attributes. But employers often want to know much more, so they hire outside agencies to conduct investigations into the background and lifestyle of prospective employees (and, often, present employees being considered for promotions as well). These are called investigative consumer reports. Millions of them are conducted each year by consumer reporting agencies for both private and public employers. The activities of these agencies are supposedly regulated by the 1970 Fair Credit Reporting Act (FCRA), but as the law was virtually written by the very industry it purports to regulate, its teeth are not very sharp.

There is no limit to the kinds of information employers may seek about a job applicant through the services of a consumer reporting agency, or to the uses they may make of the information. About all that a subject of such an investigation can hope to do, within the provisions of the FCRA, is to learn that an investigation will be made, to discover the name of the investigating agency (but only *after* the job application has been refused), to be told the general nature of the information in his consumer reporting agency file, and to ask for a reinvestigation where data are inaccurate. The remedy usually comes, if it comes at all, too late to help the person who has already lost a job prospect.

The employer who uses investigative reports is obviously looking for more than a measure of an applicant's skills and an endorsement from an earlier employer. The search is usually focused on the applicant's

Reprinted from *The Civil Liberties Review* 3, no. 3. Copyright © 1976.

personal life, and the quarry is adverse information, however the employer wishes to define that term.

The term *credit records,* in its narrow sense, refers to recorded information describing a person's previous financial transactions which bear on his present credit-worthiness. In common parlance the term also covers information about financial and employment history, character, reputation, and style of living, which may be used in deciding whether to grant a loan, a charge account, or a credit card, to insure, or to hire. The collection and dissemination of such information is a gigantic business, handled primarily by private credit reporting and consumer investigative agencies. They are estimated to hold among them some two hundred million credit and investigative files on individuals (anyone who has ever applied for credit, employment, or insurance is likely to be the subject of such a file) and to gross about a billion dollars a year.

The Fair Credit Reporting Act covers two kinds of services rendered by these agencies: the credit report, which centers on the written records of a person's financial history (payment of bills, bankruptcies, suits, tax liens, etc.), and the investigative consumer report, which goes farther afield, seeking the opinions of friends, neighbors, and employers about lifestyle, personality, drinking habits, housekeeping standards, marital problems, medical condition, and sex life. Ordinarily, credit reports are most often sold to insurance companies and employers. Under the FCRA, both types are termed consumer reports, and both kinds of agencies are generally referred to as consumer reporting agencies.

The FCRA lays down certain standards for the compilation of consumer files and reports. Agencies are supposed to set up "reasonable procedures" to assure the accuracy of their information. They are supposed to keep their files current, and specifically must not report adverse information after a certain period of time.

What the act does not deal with is the matter of relevance. There is nothing defining what kind of information is relevant to an employment or insurance decision, and permissible for inclusion in an investigative report compiled for such a purpose, nor is there anything defining what is irrelevant, and impermissible. The FCRA places nothing off-limits. Even if a person's neighbors accurately report that her kitchen floor is unwashed, how relevant is this to a decision on automobile insurance? If they accurately state that the man with whom a woman lives is not her husband, how relevant is this to an employer's decision to hire? At present, one is almost helpless to prevent such information from being collected and used. The invasion of the most private areas is, in fact, the bread and butter of most consumer investigative reporting.

One of the most deplorable aspects of the consumer reporting industry is the fact that so few people know it even exists until it is too late. The FCRA offers little remedy for this. Unless someone is suddenly seized by a fit of paranoia and decides to write to every consumer reporting agency in the nation to find out whether there is a file on him, he will probably remain unaware that a file has been opened until *after* he has been refused a loan, a job, or an insurance policy. The FCRA does not require agencies to send notification when a file is opened.

The only notification a person now receives under the FCRA is a statement from the consumer report user (that is, a prospective employer, insurer, creditor) that an investigative report may be requested. The statement is supposed to be made in writing at the time of an application, and must explain that such investigation may involve interviews with friends, neighbors, and associates to determine reputation, style of living, etc. If the person being investigated requests it, a more complete and accurate description of the "nature and scope" of the investigation must be provided. But, at this stage, he has no way of knowing which consumer reporting agency will be conducting the investigation. Only if the employment, insurance, or credit is refused, or the charge for credit or insurance is increased, based wholly or in part on information contained in the report, must a person be told the name and address of the reporting agency. Under these circumstances, it is difficult if not impossible for a person to find out what reporting agencies have files on him.

Under the FCRA, a person has the right to be told the "nature and substance" of the information in his consumer reporting agency files. This means that he need not be allowed physical access to the files or be given copies of them, nor must they be read to him word for word. The agency must, however, give a clear and accurate explanation of the *substance* of all information in the files. Thus qualified, right of access may be exercised in person or by phone, upon "reasonable notice" to the agency and the presentation of proper identification.

There are two exceptions to the access requirement: Medical information obtained from physicians, hospitals, and other medical personnel and facilities need not be disclosed. Also, the sources of information in an investigative consumer report need not be disclosed, except in a lawsuit. Thus, a person will not find out who it was that accused him of cheating on his wife, or said that his son was a pot-smoking hippie. This exemption, combined with the absence of any standard of relevance, is responsible for the enshrinement of a good deal of idle, even malicious neighborhood gossip in the files of consumer reporting agencies.

If some item in a file appears to be inaccurate or incomplete (but not, under present law, irrelevant), the agency may be asked to reinvestigate. Within a "reasonable" period of time, the agency is supposed to make a "good faith effort," which, minimally, would entail rechecking the original source of the information. In addition to the vagueness of these requirements, there is a further loophole: The agency need not reinvestigate if it has grounds to believe the dispute "frivolous" or "irrelevant."

If the agency cannot verify the disputed information, it is supposed to correct the record. If no correction is made, a person has the right to file a brief statement—up to one hundred words—setting forth his side of the story. In subsequent disseminations of the disputed data, this statement, or a summary of the nature of the dispute, must be included. Another loophole: the agency need not include the statement if it considers the dispute "frivolous."

An individual has the further right to request that previous recipients of the disputed information be notified of the correction made or be given the explanatory statement. At minimum, the agency must inform any person receiving a report for employment purposes within the last two years, or for any other purpose within the last six months.

The FCRA regulates the activities of consumer reporting agencies, defined as organizations whose business is to collect information about individuals and make reports for use in decisions concerning the granting of credit, insurance, or employment. The key here is the position of the agency as a third party, the transmitter of data from source to user. If someone applies for a charge account at Macy's, and Macy's asks Gimbels for a report on the applicant's record of paying bills there, Gimbels' answer to Macy's is not a consumer report. No information drawn from a company's own experience in dealing with a customer is a consumer report. For that reason, a reference from a former employer given directly to a prospective employer is not a consumer report either. Nor is an investigation conducted by a creditor's, insurer's, or employer's own staff solely for its own use; the FCRA covers only reports compiled for the user by an outside agency.

However, consumer reports can be made by other than actual consumer reporting agencies. Collection agencies, private detectives, and cooperative loan exchanges may from time to time make consumer reports. The files they compile in the process are subject to the same rights of access and correction and the same standards of accuracy and completeness that pertain to consumer reporting agency files.

Finally, it is important to understand how the FCRA applies to government agencies, both as users and as suppliers of consumer reports. The U.S. Civil Service Commission and many other federal government agencies collect and disseminate information of the kind and for the purposes regulated by the FCRA; yet these agencies are not covered by the act, thus denying to federal employees and others even the modest rights available under the FCRA. This omission has been partly rectified by the Privacy Act of 1974, under which most federal agency files are now opened to the persons to whom they pertain. Actually, one's rights of access and correction are much stronger under the Privacy Act than under the FCRA, and the medical information and confidential sources exemptions are much narrower.

Government agencies are also frequent users of consumer reports, both for the usual employment, credit, and insurance purposes, and for compliance with statutes requiring investigation of a person's financial responsibility before granting a license or other benefit. It is up to the consumer reporting agency to determine if a governmental request for information is to fulfill one of these purposes. The government agency has the same obligation as any other user to inform a person that an investigation is to be made, and to reveal, in case of an adverse decision, the name and address of the reporting agency.

The biggest of all the FCRA loopholes is its enforcement. The statute makes it unreasonably difficult—some would say impossible—to vindicate even the most basic rights of access and review. The Federal Trade Commission, although it can write guidelines interpreting the act, does not adjudicate individual complaints. The burden on an aggrieved person seeking help from the courts is overwhelming. Only "willful" or "negligent" noncompliance on the part of the agency can lead to the award of civil damages, and these charges are very difficult to sustain if the agency can simply show that it followed "reasonable procedures" to fulfill its obligations under the act. Such reasonable procedures are not defined, so that in most cases the simple assertion of good faith effort by the agency has been enough to prevail.

The weakness of the judicial remedies is demonstrated by the absence of any damage awards from the effective date of the act in 1971 until 1974, in the case of *Millstone* v. *O'Hanlon Reports, Inc.* Here, for the first time, a court assessed punitive damages, as well as actual damages and costs, to the victim of a prejudicial investigative report compiled by what the court termed "slipshod and slovenly" methods. Millstone's automobile insurance was cancelled after a consumer report characterizing him as a hippie and a suspected drug user had been passed on to the insurance company. The accusation was made by one former (and soon afterward deceased) neighbor. No attempt had been made to verify the accusation at the time, and the agency repeatedly refused to give Millstone access to his file. An outraged court awarded Millstone $25,000 in punitive damages, $2,500 in actual damages, and $12,500 in costs and attorneys' fees. The judgment was upheld on appeal, against the credit reporting agency's claim that its practices were protected by the First Amendment.

Other victims of consumer reporting abuses have managed to obtain a less dramatic form of satisfaction. One such example is Galen Cranz, a New Jersey woman whose auto insurance was cancelled on the basis of a report that she lived with a man "without benefit of wedlock." After months of legal wrangling, Ms. Cranz entered into a stipulation with State Farm Insurance and Retail Credit Company by which State Farm disavowed any policy of denying insurance for such a reason, acknowledged that it had improperly cancelled her insurance, and "instructed" Retail Credit not to include in any subsequent investigative reports prepared for State Farm any characterizations or "moral judgments" concerning the relationship between Ms. Cranz and other persons in the same household. State Farm, however, asserted its "legitimate underwriting interest" in learning the identity and legal relationship of any other person in the household who might be driving the insured automobile. Meanwhile, Retail Credit agreed to delete the item from Ms. Cranz's file and not to include any such item in any future reports concerning her.

The disadvantage of settlement by stipulation is that it is essentially a private arrangement. While Ms. Cranz's victory over Retail Credit and State Farm might be helpful to others victimized by these same companies because of a similar item of information, the agreement is not transferable to the operations of other companies and, of course, does not have the value of precedent like a judicial decision. In another sense, however, the Cranz settlement is significant as an indication that at least one court is prepared to deal with the question of relevance, and to say that certain things are not relevant or proper. It is quite possible that other courts may follow suit.

The decision of the Superior Court of Washington, D.C., in a suit challenging the denial of an oil company credit card based on a credit report that confused the records of two men bearing the same name (Miller v. Credit Bureau, Inc.) deserves mention because it offers some comment on the methods that constitute "reasonable procedures" to assure accuracy in the preparation of consumer reports by credit bureaus. Minimally, those include verification of the identity of a person about whom derogatory information is received (such as cross-checking the person's address), inclusion of any information mitigating the adverse item, and inclusion of any information from the bureau's files indicating that the report subject is, in fact, a responsible person.

Although the legal effect of the *Miller* decision does not reach beyond the District of Columbia, the guidelines are a useful interpretation of the extremely vague standards laid down in the FCRA. The *Miller* standards may be modest indeed, but they provide more than one can find in the act. Until Congress puts real clout into the law, giving the victims of consumer reporting abuses some feasible means of seeking redress (preferably by administrative as well as judicial procedures), the FCRA will continue to favor the interests of the industry over the interests of individuals and their right to privacy.

Dilemmas Facing Occupational Health Surveillance

Alan F. Westin

The complex of institutions and rules under which both workplace medicine and basic research into worker-consumer health is conducted is caught up today in a group of troublesome problems. This centers on the way in which individual surveillance of worker health is to be conducted as well as whether large-scale data systems building on such individual records can be developed and effectively utilized. Without oversimplifying, and though many other issues are intertwined with it, the basic problem turns on how to collect personal health data without violating individual rights of privacy, confidentiality, and due process.

1. At the individual facility level—the plant, office, or processing site —existing legal doctrines as to the civil liability of the employer produce heavy *disincentives* for the employer to collect individual case histories and map early trends. Such activities, under many current legal measures of notice of risk, could constitute documentation for lawsuits against employers who were seeking to identify risks and harms at the earliest possible moment and act, prudently, upon these problems.

2. Practitioners of occupational medicine have not always been clear themselves whether they should conduct the more frequent, intensive, and heavily documented examinations and case-taking of individual workers, their spouses, and children, or whether this should be done by care-providers outside the workplace, such as family physicians, private clinics, or local-government facilities.

3. Practitioners—and organizational managements—have been concerned about the view that workers—and the labor unions representing them in unionized establishments—would take of such medical surveillance and record keeping. Not only is this different from much of the

customary practice ("Joe, I think you have a problem; why don't you see your own doctor."), but it also raises issues of whether the individual workers, the labor union, the Occupational Health and Safety Administration and other government health agencies, and other possible groups are to have access to individual case histories. Existing law at the state and federal levels is not adequate in providing guidelines for such collection, storage, sharing, and withholding of such patient data.

4. Leading practitioners of epidemiology and managers of the national health statistics system are deeply worried about the effects of recent legislation such as the Federal Privacy Act of 1974 and the expansion of the approach of that act into the private sector upon the ability of researchers and data-system managers to do the record linking and the longitudinal studies that they believe to be absolutely essential. They also are concerned that individual programs of medical surveillance, in industry and government, will not have the uniformity and scope that our national health surveillance program requires, a problem that would also require guidelines that meet safeguard requirements.

5. The role of insurance carriers who cover workers in the overall research and trend analysis is also unclear at present. Should the vast, automated records of the insurance industry be brought into the occupational health surveillance data system, and if so, again how will questions of individual confidentiality and access be handled?

6. The role of OSHA, the National Center for Health Statistics, the Social Security Agency's disability program, state workmen's compensation boards, and similar government agencies has to be clarified in a comprehensive approach. Yet the participation of government agencies, given the general public climate of concern over government's handling of confidential data in the post-Watergate era and the concerns of medical practitioners and associations on this score, point up the need for clarifying the rules and practices to be followed, not simply assuming all will be handled satisfactorily. The likelihood of our moving into national health insurance, by whatever series of steps and with whatever final model of this system, will also require the coordination of occupational health surveillance and treatment with the record-keeping system of such a national health insurance plan.

We have been warned by many students of our comprehensive health care system that a greatly expanded national system of *occupational health surveillance* of individual workers, their families, and affected segments of the general population should be a national priority. The need for regional and national data banks of statistical information, based on linked, longitudinally based records, has also been strongly articulated. Yet the roles of occupational physician and staff, employer, statistical agencies, and government supervisory authorities in this future system are far from clear. The legal rules of civil liability are uncertain. Legal protection of confidentiality and patient access is not in place. The experience of the Federal Privacy Act on the occupational health activities of civilian and military agencies has not yet been assessed.

Health and Privacy

Anthony Mazzocchi

Let's for the moment examine the role of management in relation to a third-party payor insurance carrier. Most employees are covered by some form of insurance provided by third-party payors. Essentially the employer pays a premium on a result of collective bargaining or otherwise, to an insurance company which provides medical-surgical coverage and a major medical coverage.

In many instances, especially among large corporations, the plans are experience-rated. In a number of these situations the claims form filled out by the doctor and the hospital, if there is in-hospital care, goes directly to the employer for his approval before authorization is given to the insurance company to pay the claim.

This means that the company, usually the personnel department, is aware of every medical problem of both the employees and their family members. This information, many times, is used to discriminate against the employee in that job promotion may be denied or the job downgraded or, as happens, the employee discharged because of a medical problem. The company only becomes aware of these problems as a result of their access to the most intimate medical data dealing with a non-occupation-caused illness. The employer has the power to transmit this information along to anyone else.

Company medical departments acquire a great deal of data on employees that are accessible to the personnel departments and that can be and are used prejudicially against employees. Not only is this information available to whomever the company wants, it is denied to the employee. In fact, companies can extract blood, urine, or whatever else they choose from an employee and then refuse to tell the employee the nature of the test or its results. If the employee requests that the results be sent to his or her doctor, the company, in most

Excerpted from statement before the Privacy Protection Study Commission, December 17, 1976.

instances, will not do so, claiming management prerogatives. . . .

Not only are data accumulated on employees, the employees are denied access to data that would allow them to make decisions that can protect their very lives in the workplace. . . .

The gathering and transmission of vital health data by companies and their denial to the employees, at risk, is the ultimate in invasion of privacy, because the consequences can be death.

The collection of epidemiological data on employees and their submission to trade associations for studies without ever telling the affected employee is another common practice in industry. Only when the victim becomes highly visible as a result of an epidemic does the affected work population first become aware that he or she is being studied (the vinyl-chloride cancer epidemic is a classic case in point).

Clear rules must be established on health data. These are implicit rights in collective bargaining agreements that we are now beginning to exercise. However, 75 percent of the working population is without union protection and there has to be uniformity of rights.

Privacy in the Workplace Is an Important Benefit

Robert Ellis Smith

Social scientists and psychologists will tell you that privacy is a basic yearning in all people. As Justice Louis Brandeis said, it is "the most comprehensive of rights and the right most valued by civilized men."

In earlier days, privacy in the workplace could be taken for granted. Most rural work is done alone, so is household work, and even much factory work afforded more solitude than a person wanted. But as twentieth-century work has moved to crowded assembly lines, office complexes, and large retail establishments, privacy for the working person has nearly disappeared. Because of this, there seems to be a revival of interest in privacy as a working condition when it's time to renegotiate labor agreements. Many unions, for instance, now insist that an individual member have access to records about him held by the employer, to satisfy himself or herself that the files are accurate and fair. And the Retail Clerks Union includes in its contracts prohibitions against use of lie detectors as a condition of employment, in large part because the practice invariably invades the privacy of individual workers.

There are far more privacy issues emerging in the workplace, as workers in crowded environments realize that their efficiency, their concentration and peace of mind, and—most of all—their dignity require a measure of privacy. Here are some of those issues:

Disclosure of personal information. Many companies are discovering that not all workers welcome a public announcement of a promotion or other work change, nor does everybody like to have news of his or her latest illness posted on the bulletin board without permission. In

Reprinted from *Retail Clerks Advocate*, April–May 1977. Copyright © 1977 by *Retail Clerks Advocate*.

one sense, the essence of privacy is control over information about ourselves. In this regard, an individual has the right to consent before the company discloses personal information, regardless of how innocent that information appears. This should include the release of salary information to the placement officer at one's former high school or college, or the release of employee information to a government investigator. A particular bone of contention is the use of lists showing salary level and prior contributions, in order to beef up employee giving to charity campaigns like the United Fund. Ohio Bell Telephone Company suspected that some employees were making inflated pledges to keep supervisors and fellow workers off their backs, and then submitting reduced or cancelled pledges. The company circulated a computer printout of these pledge changes to supervisors and union leaders for "review." This type of coercion in federal employment was one of former Senator Sam J. Ervin's pet peeves and he always sought legislation to stop it. Ironically, or perhaps not so ironically, when a Cleveland news reporter asked the business executive who headed that city's United Torch Services to reveal his personal gift to the drive, he refused, saying it was a "private matter."

Surveillance. Retail clerks work in an environment that is normally surveyed by closed-circuit television cameras. Labor arbitrators have ruled that the TV cameras may be used for store security, but not for catching employees goofing off on the job. The American Civil Liberties Union in Cleveland objected a couple of years ago when it discovered that a factory owner concealed a microphone in the ladies' washroom and connected it to a speaker in the front office. The company further adopted a shop rule that employees had to notify the plant foreman before using the restroom. Workers suspected that the owner wanted to monitor workers' gossip about upcoming labor negotiations.

Most department stores use two-way mirrors or peepholes in customers' dressing rooms. The intention, clearly, is to reduce shoplifting, but workers should insist on guidelines restricting the use of such devices to spy on store employees themselves.

The law may help workers subject to such snooping, but it apparently does not protect workers who are subject to wiretapping by their bosses. The telephones, after all, belong to the company, and, under the law, if one party to the conversation consents to the wiretap it is not illegal. Federal law also permits electronic eavesdropping by the "operator of a switchboard . . . for mechanical or service quality control checks." That implies that the wiretapping must be for the purpose of *equipment* quality control, but a federal court in San Francisco has ruled that Macy's department store there did not violate the law when it tapped its own phones in order to catch employees who were pilfering merchandise. Preventing pilferage, the court decided, was "quality control."

Peace and Quiet. At the drop of a hat, experts will tell you that Muzak and other forms of programmed music give a lift to workers and customers alike, give you something to look forward to, break the monotony, eliminate excessive talking, increase productivity and, most important, inspire more purchasing. But how about the minority of persons who find such noise irritating and distracting? For workers in an environment where piped music or announcements are necessary to promote sales, shouldn't the employer provide a place where staff may enjoy a respite from the noise pollution during break-time?

And aren't hourly workers entitled to restrooms, changing rooms, and lounges that afford the maximum amount of physical privacy during breaks? American business provides a higher measure of physical privacy during non-work time to its high-level executives, who have less need of it because, like the rural workers of an earlier day, they already have a large measure of solitude during their work time. Yet business provides very scant physical privacy during work breaks to hourly workers, whose duty hours are spent often in a crowded, noisy, and unprivate environment. And, of course, it's the hourly workers who would also be less likely to enjoy much privacy in their commuting to and from work or in their own homes.

After Hours. Some companies make sure that telephone calls are made to employees' homes during off-duty hours only if the calls are essential. Some workers get overtime pay for receiving calls at home that involve work-related problems, and that seems to limit the calls to essential business, but other firms are not even sensitive to this further invasion of privacy. Further, some companies worry excessively about employees' behavior, political beliefs, and modes of dress when off duty. The main victims of this off-hours harassment lately have been employees of energy utilities who campaign for effective controls of nuclear energy development. There are other victims: Employees are often punished for unorthodox religious practices, for the misdeeds of a relative, for being "controversial," and for union activities. For an individual, each of these matters, in the classic privacy sense, is "none of your business."

One of the toughest decisions for a supervisor or union official to make is determining when private behavior—like alcohol or drug abuse, time-consuming individual projects, or physical or mental illness —affect job performance or attendance and therefore become the employer's concern.

It is not surprising that in a time of economic slowdown American workers have concentrated on bread-and-butter issues instead of working conditions, like privacy. But the time is not far off when privacy in the workplace will be a major concern among workers renegotiating contracts. A person can never truly possess the right to privacy if that right disappears during working hours.

Medical Confidentiality in the Work Environment

G. H. Collings, Jr., M.D.

Existing and pending legislation and regulation reflect the current widespread concern that people have about the privacy issue generally and about numerous sometimes knotty specific problems within this general area. Your attendance here today is evidence of your organization's interest in the changing attitudes on this subject and their possible effect on the business community.

My topic today deals with one aspect of this interest, namely, questions of medical confidentiality in the business world. The ethic of confidentiality has of course long been accepted and practiced by successful medical professionals. However, confidentiality still means different things to different people, and whereas almost all physicians would subscribe to the general principle of privacy in medical matters, closer inquiry would reveal wide individual interpretation of what is included as confidential, and even wider individual variation with respect to the day-to-day practice and maintenance of that confidentiality. Whether so expressed or not, many physicians feel that they should be the judge of what is to be handled as confidential and that they alone should make appropriate decisions regarding the protection of "the patient's best interest" on a day-to-day basis, considering each case and each situation on its merits.

This approach has generally served its purpose without producing any significant number of problems as long as the physician-patient relationship rarely involved third parties and as long as patients acquiesced to a dominant role by the physician on their behalf. However, with the disappearance of the passive patient and with the development of complex social structures presenting multiple third parties who have legitimate needs for at least certain parts of that previously privileged body of patient information, there has also come the necessity for a revised approach to dealing with the confidentiality question.

Nowhere is this brought into sharper focus more than in the field of occupational medicine, where there is continuous commingling of third-party interests with those of the patient. In fact, the fundamental reason for the existence of occupational medicine is to bring together competency in medicine with a thorough understanding of work conditions and requirements in order that better decisions relating to that relationship can be made. To say that the occupational physician should deal with his patient in complete secrecy begs the question, for if the occupational physician is prohibited from responding to the needs of the work situation then that function will simply have to be transferred to some other person. Such a transfer to a non-medical person will not work because he would have no medical competence, and to transfer to another independent physician would require that he be provided with the necessary patient medical information; this would raise the whole confidentiality question all over again and would solve nothing.

Realizing their essential role in the relationship between employee-patient and employer, progressive corporate medical departments have long since worked out successful ways of meeting the simultaneous requirements to provide a comfortable situation in regard to confidentiality for the patient while supplying the necessary counsel for proper business decisions. Experience from these operating programs over many years has established basic principles, which, if observed, will permit a successful outcome to be achieved.

Before discussing these principles, I would like to make an observation with respect to motivation which is not generally understood and which when understood has an important bearing on the posture of occupational medical departments.

Confidentiality is ordinarily viewed as a patient requirement. That is to say, confidentiality must be provided because the patient wants it. But experienced occupational physicians recognize that they need confidentiality of patient information as much or more than the patient does. This arises from a simple but seldom stated fact that much of the useful information that a doctor can acquire about the patient comes from what the patient tells the doctor. If the physician were reduced to dealing with only the information that could be acquired by examining the patient, much of the critical input into the very decisions that the occupational physician is asked to make would be missing; therefore, the whole function of occupational medicine would be significantly limited, or thwarted altogether. Put another way, in order to function properly, the occupational physician needs a cooperative patient, and in order to get a cooperative patient who will tell the doctor all of his symptoms and all of the pertinent facts and relative circumstances (about some of which he may be very sensitive), the patient needs to feel secure that this information will not go beyond the doctor.

When apprised of this situation, corporate managements who may have been intially resistant to the idea of confidentiality in the company medical department recognize the necessity for such confidentiality if their medical departments are to function effectively. For without that confidentiality, in many cases there will be no information and there will be no opportunity to achieve the salutary contribution that a good occupational medical department can otherwise make to this business.

Let us conclude, therefore, that to the experienced occupational medical department confidentiality is both a self-serving necessity and a patient need. That should provide abundant motivation to establish adequate confidentiality policies and practices. But in addition to policy on confidentiality, the occupational medical department must have the courage of its convictions, must practice what it preaches, and must expect to have to defend its confidentiality principles with unyielding commitment, because there are forces in the employee-union-management complex that will continuously test that confidentiality.

Now I want to mention the fundamentals that experience has shown must be understood and observed if the successful outcomes previously mentioned are to be achieved.

1. The first principle is implicit in what has already been said: *A conceptual difference must be accepted between (a) "information" and (b) "conclusions or judgments."* Information includes what the patient tells the doctor; facts about the patient's life, feelings, and attitudes; results of tests and measurements; diagnoses; the identity of the patient's disease(s); etc. Conclusions or judgments, on the other hand, are outcomes that the doctor reaches as a result of his assessment of the information. Those conclusions or judgments that relate to the work situation of an employee are not necessarily confidential and should not be considered part of the confidential information about the patient.

This does not mean that conclusions and judgments are therefore broadcast to anyone without circumspection. It does mean that the physician's conclusions or judgments are his own and can be expressed whenever he feels they are legitimately needed.

Experience has shown that employees universally respond favorably to a medical-department policy that guards information with the tightest possible security while permitting the judicious advice of appropriate authorities with respect to conclusions or judgments reached. Provided that the employee is informed and that conclusions and judgments are not released willy-nilly or to persons who do not have a legitimate and authorized need to know, employees find this solution to the confidentiality issue one that they can embrace with comfort, and the occupational health physician finds that patients who are comfortable in the knowledge that their personal information is jealously protected readily and voluntarily provide the information necessary for occupational medical practice.

On the other hand, it has also been repeatedly demonstrated that employees regard with distrust and suspicion any medical department where confidentiality exists in name only. This brings us to the second basic principle.

2. *Confidentiality of medical information must be absolute and uniform.* Partial confidentiality, or confidentiality when convenient, or confidentiality under some conditions but not under others will not work and for all practical purposes is no confidentiality at all. The real test of the existence of confidentiality is whether the employee-patient will voluntarily provide information and cooperate comfortably with the system.

3. *Determination of what information is to be kept confidential and what may be released is the prerogative of the patient, not of the professional.* This principle, if followed faithfully, would be almost sufficient in itself to protect the privacy of the individual. It is difficult, however, for the professional to resist the temptation to substitute his own value judgment for the patient's as to what is confidential. Yet the physician must resist this urge absolutely, since it is impossible to predict what the attitude of each patient will be. One patient may not be concerned at all if people find out he has syphilis, while another may be upset significantly by disclosure of his weight even though it is apparent to even the casual observer that he is grossly obese. Similarly, most people guard their age as a personal secret, yet it can be estimated within a few years one way or the other by their appearance.

Thus it is not sufficient to keep confidential only that information that appears to the professional to be "sensitive." All information must be protected with equal care. Furthermore, any successful program will have a practicable method to obtain the patient's approval for release of medical information on those few occasions when release is necessary and will document the fact that release permission has been given.

Here is an area commonly leading to misunderstanding unless particular attention is given to informing the employee-patient. While it is true that confidential information is not released without the patient's permission, there are two circumstances where the patient may not realize that he has in fact given permission. The courts of most states have held that when an employee files a claim for workmen's compensation, he has given permission for the release of information pertinent to that claim. Similarly, either the law or court orders (presumably acting on behalf of the individual) may require the release of otherwise confidential information. Unless the employee-patient is aware of these possible releases, his confidence in the integrity of the medical department may be undermined when such instances occur.

4. The fourth principle deals with the handling of conclusions and judgments. *Confidentiality is not synonymous with abdication of responsibility on the part of the professional, nor does it signify protection of the patient against the possible adverse effects of the professional's best judgment.* Sometimes professionals and/or patients seem to feel that because the professional is subservient to the patient's desires or even his whims with respect to confidentiality of information, the professional should also be subservient to the patient's desires in all other matters. This, obviously, cannot be allowed to happen, because it is not in the patient's best interest. For example, a physician whose best judgment tells him that a particular patient requires a dangerous operation does not change that judgment just because the patient fears the operation. Instead, he tries to get the patient to understand the need for surgery and tries to help the patient through the ordeal. Similarly, the occupational physician does not change his best judgment because that may portend difficulty for the patient. Instead, he tries to get the patient to understand and accept the validity of his judgment and helps the patient accommodate to the undesirable effects of that judgment.

In all such situations, the occupational physician will make sure that the patient is advised of conclusions or judgments that have been reached, and a particular effort will be made to help the patient understand the validity of those decisions that may run counter to his wishes.

When the foregoing basic principles are understood, accepted, and scrupulously practiced by medical professionals, and when the employee-patient is adequately informed, the basis has been established for resolution of the otherwise thorny issue of medical confidentiality in the workplace. Experience over many years in many companies has demonstrated the soundness of these principles and of their success when faithfully implemented in protecting the interests of the employee-patient while providing necessary support to operating business decisions.

IBM's Guidelines to Employee Privacy

An Interview with Frank T. Cary

HBR: *Mr. Cary, you and other members of IBM's top management have spent a great deal of time working out an original approach to employee privacy. Why does this problem concern you so much?*

CARY: Organizations have invaded people's privacy with steel file cabinets and manila folders for years. But computer systems with remote access have intensified both the problem and public concern. When I became chairman [of IBM] it seemed to me that this subject was going to become an issue for us, as auto safety has become a major issue for Ford and General Motors. In years past we tended to step back, in the belief that others should take the lead—professors, politicians, lawyers. Now we have got to take some leadership and try to think our way through the subject. Privacy is not a passing fad.

Are the policies adopted by IBM applicable to business and government organizations in general?

Some of the things we've done are feasible in other organizations, but we have long recognized that we cannot solve many issues of individual privacy before the country solves them. We have to keep our efforts in the context of our business—we don't have any special competence to tell the world how legislators and privacy commissions and other groups should resolve all the questions being debated.

What part of the privacy issue, then, is of most concern to IBM?

Personal information about employees—the material that management keeps in files and data banks. This is a big part of the privacy issue but certainly not all of it. For instance, some hotly debated questions

Reprinted with permission from the *Harvard Business Review* 54, no. 5. Copyright © 1976 by the President and Fellows of Harvard College.

have to do with protection against intrusion by government agencies and the collection of census data. We don't have special competence in matters like those.

Have IBM employees influenced your concern with privacy?

Thomas Watson, Sr. and Jr. both had very strong beliefs in the dignity of the individual, but privacy in particular didn't begin to get special attention until the middle 1960s. That was when an IBM employee asked one day to see his personal folder. The question ended up in the office of Thomas J. Watson, Jr. After he reviewed it thoroughly, his answer to the employee was yes. He then wrote to all IBM managers, saying that employees throughout the company ought to be able to see their personal folders. The subject has been growing with us ever since.

After becoming chief executive in 1973, you began giving privacy a higher priority than it had received in the past. How did you decide you had a problem?

When we looked at employee privacy in IBM from the top down, things appeared to be pretty good. We seemed to be handling personal data in a sensitive and careful way. But then we organized a corporate task force to look at the subject from the bottom up. At different IBM sites, local task forces were organized to find out what actually was being done. We found that in some cases information about employees was being handled in a way that we didn't like, that seemed to violate our principles.

What sorts of things?

Oh, information in managers' informal files that shouldn't have been there, such as a piece of hearsay. Uses of information that shouldn't have been allowed, such as when an outsider requested more than routine facts about an employee.

Then how did you go about changing these practices?

I assigned some of our very best people to work on the problem. Also, I brought in Professor Alan Westin of Columbia, an authority on civil liberties, to serve as a consultant. After much creative thought and analysis, they would bring their ideas and proposals to me, and then I'd do what I like to call "put English on the ball." That is, I would give the recommendations some thought of my own and add my personal support in implementation—meetings with key management people, speeches, letters, and editorials in *Think,* our employee publication.

Was there much employee reaction to your efforts?

The changes we made weren't being demanded by employees and didn't come as any great surprise to them, because in the past we had been paying attention to some of these needs. But I think that what we've done generally is considered by employees to be a good thing. Of course, we don't have all the answers even today. Our approach and thinking keep evolving.

What kind of feedback do you get from employees?

We use opinion surveys a lot in our business to find out how employees feel about certain things. Periodically we include a question about whether the employee feels that his or her manager and the IBM company in general treat personal information in a confidential enough way, or appropriately—something like that. The great majority (close to 85 percent) feel that personal information is handled with sensitivity by IBM, and this feeling grows over time.

In a company with 160,000 employees in the United States, there are bound to be some people with legitimate grievances about privacy. Do you hear from these employees?

We do get some feedback on privacy questions through our "Speak Up!" program. "Speak Up!" is a system of communicating problems and questions to higher levels of management when they're not handled to an employee's satisfaction by his or her manager. The employee remains anonymous—no one knows the employee's name except the coordinator in the "Speak Up!" office. "Speak Up!" complaints about privacy have been minimal, but they indicate a widespread awareness of the issue.

After you decide on privacy guidelines, how do you make sure they're followed?

We try to make it very, very clear to managers what's expected of them. The rules for handling personal information are incorporated in our management training programs. We describe the principles we want followed, and we walk them through the specific dos and don'ts of practicing the rules. We try to produce uniform understanding on this. Within thirty days of becoming a manager, every first-line manager begins to receive basic training.

In addition, we ask all IBMers to help by bringing to management's attention infringements of personal privacy in their areas of the business. And we ask every employee to refrain from any practice that would unnecessarily invade the privacy of others.

What happens to a manager or other employee who violates a guideline?

Depending on the violation, the manager may be subject to dismissal. It's very clear-cut what we're trying to do, and I think everyone understands that we mean it. If there's confusion for some legitimate reason —and there may be, because it's hard to anticipate all situations—we make allowances for error. But there have been cases when the manager has gotten into trouble.

Is it fair to say that people are penalized more severely for infractions of ethical standards at IBM than for, say, lapses in performance?

I think that failures in ethics and integrity here are less excusable than errors in performance. People can perform their jobs on a range from satisfactory to outstanding, but there's only one standard of ethics and integrity that we recognize. So, yes, there are two levels of assessment.

What kinds of problems has IBM had in developing general understanding of your privacy guidelines?

We've had little difficulty communicating the procedures. What information it is permissible to ask a job applicant for, what information goes where, who can use it, what is available to line managers versus what is available only to medical people—all of that has been formalized, and there's been little confusion about it. Where there's been a problem is in what the privacy rules mean for the manager-employee relationship. There was a tendency for some managers to think that privacy meant a change in the way they should be involved with their people.

What mistakes were your managers making?

They were withdrawing. This really worried me. We've always encouraged managers to have strong relationships with employees and to be interested and helpful to them. Partly because of the term *privacy,* I think, some managers began retreating from involvement. That wasn't what we wanted them to do.

Could you give us an example of managerial withdrawal?

I'll have to make it a hypothetical case. Suppose one of our managers got an anonymous letter giving strong indication that an employee was a child beater. The manager might judge this to be a private matter and not investigate. Of course he would be wrong. Humanitarian considerations aside, an accusation such as this, if true, might affect both the employee's performance and—if there were contact with customers—ability to represent IBM. The manager should not leave the problem unattended. He would have to investigate the situation.

The manager should not interpret privacy to mean "Let people alone"?

That's right. To give you a real, rather extreme example, a group of employees who listened to what we were saying about privacy mistakenly applied the idea to office design. They said we weren't respecting the privacy of employees because we weren't letting them have private offices. Finally, we realized what was happening. Some employees were reading into the word *privacy* their concerns for physical privacy. So we decided to be more precise by using the term *personal information*.

IBM employs some 130,000 people in countries overseas. Are they subject to the same guidelines as people in the United States?

The rules aren't applied formally in all other countries, because of differing customs and traditions. For instance, it wouldn't make sense to apply the same rules to IBMers in Japan. But the basic principles of our approach have been adopted in other countries like these, or are under review there, and I think these principles will be in practice in all countries before long.

Let's turn now to the specific everyday rules that IBM follows—the practices and policies that make this subject real from the standpoint of employees. We would like to start at the beginning, when information on an employee first accumulates. What personal information do you ask for from a job applicant?

Only what we think is necessary to make the employment decision —name, address, previous employer, education, and a few other basic facts. We don't even ask for date of birth at this time, although if the person is hired we will need to get his or her age. We don't ask about the employment of the applicant's spouse, about relatives employed by IBM, or for previous addresses. We don't ask about any prior treatment for nervous disorder or mental illness. We don't ask about arrest records or pending criminal charges or criminal indictments. We do ask about convictions—but only convictions during the previous five years.

IBM used to ask for some of the information now omitted. What made you change your mind?

We were getting a lot of data we really didn't need. It was cluttering up the files. Worse than that, it was tagging along after people. Particularly in the case of unfavorable information about an employee, there's a tendency for the material to follow the person around forever and to influence management decisions that it shouldn't. It's better not to have the data in the files in the first place.

But can you be sure in advance what personal information is going to be relevant?

No. But you know what you need at the time, for just this decision. Later you can collect more data as needed. This is part of the problem, you see. There's a common attitude that "it doesn't hurt to have all this information; it can't do any harm, so why not get it?" That's what we're working against. When we looked into this problem a few years ago, we found that it could indeed do harm to have information that wasn't of current relevance. For example, information about how young or how old a person is, or about an arrest a couple of years ago—it shouldn't influence the hiring decision, but it might do so if it were on hand. So we decided the best thing to do was simply not to collect it.

What about appraisals of the applicant's strengths and weaknesses—do you cut back on that information, too?

Not at all. Just the opposite. Good interviewing becomes the key. Our people are very good at this, and we count on them to draw applicants out and understand their interests.

What about verifying the statements an applicant makes?

We used to employ outside credit agencies to do background checking on prospective employees, but not any more. When we feel that a reference on education or previous employment should be checked, our own people do it. Incidentally, they do it with the knowledge and consent of the applicant.

Inevitably there are some things we don't catch, but I don't think they are material enough to make it worthwhile to go through all the routines we used to have to go through. When we used to do background checks on applicants, for example, the information gathered would sometimes include data that just wasn't germane.

We're interested in employment testing. Some critics feel that tests can be an invasion of privacy. What's IBM's stance here?

We have stopped excursions into applicants' emotional and private lives through the use of personality tests. We don't use polygraphs in hiring or at any other time—we never have. But we use aptitude tests and consider them useful. Some tests have credibility, for instance, in forecasting a person's aptitude for programming, or typing, or certain other types of occupation. Also, this sort of information isn't so personal or sensitive. It's more job-related than personality tests are.

What about tests of an applicant's general intelligence?

They don't help us much, either. Many of the people we hire have college backgrounds, and their records in college seem to be as good an indicator as any I.Q. test. So here again, since there are other ways of making the evaluation we need—ways that can't be called intrusions —we use them instead.

This brings us to the next stage. Do you try to control the buildup of personal information on an employee after he or she is hired?

Yes, we work pretty hard on that. We keep purging data that no longer seem relevant. Performance appraisals usually are kept for three years only—in unusual cases, for five years. All grades and appraisals from IBM course instructors are kept for three years only. A record of a conviction is thrown out after three years. Then there's all that information many managers keep on an employee's attendance, performance, vacation schedules, and so on. We tell managers to keep this material for a limited time only.

How much of the onus is on operating managers, rather than on the personnel department, to keep the files stripped down to essentials?

Since there are some files operating managers never examine, obviously the personnel department has to purge them of old data. But we hold individual managers responsible for seeing that job-related information, which they do see, is kept to a minimum. Now, the personnel department is responsible for developing guidelines, and it may check up on the manager to see that the purging is done, but he or she can't pass the buck. We say, in effect, "This is your job, and you know what the rules are—they're not terribly complex. It is up to you to see that the rules are followed."

Let's talk now about who can look at an employee's files. First, what can IBM line managers see?

Any job-related information they are allowed to see. The distinction between job-related and non-job-related is important to the privacy question. An employee's performance appraisals, performance plans, letters of commendation, records of awards, sales records, production assignments, and so on—all such job-related information is kept available for the line manager to see. The manager needs to see it to make decisions. The only other people who can inspect this material are those with a need to know, such as a manager considering the employee for a new position.

Is there anything the line manager can't see?

Yes. Every large company has to have quite a bit of personal information on an employee that has little or nothing to do with work performance. So this information is out of bounds for the line manager. This file is open only to the personnel and financial departments. It includes medical benefits data, records of personal finances such as wage garnishments, payroll deductions, life insurance beneficiaries, payments for educational programs, house valuations, and so on. These items are required to administer benefit plans, to meet the company's legal obligations, and to carry out other aspects of personnel administration, but the operating manager does not need to know them.

By this division, we protect the individual from having facts about his or her life accessible to people who should only be concerned with specific areas.

Numerous employees, attorneys, and civil liberties leaders are incensed because much personal information in the files of many employers may be released to outsiders—often without the employee's knowledge. How does IBM handle that issue?

If an outsider wants to verify that a person works for us, we will release the most recent job title the person has, the most recent place of work, and the date of employment at IBM. We'll do this much without contacting the employee. But if the outsider wants to know the person's salary, or wants a five-year job chronology, we don't give out that information without written approval from the employee.

As for creditors, attorneys, private agencies, and others desiring non-job-related information, we give out none of it without the employee's consent, unless the law requires disclosure by us.

We honor legitimate requests for information from government agencies, though we require the investigators to furnish proper identification, prove their legal authority, and demonstrate that they need the information sought. If a district attorney's office is making a criminal investigation, we cooperate within limits. It's hard to make rules to cover all situations that may arise, but we have specialists in the legal and personnel departments who use their judgment in an unusual situation, and they handle these problems pretty well.

Do you protect IBM's 600,000 or so stockholders in the same way?

Yes. Not long ago, for example, a U.S. senator wrote us asking for the names and holdings of IBM's thirty top stockholders. He had no subpoena. He would give no purpose for his inquiry, even after we asked. So we refused to give him the data he wanted. Suppose he had spelled out his purpose. Then, I suppose, we might have taken the next step and asked the permission of the thirty stockholders involved to release the facts.

Social security numbers have been a sore spot with people concerned about privacy. How does IBM deal with this problem?

In 1973 we looked into the use of social security numbers and agreed that thereafter we would release them only to satisfy government and legal requirements—at least, until some national consensus was arrived at on the use of universal identifiers, or until new legislation was passed. So we don't give outside private organizations an employee's social security number without the person's consent; we don't even supply the number to the organization that administers our company scholarship program.

But social security numbers are useful for personal identification, aren't they?

Some organizations seem to think so, but we won't put social security numbers on company badges or identification cards. Also, we have taken them off all IBM medical cards; insurance companies get an IBM employee identification number when they process a medical or a dental claim.

We've discussed access to an employee's files by operating managers, the personnel department, and outsiders. What, if anything, can the employee himself or herself see?

With just a few exceptions, employees can see what's in their personnel folders—job-related information as well as non-job-related. We want them to know what's there—no surprises. If they find something to quarrel with, they can ask for a correction. The key document, of course, is the performance appraisal. But there's less curiosity about this than you would think, and the reason is that the manager has already told the employee how he or she was rated. That was done when the appraisal session was held. In fact, the manager's appraisal that contains the ratings is reviewed by the employee, at which time he or she can add comments.

What are the exceptions—what data cannot be seen?

Employees can't see notes on "Open Door" investigations of complaints they made. At IBM, the "Open Door" is a system for allowing employees to take a grievance over their supervisors' heads to a higher management level. The employee identifies himself or herself (in this respect, the "Open Door" system is different from "Speak Up!"), so the case goes into a special file, which, by the way, has very stringent access and retention standards. As chief executive, I'm the court of last resort, so to speak, and many cases come to me. I assign an executive to investigate each situation, and I personally review the findings. During the investigations, these senior managers talk to many people and get honest, frank answers to many tough questions. They couldn't get such candid answers if they didn't talk off the record, in strict confidence. So we don't allow an employee to see the notes made on a case he or she was concerned with. If we did, the "Open Door" system wouldn't work.

Can the employee learn anything at all about the investigation?

Oh, yes. The investigator sits down with the employee after the inquiries are completed and reports the conclusion. Some of the specific findings may be discussed. But the investigator doesn't quote the people interviewed, and doesn't show the file to the employee concerned.

Do some of your assistants specialize in "Open Door" cases?

No one spends full time on them. We select different people on the basis of position occupied, objectivity, reputation for fairness, and so on. Also, we never ask the manager who has been criticized to do the investigation. We have strict ground rules for this, and I do have assistants who spend considerable time overviewing the system and seeing that the rules are followed. That the investigators start out taking the side of the complainants is an important rule. Quite often, they end up on that side—they find that the complainant is right.

Can an employee see information about salary plans for himself or herself?

Our managers make salary forecasts for their employees as a matter of course in business planning. In effect, a manager says, "I expect to increase so-and-so's salary by this much on such-and-such a date." We don't consider this personal information. It's business planning information and subject to change. Once the increase is acted on, the data become personal information, but until then the figures are not available to the employee concerned.

In fact, such figures are not kept in the employee's file but in some place like the desk drawer of the manager.

Is information about an employee's promotion prospects handled in the same way?

Yes. Again, it's just good planning technique to know who is ready to take over the management jobs at certain levels. We prepare replacement tables with the names of, say, the top three candidates for every one of those jobs. Now, there are surely people who would love to see those tables and know who will be moved up if a certain individual gets hit by a streetcar the next day. But this, too, is business planning, not personal information, and so it's not available for employees to see. Besides, it would be misleading and misunderstood. We do not always do what is written in the replacement planning tables. Nor do we always give the amount of salary increase that is forecast.

Another thing many civil liberties spokesmen and others are unhappy about is the practice of recording employee conversations without the person's consent. What is IBM policy here?

There's absolutely no taping of a person's conversations on the telephone without express permission, or at business meetings without prior announcement. I consider this a simple matter of respect for the individual.

Were conversations ever recorded in the past?

Yes, I think it was done sometimes. Some time ago, an employee had a hidden tape recorder he used for recording some sales calls he made on customers. He did it innocently, I think—for his own use to analyze what transpired. I think you just do not record conversations with customers or prospects or anyone else without telling them first. People act differently depending on the kind of talk they think they're having —recorded or not recorded, on the record or off, for a newspaper or for TV. As the saying goes, the medium is the message. I think it's the same principle that has influenced the courts to keep television out of the courtroom.

What about an employee's off-the-job behavior? Many Americans apparently feel that employers want to know too much about what an employee does after hours.

We're careful about that, too. In 1968 Thomas Watson, Jr., then chairman, wrote a letter to managers stating that management was concerned with off-the-job behavior only when it impaired a person's ability to perform regular job assignments—their own or others—or when it affected the reputation of the company in a major way. That statement has continued to be our guideline.

Yet IBM has a reputation for being solicitous about employee welfare, as you pointed out earlier. Isn't it hard to draw the line?

Yes, because when a manager is trying to be helpful and when he's getting "nosy" is something that different people see in different ways.

So you have to use judgment here. You can't have hard and fast rules. Certainly, spying of any kind is out. But what about a manager who visits an employee who is sick in the hospital or at home? Such a visit *can* be considered an invasion of privacy, given certain circumstances. So the manager has to be sensitive to the person and situation in order to do the right thing.

In Think, *IBM's publication for employees, an interesting problem was posed: An engineer goes on vacation and forgetfully leaves some confidential new product specifications in his desk drawer. Is his privacy being invaded if his manager goes into the drawer to get the specifications when needed?*

In one sense, there's no violation, because desks and files are IBM property. But the manager must have a very good reason for looking. No one should be fooling around in someone else's papers. Of course, it's important to try to avoid this sort of situation. When a person leaves on vacation or a trip, he or she should leave any business documents that might be needed in the hands of someone else who will carry on.

One hotly debated topic is management control of an employee's involvement with outside organizations. Could you comment on this question?

We ask employees who want to become involved in public problems and want to take a position on them to do so as private individuals, not on behalf of IBM. They should make that clear to the press. But only if there is a potential conflict of interest do we ask employees to excuse themselves from the discussion and any decision or to vote on it. This might be the case if, say, the employee sat on a board of education and the board were going to vote on an IBM proposal.

A Profile of Bank of America's Privacy Experience

Alan F. Westin

The best way of tracing Bank of America's changing standards of relevance of information is to study the evolution of its employment application forms. The present form, revised in March 1976, is headed "All applicants will receive consideration for employment without regard to race, color, religion, sex, age (40–65), national origin, or handicap." It is a one-page document, divided into five categories:

1. *Identification:* name; other or former name; social security number; present address and how long living there; telephone number.

2. *Position objective:* position desired; salary expected; full time or other; shift desired; by whom referred; and "Have you previously applied to Bank of America?"

3. *General information:* military status and background, including "If other than Honorable Discharge, explain circumstances" (veterans must submit a copy of their discharge papers); "Have you ever been convicted of anything other than a minor traffic offense?"; "Have you ever been refused a fidelity bond?"; "Are you currently involved in the operations of any other business?"; "If hired can you furnish proof of age?"; "Proof of citizenship or authorization to work?"; "Do you have any relatives employed by Bank of America?"

4. *Health:* "Do you have any condition, illness, or disability, either temporary or permanent, which may affect your ability to do the work in the position applied for?" According to bank policy, "Physical examinations are not required except for doubtful health cases or when specifically requested by Personnel Administration."

Excerpted from Alan F. Westin, *Privacy and the Employment Relationship: A Study of Computer Use in Personnel Administration.* Sponsored by the Institute for Computer Sciences and Technology, forthcoming.

5. *Employment and educational experience:* "Do you have any qualifications that you feel are applicable for the position applied for?" "List educational background; list employment experience." The application form does not say so, but the hiring team is instructed to require employment experience only for the last five years. "Have you ever been employed by Bank of America? Have you ever been involuntarily discharged or fired? If yes, explain circumstances."

A notice on the bottom of the form states: "I understand that proof of citizenship, proof of age, and fingerprinting will be required upon employment." (The decision to require fingerprinting for all new employees was instituted in 1975; previously, some units required this but others did not. When the bank's legal department noticed this, and considered the Federal Deposit Insurance Corporation rule that FDIC approval must be secured to carry on an insured bank's payroll a person convicted of a crime or dishonesty or breach of trust, it decided that all new employees should be fingerprinted.)

The previous form, revised in June 1973, has the same anti-discrimination heading except that it does not have (40–65) next to "age" and does not include "handicap." In addition to asking all of the questions contained in the present form, the 1973 form required the following *additional* information in each of the five categories treated:

1. *Identification:* "How long have you lived in this area?" Familiar name.

2. *Position objective:* no change.

3. *General information:* reserve military status; "Do you own home, rent, or live with friends or relatives? How long have you lived in this state? Do you have friends, relatives living in area?"; approximate travel time to this office, round trip; "Do you plan to commute?"; date of birth, age; spouse's first name; spouse's date of birth; "Is your spouse employed?"; spouse's occupation; spouse's employer.

4. *Educational and employment background:* education—grade averages and majors. Employment—supervisor's name, department title, description of duties, reason for leaving; list periods of unemployment.

5. *Health:* height, weight, date of last physical, number of school or work days missed last year because of illness; because of personal reasons. "Do you have any condition, illness, or disability, temporary or permanent, which puts you under a doctor's care? Has the doctor recommended a restriction or limitation on your activities?"; explain. This is followed by a check list of nineteen conditions including "frequent headaches, asthma, hay fever, epilepsy, emotional disorder," plus a box to check for "rejected for life insurance" and "collected workmen's compensation or disability insurance."

In addition, the 1973 form featured a set of questions on *financial information.* It asked: "Do you have income other than your salary? If yes, specify source and amount. Do you have a checking account? savings account? savings and loan account?" *Loan history:* "How much is owed on automobile? home loan? bank loan? installment payments?" List repayment schedules.

The scope of information collected from applicants was much greater in 1950. The 1950 application form was a six-page document. Besides the questions asked on the 1973 and 1976 forms, it required information on the following:

State whether you are right-handed or left-handed.

Marital status: single, married, separated, divorced, widowed.

Are you personally well acquainted with anyone connected with Bank of America (not a relative)?

Have you ever been seriously ill? Do you have relatives suffering from ill health?

List names, occupations, and home addresses of father, mother, sisters, brothers.

Are you self-supporting? Do you own a car? Is the car insured?

How many dependents? Relationship to you.

Do you have life insurance? How much?

What do you estimate it costs you to live per month?

In what extracurricular activities did you participate in school?

Did you help finance your college education?

As to schooling beyond college: Why did you take this additional education? How was it financed?

Employees' files used to contain their photographs. They are now no longer required, and are not in employee files.

None of these three forms asks for racial data. Now that the bank has an affirmative action program and is required to keep racial statistics to document its efficacy, the hiring team is instructed to have the applicant complete a separate form identifying his or her status under one of five categories: 1. Black; 2. Asian American; 3. American Indian or Eskimo; 4. Spanish surname; 5. Caucasian. The hiring team is prohibited from asking the new employee about his or her racial grouping, or make a "visual" determination. The form is then kept separate from the application.

The marked differences between the old and new application forms reflect not only the bank's awareness of privacy and antidiscrimination issues but also its recognition that it was collecting a lot of material that it never used. Even before the latest application form revision, a research department official told an interviewer that such questions as whether employees own their own homes or rent, how long the commute was, and so on, were not used in decision making, but only in research.

Similarly, when an employee using the bank's Open Line (see below) wanted to know why the Bank of America needed to know whether he was divorced or not, the bank realized that they asked that question only because they had always asked it, and not because they found it useful. It was dropped.

Investigations

Previous employers for the past five years are mailed a form to complete, as is the last educational institution attended. Personal references are required only when there is no previous employment history or when "unusual" circumstances exist. In past years, the bank sometimes used Retail Credit Company for investigative reports on applicants, but since the passage of the Fair Credit Reporting Act in 1970, it has abandoned this practice. "We have not suffered any loss in quality of employees as a result of not getting an investigative report," a bank spokesperson said.

Each newly hired employee is fingerprinted and the fingerprint card is sent to the FBI. If conviction information turns up as a result of this check, the results are reviewed by the hiring unit, which may call for further investigation or may give the applicant an opportunity to refute or explain the FBI information.

Thus, in addition to the application form, personal information about a new employee comes from reference checks, confirmation from employers and schools, an FBI check, and from military discharge papers. Newly hired employees who are handicapped may, if they wish, identify themselves as such so that their progress can be observed and positive affirmative action measures can be taken.

CHANGING STANDARDS OF EMPLOYEE SUPERVISION

Re-examination of the relevance and/or usefulness of the personal information collected about applicants was paralleled by the bank's gradual abandonment (as in many other corporations) of policies setting rather extensive behavior norms for employees on and off the job.

These changes can be seen by comparing the bank's recently adopted (1977) rules governing conflict of interest and outside activities of staff members with the regulations in effect in 1971 and 1972. The bank's concern then and now was on situations in which the employee might benefit or appear to benefit from his or her connection with the bank, to be involved in competing or conflicting business activities, or to be pursuing activity which might impugn the public integrity or reputation of the bank. Even when some of the rules remain the same, the tone is significantly different.

Old manual: "A staff member must not purchase stocks or other securities for investment or otherwise beyond his independent financial ability to meet his commitments."

New Manual: "While it is recognized that staff members have the right to make private investments, sound judgment must be exercised to avoid any involvement, either direct or indirect, which might convey even the appearance of impropriety . . . [such as] . . . purchasing stocks or other securities . . . beyond the independent financial ability to meet his or commitments."

Old manual: "Staff members should avoid accepting fiduciary appointments, such as executor, administrator . . . etc., except those involving members of their immediate families."

New manual: "Staff members who accept fiduciary appointments . . . do so as individuals and not in any way as representatives of the bank. This distinction must be made clear at every step."

The old manual had a section prohibiting "all forms of gambling" and attendance at "horse racing and dog racing." The new manual eliminates this.

The change in supervisory standards was also reflected in observations by various bank officials to an interviewer:

• Employees may have a free checking account at the bank. Formerly, if an employee wrote a bad check, that branch would notify the employee's supervisor who would "counsel" the employee. "We don't do that any more. It's treated just as any other customer writing an overdraft."

• The bank used to have a uniform dress code which was rigidly enforced. Now the bank leaves this question up to the local manager, who is meant to take community standards into account. The new branch in Berkeley, for instance, permits male employees to wear beads and sandals, provided they are neatly groomed.

• Ten years ago, some supervisors would not have hired a known homosexual and would have fired such a person if his status became known in the community. Some supervisors would also have fired a pregnant unmarried employee, especially in a small town where that condition would have been considered detrimental to the bank's good reputation.

• An unsuccessful effort was made a few years ago to unionize a Bank of America location. One union activist asked to see his file and was pleased to discover that it contained no "black mark" or indication of his union activity in it.

• Previously, when anyone sent anything to record clerks to file, it went in. Files got "fat and full of garbage. . . . It was easy to put things in and there was no purging procedure to take them out." Starting in the early seventies the bank issued new regulations on what could be contained in personnel files, and starting in 1975 it reviewed all the old files to determine what should be destroyed.

The bank's affirmative action programs in behalf of women and minorities have produced three significant changes in record-keeping practices:

1. Salary history cards are no longer kept in personnel folders. Earlier, a problem had been seen in keeping women's salary cards since their historically lower salaries might lead supervisors or personnel administrators not to equalize their salaries with men doing equivalent jobs. As one bank official interviewed put it, maintaining such salary records now would be "improperly allowing history to control, and letting 'the record' perpetuate the harm."

2. Some records for men employees sometimes used to include notations that "he's clubbable," meaning that the employee could get into the "right" clubs that would be good for business. Since the "right" clubs almost invariably excluded women and minority-group members, this could have impeded promotions of female and minority employees. Such notations are no longer made.

3. EEO proceedings and the consent decree in a women's lawsuit have led the bank to maintain records on the number of minority members and women in particular selection pools for hiring or advancement, and to be sure to have full documentation of the reasons for advancement or failure to advance in individual cases.

One of the ways in which the Bank of America gauges the social climate upon which its behavior criteria should be based is through Open Line. This is a suggestion channel through which employees are encouraged to complain, comment, or inquire about bank activities. The subjects are not limited to employee practices, but may cover such matters as policies toward customers, loan programs to minority contractors, etc. When the Open Line coordinator receives an employee communication, he forwards it to the appropriate bank department for an answer, but first removes the employee's name and anything else that might identify him or her. The responding officer sends the answer back to the coordinator, who in turn mails it to the employee's home so that none of his or her colleagues or supervisors can learn of the correspondence. (Employees may request that their letters be printed in the bank's house organ, or they may request an interview with the appropriate official to help resolve a problem, but unless they make such specific requests, only the coordinator of Open Line knows the names of the correspondents.)

CONFIDENTIALITY OF PERSONNEL RECORDS

Internal Confidentiality Policies

Bank of America has traditionally been highly sensitive to the confidentiality of its customer records, and this attitude has carried over to employee records. In general, the bank protects confidentiality within the bank by compartmentalizing it so that a particular department has access only to the specific information it needs to function, and not to the employee's whole file. Thus, the training department has access only to matters pertaining to course attendance, reimbursed tuition by the bank, etc. The benefits section has access only to information about medical and other claims, and this information is not shared with the employee's supervisor. Also kept confidential from supervisors or personnel officers are benefits payments to the employee for alcoholism or drug treatments and up to $1,000 a year for psychiatric treatments. The auditing department does security investigations for bonding purposes, and supervisors do not have access to this information either.

Access to the personnel files kept by each branch or department on its own employees is restricted to the office manager or operations officer. That official is permitted to keep a temporary desk file covering an ongoing personnel problem. If, for example, a pattern of coming in late began to develop, the office manager would keep notes in his desk until the matter was resolved. If the problem was resolved, all the records and notes would be destroyed. If it was found to be true, it could be the basis for an action in which the employee got to tell his or her side, but in such a case, case statements taken from colleagues would not be shown to the employee. In any case, the policy about such manager's notes is either to destroy them at the end of a year or to send a memo to the personnel file; if the latter, the employee can review the memo along with the rest of his or her personnel file.

Applicant files are kept by the employment office. Interview cards are kept separately in active files for three months, in inactive files for an additional five months, and then destroyed unless the applicant is hired. Fingerprint information is kept locked and separate, and employees with access to it are alerted to the "extremely confidential nature of the fingerprint cards and the accompanying rap sheets. No information from rap sheets is divulged."

Although the bank takes pride in its confidentiality protection measures, a 1974 internal report, "The Privacy of Bank Records," noted that "there is a significant trading of personnel information between the Regional VPs and Employee Loan Department and the Personnel Department. Much of this is oral. . . . We were satisfied during our review that the officers in charge of personnel records . . . were aware of the proper limits for exchange of information and screened access carefully. However, there are no written guidelines in this area and officers in Personnel have indicated they would welcome such guidelines. Even standards should be applied so that personnel data is confidential at all levels of employment."

The report noted one other area in which more specific confidentiality guidelines would be useful, and that is access to the employee's computerized files in the Personnel Information Center. These files contain no subjective information except for a coded performance rating. The manual files in individual branches and offices are "richer," so the PIC files are less likely to lead to confidentiality abuses. Still, the report noted, "once [the information] is in 'hard' copy, [it] loses its visual semblance to something 'confidential' and is often widely distributed without proper screening for authorized access." Guidelines were drafted to implement the policy and special arrangements were made by PIC administration to monitor the systems logs to review the output of programs and the numbers of copies and recipients.

Dissemination of Personnel Information
Outside the Bank

The bank's policy is not to share employees' names and addresses with any other organizations for the purposes of commercial or nonprofit solicitation, either through rental or exchange of mailing lists. For its own house organ, which is delivered to employees' homes, the computer system produces name and address labels which are delivered to a mailing house, one set at a time, where they are locked up until used.

Since the bank processes its own benefit programs and claims, large-scale exchange of personal information with outside insurance companies does not arise. (There is *some* disclosure, as with coordination of benefits with an outside insurance company covering a spouse.) Employees submit claim forms to a single claims unit in the San Francisco personnel department, whose staff is under strict rules for the confidential handling of such information. No medical-claims information about individual employees is shared with immediate supervisors or unit managers.

According to bank officials, in former years Bank of America used to cooperate fully with law enforcement agencies when they requested information on an employee in the course of a local investigation—e.g., an employee of the bank who was also collecting welfare payments, or employees suspected of drug use. "Now we insist on a subpoena for such information, and notify the employee before we comply."

Physical Security

Physical security of personnel records is given a high priority at Bank of America, in keeping with its special concern for the safety of its cash and other convertible assets. Manual personnel records with sensitive materials in them are kept under lock and key. Computer facilities are guarded and require special access codes that specify the limits of the access.

EMPLOYEE ACCESS TO PERSONNEL RECORDS

Prior to 1968, Bank of America resembled most large corporations in that there was no formal policy allowing employees to see what was in their personnel records, either at the local or regional location or the central personnel headquarters. Beginning in 1968, the bank's top management decided to open the personnel record—with some exceptions —to any employee who asked to see it. The exceptions included letters of reference and recommendation obtained at the time of applying for employment; ratings of promotability and potential assigned by supervisors; reports arising from security investigations; and a few similar items.

By the early 1970s, this policy was firmly in place and had been communicated to all bank employees. Employees could review their files with a member of the personnel department. Employees responded by seeking such reviews of personnel folders in what one bank official called "small but significant" numbers. By "significant," he explained, he meant that "it only took reviews of the records by a few people in a location to get the word out to other employees about what was and wasn't in the files. By the early 1970s, we had purged a lot of the wide-ranging materials that had been in files, and what was left was, for the most part, what our employees regarded as appropriate information for the Bank to be maintaining. From then on, it has been a small but steady stream of employee access requests, about 75–80 a month."

When the computerized personnel data system went into effect, the right of access was extended to that also. A 1974 in-house report on privacy of bank records noted that "employees can request to see a display of information concerning them kept on the computer file." Because "much of the information is abbreviated, a personal interview with a PIC employee would be required. No such interview or computer display has been requested to date." According to this report, "No subjective information is kept on the computer other than the performance rating, as represented by a number 1–4 and details supplied by the employee himself relative to activities outside the Bank."

A bank official noted that their Career Profile used to have two codes on it that they wouldn't let an employee see. One was "promotability," which included a projection of the *level* of promotion that the employee might reach ("lateral move, 1 grade, 2 or more grades") and his or her "readiness" (such as: "immediate promotion, by next review, in 18 months to 2 years," etc.). "Potential" was coded in a number scale to indicate a range from "limited" to "exceptional." "The idea was to see whether Joe Smith or Jane Doe might become General Counsel or Vice President for Personnel at the Bank some day. We don't use those now; they proved not to be valid and not needed. All we have today is a small research study, off the computer, to compare those codes when we did them with the career paths of a selected group of people."

Employee access has also been extended to the bank's performance appraisal system, an annual review in which the supervisor sits down with each employee to review and evaluate work performance against job standards, set future goals for the employee, and review salary status against job performance to make "equitable salary decisions." The guidelines for performance appraisal caution: "Remember, you are evaluating *performance* . . . you are *not* asked to evaluate the underlying motivations or personality characteristics of an individual."

The bank's guidelines also stress that performance appraisal "provides a form of documentation for personnel decisions."

The day when management decisions went unquestioned is long past. Individual employees, special interest groups and both federal and state governments are challenging and questioning all employers. Increasingly, we are asked to explain why a promotion was given or denied. The recollection of a supervisor is not sufficient. What is needed is a careful system of performance evaluation to serve as a basis for and to document important personnel decisions. In short it helps guarantee each employee fair treatment.

By the mid-1970s, the bank had evolved a policy of full access by the employee to his or her performance appraisal, including the numerical rating assigned by the supervisor at the end of the interview. The bank's instructions state:

Employee Review of the Report:

During the interview, the report should be completely reviewed with the employee. At some time in your discussion, give the employee an opportunity to read the report and make comments on your ratings. *It is our firm policy that employees have the right to know everything that appears on their performance report—and the right to discuss it with you freely.* If there are any differences of opinion, it is your responsibility to make an honest effort to resolve them. In any situation where differences are not resolved satisfactorily, you should encourage the employee to take the problem to the next level of supervision or to go directly to the District Administrator or to an Employee Relations Officer in Personnel Administration.

The employee is also given copies of various forms when they first originate or when they are updated, some of which, such as benefit claims and medical information, are not shared with the supervisor. Officers can see their progression file, which is maintained on every officer in the bank. However, the officer is not permitted to see comments evaluating others in comparison to him or her where other individuals are competing with the officer for an executive opening; nor is the officer given letters solicited and received from former employers, and he or she is informed of these two restrictions.

On January 1, 1976, a new California law went into effect that provided that

every employer shall, at reasonable times upon the request of an employee, permit that employee to inspect such personnel files which are used or have been used to determine that employee's qualifications for employment, promotion, additional compensation, or termination or other disciplinary action.

This section does not apply to the records of an employee relating to the investigation of a possible criminal offense. It shall not apply to letters of reference.

When the new California law was passed, the bank was in a good position to determine whether or not it was in compliance with it. A year earlier, shortly after the passage of the Privacy Act of 1974, and while its proposed California counterpart, AB 150, was being considered, the bank undertook a department-by-department study to determine its practices as to access, confidentiality, and relevance. It was able to identify twenty-one personnel record systems and to conclude that six of them were not covered by the law. Of the twenty-one, four were duplicative with the information contained in individual personnel files; six fell under the law, and the bank's practices were already in compliance with it; and five required further legal study to see whether they were covered.

Following enactment of the access law, the bank revised its personnel manual by adding a directive to each operations officer to allow employees access under the law. It also issued to supervisors a separate circular with the same information but adding an additional warning: "Be sure contents are NOT removed from the files. . . . Employees who wish to see files that pertain to them other than those kept in individual branches and departments are to be referred to the Employee Relations Department."

Aside from these two notices, the bank has not conducted a campaign to inform employees about the access law, although bank officials state that any employee could see all of the records pertaining to him or her upon request. The reason the bank did not advertise the access law more widely is that it feared a deluge of requests that would be time-consuming and costly. Requests to review files are at about one hundred a month, up 20 percent since before the law. So far nobody has asked to see the computerized files in PIC, presumably because all of that information is in the manual file in more readable form.

One problem of access arose when an ex-employee filed a complaint with the California Department of Labor that the bank would not make their file available to her in the community where she had worked but had required her to come to San Francisco to see the central file. The bank responded by sending the employee's file to the regional office near her home. Although this particular case was resolved without difficulty, the bank is concerned about the possibility of having to send files to more than two thousand branch and departmental offices all over California.

Another problem of access is the request by ex-employees not only to inspect their files but to copy them. The bank maintains that this cost would be excessive, since there are about one hundred documents in a typical file, and if the law were interpreted to require permission to copy the file, it would cover all sixty thousand employees.

While the bank has not found the access law difficult to administer, it has serious concern over the broad proposed privacy legislation (such as the Koch-Goldwater Bill, H.R. 1984, introduced in 1974) to private business. It believes that the timetable and methods for purging old data and for maintaining data control would be terribly costly. As for dropping the social security number as an identifier, it would cost hundreds of thousands of dollars to reprogram its numbering system and change all of their forms. Since the bank has not identified any abuses of the social security numbering system, they believe that this cost would not be justified.

CURRENT PRIVACY REVIEWS

While its policies on employee privacy are much more detailed and have probably been in place longer than any other American corporation except IBM, Bank of America is still in the midst of refining its policies, applying them in new record-keeping and confidentiality situations, and relating them to external legal and social developments.

For example, the bank's 1975 report on privacy in employee records and its 1976 task force made a series of recommendations that the bank has been responding to in 1977. For example:

• It was recommended that the bank take the five principles of fair information practices enunciated by the HEW Report of 1973 and embodied in the Federal Privacy Act of 1974 for federal agencies and put these in the Bank's Standard Practice Manual; it was also recommended that a statement about what is in each of the bank's employee record systems, manual and computerized, should be in the Standard Practice Manual. The legal department is proceeding with that now.

• It was recommended that, after determining the legitimate needs of potential users within the bank, a set of guidelines on access for those users be drawn up and disseminated. This has been done.

• All computer system output should be reviewed to see if programs used need to disclose personal data or could do without that. The legal department is now reviewing all computer output and forms to do that.

• It was recommended that destruction dates be set for files and record elements, to insure that only needed information was retained. The bank's Standard Practice Manual now directs that no outdated information should be kept, and some destruction dates have been set. However, the legal department has found that EEO regulations and litigation possibilities force the bank to keep some personnel records longer than it would otherwise want or need to.

• It was recommended that no employee should photocopy his or her personnel file without the need to do so and authorization from a supervisor or manager. Following the California Labor Code, bank policy now is to allow employees to inspect all files that are used or have been used "to determine that employee's qualifications for employment, promotion, additional compensation, termination or other disciplinary action."

• It was recommended that the contents of all employee files should be reviewed for legal content. This was done by the legal department during 1976–77. "We did set rules to dispose of many irrelevant items," one official noted, "such as letters of recommendation." In addition, a list was drawn up of the documents that can be kept in the local personnel file at the operating unit.

• It was recommended that the older manual personnel files be examined and obsolete material removed from them as part of the move to putting such records on microfiche. The bank found this to be such a time-consuming and expensive task, and with so little value in terms of current personnel decisions not being based on review of those records, that they decided not to do this. They feel that the greater physical security controls that are part of handling microfiche records will insure that when a query is made about a particular record, improper material will not be made available.

• It was recommended that the bank's training films on video tape for managers should include a privacy unit. These are being produced now.

Beyond carrying out its own in-house recommendations, the bank has re-examined some of its employee privacy policies in light of its new Voluntary Disclosure Code for providing public information about the bank's affairs. In setting out its code, the bank's president, A. W. Clausen, noted that "the most perplexing problem was how to provide maximum, meaningful information without violating the rights of customers and employee privacy." While the innovative aspects in the code involve disclosure of bank operating policies and procedures to the press, public-interest groups, and bank customers, the code also includes a section on what the bank's own employees are entitled to know about administration of the bank's compensation policies. Thus the bank will now disclose to employees, among other things, the following:

1. Criteria used in setting salary structures; information on the salary grade system and salary ranges within grades

2. Information on salary surveys, and policy on the competitiveness of salaries

3. Special compensation benefits and other programs available to employees; how employee benefit plans are funded

4. Compensation and benefit plans extended to U.S. employees stationed abroad

5. The number of overseas employees, including expatriates, third-country nationals, and local employees

6. Policy on extending credit to employees

OBSERVATIONS

Looking back on Bank of America's employee privacy initiatives during the past decade suggests some useful overall observations. The bank began these initiatives in 1968 by focusing on giving employees an opportunity to see their personnel records, if they wished to do so. In 1969–71, the same issue was further treated in terms of implementing the bank's new automated personnel data system, with the concept established that it would be good for insuring accuracy and timeliness to have employees review and update a printout of their basic employee profile once each year. In 1971, the bank ended its previous practice of buying investigative reports on job applicants. In 1973–74, the bank mounted a general review and reform of its policies for handling customer, employee, and third-party data. Finally, in 1976, the bank conducted its most extensive privacy review, a year-long internal survey of all data practices conducted by two full-time bank executives.

What is worth emphasizing is that this decade of policy reviews and new data practices was *not* a response to pressures from disgruntled employees or outside protest groups. Nor were the bank's privacy changes spurred on by litigation or government regulatory-agency orders.* The privacy reviews were basically *management* initiated. Partly, this was a result of the need to formulate clear policies for new automated personnel data systems. Partly, the bank sought to anticipate and solve any policy shortcomings *before* state or federal privacy legislation might force such measures, and to see from internal examination which proposed federal or state privacy laws to oppose publicly

---

*Because the Fair Credit Reporting Act of 1970 did not forbid the use of pre-employment reports, the bank's decision to eliminate these is not properly classified as compliance with outside legislation or regulation.

as unnecessary, unwise, or over-costly measures.

Anticipating outside regulation was especially important in the 1973–77 period. "Without the threat of congressional privacy bills like H.R. 1984 that would regulate the private sector, and similar bills in the California legislature," one bank executive commented to us, "I don't believe we would have taken all the time and spent all the money to look over our record-keeping practices. That just isn't the kind of thing that a busy, profitable enterprise does unless it thinks that it had better get its house in order before a storm may hit."

What was distinctive about Bank of America's approach to possible state of federal privacy laws regulating private industry was that it had tremendous resources to commit to such efforts; that it decided to solve the privacy problems, not dig defensive trenches against outside criticism; and that it did so essentially on its own—without linking its making internal reforms to similar actions being followed by other California banks or corporations, or to state and national banking associations.

Furthermore, since it carried out its reforms in application procedures, employee records, and access policies over almost a decade, the bank was able to pay the costs of such changes gradually, as part of its regular updating and revision of forms, creation of new automated files, training of managers, etc. "The costs of setting new privacy and employee access policies in the bank was quite bearable to us," one official commented.

Has all of this activity on employee privacy been of concern and importance to employees and executives at Bank of America? We did not do an employee survey to answer that question scientifically. However, in four site visits to various San Francisco offices and operating units of the bank running from 1970 to 1976, and conversations as recently as February of 1977, we found that employees and executives we talked with expressed a common satisfaction with these policies. One official in the legal department who conducted widespread interviews with bank employees on these matters explained it this way:

> Our employees want to know what is in their records. If you were to ask a cross-section of them, Does it matter to you that you can see your record if you wanted to? the great majority would say yes. They want to know anything that can affect their lives and careers, so it's not mere curiosity. Also, people today are more willing to speak out, they're not afraid of management. It's also tied to the rising general awareness of privacy issues, and when employers are being held to account in government, that reflects inside corporations. Americans of all kinds today want both government and private employers held to account for what

they decide about people. Our younger employees are the ones who are pushing most actively for such rights, but even the older ones have been affected by the general national climate.

However, Bank of America officials describe themselves as "essentially nonmissionary" with regard to their employee privacy policies. They are glad to tell other corporations what they have done, but they have not initiated a public-relations campaign to tell "their privacy story," as they *have* done with their Voluntary Disclosure Code. Bank executives say they would be glad to join industry association groups in defining model organizational behavior in this area.

Another important observation involves the relation of computer technology to privacy policies. When the bank first automated personnel data in 1970–71, the costs of converting data from eye-readable to machine-readable form, and of storing and accessing each bit of information, were so great that this provided a serendipitous protection to privacy. Each element of information had to prove its "worth," and such pressure for relevance helped prevent broad data collection in the computer files. Today, however, the costs of data conversion and storage have gone down so dramatically that they represent a minor constraint. "When we did the PDS system in 1972," one bank official observed, "we cut out items because of cost. Now, everything is so cheap that if we feel we need it, and it meets our privacy policies, we computerize it."

The comparisons between old and new employee information practices—given this profile's perspective that the new is an improvement on the old—may leave the cumulative impression that in the "olden" days, employees were beaten-down Bob Cratchits who were virtually chained to their desks, while under the new procedures a Nirvana of enlightenment has been achieved. Neither of these black and white perceptions is true, and a relatively brief profile does not allow enough room to highlight all the gray areas. For example, there are some employees who are still dissatisfied with what they regard as the bank's slow movement toward racial and sexual equality; who are dissatisfied with the bank's promotion and assignment policies because they rely too heavily on subjective supervisory endorsements; who are pushing for greater rights of access; who resent lingering regulation through local definition of dress requirements, financial disclosure requirements, and similar policies.

There are also some bank officers who view the bank's new access and privacy policies as consumerism and radicalism; who resent the abandonment of bank-wide standards governing appropriate dress and per-

sonal behavior; and who believe the bank should be affirmatively helpful, and not neutral, in response to requests for assistance from law
enforcement officers without legal process.

For those directing the bank's privacy policies, however, the present
approach seems to be just the right amount of innovation.

THE EQUITABLE LIFE ASSURANCE SOCIETY
PRIVACY PRINCIPLES

Office of The President

General Operating Policy No. <u>IV-5</u>

Subject: Privacy Principles **Date:** March 19, 1976

In recognition of the rights of all individuals, it will be our policy and practice to so conduct our business as to protect the rights and privacy of all our customers, Agents, and employees. We shall do this in ways that are reasonable and consistent with good business practices; with the rights of individuals as our ultimate guideline.

In the on-going pursuit of this principle, we shall:

1. Request and use only that personal information which is pertinent to the effective conduct of business.

2. Consider personal information collected and maintained to be of a confidential nature, recognizing our responsibility to provide adequate safeguards to maintain that confidentiality.

3. Refuse to make available, without the knowledge of the individual, personal information outside The Equitable or its subsidiaries, except to provide routine service or as required by law.

4. Make available to employees and Agents, upon proper request, any information we maintain on them; recognizing our obligation to protect the privacy of the source of the information.

5. Make available to policyowners and applicants, upon proper request, any information we maintain on them, recognizing our obligation to protect the privacy of the source of the information, and in the case of medical information, supplying that through the individual's designated physician.

6. Correct or delete any information found to be inaccurate, thus recognizing the importance of using timely and accurate information so that action adverse to an individual is not based on erroneous data.

7. Expect all employees and Agents to conform to our well-established ethical standards as to the confidentiality of personal information held by The Equitable.

The Problem of Employee Privacy Still Troubles Management

Alan F. Westin

The long-running public debate over the rights and rules governing employee privacy has lately taken the shape of a baffling paradox. More insistently than ever, the advocates dedicated to guarding this privacy are arguing the need for tougher action and legislation to support their cause. Yet at the same time, a great many business leaders are responding with equal conviction—and some bewilderment—that they cannot comprehend such agitation over what appears to them a cause already largely won. The consequent paradox turns on the fact that both sides in this dispute may, essentially, be quite right.

PUBLIC SUPPORT FOR NEW LAW

The champions of employee privacy can cite much evidence to support their call for new federal or state legislation to guarantee rights of confidentiality and access to files for 70 million Americans working in business establishments. They point to such persistent practices as the use of lie detectors for pre-employment screening in industries like trucking, pharmaceuticals, and food chains; the questioning of applicants about whether they have had psychiatric or psychological treatment; and the use of personality tests by some employers (including one large newspaper chain). They note the fears of professionals and executives that sensitive health information contained in claims filed with insurance carriers can make its way back to management to be used in promotion decisions. Hence, the time has come—so these critics say—to put employers under the rule of law on privacy matters.

There appears strong public support for these perceptions, moreover, in a major opinion survey on privacy released on May 3. Conducted by Louis Harris & Associates and sponsored by Sentry Insurance, this study showed that 62 percent of the public and 65 percent of employees want Congress to pass legislation regulating and defining the information that private employers can collect about individuals. Even larger percentages favor laws to give employees access to their files and to forbid employers to use lie detectors in hiring, or watch worker efficiency on closed-circuit television, or monitor employee conversations for personnel supervision.

The heads of many corporations profess astonishment at all this clamor. "My God," they are apt to exclaim, "there has never been a time when corporations are collecting *less* personal information about job applicants, or when so *much* confidentiality is observed." They go on to point to the employee-privacy programs voluntarily initiated by companies like IBM, Bank of America, Aetna Life & Casualty, and Cummins Engine. They also contend that most companies at the Fortune 500 level have recently adopted policies allowing employees to see their personnel files.

The defenders of business on this issue can draw considerable support from the Sentry Privacy Survey too, for 64 percent of the public and 69 percent of employees acknowledged that employers do limit their collection of personal information to what is really necessary, and 56 percent of the public and 57 percent of employees declared that employers are already doing enough to protect confidentiality. Among employees, 76 percent found it "not at all likely" that their employer has ever improperly released information from their personnel files. And overwhelming majorities of employees stated that they have never been turned down for a job or promotion because of information that was inaccurate (86 percent) or unfair (83 percent).

What, then, is the basis for the argument—and how can both sides be largely right? The answer is to be found, I believe, in the somewhat circuitous history of the evolution of policy on employee privacy over the last two decades.

In the 1950s and early 1960s, almost all American corporations engaged in practices that today would be considered improper by employees and the public. Most did use deep-probing selection interviews, psychological testing, investigative reporting, or lie detectors. Most managements did try to prescribe standards of dress, ideology, and lifestyle—even through "loyalty" tests and blacklists. Few employers let employees examine their personnel files—even while making the data therein available to law-enforcement officials or credit bureaus. On the whole, moreover, these practices were accepted by the general public's view of who was "entitled" to employment and advancement. The demands for equality had not yet taken hold, and employee privacy was virtually an unknown concept. Anyone who would not accept the employer's right to collect and use extensive personal information had only one remedy—to quit his job.

During the late 1960s and early 1970s this picture started to change significantly, as a few pioneering companies began to undertake new employee-privacy programs. These companies included IBM, Bank of America, Prudential Insurance, and Atlantic Richfield. Generally, these are corporations with a strong tradition of anticipative management, which pride themselves on foreseeing major social changes and instituting appropriate new policies before these might be required by law or regulation. Such corporate leadership realized that the complex social revolution of the sixties would require major changes in employee-information policies.

IBM CHANGED ITS WAYS

For IBM—as its chairman, Frank Cary, put it—this meant redefining for a new era just what IBM's traditional principle of "dignity of the individual employee" now meant. In a company famous before the 1960s for its white-shirt and dark-suit dress standard, and its company songbook, all the personal authority of IBM's chairman was needed to launch a new approach—especially since there were no laws requiring it and few guidelines to point the way.

The world's largest manufacturer of computers had, of course, special interests at stake here. IBM welcomed the chance to demonstrate that the growing data banks of personal information in use throughout the corporate world could be controlled by progressive rules on privacy. For this would help shift the general debate on privacy from wrongheaded attacks on "the machines" per se to a proper concentration on the social policies that govern how computers process information.

But by the mid-1970s, even after passage of the Equal Employment Opportunity Act, only a handful of the nation's 80,000 business establishments employing more than a hundred employees had adopted specific policies recognizing the rights of privacy. What has happened throughout business since the late 1960s, however, has been a spreading of awareness that new social attitudes about equal-employment opportunity required management to cut back sharply on the range of questions it could ask job applicants. Direct questions about race, religion, nationality (and, later, sex, age, and handicap) had to be eliminated—as well as questions about arrest-only records, since these incorporated potentially discriminatory standards into hiring. It also caused personality testing to be restricted sharply, since EEO required proof that such tests were truly job-related.

FILLING THE FILES AGAIN

Another force that had a "fallout" effect was the move of many large corporations to develop more refined personnel data systems. These were needed to handle such reporting duties as were required by EEO and to build up general "Human Resources Information Systems." Given the high costs of data conversion, storage, and transmission, the corporations' personnel officers were forced to reduce information on employees to what was really relevant and accurate enough to merit automation in centralized data systems.

While EEO and computerization were thus thinning out employee files, however, a host of record-keeping duties under new laws and the installation of corporate benefits programs were demanding ever-larger accumulations of sensitive data in company files. Federal regulations required race, sex, age, and handicap data on all employees, to document that there had been no discrimination. Statutes covering workmen's compensation, occupational health and safety, and employee pensions called for extensive personal records—as did new programs for health insurance, or alcohol and drug rehabilitation.

Spurred on by such developments, Congress in 1974 passed the Privacy Act, placing all federal agencies under a code of fair information and employment. At the same time, Congressmen Edward Koch (now mayor of New York) and Barry Goldwater, Jr. jarred the business community by proposing legislation (H.R. 1984) to put all the customer, client, and employee information practices of private business under standards even more closely regulated—and more costly to follow—than those of federal agencies.

Fortunately for business, the Privacy Act had created a Privacy Protection Study Commission that was directed to spend two years (1975–77) investigating what rules ought to be applied to the private sector. On the federal level, this assured a spell of watchful waiting. But action on the state level quickened when, in 1975, California adopted a law giving people in private employment the right to examine their personnel files. In the next two years, Maine and Oregon enacted similar laws.

Facing the prospect of onerous H.R. 1984–type bills in many state legislatures, more than fifty large companies began to formulate new employee-privacy programs in the years 1975–77. They recognized that a wide range of companies would be called to testify on their practices by the Privacy Protection Study Commission, and they knew that the voluntary policies of the pioneering companies seemed to be working effectively. Nonetheless, the overwhelming majority of companies were not yet convinced that the issue was important enough to justify the costs of cleaning up their personnel files or making major changes in hiring, evaluation, and promotion policies.

This sedentary posture was disturbed by the publication of the Privacy Protection Study Commission's report in July 1977. The commission made thirty-four recommendations to assure fair employment practices. These called for observing standards of propriety in the collection of information; increasing the accuracy and completeness of records; guarding confidentiality along need-to-know principles; giving employees access to their own records; and putting controls on the release of data outside the company.

The Privacy Commission cheered business leaders by advocating that most of its recommendations be adopted "by voluntary action." (The few exceptions were such areas as the use of polygraphs or arrest-record inquiries in pre-employment, where the commission favored outright bans.) The commission recognized the great diversity of employment environments and job qualifications, as well as the difficulty of determining the role of any record in personnel decisions. But it warned that a failure by employers to develop "a conscientious program" would mean that "a future commission or legislative bodies may have to consider compulsory measures." This voluntary approach was accepted by the Carter Administration in its recommendations sent to Congress last April. The only federal legislation proposed in the employment area was a limit on the use of lie detectors.

THE MICHIGAN FORMULA

The momentum for stricter legislation has nevertheless continued on the state level. In 1978, Michigan enacted a broad "Employee Right to Know" law. Covering all enterprises with four or more employees, this law grants employees the right to see any information in their personnel files (with a few exceptions) used "in determining employment, promotion, transfer, additional compensation, or disciplinary action." Employees have the right to put in their files a written rebuttal of any information felt to be incorrect or unfair. The law also prohibits employers from including in personnel files any information relating to an individual's associations, political activities, publications, or communications on non-employment activities, unless the employee gives written permission. The employer is also required to give his employees written notification whenever disciplinary reports or letters of reprimand are disclosed to a third party, unless the employee waives this requirement. Any derogatory information more than four years old may not be sent to third parties. No state agency is charged with administering the law, but an employee can sue to recover actual damages, a $200 penalty, court costs, and "reasonable attorney's fees."

With the commission's 1977 blueprint as a guide—and with leading business groups urging voluntary action—perhaps as many as two-thirds of the Fortune 500 industrials have issued, or are now writing, new employee-privacy rules. Yet far from these rules satisfying employee concerns, there is stronger demand than ever for protective state or federal legislation. Are we to conclude that this reflects the critics' belief that only legal rules can carry out the Privacy Commission's recommendations? Or is this a classic "regulatory versus voluntary" conflict at work?

MORE THAN COSMETICS

It first might be noted that even if *all* the Fortune 500 industrial firms and their large, nonindustrial counterparts were assumed to have privacy policies, this would cover only 20 million out of the 70 million employees working for business firms. Many students of personnel administration argue that it is precisely the medium- and smaller-sized firms *outside* the Fortune 500 mold that are slowest to recognize the rights defined by the Privacy Commission.

The issue turns on not only the quantity but also the quality of employee-privacy programs. Much of what is being promulgated might be called "privacy boiler plate"—some splendid but vague declarations of intent or a numbingly detailed code of procedure that contributes little to fair information practices. But honest employee-privacy policies require a humanistic approach to personnel administration, not just a cosmetic brushup.

What it takes to make these programs work became clearly apparent in 1978, when executives from eleven companies analyzed aspects of their programs at the First National Seminar on Individual Rights in the Corporation. The participants were Aetna Life & Casualty, American Telephone & Telegraph, Atlantic Richfield, Control Data, CPC International, Cummins Engine, Du Pont, IBM, Prudential Insurance, Standard Oil (Indiana), and TRW. These companies maintained that their programs had not crippled good personnel management. They had found, in fact, that the opening of personnel files to employees—far from making supervisors less candid in their appraisals—had helped to sharpen management judgment.

The companies also shared four other key conclusions. First, that truly fair information practices call for an open process, in which employees share to the greatest extent possible the facts on just how decisions about people are really made. Second, that a clear definition of merit and demonstration of equitable treatment are vital to the credibility of management. Third, that organizations must provide explicit mechanisms for fair procedure, making plain what information is used to make decisions. Finally, all company policies, from the organization of work to handling of employee discipline, must take into account every employee's need for self-expression and individual dignity. Without such a spirit animating management, all privacy policies are mere exercises in bureaucracy, where the letter killeth.

These principles do not mean that there is one perfect set of privacy policies and procedures apt for every company. Each business has its own requirements and traditions. The applying of fair practices must follow from sensitive designing, not buying "off-the-shelf" guidelines. What really matters is not the details but the overall spirit of a privacy program. As with other areas of employee rights, the test is not the text of an employee handbook but the perceptiveness and sensitivity of personnel administration.

In this spirit, I would reject any "full code" model of regulation, either federal or state, to specify what information was appropriate to collect and use in employment, or to prescribe the use of personal data inside or outside the company. Such a detailed code would be rigid and costly. By extending regulatory-agency or judicial intervention into the delicate choice-making of personnel administration, it could not only warp responsible employment policies; it might also poorly serve employee interests, with managements complying with the letter of regulations but not moving any closer to a humanistic style of corporate performance.

And yet—the purely voluntary procedures do not seem to me to suffice. I worry, for example, that more than a third of the business employers on the Fortune 1,000 list sampled in the Sentry Study acknowledged that they did *not* want to be "pioneers" in new employee-privacy protections. Instead, they agreed with the statement, "We want to wait until laws are passed that define what is proper . . . and we would then comply as good citizens."

FOR FUTURE DECISION

In these circumstances, I think it reasonable to argue for a "minimum-rights" legislative approach with remedies by individual lawsuit. This would give every employee the right to examine his or her personnel data, in situations as defined by the Michigan law. It would also set rules to govern release of employee data outside the firm, much as Michigan does. I would also favor outlawing completely certain specific practices, such as the use of polygraphs and Psychological Stress Evaluators in hiring. Yet I would not attempt otherwise to specify or regulate what types of information to collect for effective personnel administration.

Such an approach reserves for voluntary action those areas where differences of function, organization, and style matter most in the selection of personnel. But it also makes open and clear—to employee and public alike—the facts on just what is being collected by employers and how it is being used. This would allow American society to decide—three or five years from now—whether business's response has been good enough or whether additional laws may be needed. And this seems both a just balance and a fair test.

STATE OF NEW YORK ACT TO
AMEND THE LABOR LAW

STATE OF NEW YORK

6140

1977–1978 Regular Sessions

IN ASSEMBLY
March 1, 1977

Introduced by M. of A. POSNER—read once and referred to the
Committee on Labor

**AN ACT to amend the labor law, in relation to the prohibition of
psychological stress evaluator examinations**

*The People of the State of New York, represented in Senate and Assembly,
do enact as follows:*

Section 1. The labor law is hereby amended by adding thereto a new
article, to be article twenty-B, to read as follows:

ARTICLE 20-B

PSYCHOLOGICAL STRESS EVALUATORS AND EMPLOYMENT

Section 733. Definitions.

734. Practitioner limitations.

735. Employer limitations.

736. Employee rights in related proceedings.

737. Supplemental provisions.

738. Actions for damages.

739. Applicability of article.

§ *733. Definitions. As used in this article:*

*1. "Employer" means any individual, person, corporation, department,
board, bureau, agency, commission, division, office, council or committee
of the state government, public benefit corporation, public authority or
political subdivision of the state, or other business entity, which employs
or seeks to employ an individual or individuals. All provisions of this article
pertaining to employers shall apply in equal force and effect to their agents
and representatives.*

2. "Employee" means an individual employed by an employer.

*3. "Prospective employee" means an individual seeking or being sought
for employment with an employer.*

*4. "Psychological stress evaluator" means any mechanical device or
instrument which purports to determine the truth or falsity of statements*

EXPLANATION—Matter in *italics* is new; matter in brackets [ ] is old law to be omitted.

made by an employee or prospective employee on the basis of vocal fluctuations or vocal stress.

5. *"Psychological stress evaluator examination" means:*

(a) the questioning or interviewing of an employee or prospective employee for the purpose of subjecting the statements of such employee or prospective employee to analysis by a psychological stress evaluator.

(b) the recording of statements made by an employee or prospective employee for the purpose of subjecting such statements to analysis by a psychological stress evaluator; or

(c) analyzing, with a psychological stress evaluator, statements made by an employee or prospective employee for the purpose of determining the truth or falsity of such statements.

§ 734. Practitioner limitations. 1. It shall be unlawful for any individual to knowingly administer or participate in the administration of a psychological stress evaluator examination of an employee or prospective employee as defined in section seven hundred thirty-three of this chapter.

2. Any individual violating any of the provisions of this section shall be guilty of a class B misdemeanor upon the first conviction and upon any subsequent convictions shall be guilty of a class A misdemeanor.

§ 735. Employer limitations. 1. No employer or his agent shall require, request, suggest or knowingly permit any employee or prospective employee of such employer to submit to a psychological stress evaluator examination and no employer shall administer or utilize the results of such test within or without the state of New York for any reason whatsoever.

2. A violation of any of the provisions of this section shall be a class B misdemeanor upon the first conviction and upon any subsequent conviction a class A misdemeanor.

§ 736. Employee rights in related proceedings. No employee shall be discharged, disciplined or discriminated against in any manner for filing a complaint or testifying in any proceeding or action involving violations of the provisions of this article. Any employee discriminated against in violation of the provisions of this section shall be compensated by his employer for double the amount of any loss of wages and benefits arising out of such discrimination and shall be restored to his previous position of employment.

§ 737. Supplemental provisions. No individual shall administer or participate in the administration of a psychological stress examination within the state to any individual seeking employment outside the state of New York or for the purpose of continuing employment outside the state of New York. Any individual violating the provisions of this section shall be guilty of a class B misdemeanor upon first conviction and upon any subsequent convictions shall be guilty of a class A misdemeanor.

§ 738. Actions for damages. Any employee or prospective employee damaged as the result of a violation of any of the provisions of this article shall be entitled to file an action for damages in the supreme court of this state.

§ 739. Applicability of article. This article shall only apply to employee and prospective employee-employer relations.

§ 2. This act shall take effect one hundred eighty days after it shall have become a law.

STATE OF MAINE ACT TO PERMIT AN EMPLOYEE TO REVIEW HIS PERSONNEL FILE

FIRST SPECIAL SESSION

ONE HUNDRED AND SEVENTH LEGISLATURE

Legislative Document   **No. 2270**

H. P. 2121   House of Representatives, February 27, 1976
Reported by Mr. Faucher from the Committee on Legal Affairs pursuant to H. P. 1597 and printed under Joint Rules No. 3.

EDWIN H. PERT, Clerk

Filed under Joint Rule 3 pursuant to H. P. 1597.

STATE OF MAINE

IN THE YEAR OF OUR LORD NINETEEN HUNDRED SEVENTY-SIX

AN ACT to Permit an Employee to Review His Personnel File.

Be it enacted by the People of the State of Maine, as follows:

Sec. 1. 5 MRSA § 638 is enacted to read:

§ 638. Employee right to review personnel file

The director shall, upon written request of an employee, make available to that employee during his normal working hours his personnel file if the director has a personnel file for that employee. For the purposes of this section, a personnel file shall include, but not be limited to, any formal or informal employee evaluations and reports relating to the employee's character, credit, work habits and compensation and benefits which the director has in his possession.

Sec. 2. 26 MRSA § 631 is enacted to read:

§ 631. Employee right to review personnel file

The employer shall, upon written request of an employee make available to that employee during his normal working hours, his personnel file if the employer has a personnel file for that employee. For the purposes of this section, a personnel file shall include, but not be limited to, any formal or informal employee evaluations and reports relating to the employee's character, credit, work habits and compensation and benefits which the employer has in his possession.

Sec. 3. 30 MRSA § 64 is enacted to read:

§ 64. Employee right to review personnel file

The county commissioner shall, upon written request of an employee, make available to that employee during his normal working hours, his personnel file if the county commissioner has a personnel file for that employee. For the purposes of this section, a personnel file shall include, but not be limited to, any formal or informal employee evaluations and reports relating to the employee's character, credit, work habits and compensation and benefits which the county commissioner has in his possession.

Sec. 4. 30 MRSA § 2257 is enacted to read:

§ 2257. Employee right to review personnel file

The municipal officer shall, upon written request of an employee, make available to that employee during his normal working hours his personnel file if the municipal officer has a personnel file for that employee. For the purposes of this section, a personnel file shall include, but not be limited to, any formal or informal employee evaluations and reports relating to the employee's character, credit, work habits and compensation, and benefits which the municipal officer has in his possession.

STATEMENT OF FACT

This bill resulted from the Joint Standing Committee on Legal Affairs' study of record keeping, H. P. 1597. It will provide an employee, in both the public and private sector, with the right to review his personnel file.

The Privacy Commission Recommendations on Employee Access

FAIRNESS IN USE

Access to Records

Fairness demands that an applicant or employee be permitted to see and copy records an employer maintains about him. Allowing an employee to see and copy his records can be as advantageous to the employer as to the employee. As discussed earlier, employment records in the private sector are generally regarded as the property of management.[1] Except where limited by state statute, as in Maine[2] and California,[3] or where controlled by collective-bargaining agreements, all the rights of ownership in employment records vest in the employer. Although many firms permit, and some even encourage, employees to review at least some of the records kept about them, there is no generally accepted rule.[4] Where records are factual, e.g., benefit and payroll records, or where they are the sole basis for making a decision about an individual, such as in a seniority system, the advantages of employee access to assure accuracy are rarely disputed. However, many employers do not give their employees access to promotion tables, salary schedules, and test scores. Some employers believe that employee access to information may weaken their position when they are potentially in an adversary relationship with an employee, e.g., in a dispute regarding a claim for benefits. Most employers do not want employees to have access to information they believe requires professional interpretation, such as medical records and psychological tests. In addition, employers are reluctant to give employees access to information supplied by sources requesting an assurance of confidentiality. While testimony before the Commission suggests that this last problem is diminishing as reliance on references diminishes,[5] in the academic community, where candi-

Excerpted from the Report of the Privacy Protection Study Commission, July 1977, U.S. Government Printing Office.

dates for tenure are traditionally evaluated by unidentified peers, concern about access to letters of references is great.[6]

Although union contracts rarely address the access issue, where formal grievances are filed, the records supporting management's decisions must, by law, be shared with the union and with the grievant. Also, certain information, such as seniority, salary, and leave, must be posted.[7] Unions have won access to particular records in specific circumstances by arbitration, and even where there is no union some employers have grievance and arbitration procedures. Without a union, however, employees who complain of violations of an internal policy on employee access to records have little protection from reprisals and no right of appeal if their complaints are ignored.

Furthermore, a right to see, copy, and request correction or amendment of an employment record is of little value, so long as an employer is free to designate which records will be accessible and to determine the merits of any dispute over accessibility or record content. Nonetheless, a well-considered access policy, consistently carried out, is strong evidence of an employer's commitment to fair practice protections for personal privacy. Such a policy gives an employee a way to know what is in records kept about him, to assure that they are factually accurate, and to make reasoned decisions about authorizing their disclosure outside the employing organization.

While recognizing that periodic evaluations of employee performance contain subjective information developed by the employer for its own use, the Commission believes that employees should have a right of access to those records also. Many employers do, in fact, share performance evaluations with their employees, as guidance on how to improve performance is generally regarded as one of the more important functions of these evaluations.[8] The employee's interest in these records is obvious, since negative evaluations can deny an employee opportunities for promotion or placement. They may also disqualify him from entering the pool of employees from which such selections are made. Furthermore, records pertaining to employee performance are usually maintained in individually identifiable form and could be disclosed in that form to outside requestors.

When it comes to evaluations of an employee's *potential,* however, the testimony suggests that the resulting records frequently are not shared with employees.[9] The Commission finds it difficult to justify the difference in treatment. Performance evaluations and evaluations of potential are intimately related. Moreover, where an employee does not have access to both, supervisors can evaluate an employee one way to his face and another way behind his back, so to speak, making it impossible for him to assess his standing.

The Commission recognizes a valid difference between performance and potential evaluations when a separate set of records pertains to employees thought to have a *high potential* for advancement. Since such records are mainly a long-range planning tool of management, employees should not necessarily have a right to see and copy them, whether or not they are maintained in individually identifiable form. The mere existence of such records, however, should not be kept secret from employees.

Another type of evaluation record an employer might justifiably withhold from an employee is the security record concerning an ongoing or concluded investigation into suspected employee misconduct. Although employees have a right to know that their employer maintains security records, a general right to see, copy, and request correction of such records would seriously handicap security investigations. Nonetheless, as the Commission contends later in this chapter, access should be allowed to any information from a security record that is transferred to an individual's personnel file.

The Commission strongly believes that employees should be able to see and copy most employment records. If an individual cannot conveniently do this in person, he should be able to arrange to do so by mail or telephone, provided the employer takes reasonable care to assure itself of the identity of the requestor. Nonetheless, as the Commission has already emphasized, to legislate a right of access to records without a more general scheme of rights to protect the employee who exercises it could be futile. When the employee-employer relationship is defined by collective bargaining, access to records is an obvious topic for contract negotiation and the resulting provisions would then be binding on the parties. When, however, employee access rights are not defined by contract, or enforceable by a government agency with rule-making powers, individual employees are in a poor position to resist their employer's refusal to honor their access and correction rights. As indicated earlier, there were differences within the Commission as to whether such a right need be a right without a remedy, and thus a right that should not be legislated. Recognizing that employers have discretion to determine which records they will make available to their employees, the Commission believes that employers should develop and promulgate access and correction policies voluntarily. Accordingly, the Commission recommends:

Recommendation (17):

That as a matter of policy an employer should

(a) designate clearly:

    (i)   those records about an employee, former employee, or applicant for employment (including any individual who is being considered for employment but who has not formally applied) which the employer will allow such employee, former employee, or applicant to see and copy on request; and

    (ii) those records about an employee, former employee, or applicant which the employer will not make available to the employee, former employee, or applicant,

except that an employer should not designate as an unavailable record any recorded evaluation it makes of an individual's employment performance, any medical record or insurance record it keeps about an individual, or any record about an individual that it obtains from a consumer-reporting agency (as defined by the Fair Credit Reporting Act), or otherwise creates about an individual in the course of an investigation related to an employment decision not involving suspicion of wrongdoing;

(b) assure that its employees are informed as to which records are included in categories (a)(i) and (ii) above; and

(c) upon request by an individual applicant, employee, or former employee:

    (i)   inform the individual, after verifying his identity, whether it has any recorded information pertaining to him that is designated as records he may see and copy; and

    (ii) permit the individual to see and copy any such record(s), either in person or by mail; or

    (iii) apprise the individual of the nature and substance of any such record(s) by telephone; and

    (iv) permit the individual to use one or the other of the methods of access provided in (c)(ii) and (iii), or both if he prefers,

except that the employer could refuse to permit the individual to see and copy any record it has designated as an unavailable record pursuant to (a)(ii), above.

Access to Investigative Reports

The Fair Credit Reporting Act requirement that an employer notify an individual when information in an investigative report that was the basis for an adverse employment decision about him is inadequate. That an individual, so notified, can go to the investigative-reporting agency that made the report and demand to know what information is in it gives him some protection. [*15 U.S.C. 1681h*] The Commission believes, however, that in employment, as in insurance, the subject of an investigative report should have an affirmative right to see and copy it, and to correct, amend, or dispute its contents. When corrections, amendments, or dispute statements are entered into a report by an employer, it should so inform the investigative-reporting agency so that its records may also be altered. Finally, it is important for an individual to be notified in advance of his right to see, copy, correct, amend, or dispute a proposed report, and of the procedures for so doing.

The Commission's recommendations in Chapter 5 [of the *Report*] on the insurance relationship specify that the subject of an investigation has a right to see and copy, in two places, the report prepared by a support organization in connection with an underwriting investigation: at the office of the insurer that ordered it, and at the office of the firm that prepared it. Hence, the Commission does not recommend that the insurer or investigative agency routinely provide the individual with a copy of the report, either before or after using it to make a decision about him. To do so would be costly because of the volume of reports insurers order, many of which do not result in adverse decisions, and because *Insurance Recommendation (13)* on adverse underwriting decisions, would immediately expose a report that did result in such a decision.

In the employment context, however, several considerations urge a different approach. First, all the evidence available to the Commission indicates that there are far fewer investigative reports prepared on job applicants and employees than on insurance applicants.[10] Second, the Commission's recommendations on employment records provide no guarantee that an employee will be able to see and copy an investigative report on himself that remains in an employer's files after he is hired, even though the report could become the basis for an adverse action in the future. Third, while the Commission considered tying a see-and-copy right to the making of an adverse employment decision, it rejected the proposal because the relationship between items of information and employment decisions is not always clear enough to make such a right meaningful. Fourth, it seemed to the Commission that for a rejected applicant to exercise a see-and-copy right would be awkward at best.

Hence, to balance an employer's legitimate need to collect information on applicants and employees through background checks against the procedural protections needed to insure fairness to the individual in making such investigations and using the information so acquired, the Commission recommends:

Recommendation (18):

That the Fair Credit Reporting Act be amended to provide:

(a) that an applicant or employee shall have a right to:

(i)   see and copy information in an investigative report maintained either by a consumer-reporting agency (as defined by the Fair Credit Reporting Act) or by the employer that requested it; and

(ii) correct, amend (including supplement), or dispute in writing, any information in an investigative report maintained either by a consumer-reporting agency (as defined by the Fair Credit Reporting Act) or by the employer that requested it;

(b) that an employer must automatically inform a consumer-reporting agency (as defined by the Fair Credit Reporting Act) of any correction or amendment of information made in an investigative report at the request of the individual, or any other dispute statement made in writing by the individual; and

(c) that an employer must provide an applicant or employee on whom an investigative report is made with a copy of that report at the time it is made by or given to the employer.

Access to Medical Records

The medical records an employer maintains differ significantly in character and use from the other records created in the employee-employer relationship. Responsibility for giving physical examinations to determine possible work restrictions and for serving as primary medical-care providers is falling ever more heavily on employers, giving them increasingly extensive medical files on their employees. These records, and opinions based on them, may enter into employment decisions, as well as into other types of non-medical decisions about applicants and employees. Hence, the Commission believes that access to them should be provided in accordance with the Commission's recommendations on medical records and medical-record information in Chapter 7. That is, *when an employer's relationship to an applicant, employee, or former employee is that of a medical-care provider,* [11] the Commission recommends:

Recommendation (19):

That, upon request, an individual who is the subject of a medical record maintained by an employer, or another responsible person designated by the individual, be allowed to have access to that medical record, including an opportunity to see and copy it. The employer should be able to charge a reasonable fee (not to exceed the amount charged to third parties) for preparing and copying the record.

However, when the employer's relationship to an applicant, employee, or former employee is *not that of a medical-care provider,* the Commission recommends:

Recommendation (20):

That, upon request, an individual who is the subject of medical-record information maintained by an employer be allowed to have access to that information either directly or through a licensed medical professional designated by the individual.

In Chapter 7, where the rationale for these recommendations is presented in detail, "medical-record information" is defined as:

Information relating to an individual's medical history, diagnosis, condition, treatment, or evaluation obtained from a medical-care provider or from the individual himself or from his spouse, parent, or guardian, for the purpose of making a non-medical decision about the individual.

As to *Recommendation (19)*, the Commission would urge that if a state enacts a statute creating individual rights of access to medical records pursuant to *Recommendation (2)* in Chapter 7, it encompass within the statute medical records maintained by an employer whose relationship to applicants, employees, or former employees is that of a medical-care provider.

Access to Insurance Records

In their role as providers or administrators of insurance plans, employers maintain insurance records on employees and former employees and their dependents. Since the considerations governing access to these records are largely the same as when the records are maintained by an insurance company, the Commission believes that employer policy on access to them by the individuals to whom they pertain should be consistent with the recommendation on access in Chapter 5 [of the *Report*]. Accordingly, the Commission recommends:

Recommendation (21):

That an employer that acts as a provider or administrator of an insurance plan, upon request by an applicant, employee, or former employee should:

(a) **inform the individual, after verifying his identity, whether it has any recorded information about him that pertains to the employee's insurance relationship with him;**
(b) **permit the individual to see and copy any such recorded information, either in person or by mail; or**
(c) **apprise the individual of the nature and substance of any such recorded information by telephone; and**
(d) **permit the individual to use whichever of the methods of access provided in (b) and (c) he prefers.**

The employer should be able to charge a reasonable copying fee for any copies provided to the individual. Any such recorded information should be made available to the individual, but need not contain the name or other identifying particulars of any source (other than an institutional source) of information in the record who has provided such information on the condition that his or her identity not be revealed, and need not reveal a confidential numerical code.

It should be noted that this recommendation as it would apply to insurance institutions (see Chapter 5) would not apply to any record about an individual compiled in reasonable anticipation of a civil or criminal action, or for use in settling a claim while the claim remains unsettled. After the claim is settled, the recommendation would not apply to any record compiled in relation to a third-party claimant (i.e., a claimant who is not an insured, policy owner, or principal insured), except as to any portion of such a record which is disseminated or used for a purpose unrelated to processing the claim.

Inasmuch as this recommendation and *Recommendation (25)*, below, are proposed for voluntary adoption by employers, it should be noted that there is a gap in the Commission's recommendations regarding records generated in the insurance relationship (Chapter 5) and that it may affect a substantial number of individuals, given the proportion of the work force currently insured under employer-provided or employer-administered group plans. Thus, while the Commission hopes that employers will voluntarily adopt *Recommendations (21)* and *(25)*, it also hopes that because their adoption must be voluntary, employers will not seize on self-administered insurance plans as a way of avoiding the statutory access and correction requirements recommended for insurance records in Chapter 5.

As to medical-record information maintained by an employer as a consequence of its insurance relationship with an individual employee or former employee, the Commission's intention is that *Recommendation (20)* apply.

Correction of Records

Any employee who has reason to question the accuracy, timeliness, or completeness of records his employer keeps about him should be able to correct or amend those records. Furthermore, the procedures for correcting or amending employment records should conform to those recommended in other chapters of this report. For example, when an individual requests correction or amendment of a record, the employer should notify persons or organizations to whom the erroneous, obsolete, or incomplete information has been disclosed within the previous two years, if the individual so requests. When the information came from a consumer-reporting agency (as defined by the Fair Credit Reporting Act), any corrections should routinely be passed on to that agency so that its records on an applicant or employee will also be accurate. When the employer rejects the requested correction or amendment, fairness demands that the employer incorporate the employee's statement of dispute into the record and pass it along to those to whom the employer subsequently discloses the disputed information, as well as to those who need to know the information is disputed in order to protect the individual from unfair decisions being made on the basis of it. Moreover, if an employer attempts to verify allegedly erroneous, obsolete, or incomplete information in a record, it should limit its investigation to the particular items in dispute.

The Commission does not intend that the correction or amendment procedures alter any existing retention periods for records or require employers to keep an accounting of every disclosure made to a third party. However, when an employer does keep an accounting of disclosures to third parties, for whatever purpose, it should let an employee use it in deciding to whom corrections, amendments, or dispute statements should be forwarded. Accordingly, the Commission recommends:

Recommendation (22):

That, except for a medical record or an insurance record, or any record designated by an employer as an unavailable record, an employer should voluntarily permit an individual employee, former employee, or applicant to request correction or amendment of a record pertaining to him; and

(a) within a reasonable period of time correct or amend (including supplement) any portion thereof which the individual reasonably believes is not accurate, timely, or complete; and

(b) furnish the correction or amendment to any person or organization specifically designated by the individual who may have, within two years prior thereto, received any such information; and, automatically to any consumer-reporting agency (as defined by the Fair Credit Reporting Act) that furnished the information corrected or amended; *or*

(c) inform the individual of its refusal to correct or amend the record in accordance with his request and of the reason(s) for the refusal; and

   (i) permit an individual who disagrees with the refusal to correct or amend the record to have placed on or with the record a concise statement setting forth the reasons for his disagreement;

   (ii) in any subsequent disclosure outside the employing organization containing information about which the individual has filed a statement of dispute, clearly note any portion of the record which is disputed, and provide a copy of the statement along with the information being disclosed; and

(iii) furnish the statement to any person or organization specifically designated by the individual who may have, within two years prior thereto, received any such information; and, automatically, to any consumer-reporting agency (as defined by the Fair Credit Reporting Act) that furnished the disputed information; and

(d) limit its reinvestigation of disputed information to those record items in dispute.

The procedures for correcting and amending insurance and medical records which the Commission recommends in Chapters 5 and 7 [of the *Report*] should be voluntarily adopted by employers who maintain such records. Thus, with respect to a medical record maintained by an employer whose relationship to an employee is that of a medical-care provider, the Commission recommends:

Recommendation (23):

That an employer establish a procedure whereby an individual who is the subject of a medical record maintained by the employer can request correction or amendment of the record. When the individual requests correction or amendment, the employer should, within a reasonable period of time, either:

(a) make the correction or amendment requested, or

(b) inform the individual of its refusal to do so, the reason for the refusal, and of the procedure, if any, for further review of the refusal.

In addition, if the employer decides that it will not correct or amend a record in accordance with the individual's request, the employer should permit the individual to file a concise statement of the reasons for the disagreement, and in any subsequent disclosure of the disputed information include a notation that the information is disputed and the statement of disagreement. In any such disclosure, the employer may also include a statement of the reasons for not making the requested correction or amendment.

Finally, when an employer corrects or amends a record pursuant to an individual's request, or accepts a notation of dispute and statement of disagreement, it should furnish the correction, amendment, or statement of disagreement to any person specifically designated by the individual to whom the employer has previously disclosed the inaccurate, incomplete, or disputed information.

As with *Recommendation (19),* the Commission would urge that if a state enacts a statute creating individual rights regarding the correction of medical records pursuant to *Recommendation (2)* in Chapter 7, it encompass within the statute medical records maintained by an employer whose relationship to applicants, employees, or former employees is that of a medical-care provider.

In addition, when an employer maintains medical-record information about an individual applicant, employee, or former employee, the Commission recommends:

Recommendation (24):

That notwithstanding *Recommendation (22),* when an individual who is the subject of medical-record information maintained by an employer requests correction or amendment of such information, the employer should:

(a) disclose to the individual, or to a medical professional designated by him, the identity of the medical-care provider who was the source of the medical-record information;

(b) make the correction or amendment requested within a reasonable period of time, if the medical-care provider who was the source of the information agrees that it is inaccurate or incomplete; and

(c) establish a procedure whereby an individual who is the subject of medical-record information maintained by an employer, and who believes that the information is incorrect or incomplete, would be provided an opportunity to present supplemental information of a limited nature for inclusion in the medical-record information maintained by the employer, provided that the source of the supplemental information is also included.

Although *Recommendations (22), (23),* and *(24)* appear complex, they contain only two key requirements:

1. that an individual have a way of correcting, amending, or disputing information in a record about himself; and

2. that the employer to whom the request for correction or amendment is made shall have an obligation to propagate the resulting correction, amendment, or statement of dispute in any subsequent disclosure it makes of the information to certain prior or subsequent recipients.

Finally, with respect to the correction or amendment of insurance records maintained by an employer, the Commission recommends:

Recommendation (25):

That when an employer acts as a provider or administrator of an insurance plan, the employer should:

(a) permit an individual to request correction or amendment of a record pertaining to him;

(b) within a reasonable period of time, correct or amend (including supplement) any portion thereof which the individual reasonably believes is not accurate, timely, or complete;

(c) furnish the correction or amendment to any person or organization specifically designated by the individual who may have, within two years prior thereto, received any such information; and, automatically, to any insurance-support organization whose primary source of information on individuals is insurance institutions when the support organization has systematically received any such information from the employer within the preceding seven years, unless the support organization no longer maintains the information, in which case, furnishing the correction or amendment would not be necessary; and, automatically, to any insurance-support organization that furnished the information corrected or amended; *or*

(d) inform the individual of its refusal to correct or amend the record in accordance with his request and of the reason(s) for the refusal; and

   (i) permit an individual who disagrees with the refusal to correct or amend the record to have placed on or with the record a concise statement setting forth the reasons for his disagreement;

   (ii) in any subsequent disclosure outside the employing organization containing information about which the individual has filed a statement of dispute, clearly note any portion of the record which is disputed and provide a copy of the statement along with the information being disclosed; and

   (iii) furnish the statement to any person or organization specifically designated by the individual who may have, within two years prior thereto, received any such information; and, automatically to an insurance-support organization whose primary source of information on individuals is insurance institutions when the support organization has received any such information from the employer within the preceding seven years, unless the support organization no longer maintains the information, in which case, furnishing the statement would not be necessary; and, automatically, to any insurance-support organization that furnished the disputed information; and

(e) limit its reinvestigation of disputed information to those record items in dispute.

FAIRNESS IN INTERNAL DISCLOSURES ACROSS RELATIONSHIPS

Just as fairness must be a concern of employers when gathering information from external sources, they have a duty to see that information generated within the several discrete relationships subsumed under the broad employee-employer relationship is not shared within the employing organization in ways that are unfair to the individual employee.

As a rule, employers large enough to have separate functional units for personnel, security, insurance, and medical-care operations have voluntarily taken steps to assure that the records each of these units generates are maintained separately and not used improperly. The biggest problems are in small organizations that cannot realistically segregate record-keeping functions. Another potential problem is the impact of technology which could make retrieval of information stored in a common data base by unauthorized persons easier than is currently the case.

Personnel and Payroll Records

As personnel planning and management systems have become more elaborate, so have the personnel files and payroll records an employer keeps on its employees. This is not to say that all employees expect personnel and payroll records to be held in confidence within the employing organization. Some may not; but out of consideration for those who do, the Commission believes that an employer should limit the use of personnel and payroll record information to whatever is necessary to fulfill particular functions. Therefore, the Commission recommends:

Recommendation (26):

That an employer assure that the personnel and payroll records it maintains are available internally only to authorized users and on a need-to-know basis.

Security Records

Security records differ from personnel records in that they frequently must be created without the employee's knowledge. Sometimes the information in them is inconclusive; sometimes the problem that precipitated the security record is not quickly resolved. Nonetheless, an employer may have to keep security records in order to safeguard the workplace or corporate assets. As a rule, employers document any action resulting from security investigations in the individual's personnel file, but do not include the details leading up to the action.[12]

Security departments usually work with personnel departments in the course of investigating incidents involving employees.[13] When the security function is separate from the personnel department, however, security records are generally not available to management and are frequently, though not always, filed by incident rather than by name, at least until the case is resolved.[14] Since security records maintained apart from personnel records can have little impact on personnel decisions about an employee, and since employee access to security records could substantially hamper ligitimate security investigations, allowing the employee to see and copy them while they are being maintained as security records seems hard to justify. If, however, information in the security record of an employee is to be used for other purposes, such as discipline, termination, promotion, or evaluation, fairness demands that the employee have direct access to it. Thus, the Commission, again taking the voluntary approach, recommends:

Recommendation (27):

That an employer:

(a) maintain security records apart from other records; and
(b) inform an employee whenever information from a security record is trans-
    ferred to his personnel record.

Medical Records and Medical-Record Information

As indicated earlier, an employer may maintain both medical-record
information and medical records: the former as a consequence of requiring it as a condition of employment, placement, or certification to
return to work; the latter as a consequence of providing various forms
of medical care, including routine physicals. However collected, there
is a case for requiring employers to restrict the circulation of medical
records and medical-record information outside the medical department. Corporate physicians are sincerely concerned about possible
misuses of the records they maintain. No matter how hard they may
strive to be independent of the employing organization their allegiance
is ultimately to the employer.

Many large employers have procedures that guarantee the confidentiality of medical-record information in all but the most extreme circumstances; and many corporate medical departments only make
recommendations for work restrictions, carefully refraining from passing on any diagnosis or treatment details in all but the most extreme
circumstances.[15] Nevertheless, it is the duty of the corporate physician
to tell his employer when he finds in an individual a condition that
could negatively affect the interests of the employer or other employees.[16] Furthermore, employers rely on corporate physicians for
evaluation of an applicant or employee's health in making hiring and
placement decisions. A further complication arises if, as often happens,
the corporate physician also provides regular medical care for employees outside of the employment context, perhaps functioning as the
family doctor.

An employee availing himself of medical services offered by his employer does so at some risk to the traditional confidential relationship
between physician and patient, unless great care is taken to insulate that
relationship from the usual work-related responsibilities of the medical
department. Thus, when a medical department provides voluntary
physicals or routine medical care for employees, the resulting records
should be maintained separately from the records generated by work-
related contacts and should never be used to make work-related deci-

sions. This is a difficult policy to enforce and can work only where management understands and respects the need to separate the compulsory and voluntary functions of the medical department. Thus, the Commission recommends:

Recommendation (28):

That an employer that maintains an employment-related medical record about an individual assure that no diagnostic or treatment information in any such record is made available for use in any employment decision; and

Recommendation (29):

That an employer that provides a voluntary health-care program for its employees assure that any medical record generated by the program is maintained apart from any employment-related medical record and not used by any physician in advising on any employment-related decision or in making any employment-related decision without the express authorization of the individual to whom the record pertains.

Insurance Records

Insurance claims records often contain information about medical diagnosis and treatment. This information is given to the employer to meet a need of the employee; that is, to protect the employee against loss of pay due to illness or to arrange for medical bills to be paid. Where an employer either self-insures or self-administers a health-insurance plan, it necessarily maintains a significant amount of information about employees and their families. Some of this information can be useful in making personnel decisions, especially if it gives details of the diagnosis or treatment of a mental condition, a terminal illness, or an illness that drains the emotions of an employee. Testimony before the Commission indicates that many employers guard claims information carefully, apparently understanding how unfair it is to make an employee choose between filing a legitimate insurance claim and jeopardizing future employment.[17] Some physicians say, however, that this kind of information is available for use in personnel decision making,[18] and there is evidence of its unauthorized use in making decisions unrelated to claims payment.[19]

In its consideration of insurance institutions and the records they maintain, the Commission saw how important a confidentiality policy is to insureds. It believes that such a policy is no less important when the insurance plan is administered by an employer. Although it may be difficult to segregate insurance claims records completely, fairness demands that the claims process be walled off from other internal functions of the employing organization.

Employment-related insurance, such as disability or sick pay, usually involves the corporate physician in claims processing, as it is his function to evaluate the medical evidence on which the claim is based. Thus, corporate physicians must have access to information about these claims. They do not, however, have to use information thus obtained in making decisions that are unrelated to the claim. If asked for an opinion of a candidate for transfer to a job at a new location, for example, the physician can determine a person's physical capacity by examination without delving into claims records for clues to potential medical problems. Nor should these records influence other employment decisions, such as determinations of tenure, promotion, or termination. Accordingly, the Commission recommends:

Recommendation (30):

That an employer that provides life or health insurance as a service to its employees assure that individually identifiable insurance records are maintained separately from other records and not available for use in making employment decisions; and further

Recommendation (31):

That an employer that provides work-related insurance for employees, such as worker's compensation, voluntary sick pay, or short- or long-term disability insurance, assure that individually identifiable records pertaining to such insurance are available internally only to authorized recipients and on a need-to-know basis.

Notes

1. Letter from the Association of Washington Business to the Privacy Protection Study Commission, November 22, 1976; and Letter from the Standard Oil Company to the Privacy Protection Study Commission, October 18, 1976.

2. Maine Rev. Stat. Ann. Tit. 5, Sec. 638; Tit. 30, Sec. 64 and 2257.

3. California Labor Code, Sec. 1198.5.

4. See, for example, Testimony of General Electric Company, Employment Records Hearings, December 9, 1976, p. 235; Testimony of Cummins Engine Company, Employment Records Hearings, December 9, 1976, pp. 58–59; and Testimony of Inland Steel Company, Employment Records Hearings, December 10, 1976, pp. 370–73.

5. See, for example, Testimony of General Electric Company, Employment Records Hearings, December 9, 1976, pp. 279–80; and Testimony of Cummins Engine Company, Employment Records Hearings, December 9, 1976, p. 68.

6. See, for example, Testimony of Harvard University, Employment Records Hearings, December 17, 1976, pp. 864–902; Letter from Jean Mayer, President, Tufts University, to Roger W. Heyns, President, American Council on Education, August 9, 1976; and Sheldon Elliot Steinbach, "Employee Privacy, 1975: Concerns of College and University Administrators." *Educational Record* 57, no. 1 (1976).

7. Labor Management Relations (Taft-Hartley) Act, 29 U.S.C. 141 *et seq.* (1947).

8. See, for example, Testimony of Cummins Engine Company, Employment Records Hearings, December 9, 1976, pp. 46–47; Testimony of Equitable Life Assurance Society of the U.S., Employment Records Hearings, December 9, 1976, pp. 131–32; and Testimony of J. C. Penney Company, Employment Records Hearings, December 10, 1976, pp. 464–65.

9. Testimony of Manufacturers Hanover Trust Company, Employment Records Hearings, December 16, 1976, p. 653.

10. See, for example, Testimony of Equifax Services, Inc., *Credit Reporting and Payment Authorization Services,* Hearings before the Privacy Protection Study Commission, August 3, 1976, pp. 162–63; Testimony of Wackenhut Corporation, Private Investigative Hearings, January 26, 1977, p. 29; and Testimony of Inland Steel Company, Employment Records Hearings, December 10, 1976, p. 349.

11. The term "medical-care provider" includes both "medical-care professionals" and "medical-care institutions." A "medical-care professional" is defined as "any person licensed or certified to provide medical services to individuals, including, but not limited to, a physician, dentist, nurse, optometrist, physical or occupational therapist, psychiatric social worker, clinical dietitian or clinical psychologist." A "medical-care institution" is defined as "any facility or institution that is licensed to provide medical-care services to individuals, including, but not limited to, hospitals, skilled nursing facilities, home-health agencies, clinics, rehabilitation agencies, and public-health agencies or health-maintenance organizations (HMOs)."

12. See, for example, Testimony of Inland Steel Company, Employment Records Hearings, December 10, 1976, p. 388; Testimony of Ford Motor Company, Employment Records Hearings, December 16, 1976, p. 576; and Testimony of International Business Machines, Employment Records Hearings, December 10, 1976, p. 309.

13. See, for example, Testimony of Cummins Engine Company, Employment Records Hearings, December 9, 1976, p. 19; and Testimony of Ford Motor Company, Employment Records Hearings, December 16, 1976, p. 556.

14. See, for example, Testimony of Inland Steel Company, Employment Records Hearings, December 10, 1976, p. 388; and Testimony of Ford Motor Company, Employment Records Hearings, December 16, 1976, p. 576.

15. See, for example, Testimony of Dr. Bruce Karrh, Assistant Medical Direc-

tor, du Pont de Nemours and Company, Employment Records Hearings, December 17, 1976, pp. 782–83; and Testimony of Dr. Norbert Roberts, Medical Director, Exxon Corporation, Employment Records Hearings, December 17, 1976, p. 785. This is also the policy of the Ford Motor Company and the Atlantic Richfield Company. See "Employee Records & Personal Privacy: Corporate Policies & Procedures," McCaffery, Seligman & von Simpson, Inc., November 1976, pp. 105, 139.

16. See, for example, Testimony of Ford Motor Company, Employment Records Hearings, December 16, 1976, p. 587; and Testimony of Dr. Bruce Karrh, Assistant Medical Director, du Pont de Nemours and Company, Employment Records Hearings, December 17, 1976, pp. 781–83.

17. See, for example, Testimony of Inland Steel Company, Employment Records Hearings, December 10, 1976, p. 334; and Testimony of General Electric Company, Employment Records Hearings, December 9, 1976, pp. 248–50.

18. "Confidentiality and Third Parties," The American Psychiatric Association Task Force of June 1975, Appendix Vol. H, p. 53.

19. Ibid., p. 55.

A Businessman's View of the Privacy Commission's Employment Recommendations

Allan H. Knautz

Privacy is no longer an issue that affects just a handful of specialized businesses. Since the publication of the Privacy Protection Study Commission's report on July 12 of last year, it has become an issue that should be on the mind of every businessperson in the country. For included in this report are thirty-four recommendations that may directly affect the way businessmen handle records and information pertaining to their employees. Although many of the recommendations call for voluntary action on the part of the employer, there is still a strong potential for legislation that would cause drastic changes in the way we, who are involved in employing people, conduct our business.

The uncovering of Watergate abuses lent impetus to the passage of the Privacy Act of 1974, which established the Privacy Protection Study Commission in addition to regulating information uses by agencies of the federal government. For two years the Commission heard testimony concerning the handling of personal information in the private sector. Its goals were

> to foster public awareness of privacy protection issues and of the fair information practice principles established by the Privacy Act of 1974; to have a lasting impact on the way privacy protection issues are perceived and addressed; to acquire and promote accurate understanding of current practices with respect to the collection, use and dissemination of recorded information about individuals and of the dangers and protections for personal privacy that are inherent in those practices; to assess

the degree to which the fair information practice principles established by the Privacy Act of 1974 are already being adhered to in practice, and the reasons why; and to make recommendations that seek to promote a fair balance between the personal privacy interests of the individual on the one hand and the institutional and societal needs for information on the other.

Judging from the volumes of testimony and the very weight of the report, it would appear that these goals have been at least partially reached. To be sure, the study fostered public awareness in privacy issues, and it will have a lasting impact. Also, the Commission made a serious and studious effort to understand the current practices involving the handling of information, but their report indicates that this understanding is not yet complete. Much testimony was heard in regard to private businesses' adherence to fair information practice principles, but assuredly more input is needed.

Although the Commission's performance of this difficult task is admirable, it is doubtful that all these recommendations will truly result in a fair balance between personal privacy interests and institutional and societal needs for information.

It is difficult to determine which recommendations may finally be hammered into law. However, the most obvious implications are that (1) the information upon which businessmen base employment decisions may be greatly restricted, and (2) the manner in which we maintain and use applicant, employee, and former-employee records may become a matter of legislation. Viewing this as a businessman, I see the probable long-term impact as an increase in the cost of doing business which would be manifested in two ways: directly, in the form of multiple filing systems and additional clerical help; and indirectly, in higher personnel turnover, lower production, and an increased incidence of employee theft.

At present, we depend upon information about applicants in order to make hiring decisions. Information from educational institutions, former employers, medical records, and conviction records is pertinent in determining whether the applicant's training, experience, health, and temperament are compatible to the job and the company. Several of the Privacy Commission's recommendations could form the basis for legislation that would greatly restrict this information for use in making employment decisions.

Recommendation 16, for example, provides for selective authorization on the part of the job applicant. If passed into law, background information on the applicant that the employer would be allowed to obtain would be restricted to only that which the applicant feels is desirable. If the applicant had a past record showing dishonesty, absenteeism, or any negative quality that he would not want disclosed, the employer most likely would not be aware of it until after valuable company assets were committed to hire and train the new person. Since screening procedures would be weakened, employee theft would be an obvious factor increasing costs.

But beyond this, we must also consider the cost to the current employees as well as the newly hired employee. An employer does not hire a person with the idea of soon letting that person go. Instead, most employers want to give a new employee enough time to learn the job and hopefully to become an asset to the company. This time varies with the individual, and the realization that the employee is not capable of handling even the minimum responsibilities of the job or that he lacks integrity comes slow and hard to the employer. But the new employee, realizing his inability, soon becomes worried and unhappy. Seasoned employees who must take up the slack created by the inept person become alienated. Employee turnover increases and the cost of personnel administration rises. In the meantime, production decreases and cost per unit goes up. This hypothetical situation could become reality if the necessary information is not available when the employer needs it to make a decision.

An added expense may result from the recommendations that lay guidelines for the maintenance of certain records and files. For instance, several recommendations call for the separation of certain information into individual files. In many cases, this would require multiple filing systems, necessitating additional floor space, filing cabinets, and clerical help. Some large companies already have separate systems for one or two of these categories and even these firms may find their record-keeping costs increasing dramatically in the wake of stiff government regulation.

Also, there is again a cost to the employee, especially in regard to the recommendation concerning conviction records. The cost would not be in dollars, but in confidentiality of this information. A separate system that would segregate conviction records from the main body of personnel information would be more apt to call attention to the conviction. In many cases, where conviction records are kept separately, a note to cross-reference the conviction file may be included in the main personnel file, thus referring to the conviction in two places. Confidentiality of conviction records, which is the intent of this recommendation, is in more danger because of the multiple filing system.

Naturally, any law stemming from this recommendation would probably have the greatest impact on the smaller firm, which may not have the assets, space, and personnel to set up such redundant systems.

The implications of the Privacy Protection Study Commission's recommendations cannot be fully realized until specific legislation is proposed. But it is obvious that the greatest impact will come in the form of increased costs: costs that can be measured in dollars spent for additional personnel and systems to assure compliance and in dollars lost because of incompetence, theft, employee dissatisfaction, and high turnover rates.

The degree of impact depends on whether we who are involved with personnel administration will continue to be allowed access to the pertinent information necessary to make intelligent employment decisions that will benefit both the company and the applicant; whether we are allowed to keep filing systems in a manner that is the most efficient and practical for our particular business; and whether the guidelines for voluntary action set forth in many of the Commission's employment recommendations remain voluntary after the legislative rush is over.

It is incumbent upon all of us as responsible professionals to monitor all legislative efforts when they appear and provide our lawmakers with sufficient input to enable them to achieve the fair balance outlined in the Commission's goals. In this regard, we must work through our various business associations to make legislators, both on the state and federal levels, aware of existing Fair Information Practice policies within our own industries. They should be told of the specific problems that would be inflicted upon our businesses by additional restrictions. And they should be apprised of the detrimental effects of such legislation upon our employees and prospective employees.

With our efforts focused in this direction, individual privacy can be protected and the flow of information needed for all of us to make sound employment decisions will continue.

VI.

The Rights
of Fair Procedure:
Union and Nonunion

What Price Employment?
Arbitration, the Constitution,
and Personal Freedom

Julius G. Getman

In reading over past proceedings of the [National Academy of Arbitrators] in order to prepare for this session, I was struck by the variety of roles suggested to arbitrators. They range from the common suggestion that arbitrators are employees chosen to perform a specific task of contract interpretation to the suggestion that arbitrators should consider themselves the "supreme court" of industrial relations. Because the subject assigned to me involves the relationship among arbitration, the Constitution, and personal freedom, it is with the usefulness of the latter model that I am concerned. My conclusion is that the analogy, though far from perfect, has much to commend it as a description of how arbitrators have functioned in discipline cases. It also provides a guide for the solution of vexing problems involving conflict between individual rights and management prerogatives.

Since my subject concerns discipline, the focus of my discussion will be on the Supreme Court's role in criminal cases and in cases involving the disciplining or discharge of governmental employees. My discussion presupposes a typical "just cause" provision and does not question the duty of the arbitrator to follow whatever other standards the parties explicitly established by contract.

Reprinted by permission from *Arbitration 1976, Proceedings of the Twenty-Ninth Annual Meeting, National Academy of Arbitrators,* copyright © 1976 by The Bureau of National Affairs, Inc., Washington, D.C. 20037. Most footnotes deleted.

BASIC PROCEDURAL RIGHTS

A major function of the U.S. Supreme Court in criminal cases has been to monitor the actions of government officials prior to arrest and immediately afterward in order to ensure that certain standards of conduct have been met. Arbitrators have similarly used their power to monitor the behavior of company officials prior to discharge and during the early stages of the grievance machinery. Thus they have insisted that employees be given adequate notice of what constitutes grounds for discharge and that the accused be given an opportunity to be heard before discipline is administered. They have, in general, held that an employee accused of a serious infraction has the right to representation. In addition, arbitrators have rejected improperly obtained evidence. When company officials or security personnel have tricked, coerced, or misled employees into harmful admissions, arbitrators have refused to admit or consider them. Thus arbitrators have with considerable consistency incorporated basic concepts of due process into the definition of good cause.

Although this practice has been noted before, there has been surprisingly little challenge to it. The early cases in which due process or equal protection concepts were first adopted apply them without discussion —almost as a matter of course. Later cases more openly enunciate the role of the arbitrator as monitor of the processes of discharge, but they treat the function as being so well settled as not to require justification. For example, arbitrator Carroll Daugherty, in a series of opinions, has attempted to define "good cause" as the concept has evolved in arbitration.[1] He has focused almost exclusively on the procedures used by management in establishing and administering discipline. I believe that Daugherty's definition is somewhat too formal and does not encompass enough of the role of the arbitrator as a trial court judge to find facts and to pass on the adequacy of grounds offered in justification for company action. It is noteworthy, however, that an able, experienced arbitrator would focus the appellate aspect of the arbitrator's role as the distillation of arbitral experience in defining the concept of just cause.

If the role of arbitrator were as modest as speakers at these meetings sometimes pretend, a different approach could easily have been taken. Arbitrators might have stated that they were entrusted solely with the task of deciding whether a particular employee had done anything that justified his discharge. If it was proven that he had, that ended the matter—grievance denied. Arbitrators have seldom taken this position; they have rarely even seriously considered it, which reflects the importance of procedural fairness to anyone who determines the legitimacy of punishment. The existing practice also demonstrates how well accepted is the notion that the arbitrator's role is the culmination of a process of self-regulation, with the arbitrator, like the Supreme Court, having responsibility for the workings of the other parts of the process.

BASIC SUBSTANTIVE RIGHTS

The Supreme Court's role in criminal cases also involves articulating fundamental liberties—areas of behavior in which an individual's actions are presumptively immune from state interference or criminal penalties. Thus far, however, there is no comparable, recognized concept of fundamental rights in arbitration. Although a perceptible movement toward recognition of individual rights exists, arbitrators have not developed a consistent response to claims that constitutional rights should be recognized in arbitration. Some arbitrators have implicitly accepted this contention; some have rejected it. For the most part, however, arbitrators have been ambivalent and have shown a marked reluctance to deal with the question directly. Many opinions contain alternative analyses arguing both that constitutional rights are not applicable and that in any case they are not infringed. For example, in *Great Lakes Steel Co.,*[2] the arbitrator upheld a company rule forbidding employees "to bring or distribute on Company property literature which is scurrilous, abusive or insulting." The grievant's First Amendment claim was initially rejected on the ground that "the rule in dispute . . . is not a Congressional act." The arbitrator also concluded that in any case the literature was beyond the protection of the Constitution, but the analysis was perfunctory. Had the arbitrator been willing to recognize its applicability, I think he would have recognized that the First Amendment applies even to "criticism . . . beyond all reasonable grounds."

In addition, cases that raise claims of the applicability of constitutional rights are frequently decided on other grounds. This hesitation to address directly the applicability of basic constitutional rights in arbitration, though understandable, is unfortunate. Arbitrators should recognize that certain interests, such as freedom of speech and religion, are so fundamental to individual liberty that they can be limited and made the basis for disciplinary action only when management can demonstrate an overriding economic need. In considering claims of fundamental rights, arbitrators should familiarize themselves with court decisions construing the Constitution. Such decisions are valuable because they articulate the significance of individual liberties, provide a sense of their reach, and state the policies that are advanced by their recognition. Court opinions also suggest techniques for the accommodation of important interests when they are in conflict or when they infringe upon some fundamental opposing interest.

I recognize that the validity of the constitutional analogy I propose as a starting point for evaluating individual rights and the practice of considering judicial opinions may be contested from a variety of perspectives. It might, for example, be claimed that such constitutional rights are less important in the industrial setting than they are in the political. Although there are factors that might be pointed to, such as the ability to change jobs, that differentiate the industrial process from the political process, they do not bulk large. We have come to recognize that the job environment is one of the most significant aspects of a person's life. Most people spend more of their waking time at work than they do anywhere else. My own recent field research,[3] which has involved extensive interviews with hundreds of workers, has made me realize how deeply held feelings about work are and how closely related these feelings are to basic self-image. Thus, just as we recognize that the possession of certain rights is crucial to political freedom, it should seem obvious that they or similar rights are also vital to industrial dignity and self-respect.

This is not to say that there must be a one-to-one correspondence between constitutional rights and fundamental rights recognized in arbitration. There are rights customarily observed in arbitration, such as the right to be judged solely by one's performance on the job, that are only metaphorically related to political rights. Similarly, fundamental political rights, such as the right to vote, are not easily translatable to job rights. Nevertheless, the fact that certain interests are constitutionally recognized should be a powerful argument to arbitrators that such rights should also be recognized in arbitration. Thus, for example, the constitutional commitment to robust and "open" debate of public issues should be recognized in the plant environment. Freedom of expression at work should be limited only when a strong showing can be made that the expression of ideas or the use of words is likely to cause serious disruption. Similarly, our commitment to free exercise of religion should make arbitrators most reluctant to uphold discharges based upon religious observance, and the existence of a constitutional right of privacy should make arbitrators suspicious of discipline based on sexual behavior that does not pose a threat to the functioning of the company. The fact that the exercise of such rights is unpopular with other employers should not be a basis for their limitation.

The method of analysis that I am urging was employed by arbitrator Adolph Koven in *California Processors, Inc.*[4] The grievant in that case was indefinitely suspended for refusing to remove a poster of Emiliano Zapata that contained a slogan "Viva la Revolución." Koven, citing the Supreme Court's decision in *Tinker* v. *Des Moines School District,*[5] dealing with the right of students to distribute literature, rejected the company's ban. He stated, "Not even a scintilla of evidence was produced to show that an absolute ban on the Zapata poster was called for pursuant to the requirements of *Tinker.*"[6]

Such analysis might be attacked as inconsistent with a proper appreciation of the arbitrator's role. The concern has frequently been expressed at these meetings that arbitrators not overstep their institutional limitations and give way to that most seductive of perfidious impulses, the desire to do good. We are hired to interpret contracts, not to indulge our fantasies of being on the Supreme Court. However, the task of contract interpretation varies with the nature of the issue and breadth of the language used. The language of just cause is so general that it cannot be construed in terms of the precise intent of the parties. The most that can be said is that by the use of such language, the parties have manifested an intent to refer in discharge cases to the moral standards of the community modified for the industrial setting. The Constitution and the decisions that interpret it both reflect and shape contemporary standards of morality. As such, they are valuable sources of guidance to arbitrators in determining whether specific conduct is sufficiently reprehensible to justify discharge.

Notes

1. See *Combustion Eng'r,* 42 LA 806 (1964); *Enterprise Wire Co.,* 46 LA 359 (1966).

2. 60 LA 860 (Richard Mittenthal, arbitrator, 1973).

3. See Julius G. Getman et al., *Union Representation Elections: Law and Results* (New York: Russell Sage, 1976).

4. *California Processors, Inc.,* 56 LA 1275 (1971).

5. 393 U.S. 503 (1969). The arbitrator, however, applied the rule that the grievant should have obeyed the rule and filed a grievance. This conclusion is highly questionable in this setting.

6. *Supra* note 4, at 1275.

Arbitration and the Constitution

John E. Dunsford

Professor Getman appears to be recommending something remarkably different from the simple notion that the arbitral approach, like that of the Supreme Court, must recognize the institutional setting in which the terms of a basic compact operate. He is saying that although the mandates of the Bill of Rights are not legally operative in the private employment relationship, arbitrators ought consciously to work toward incorporating them into collective bargaining relationships wherever feasible. The underlying premises for this theme must be (1) that the questions of procedural fairness and personal liberties that surface in the arbitration process are often (though not always) indistinguishable from those with which the Supreme Court must deal; and (2), accordingly, that arbitrators should deliberately (though with care and sophistication) look to Supreme Court decisions for guidance in the resolution of these matters. While I have the highest respect for the scholarship of our speaker and find him a stimulating and creative thinker, I am compelled to disagree with his Bicentennial message.

It is possible, of course, to see some similarities in the subject matter of cases in arbitration and those that come before the Supreme Court. Both may pose a question of speech, for example; both may call for consideration of the fairness of the procedures leading to the sanction. In addition, the underlying standards that arbitrator and judge apply to the issues may have the same resonances: due process, equal protection, just cause. Instructive comparisons can certainly be made between the reasoning and results produced in the two forums. And arbitrators will no doubt find profitable, in a general way, the analysis and exposi-

Reprinted by permission from *Arbitration 1976, Proceedings of the Twenty-Ninth Annual Meeting,* National Academy of Arbitrators, copyright © 1976 by The Bureau of National Affairs, Inc., Washington, D.C. 20037.

tion of the Supreme Court on such matters as the elements of due process.

But the decisive question is not whether there are similarities or analogies which can be discerned in the two systems; the question is what, if any, significance such attempted correlations may have for the sound development of the arbitration process. It is one thing to trace out the outline of a picture in the stars, but quite another to attribute a reality to the image that is projected. I can see the outline of a Big Dipper in the sky, but I find that it does not really hold water. That is my difficulty with the thesis Professor Getman is proposing.

As an academic, I am obviously in favor of comparative studies of the roles of arbitrator and Supreme Court justice; as a lawyer and an arbitrator, I endorse the proposition that an understanding of Supreme Court jurisprudence can be a helpful aid in thinking about many of these matters. Nevertheless, I do find unconvincing the further contention that the substance of the Supreme Court rulings under the Bill of Rights is in most cases readily transferable to the resolution of issues of personal freedom under the labor contract.

In support of his thesis, Professor Getman first reviews some of the procedural requirements that arbitrators through the years have developed in discipline cases. He finds that they are in many respects comparable, if not identical, to standards constitutionally imposed by the Supreme Court in criminal matters. From the similarity between the two systems, he finds support for his theme and concludes that arbitrators have "with considerable consistency incorporated basic concepts of due process into the definition of good cause." This statement rather strongly implies that there has been a conscious adoption by arbitrators of the criminal procedural standards of the Constitution. If that is not actually intended, there is in any event the intimation that what is procedurally necessary in criminal cases must therefore be desirable in arbitration. Two things are wrong with this reasoning. The first is that it neglects to inquire why these similarities have appeared and instead tends to assume that the arbitral process inherited its notions of procedural fairness directly from the criminal courts. The second is that it fails to consider the numerous ways in which the procedural requirements in discipline cases are, in fact, different from—even contrary to—the criminal law.

Professor Getman notes that, even in the earliest reported decisions, arbitrators seldom bother to discuss the meaning of "just cause." As he accurately reports, the concept is applied almost as a matter of course. But the conclusion to be drawn from this primeval reticence to expound on the meaning of "just cause" is not that the arbitrators had a ready-made source of decisional guides in criminal law, but rather that the contract phrase touches root concepts of justice and equity that demand application in specific contexts before they can be articulated in judgments and rules. On the rare occasion when an arbitrator does drop a remark about the "just cause" standard in these early years, the one thing that is clear is that his thinking is oriented to the universe of the private parties before him, not to the fate of an accused in the criminal dock of the state. For example, in an award of January 4, 1947, arbitrator Robert Brecht offered this definition: "Just cause was established by reference to such considerations as fairness, appropriateness of punishment to offense, absence of arbitrariness and capriciousness, consistency of treatment, and absence of haste and emotionalism."[1] A few months later (still almost thirty years ago) another young arbitrator named Harry Platt made this effort to explain the process of balancing the needs of the company against the interests of the discharged employee:

> To be sure, no standards exist to aid an arbitrator in finding a conclusive answer to such a question and, therefore, perhaps the best he can do is to decide what reasonable men, mindful of the habits and customs of industrial life and of the standards of justice and fair dealing prevalent in the community, ought to have done under similar circumstances and in that light to decide whether the conduct of the discharged employee was defensible and the disciplinary penalty just.[2]

This approach, it will be noticed, is a far cry from what one would expect if the arbitrator were thinking in terms of the criteria for prosecuting crimes.

It is not surprising that arbitrators, testing the limits of this embracing standard of "just" or "proper cause," began to conclude that it encompassed procedural elements of adequate notice, opportunity to present evidence, cross-examination, and similar things. This occurred because claims for procedural fairness are constantly struggling for recognition in any system where binding factual determinations are made on a record of evidence. Of course these arbitrators in the earlier years were not unaffected by their exposure to a legal system in which the courts interpreted and applied such terms as "due process" or "equal protection" in the area of crimes. But neither were they necessarily positing any formal correspondence between constitutional requirements of fair criminal procedure and the proper handling of discipline within an industrial setting. Working within the spacious boundaries of the "just cause" language, arbitrators were independently confronting questions about the ultimate fairness of plant discipline which suffered the infirmities of inadequate procedures. And they resolved some of these problems by embodying requirements of procedural fairness into their decisions. But these requirements were embraced not because they were constitutional, but because they were *due*. And they were *due* not in consideration of what might be needed to protect those accused of crimes against the overreaching power of the state, but instead what was deemed appropriate and fitting in the special relationships of the industrial community.

While admittedly there are similarities to be observed between the essential procedural protections that have emerged in both the arbitration forum and the criminal law, there are also noteworthy differences that are generally thought to be entirely justifiable. That is a second weakness in the proposition that a deliberate effort at correlation between the two systems is either necessary or desirable. In a paper delivered at the 17th Annual Meeting in 1964, Professor Sanford H. Kadish conducted a painstaking review of the sanctioning systems of the criminal law and industrial discipline.[3] Though not restricting himself to the subject of procedural mechanisms, Professor Kadish did, for example, point out the substantial differences between the two systems in regard to the provision of notice for conduct that is forbidden. The highest degree of specificity is required in the notice requirements that precede the imposition of criminal penalties. There must be no vagueness or ambiguity in the drafting of the statute that sets forth the crime. By way of contrast, the type of notice that is deemed necessary in industrial discipline depends on a variety of factors, the foremost of which is the nature of the conduct under review. Nobody in the plant has to be advised in written rules that he will jeopardize his job if he punches the foreman in the nose. But an absence of precisely such a formal prohibition of assault would invalidate efforts of the state to fine or imprison him.

Further examination of the two systems offers other striking examples of procedural variances. The privilege against self-incrimination is one of the central protections of the Fifth Amendment, and it is interpreted to forbid the drawing of any adverse inference from a failure of the defendant to testify. Yet it is commonplace for arbitrators both to expect the grievant to testify at the hearing and to draw appropriate inferences from his unwillingness to respond to the evidence adduced against him. The underlying purposes behind the constitutional privilege are not relevant to the industrial setting. They stem from concerns about abuse of governmental power going back to Star Chamber proceedings and the thumbscrew and the rack, elements that do not loom large in the modern American factory. The privilege is also understandable in the light of the severe penalties to which the defendant is potentially exposed, and the heavily adversary character of the criminal trial in which the individual citizen must face the formidable resources of the state. In the industrial relations environment, however, a different set of considerations is at work. Between the parties there is usually an expectation of mutual cooperation and respect for the other side's interests, which survives even the bitterest of disputes. Men and women who work next to each other, both in supervision and in the bargaining unit, expect each other to be open and responsive when disciplinary charges are made. The relationship of labor and management is not an isolated, impersonal affair comparable to that of a prosecutor and defendant, but an ongoing collaborative enterprise with its own unique texture.

There are other differences between the procedural requirements of criminal law and arbitration that might be mentioned. Some relate to the degrees of formality required in the handling and processing of charges. In the criminal area, the manner in which evidence is obtained, the requirement of a grand jury indictment or a prosecutor's information, the precision called for in the written specification of charges, the arraignment of the defendant—all of these are vital to the success of the prosecution in establishing an adequate basis for criminal sanction. The same format is not necessarily desirable in arbitration. The weight that comparable factors receive in arbitration usually depends upon the facts of a particular case as they bear upon the fairness of the result.

Notes

1. *Glenn L. Martin Co.,* 6 LA 501, 504 (1947).
2. *Riley Stoker Corp.,* 7 LA 764, 767 (1947).
3. Sanford H. Kadish, "The Criminal Law and Industrial Discipline as Sanctioning Systems: Some Comparative Observations," in Mark L. Kah, ed., *Labor Arbitration: Perspectives and Problems,* Proceedings of the 17th Annual Meeting, National Academy of Arbitrators (Washington, D.C.: BNA Books, 1964), p. 125.

Arbitrators and Drugs

Kenneth Jennings

Awareness of employee drug use in industry is relatively new. Few, if any, corporation executives acknowledged this issue prior to 1967. Accordingly, there have been few arbitration cases pertaining to this issue—a situation which possibly does not generate substantial guidelines for arbitral decisions. While drugs and alcohol are both labeled "intoxicants," many management representatives differentiate between the two in discharge decisions because drugs, unlike alcohol, are often illegal in the procurement, consumption, and sale to other employees.

Thus, management often uses a hard-line approach in dealing with drug offenders. Only six of the thirty-eight employees involved in the reviewed cases were assigned a penalty less than discharge. However, companies have had very limited success in having their disciplinary actions upheld by the arbitrator. In cases studied the disciplinary penalties were reduced or set aside for twenty-four of the affected employees.

This article discusses two broad questions affecting the arbitrators' decisions: (a) Does the seriousness of the drug offense warrant discharge? (b) Did management follow proper guidelines in investigating and establishing evidence?

THE SERIOUSNESS OF DRUG INVOLVEMENT

Management usually argues that the employee drug offender is deserving of discharge because he or she is violating company rules and societal laws, as well as affecting the safety and well-being of other employees.

Surprisingly, only six of the reviewed cases specifically cited a company rule prohibiting drug involvement on company property. Arbitrators have regarded the rule as appropriate in discharge considerations even if the rule was unilaterally established by management or silent on its penalty for violation. In three cases the written consequence for rule violation was "subject to discharge." Arbitrators reinstated employees in two of these cases, presumably under the assumption that "subject to discharge" carries the potential for lesser penalties.

Another disciplinary option available to management is to post a rule stating that "conviction of a penal offense in any court of competent jurisdiction" will subject the employee to discharge. Here, the employee is not technically discharged for drug usage; however, if involvement leads to a criminal conviction, the employee can be discharged on the basis of this conviction. An advantage to this approach is that the action is solely based on the objective criterion of criminal conviction; hence, the potential libel or defamation of character suits associated with drug abuse are avoided.

A grievance at National Floor Products Company protested the discharge of an employee who was convicted of possessing marijuana off company premises. The union, in protesting the discharge, made a strong argument that the offense was relatively minor and did not affect the company in any manner. The arbitrator, observing that the company was consistent in applying this rule with other employees having criminal convictions, upheld the discharge commenting:

> Precedent seems to be clear that management's right to discipline an employee for off-premises, off-duty conduct depends upon the effect of that conduct upon the company's business. However, this would not appear to be so where you have a rule such as we have here. . . . In the case at hand this arbitrator is not disposed to agree with the union that he may supplant his judgment for that of the company.

A somewhat opposite opinion about the applicability of this type of rule was given by Howard Block, who reinstated a grievant discharged for a drug-related criminal conviction:

> An arbitrator should enforce company-established rules, unless it can be shown that the application of the rule to the facts of a particular case is arbitrary, capricious, or otherwise unreasonable. In the opinion of this arbitrator, an a priori determination that every employee convicted of a crime should automatically be discharged is overboard. To the extent that the rule fails to take into account the relationship between the crime and the employment situation, as in the instant case, it is arbitrary and therefore inapplicable. As to the company's contention that the rule was uniformly applied in the past, the record reveals that there have been

only a few instances calling for its application and none of them involved conduct away from the plant.

Consequently, a rule subjecting an employee to discharge for a criminal conviction has to be consistently and somewhat frequently applied or else the arbitrator will likely interpret the rule in the context of the particular conviction.

Most of the companies surveyed had no rules regarding discipline for a criminal conviction; however, management in these instances discharged the affected employee, contending that the seriousness of the conviction warranted dismissal. Arbitrators, lacking contractual guidance, then applied several tests to determine the seriousness of the offense. One such test referred to a grievant who either received a suspended sentence, or was placed on probation. A related case occurred at Vulcan Materials where the grievant, found guilty in court of possessing marijuana, was ordered to pay a $500 fine and placed on supervised probation for two years. Management considered this offense serious enough to warrant discharge; however, the arbitrator, in reinstating the grievant with back pay, believed the company overlooked the stipulations and reasoning governing probation. The arbitrator suggested that the terms of the probation—the employee would not be involved with marijuana or its users—constituted "excellent insurance that grievant will not come to work under the influence of marijuana." Thus, the arbitrator believed that management should follow the court's example in (a) not branding the employee as a criminal, (b) holding the conviction in abeyance, and (c) erasing the conviction upon satisfactory completion of the probation.

Similar reasoning was used by an arbitrator in another case where an employee was placed on a two-year probation for possession of marijuana. Arbitrator Wyckoff reinstated the discharged employee with full back pay contending that the state, after a presumably extensive investigation, decided to "free the grievant with some restrictions" rather than place him in jail. The company, on the other hand, did not undertake a similar investigation before making its discharge decision.

THE GRIEVANT'S RECORD

The previously cited cases assume that the grievant has few or no blemishes on his or her work record, other than being placed on probation for an offense committed off company premises. A grievance at Aeromotive Metal Products protested the discharge of an employee who pled guilty to marijuana possession and was placed on probation. Arbitrator Koven, in upholding the discharge, acknowledged management's obligation to realize that probation indicates the employee can be a useful member of society with minimum guidance. However, he also stated that management had additional obligations to provide "wholesome character." In this case the employee's work record was very unsatisfactory; in addition, the employee gave management a false reason for his court appearance which resulted in receiving holiday pay.

Arbitrators, in determining the seriousness of drug use off company premises, appear to make a distinction between possession of a drug and attempts to sell the drugs to others. A somewhat common belief is that simple possession of marijuana is a relatively common occurrence, with little or no cause for concern. This is particularly true if management, as indicated in the six cases, could not establish that the grievant's actions:

1. damaged the company's reputation through adverse publicity resulting from the court trial.

2. rendered the employee unable to appear at work.

3. led to refusal or reluctance of other employees to work with the grievant.

4. resulted in poor work performance, for example, lack of timing or alertness.

5. affected the morale of other employees, or the orderly, profitable operations of the plant.

On the other hand, if management could show that the grievant's off-premises drug activity *might* affect its employees, arbitrators were likely to uphold disciplinary actions. A related case concerned the discharge of two employees for their criminal conviction: possession and intent to sell marijuana. Two of the union's contentions were: (a) marijuana was relatively harmless, and (b) the company did not present any evidence that the grievants sold marijuana on company premises or to company employees. Arbitrator McDermott, in upholding the discharges, implied that possession of marijuana was somewhat insignificant as it was labeled a misdemeanor by the state (West Virginia). However, sale (or intent of sale) of this substance was recognized by this state as a far more dangerous situation and labeled the offense a felony: "However tolerant society may be towards personal possession and use of marijuana by individuals, there is no indication that such tolerance extends to individuals who engage in the sale of the substance for profit."

The arbitrator also believed the union's second contention to be rather arbitrary, as it implied that management would have to wait until the individual seller was caught engaging in the illegal action on company premises before it could act to protect the welfare of its employees. The union's contention also implied that persons who engage in the sale of drugs for profit would necessarily refuse to sell on company property or to fellow employees even if they had the opportunity to do so. Thus, the arbitrator upheld the company's action even though the company did not present evidence that serious drug abuse existed on its premises, reasoning that the company had sufficient justification in protecting its interests as well as its employees' welfare.

TYPE OF DRUG

While almost all of the reviewed cases were concerned with marijuana, three arbitral decisions suggested that the drug itself may influence the arbitrator's decision, particularly if the drug user could seriously affect fellow employees. One employee, in applying for a crane operator's position, answered no to the company's question, "Are you taking any medication at present?" A subsequent urinalysis revealed the presence of barbiturates; consequently, management discharged the employee for making incorrect statements about his drug use. Although not explicitly stated, the arbitrator appeared to have weighed the effects of the drug on the company's operations, including its work force. Noting that the urinalysis did not reflect the quantity of drug consumption, the arbitrator sustained the grievance: "It is certainly conceivable that an employee who took a 'bennie' at a party or on an occasional Saturday night should not be classed in the same category as a daily or weekly user."

A nearly identical grievance at Southwestern Bell Telephone Company protested the discharge of an employee who was arrested (but not convicted) for possession of one amphetamine tablet. The arbitrator reinstated the grievant with the following reasoning:

> The company has argued that the possession of illegal drugs during working hours is itself so serious an offense, with such dangerous potentialities when considered in the light of the company's approximately 5,000 employees and of the company's public nature, that the automatic discharge penalty for any employee found in possession of even a single unit of illegal drug of any kind is reasonably necessary and proper. . . . Even when the necessity of deterring other company employees from like misconduct is given full weight, I find myself unable to agree that

the grievant's first offense of possession of the illegal amphetamine pill under the circumstances of this case was such as to render the discharge penalty reasonable or fair or just. I am distinguishing the mere fact of possession alone of a single pill from trafficking in or use of illegal drugs during working hours or on company premises.

On the other hand, a grievant with ten years seniority was arrested and convicted for attempting to obtain eighteen grams of cocaine through fraudulent means. Management, upon notification of the conviction, had the employee examined by a doctor who concluded (a) that the employee was unquestionably addicted to the drug, and (b) that cocaine addicts are dangerous, capable of attacking friends or other innocent bystanders. The company, on the basis of these findings, discharged the grievant, with the arbitrator upholding the discharge:

> Drug addiction not only deprives the victim, but it rightly carries a social stigma. The fact that the addiction had not yet reached the stage where it directly affected the employee's ability to properly perform his work duties is not determinative. Degeneration of the addict could at any time reach the point where it would seriously endanger the health and safety of fellow employees and company equipment.

Managerial concern over employees is sometimes reflected in preventative discipline—the grievant who is indicted for drug use is temporarily suspended pending the outcome of the trial. Unions in these instances contended that the employee is innocent until proven guilty in the courts, and that discipline before a judicial decision is reached should be regarded as arbitrary and capricious. A representative case occurred at Brown and Williamson Tobacco Corporation, where the grievant was suspended for an indictment (possession and sale of Cannabis sativa). The arbitrator, in upholding the suspension, indicated management's actions were not capricious; instead, management had cause for concern as many of its employees worked the night shift where it was difficult to keep employees under close surveillance:

> While the company is not permitted to become a censor of morals, it may take steps reasonably calculated to protect its operations. The company was alerted to the danger that the employee might be interested in drug traffic and found it prudent to exclude him from the premises, so that he would not have an opportunity to carry on this activity on company property, and thereby interfere with production.

It should be noted, however, that a company following the policy of temporary suspension would usually be obligated to pay the grievant appropriate back wages if the employee is subsequently found innocent by the courts.

PROBLEMS OF EVIDENCE AND PROOF OF DRUG INVOLVEMENT

Arbitrators regard drug use on company premises as being very serious; however, management, in attempting to justify disciplinary action to the arbitrator, sometimes has difficulty in establishing reasonable evidence. For example, in two cases arbitrators have questioned the accuracy of urinalysis techniques; one arbitrator was concerned that the lab technician was unavailable for cross-examination, while another was concerned with potential errors resulting from the handling and analysis of many samples.

Two employees at Inland Steel Container Company were discharged on the basis of an undercover agent's written findings that the employees (a) on one occasion admitted they were getting high on marijuana taken from a brown paper bag, and (b) indicated on another occasion that they were going to get high. Arbitrator Marcus found the evidence to be lacking in both instances. First, the undercover agent admitted in his testimony that the brown bag may have contained a substance other than marijuana. Also, the grievants' comments about "getting high on grass" were regarded as irrelevant to the question of marijuana possession or use. "If the statements were actually made, they could have been horseplay, or indicative of off-duty indulgence."

Management has an additional problem when using an undercover agent: namely the protection of the agent's identity. In one arbitration case, management presented its testimony on the basis of an undercover agent who was not present during the hearing. The arbitrator reinstated the discharged employee with back pay, contending that management's testimony was basically hearsay evidence. Still another arbitrator stated that the undercover agent must have corroborated evidence even if he did appear in person during the arbitration hearing. Managers at one company hired an undercover agent to examine the problem of company property theft. During the course of this investigation five employees were suspended and later discharged for possession of marijuana on company property. Arbitrator Autrey, in reinstating the grievants with back pay, expressed some concern over the lack of evidence supporting the agent's testimony. More specifically, the arbitrator indicated in his decision that (a) there was no prior evidence

suggesting a drug problem in the plant; (b) company supervisors testified that they had never seen the grievants smoking marijuana or
appear intoxicated from its usage; and (c) there were no hidden cameras
or recording devices to support the agent's testimony.

> Although the testimony of any accused person must be viewed with some
> skepticism, the testimony of an employee with a good prior work record,
> as is the case with each of the grievants, should be considered very
> carefully. While, in the opinion of this arbitrator, it is more likely that
> an accused employee will testify falsely in his own behalf than an under-
> cover agent will testify falsely against an accused employee, this arbitra-
> tor is of the opinion that the testimony of an outside investigator requires
> some corroboration for clear and convincing proof of guilt in the face of
> an emphatic denial of guilt by an employee with a prior good employee
> record.

It should be emphasized, however, that management did not have to
catch the employee in the act to prove its case if the circumstantial
evidence was overwhelming. This situation was best illustrated in three
cases where the grievants' discharges were upheld by the arbitrator. At
Howmet Corporation, a night shift foreman tailed two grievants, who,
on their lunch hours, entered a remote loft above the shipping room.
The foreman did not climb the loft because he was the only supervisor
on duty that night and he was apprehensive. However, the foreman,
noting the "unmistakable" smell of marijuana, suspended the employees; after the suspension the supervisor examined the ashes in the
loft which, unlike cigarette ashes, had a grainy appearance. The grievants categorically denied smoking marijuana; instead, they contended
they smoked cigars and cigarettes. They also stated they wanted a
secluded lunch hour, one away from the glaring lights and noise of the
general shop. The arbitrator was not very impressed with the grievants'
version, particularly since the grievants had to walk over a quarter of
a mile on the coldest night of the year to a totally unattractive place
having no heat. In addition, the arbitrator considered the foreman to
be a qualified judge of marijuana odor as he had attended a seminar on
drug control.

The second case pertained to a grievant who was observed rolling a
cigarette from a substance in a small plastic bag. Management turned
the contents of the bag over to legal authorities, who identified the
substance as marijuana. The union contended that the grievant found
the bag and was observed by management at the very moment he picked
up the bag. Accordingly, the grievant gave the bag to management who
so requested; if the bag had really belonged to the grievant, he would

have never shown its contents to management. The arbitrator doubted the grievant's contention that he was using the very narrow walkway to get to the washroom, and concluded that management's version of the incident had more merit:

> Not only the route taken contributes to the doubt but also the purpose given for his being there. . . . The grievant allegedly had been on the way to the washroom, yet, this was just shortly after he had left the locker room, which contained similar facilities. . . . There was no reason for Mr. F., who was a management representative, to manufacture this scene, at a time when he had no knowledge of what was in the bag, and he had no cause for falsely accusing the grievant of any act at all.

A supervisor at a third company received a tip from another employee that the grievant was smoking marijuana during his work break. The assistant plant manager and foreman confronted the grievant in an office, asking the grievant to empty his pockets. After emptying some of his pockets, the grievant admitted having marijuana; however, he ran out of the office when a management representative started to call the police. The arbitrator, noting that no substance was confiscated, believed the grievant's confession to be "overwhelming evidence of guilt," particularly since the grievant did not empty all of his pockets and ran out of the office.

ENTRAPMENT BY UNDERCOVER AGENTS

Finally, management, in attempting to establish its case against the employee drug user, may encounter the issue of entrapment. Unions contend that management is guilty of entrapment when it employs an undercover agent who often encourages the employee to become actively involved with drugs on the company's premises. Arbitrators appear to discount this argument given the previously mentioned qualifications attached to undercover agents. For example, the union, in one grievance, protested the undercover agent's actions—drinking intoxicants and smoking marijuana on and off company premises. The arbitrator found little merit in the union's contention stating, "Obviously, an effective undercover investigator of this type must appear to all other employees to be the regular employee he is pretending to be."

However, another arbitral decision suggests caution management should exercise in allowing its foremen to uncover drug abuse. An installer foreman, at New Jersey Bell Telephone Company, had several discussions regarding marijuana with an hourly employee. On one occasion the foreman approached several employees standing near the grievant's car, whereupon the foreman said, "I know what you fellows are up to. You better be in shape for work tomorrow." The grievant then asked the foreman if he wanted some, and handed the foreman two marijuana cigarettes when the foreman replied yes. After conferring with legal authorities, the foreman was advised to arrange a sale of marijuana. He then asked the grievant if he could purchase $5 worth, with the grievant responding in the affirmative. The foreman then notified a representative of the Morris County Prosecutor's Office Narcotics Squad, who, in turn, searched the grievant's automobile at the end of the shift, finding a quantity of marijuana. The employee was arrested for possession, and pleaded guilty, receiving a $25 fine. Management, in discharging the employee, contended that it could not have an acknowledged "pusher" on its premises. Arbitrator Weston believed the evidence did not establish the employee as being a pusher, and that the foreman provoked the employee to distribute the substance on company premises:

> X's conviction as "a disorderly person" does not constitute a ground for discharge. The conviction was based only on possession of a limited amount of marijuana. If it had been shown that X was a pusher or supplier, he would have been found guilty of a greater crime and been subjected to considerably more than a $25 fine. . . .
>
> The critical question is whether the record establishes that X acted as a pusher or supplier. There is no proof that he ever sold marijuana. His general statements to Porter [the foreman] that he had done so, in the course of friendly and casual conversation, do not establish that he actually sold the drug on any specific occasion. That he knew the prices of marijuana and was familiar with the language associated with its distribution is also not sufficient to prove that X was a pusher. . . .
>
> While X did give Porter two cigarettes, Porter initiated the conversation and, in earlier talks, had asked for marijuana cigarettes and had just indicated to the employees he suspected they were smoking marijuana and his only concern was that they report to work in good shape the following morning. X's act in giving the foreman two of his cigarettes was not a sale or form of distribution under the circumstances, particularly in view of the foreman's expressed interest in using marijuana and their friendly discussions of the subject. . . . Quite apart from the foregoing, we are impressed by the union's theory that management has an obligation to deter potential violators. The record is clear that instead of cautioning X during April against engaging in marijuana possession and activity on company property, Porter persisted in approaching him and prodding him on to commit a wrongful act. We do not condone the

practice by a supervisor of preying upon an employee's weakness in order to subject him to discipline.

It thus appears that arbitrators place strong qualifications on management's disciplinary action against drug-using employees. Companies formulating a drug-abuse policy for its hourly employees should consider a flexible approach, one that would allow consideration of the unique circumstances of each drug-related incident.

Resolving Personnel Problems in Nonunion Plants

Maurice S. Trotta and Harry R. Gudenberg

The manager of an electronics division at a United States Air Force base attended a conference on how to resolve employee grievances. The conference leader outlined a typical problem and asked the manager how he would handle it. The Air Force man gave his decision, and when asked to state his reasons for it, he replied: "It was a gut reaction." Pressed to explain "gut reaction," he was unable to do so. During the subsequent discussion many of his colleagues disagreed with his solution, and he later admitted that (1) this was the first time his personnel decisions had ever been questioned and analyzed, and (2) he now realized that making a sound personnel decision was a complex process.

Highly competent and intelligent, this electronics engineer had honestly felt that his personnel decisions were fair and sound. He was able to make sound technical decisions, but his ability to make sound personnel decisions was questionable.

CONFLICT ANALYSIS: THE DECISIONAL PROCESS

If managers were trained how to handle personnel problems and were taught something about the decisional process, many personnel grievances that now come up for adjudication would never materialize in the first place. This is a view held by experienced arbitrators, and a reading of arbitration awards published by the Bureau of National Affairs and Commerce Clearing House will confirm it.

It should also be emphasized, however, that the same lack of training among shop stewards and other union officers also provokes many grievances that are eventually submitted to arbitration.

Conflict results when two parties view the same situations, but come to different decisions. Thus, the first step toward conflict resolution is to analyze why the parties reached different conclusions. Such an effort is one of the functions of the arbitral process.

In most situations both sides believe their conclusions are sound and fair. But the arbitrator, in reviewing the reasons why two persons or sides have reached different conclusions, will often discover that there is a dispute as to facts or that lack of communication has created misunderstandings. He may also find that basic assumptions rested on shaky facts, that opinions were formed upon scanty evidence or stated by persons not competent to form a reliable opinion, and that the parties' concepts of what is a proper employee-employer relationship are diametrically opposed. Personality conflicts also cause problems.

CASE STUDIES IN PERSONNEL DECISION MAKING

The following true case studies illustrate how easy it is for intelligent, well-meaning persons to make wrong personnel decisions.

1. *The Idle Worker.* An employee in a manufacturing plant was recommended for promotion by his foreman, but the personnel division turned down the request without giving a reason. The company had a grievance procedure, and the disappointed worker filed a grievance that went to arbitration.

At the arbitration hearing, it was disclosed that the decision not to promote was made by the head of personnel. Explaining why he had ruled against the promotion, the personnel chief said he believed the employee was not a responsible person, a conclusion based on an incident that occurred one day while he was touring the plant with a group of main office executives. "I looked up and saw him [the grievant] standing on a ladder with his arms folded when he should have been working," the personnel director said.

Then the employee explained what had really happened. He was working on a high ladder in a narrow passageway transferring heavy pipe from one storage bin to another when the personnel director and his group started to walk down the passageway toward him. Because they would be passing underneath his ladder, he stopped handling the pipe for safety's sake until the group had passed. "And when I stand," he said, "I usually fold my arms."

The plant's grievance-arbitration procedure benefited both parties in the case. The workman got his promotion, and the company saved a valuable employee who otherwise might have become antagonistic and looked for another job.

2. *The Underpaid Professor.* A university faculty member complained to his dean that he had neither been promoted nor received a salary increase in many years, whereas others in his department had received regular raises and promotions. The university had a grievance procedure, and when the complaint came up for hearing, it was revealed that the department chairman had told the dean in confidence that the complainant was an unsatisfactory teacher whom no one would recommend for promotion. The testimony brought out that the dean decided not to promote the professor on the basis of the information given him by the department chairman.

Other faculty members testified, however, that their individual opinions were never sought and that no faculty committee on promotion even existed in the department. Some said that the grievant had a good reputation as a teacher and that the department chairman was antagonistic toward him for no apparent reason.

It was apparent that the dean had made false assumptions based upon erroneous information. His original decision might have been different had he given the faculty member an opportunity to explain or deny the charges against him. Without a grievance procedure, the truth would not have been disclosed.

3. *The Fired Biochemist.* A medical school biochemist was summarily discharged by his department head in the middle of the university year. The firing followed his refusal to withdraw from publication a scientific paper he had delivered at a scientific convention. The biochemist believed that the request was unwarranted and embarrassing. After his summary discharge, the man appealed to the head of the medical school, asking for a review of the action that he knew would be damaging to his career. But his request was denied without explanation.

TRENDS IN RESOLVING PERSONNEL PROBLEMS

Whenever people are supervised, personnel problems will inevitably arise. Top management invariably expresses desire for equitable personnel decisions and assumes that personnel decisions made by middle management are sound and fair and do not need to be reviewed. On the basis of arbitration awards, however, it appears that the assumption underlying this traditional approach is not always warranted.

A large percentage of cases processed through grievance-arbitration procedures is decided in favor of the grievant. For example, a recent survey found that in cases involving faculty members of institutions of higher education, 40 percent of the grievants were successful, 30 percent of all issues arbitrated involved discharge, discipline, and tenure problems of faculty, and 24 percent involved merit rates, promotion, and demotion. (Approximately the same percentages are applicable to cases submitted to arbitration by business and industry.)

The survey authors concluded that unilateral action by a board of administration should be scrutinized with greater discretion by all parties. And they predict increased use of the arbitral process in higher education.

Experience has also shown that a company or institution will have high turnover—with resultant higher labor costs and lower efficiency—if employees believe their personnel problems are consistently handled arbitrarily, with no right to an impartial review of decisions believed to be unfair. To avoid this problem, nonunion plants and nonprofit institutions are tending to establish impartial appeal procedures. Advisory arbitration, which is nonbinding, is losing favor to binding arbitration, which is enforceable in court if either party refuses to abide by the award.

Federal and state agencies as well as private industry are sending more managers to conferences for training in handling personnel problems. This is a significant trend because managers without insight into the decisional process too often aggravate personnel problems regardless of their competency in technical fields.

TYPICAL GRIEVANCE PROCEDURES

Grievance policies adopted by nonunion companies and organizations prescribe a wide range of appeal and decision procedures. Some enunciate relatively informal "open door" policies that are briefly stated in one or two paragraphs in employee handbooks. Others provide a lengthy, formalized series of checks and balances designed to assure fair treatment of workers who believe they have been wronged in one way or another.

An informal survey conducted by the authors among some one hundred companies and institutions showed that most firms contacted had installed basically formalized procedures terminating in a final decision by the general manager. But a few had adopted procedures utilizing impartial arbitration along the lines specified in union contracts.

An informal "open door" policy utilized by some firms is illustrated by the following compact statement from an employee handbook:

> All problems should be taken up initially with the employee's immediate supervisor. Most of the problems will be settled at this point to the satisfaction of the employee. There may be times, however, when the nature of the problem is such that the supervisor may not be able to give an immediate answer. In those instances where the immediate supervisor is unable to solve the problem within two working days following the date of presentation by the employee, the employee may review the problem with his departmental manager or superintendent. In situations where, after having discussed his problem with this immediate supervisor and departmental manager or superintendent, an employee still has questions, he may take the problem to the personnel manager for disposition.

Other, less informal grievance procedures extend the route for appeal past the personnel or employee relations manager to the general manager. For example, one company prescribed a three-step procedure similar to the one quoted above, but added a fourth step as follows: "If the Employee Relations Manager is unable to give you an answer that resolves your problem, he will be happy to get you an appointment with the General Manager, who will give a fair and just answer to your problem after reviewing the facts." This company then assured employees that use of the grievance procedures would not jeopardize them in their jobs: "If you follow these steps, no one may criticize you, penalize you, or discriminate against you in any way. If you have a very personal problem that you wish to discuss with the Employee Relations Manager or any member of management, just tell your immediate supervisor of this fact, and he will get you an appointment."

One of the more formal, detailed grievance procedures reported in the survey is illustrated on pages 308–10. Note how it carefully specifies action time requirements for both the employee and supervisors and states that all decisions are to be handed down in writing.

CHURCH SUPPORT FOR ARBITRATION

A major boost for use of the arbitration process in employee-management disagreements has come from the Roman Catholic church. The church has adopted final and binding grievance-arbitration procedures to resolve internal personnel problems.

Responding to a demand for more democratic procedures in establishing policy and a method of resolving personnel problems, the 1969 national conference of Roman Catholic bishops adopted a resolution recommending experimentation with procedures recommended by the Due Process Committee of the Canon Law Society of America.

Among the steps recommended were:

1. The power of administrative bodies and administrators should be carefully defined and limited to avoid overlapping." One of the great causes of unrest . . . [is] lack of knowledge as to who made a particular decision."

2. Administrative bodies and administrators should publish written policies and standards. "It is crucial to the minimization of disputes that there be known what standards and criteria will be used by particular administrators . . . in reaching decisions in individual cases."

3. Persons who will be affected by policies should be encouraged to participate in the formulation of these policies.

4. Administrative decisions in individual cases should be accompanied by clearly stated findings of fact and supporting reasons. "Few things . . . spawn unrest and cater to the human fear of the unknown as much as administrative decisions secretly made, isolated from criticism, unsupported by findings of fact, unexplained by reasoned opinions, and free from any requirement that they be related to past precedents."

5. Not only should decision-making procedures on all levels in a diocese be fair, but they also should be recognized as fair. In accordance with this principle, when any administrative action affects a person adversely, he should be notified of the action before it takes place, and the information used in reaching an administrative decision should be made known to the parties concerned.

6. Conciliation, arbitration, and adjudication should be applicable to disputes arising out of the exercise of administrative authority on all levels." Mere administrative avenues of recourse for the resolution of such disputes are not effective."

KEY ELEMENTS OF GRIEVANCE PROCEDURES

To be effective, employee grievance procedures should contain the following features:

1. Three to five steps of appeal, depending upon the size of the organization. Three steps usually will suffice.

2. A written account of the grievance when it goes past the first level. This facilitates communication and defines the issues.

3. Alternate routes of appeal so that the employee can bypass his supervisor if he desires. The personnel department may be the most logical alternate route.

4. A time limit for each step of the appeal so that the employee has some idea of when to expect an answer.

5. Permission for the employee to have one or two co-workers accompany him at each interview or hearing. This safety-in-numbers approach helps overcome fear of reprisal.

Employees are entitled to know the reasons for decisions affecting them. Thus some procedure is necessary to examine the basis for decisions that employees believe to be unfair.

Personnel decisions are frequently unfair because the manager is not trained in the decisional process and is unaware of his biases. Therefore, when a grievance procedure gives the final say to a management representative, that executive or supervisor should be required to take an intensive course in the decisional process in order to improve the chances for a sound personnel decision.

ONE COMPANY'S "ACTION REVIEW" OF SALARIED EMPLOYEES' GRIEVANCES

Policy. It is our policy to provide a pleasant working environment for all employees. This is achieved by developing and maintaining cooperative working relationships among employees based on mutual respect and understanding. We recognize the need for a procedure that will allow employees to call attention to work-related matters that they feel need correction. The following procedure may be used for resolving such work-related problems.

Procedure. A grievance is defined as an alleged violation by the company of its established policies and/or practices with respect to wages, hours, or conditions of work, or where an employee claims that the company has shown discrimination among employees in the application of its policies and/or practices.

It is the employee's right to make his grievances known. Any employee who feels that he has a just grievance is encouraged to make use of the following procedure with the guarantee that in so doing he will in no way place his standing or job in jeopardy. If the basis of his complaint is found valid, immediate steps will be taken to correct the matter.

The employee-relations specialist is available upon request by the employee to assist in preparation and presentation of grievances at any step. The employee should be advised of this service

Step 1. Immediate Supervisor

A. The employee normally is expected to present his grievance to his immediate supervisor either verbally or in writing, but must do so within three working days of the alleged violation.

B. In unusual cases where the grievance is of a personal nature, the employee may discuss it with the employee-relations specialist. The employee-relations specialist will then arrange a meeting between the employee and his supervisor, and the employee-relations specialist will attend if the employee so requests.

C. The immediate supervisor will, within three working days, give the employee an answer (in writing if the employee so requests).

To retain flexibility and to reduce the number of formal steps in this procedure, the immediate supervisor should confer with all appropriate line management below the level of department head where it is deemed necessary. The answer given to the employee will then represent the combined opinion of the section head, foreman, assistant foreman, etc.

Step 2. Department Head

A. If the grievance is not resolved in Step 1 above, the employee may, within three working days, state his grievance in writing. Grievance forms may be obtained from the immediate supervisor or the office of the employee-relations specialist.

B. The immediate supervisor will add his answer to the written grievance and immediately submit it to the department head.

C. The department head will, within three working days, meet with the employee.

All levels of supervision involved in the Step 1 answer shall initial the written grievance before it is sent to the department head.

The employee-relations specialist shall be notified by the immediate supervisor of any grievance reduced to writing for Step 2 consideration.

The department head will discuss the grievance with the immediate supervisor and other appropriate supervisors before meeting with the employee and may call the immediate supervisor into the meeting to clear up any conflicting information given by the employee during the meeting.

Step 3. General Management Review

A. If the grievance is not resolved in Step 2 above, it may be referred to the director of personnel who will, within five working days, establish a date for a meeting with the general manager and the employee.

The department head shall refer the grievance to the director of personnel in all cases requiring Step 3 consideration. The director of personnel shall contact the employee to orient him to his Step 3 session with the general manager.

The general manager will discuss the grievance with the immediate supervisor and other appropriate supervisors before meeting with the employee and may call the immediate supervisor into the meeting to clear up any conflicting information given by the employee during the meeting.

B. After hearing the facts presented by the parties, the general manager will, within five working days, render his decision in writing to the employee through the employee's immediate supervisor.

The View from the Ombudsman's Chair

Frederica H. Dunn

In most companies an employee who feels he has been wronged has little recourse. He can go to his boss, who may be the source of the problem, he can go over his boss's head, which may pay off in the short term, he can suffer silently, or he can quit.

Neither the needs of the individual employee nor of the company are adequately served by these options. When I joined General Electric as an ombudsman, Gerhard Neumann, the executive vice president in charge of the Aircraft Engine Group, expected me to do these four things:

1. review the methods for handling complaints from employees and develop programs to correct any deficiencies.

2. improve communications between management and employees to eliminate cases where a complaint is unfounded but derives from the company's failure to explain its policies adequately.

3. work to reverse unfair decisions when valid complaints were made.

4. assure an impartial outlet for employee grievances.

The aircraft engine business is hectic and deadline-oriented. Missing a deadline delays completion of a program and defers the payoff that comes when an engine moves into production and starts earning, rather than absorbing, money.

Because of deadline pressures, managers often simply didn't have enough time to investigate employees' complaints, or employees were reluctant to "waste" an executive's time with "trivial" complaints, so they suffered in silence—at reduced rates of efficiency.

Generally, the existence of an ombudsman was welcomed by managers and employees alike. In the first year, over half of the three hundred cases that I investigated dealt with promotional opportunities and job search.

These issues were especially sensitive at this time, because the aircraft engine business was shrinking and a number of professional employees were receiving termination notices. There simply was not enough work for them. Generally, these were employees who ranked at the bottom of their job groups, based on performance.

In too many cases, I found that management's evaluation of their status in relation to others had never been communicated to them— even at the point when they were given their termination notices. In some extreme cases, some employees were given a raise one month and a termination notice the next, reflecting poor communications or the slowdown in business.

My extensive interviews both with the people who had received termination notices and their managers showed that in many cases the managers had been passing the buck—"Hate to let you go, Henry, I fought it up the line but couldn't do anything" or "They're making the cuts up the line, and I really don't have any say."

In isolated cases, where the manager had leveled with the affected employee well before the termination, the employee often chose not to hear what he was being told. As a result of these termination-oriented cases, new emphasis on candid, honest performance appraisals came from the vice president's office.

The sheer numbers of cases involving promotional opportunities and job search, as well as the depth and conviction of employees who felt they had been wronged, overlooked, or otherwise mistreated provided a strong basis for suggesting an in-depth look into the way professional jobs were being filled.

I found that, while many, if not most, jobs at this point were being filled with the most qualified candidates, many employees felt that "pull" and influence were more important than actual qualifications when an opening was filled.

As a result of information that I gathered and from other data provided by the personnel department and by employees, an employee panel studied the whole area for almost a year and came up with a staffing system, still in operation, that relies on the posting of all open positions exempt from union jurisdiction.

Some early cases that I dealt with involved minor housekeeping complaints: office too hot, copier won't work, etc. But as the ombudsman role became more clearly defined, these subsided. A sampling of cases from a typical month might include the following:

• A manager asking the ombudsman confidentially to find out where he stands. Through an organizational change, he had lost some of his responsibilities. Finding: He was still very highly regarded and the change was made to prepare for an anticipated work load increase in the area he retained.

• A complaint about "forced" overtime among engineers. Finding: The company policy was fair and correct, but some managers were operating by their own interpretations, which were not always correct. A frank letter from the vice president helped, but did not entirely eliminate these abuses.

• The denial of medical insurance payments to an employee for reasons unclear to him. Finding: The claim was payable and the man got his money.

The mere existence of the ombudsman encourages managers to be sure they can justify their actions. This preventive aspect is due largely to the high visibility the position is given, as well as to its high level organizationally—reporting directly to the top man. It would seem that trying to establish the role at a lower level or with less exposure could only result in failure.

Interestingly, although I expected to experience rebound cases, where a person would come to me for help with a problem and later return, claiming he had been subjected to retribution for using the ombudsman's office, no such cases ever materialized. I attribute this happy surprise to the visibility of the office and the fact that many managers viewed the ombudsman as an aid to reducing their work load, rather than as an adversary.

So far, I have discussed what an ombudsman *can* do. But there are plenty of things that the office *cannot* do. Among them:

1. Please people whose idea of justice is having their own way, even when it is objectively wrong.

2. Change managerial styles, even when they could objectively be considered wrong.

3. Replace the vital need for an employee and his manager to be honest and open with each other.

Besides considering what an ombudsman can and cannot do, it is important to evaluate what an ombudsman should be. I have some strong feelings in this area.

In my own case, I came to the role from outside the company. Hence, there were no skeletons in my closet, and I was starting with a clean slate. Selecting an ombudsman from the ranks of current employees would call for utmost care. The person should have an unassailable reputation for honesty and evenhandedness, or he will never generate the trust needed to make the role work.

The tenure of office for an ombudsman also should be considered. I favor two extremes: either a brief appointment of perhaps two years or a "lifetime" contract not unlike that of a Supreme Court justice.

In large companies, it would seem best to insure that the ombudsman could move from that position to an entirely different component or division. Otherwise, the conflict might emerge of trying to engineer your next job while trying to serve aggrieved employees in complete fairness. Certainly, this conflict could affect the ombudsman's performance and whose toes he chooses to step on.

At General Electric I held the ombudsman's position for two and a half years, and I welcomed the opportunity to move to a different kind of job in the International and Canadian Group, where I could utilize some of the experience that I obtained before joining the company. The Aircraft Engine Group now has two ombudsmen, and at least two other companies have started similar programs.

Making Unions Unnecessary:
The Open-Door Policy

Charles L. Hughes

What makes employees want to join a union? There are many reasons, and some of them may not even have occurred to you. What comes to mind first, of course, is *money*. Like all of us, your employees want to earn enough money to meet their needs and enable them to live the kind of life they feel they deserve for themselves and their families. If they are not being paid fairly for the work they do, money can be an important issue.

Surprisingly enough, however, money is not always as important as one may think as a factor in encouraging employees to turn to a union. If their salaries are in line with community standards, your employees' demands for more money may be a substitute for some of the other satisfactions that they aren't getting from their jobs. It's easier for them to demand higher wages than it is for them to put into words the other needs they have that they feel the organization isn't meeting.

Recent studies have shown that the needs employees feel most strongly are job security, confidence in management, and assurance of equal treatment. When needs like these aren't met on the job, employees often turn to demands for higher wages as a substitute for the things that they really want but aren't getting.

One of the strongest arguments a union makes when it is trying to organize a bargaining unit is that it can make management listen to employee problems and do something about them. In practical terms, you, the supervisor, *are* management to the employees who report to you. This means that how well you listen to the problems and complaints of the people in your unit directly affects how much appeal a union will have for them.

One important way in which you, as a supervisor, can provide the people who work for you with satisfactions for the non-monetary needs that they feel so strongly—and, at the same time, make it clear to them that they don't need a union to get what they want from their jobs—is by maintaining an open-door policy, which simply means letting your employees know that when they have a gripe, a complaint, or a problem, your door is always open to them—you are always there to listen to them and to do whatever you can for them.

KEY REQUIREMENTS

Here are the key requirements for conducting an effective open-door policy:

Let employees know about it. Use meetings, memos, face-to-face communications—any way that works. Let the people you supervise know that whenever they have a complaint or a problem, you will be there to help. In other words, be sure they know that your door is always open.

When people come to see you, be sure you talk to them right away. If you're pressed for time, make an appointment to see them later—within a day or two. But make it definite—not "Come back when I'm not so busy." If you seem to be putting them off indefinitely, they'll think that your open-door policy is nothing more than a gimmick.

After hearing the complaint, ask for any additional information you need to act on it.

If you can't solve the problem on the spot, say so. Tell the employee that you'll take it to your boss or another appropriate authority, or that you'll take some other specific action to get it resolved.

Tell the employee when you'll have an answer, and be sure to get back to him at that time. If you still don't have an answer then, explain why, and set up a new time.

Send the employee to see your boss when it is necessary. When employees' complaints are in areas in which they are questioning your authority or judgment—for example, such areas as shift scheduling, attendance problems, overtime assignments, or performance evaluations—it's to everyone's benefit for you to open the door to higher management. In most instances, of course, your boss will want you to attend any meetings with the affected employees or will at least want to hear your side of the story before making a decision. But supervisors who help employees see higher-level managers when it is appropriate are usually highly regarded and considered self-confident by their bosses. The weak supervisor tries to hide problems from higher management and is often instrumental in causing employees to join unions in order to be heard.

GIVING ANSWERS

When answering questions brought to you through your "open door," keep these points in mind:

Concentrate on what's right, not who's right. Base your decisions on company policies and regulations, not on personalities—who you like and who you don't like.

Phrase your responses in objective language. Avoid words that create a win-lose, me-you atmosphere. Stick to the facts when you're giving an answer to an employee complaint. It's fine to say, "I spoke to my boss, and he said that two days' notice on a shift change is sufficient." It's another thing to say, "I spoke to my boss and he backs me up all the way. You don't know what you're talking about." Rubbing it in creates resentment and undermines the whole purpose of an open-door policy.

If you're wrong, admit it. Everyone admires a person who's big enough to admit mistakes. Keep personal pride out of it. You make yourself bigger, not smaller, when you say, "You were right—I goofed on that one." And you gain the respect of someone who might otherwise be looking for a union to fight for him against the unreasonableness of his supervisor.

Don't expect too much. When you inaugurate an open-door policy, people will be suspicious of your motives. You have to anticipate a slow start at first. This means that the way you handle the first people who come to you with complaints or problems may determine the success of your open-door program.

AVOIDING COMMON MISTAKES

The open-door policy must not only be fair—it must be *seen* to be fair. This is a case where the form is very often as important as the substance. Your solutions to employees' problems may be absolutely equitable, but your manner or your way of speaking may give them the impression that they aren't getting a fair shake. If so, your open-door policy will lose its effectiveness.

Here are some important factors to keep in mind to ensure that you don't undermine your open-door program:

Take all complaints seriously. No matter how trivial a complaint may seem to you, remember that it's important to the person who's making it. Don't brush anyone off lightly; take enough time to make it clear that you are considering the complaint seriously before you respond.

Don't make employees defend their complaints. You have to get all the information you need to deal with the problem intelligently, but don't come on like a district attorney. Your objective is not to prove how sharp you are or to puncture the case the employee is making. You must make it clear that you are interested in their problems and concerned with treating them fairly.

Listen for the real problem. The complaints that employees bring to you are not always what is really bothering them. Very often, they are less concerned with *what* was done than with the *way* it was done. If you're aware of this, you'll be able to listen to complaints to find out what the real problem is.

Apologize if it's called for. If you find that the real problem is that you were rude or unnecessarily abrupt when giving a reasonable order, don't be afraid to apologize. A sincere apology, when it's warranted, won't make you look weak; on the contrary, it will increase your employees' respect for you.

Following these guidelines will enable you to maintain an open-door policy that will convince employees that you are interested in their problems and that they don't need a union to solve their problems on the job.

CASE IN POINT: CLOSING THE OPEN DOOR

Al Turner, vice-president for production at the Conway Corporation, looked up from his desk as Harry Weingarth entered his office. Harry supervised the assembly department at Conway, and Turner had some bad news for him.

"Come in, Harry," Turner said. "Sit down. We've got a problem, I'm afraid."

"I can't say that comes as a big surprise," Harry said. "When do you ever ask me to come to your office, when we *don't* have a problem?"

"Oh, come on now, Harry, it's not that bad. But this time we are in a little trouble," Turner said. "You heard about the fire last night in our warehouse?"

"Sure," Harry said, "I heard about it. But I understood it wasn't very serious."

"That's right," Turner said. "We were lucky. It could have been a lot worse. But there was some damage—and unfortunately, it affects us. That shipment for the Harbor Company was almost completely destroyed, and we have a solid commitment to make delivery to them on Monday."

"Great," Harry said. "So that means . . ."

"That means we're going to have to work tomorrow, Saturday, to get a new shipment together by Monday morning. I'm sorry, but your people are going to have to put in some overtime tomorrow."

Harry got up from his chair. "Well," he said, "that's not going to make anyone very happy, but I guess we have no choice. "I'll go give them the news."

On the way back to his department, Harry thought about his own plans for the weekend. He and his wife were going to take a trip to visit friends out of state—people they saw only once or twice a year. This Saturday job certainly shot down *that* idea. Harry wasn't looking forward to telling his wife that their trip was off. "These things always happen at the worst times," he thought.

He wasn't looking forward, either, to telling the assemblers in his department that their weekend plans, whatever they were, were also going to change. "Well," he thought, "it can't be helped. I might as well get it over with."

Harry walked over to the benches where the assemblers were working. "Let me have your attention, please," he said. "I'm going to make this short and sweet, and I don't want to hear any arguments. We're going to be working tomorrow, probably all day. So plan to be here at eight o'clock. We've got a lot to do." He turned and walked back into his office.

He had just sat down at his desk when Angela Alston, one of the assemblers, came into his office. "Listen, Mr. Weingarth," she said. "You kind of took us by surprise just now. What's this about working tomorrow?"

"You heard me," Harry said. "We have to work tomorrow, and that's all there is to it, so there's no point in talking about it."

"But I have plans for tomorrow, and they're very important to me," Angela said.

Harry shrugged. "We all had plans," he said.

"But this isn't fair," Angela said. "I thought it was company policy that we had to get weekend overtime assignments by Wednesday at the latest. This is Friday morning."

"Look," Harry said. "I'm not going to argue with you. You're all working tomorrow, and I expect to see you at your stations at eight o'clock. Anyone who doesn't like it had better start looking for another job."

Angela was furious when she got back to her bench. "It's just not fair," she said to the other assemblers. "He's supposed to tell us by Wednesday if we have to work on the weekend. That's always been the company policy."

"That's right," another assembler said. "Where does he get off telling us on Friday that we have to work on Saturday? There's no reason for that."

"You know what I think?" said a third worker. "I think he screwed up, and now he wants us to come in tomorrow to cover up for his bad planning. He doesn't care what the policy is as long as he looks good to management."

"Well, it really burns me up," Angela said. "We don't have to take this. I'm going to see the personnel director during the next break. Anyone want to come with me?"

During the next break, Angela and six other assemblers marched purposefully to the door of Carl Hyatt, the company's personnel director. "Mr. Hyatt," Angela said, "can we talk to you?"

"Why, yes—sure," Hyatt said. "Come on in. What's on your mind?"

Angela got right to the point. "Mr. Hyatt," she said, "it's a question of policy. Aren't we supposed to get weekend overtime assignments by Wednesday?"

Hyatt could see that the assemblers were angry. "Why, yes," he said. "That is the rule. Why?"

"Well," Angela said, "Mr. Weingarth just told us an hour ago we have to work tomorrow. Can he do that? I mean, what good is a rule if no one pays any attention to it?"

"Oh, I see," Hyatt said. "Well, look, I really don't know what the story is on this. If you'll wait here a few minutes I'll see what I can find out. I'm sure there's some explanation."

Hyatt left the office. A few minutes later, he returned with the production vice-president, Al Turner. "Thanks for waiting," Hyatt said. "I think Mr. Turner can clear this up for us."

"Mr. Hyatt told me about your complaint," Turner said. "First of all, let me tell you that this last-minute assignment wasn't Harry Weingarth's fault. He didn't know anything about it until this morning. In fact, none of us did. It's one of those things that came up all of a sudden."

"Mr. Weingarth didn't tell us that," Angela said.

"Well, he really should have," Turner said, "because it was nothing he or I could do anything about. I don't know if you heard about it, but we had a fire in our warehouse last night. One of our shipments was badly damaged—and it was a shipment we've promised to deliver on Monday. If we don't make delivery, we stand to lose a very important customer—and I don't have to tell you that could have very serious effects on our company. So we just have to get another shipment ready to send out on Monday."

"And that's why we have to work on Saturday?" Angela asked.

"That's right," Turner said. "Now, I'm not usually involved in the shift assignments, and I have to admit that I didn't know about the Wednesday rule. Mr. Hyatt has explained it to me, and you're absolutely right about it. Asking you to work tomorrow is contrary to our policy, and I apologize."

The tension in the room was beginning to ease. "But I hope you'll recognize," Turner went on, "that this is an emergency, and we really do need you to work tomorrow. In the future, we'll do everything we can to stick to our policy, but I think you realize that there are times when we have to make exceptions because we really have no choice. This is one of those times. Again, I'm sorry that it happened this way, but I hope you understand that asking you to work tomorrow is not a matter of choice—it's a matter of necessity."

There was silence for a moment, then Angela spoke up: "Okay, I guess we can understand that. And I guess it isn't as unreasonable as we thought at first. But what I don't understand is, why didn't Mr. Weingarth explain it to us right away?"

Comment

That's a good question. Actually, Harry made two mistakes. First, he gave an order that violated company policy without offering any explanation. That might be excused as an oversight, since he was upset about the situation, too. But when Angela came into his office, he compounded his error by not giving her any explanation for what seemed like an unreasonable order. What he did, in effect, was to close his "open door" and antagonize the people in this department. If the assemblers hadn't gone to see the personnel director, Harry would have had some very disgruntled employees on his hands—people who would be easy pickings for any organizer who promised that his union could protect them against such arbitrary and unreasonable treatment.

The Grievance Procedure in the Nonunion Setting: Caveat Employer

Richard L. Epstein

INTRODUCTION

It has become the pattern of nonunion employers, in their effort to remain nonunion, to offer employees the wages, programs, and job benefits which organizing unions try to convince employees are available only through unionization. That is why there is an increasing number of grievance procedures being adopted by nonunion employers. "If we have one already," reasons nonunion management, "the union can't sell our employees on needing a union to get one."

The purpose of this article is to show why it is preferable to avoid the adoption of a grievance procedure in a nonunion setting and, in the alternative, where the nonunion employer has one already in place, what safeguards should be attached to it.

THE TRADITIONAL GRIEVANCE PROCEDURE

The grievance procedure to which this discussion is addressed is the traditional type included in nearly every collective bargaining agreement. While there are variations among them, they all include these characteristics which are pertinent to the discussion:

1. A description of the cause or event in the employment relationship that entitles an employee to seek redress;

From the *Employee Relations Law Journal* 1, no. 1., Summer 1975. Copyright © 1975 by Executive Enterprises Publications Co., Inc., New York, N.Y. Reprinted by permission.

2. A printed form on which to record the nature and cause of the dissatisfaction;

3. A series of steps in which the grievant presents the matter to successively higher levels of supervision until there is either a satisfactory disposition or the final step;

4. An end to the procedure by either

 a. grievant's acquiescence to a denial of the grievance at any step; or

 b. management's granting the relief sought by the grievant; or

 c. an award by a pre-agreed third party making final disposition of the matter in dispute.

One of the foremost functions of a labor union is to provide assistance to its members (of the bargaining unit) with respect to matters of employee dissatisfaction. The usual mechanism for the performance of this function is the grievance procedure. In many ways the essence of unionization is the representative function manifest in the processing of grievances. (The other major aspect is of course related to the contract bargaining function.)

Grievance procedures are not without their logical quid pro quo, however. The concomitant to the grievance procedure is the union commitment to avoidance of work interruptions on account of disagreements arising during the term of the contract. (Some persons mistakenly view the no-strike obligation and the no-lockout obligation as the reciprocals. Not so; it is the grievance procedure and the no-strike arrangement.)

The cumulative effect of the grievance procedure in the unionized employer is substantial. It provides:

1. an employee with a means of airing a dispute without fear of reprisal;

2. knowledge by the employee that his position is supported by an organizational entity;

3. reliance on a final step to be decided by a neutral independent third party;

4. assurance on the part of the employer that the absence of grievances indicates a climate of general satisfaction, or one in which problems are being solved at relatively early stages.

NEEDS OF THE NONUNION EMPLOYER

Among the priorities of virtually all nonunionized employers who are vulnerable to unionization is to remain nonunion. Modern times have reasonably convinced such employers of two things—first, that the goal of remaining nonunion is attainable; and, second, that considerable effort and commitment are required to achieve it.

It has also been convincingly demonstrated that the success of unionization is a fairly direct function of the failure of management to discover and attend to employees' dissatisfaction. It is understandable, therefore, that the existence of the "grievance procedure" offers the nonunion employer the allure of a mechanism to solve or avoid one of management's most basic problems.

Purpose of the Grievance Procedure

The implementation of a grievance procedure by the nonunion employer is really intended by that employer to serve two purposes. First, of course, is the aim alluded to above—namely, to provide a reliable, observable mechanism to learn of and cure the various causes of employees' disgruntlement. Second is the presumed dividend of removing an enticing key benefit from among the wares of a campaigning union. The net result is that the nonunion employer understandably is inclined to view the grievance procedure as a must in its program to remain nonunion. The balance of this discussion will examine whether the employer's approach is sound. The reasons why it is not will be suggested.

FAILURE IN THE NONUNION SETTING

Procedural Requirements Absent

Commendable or understandable as the nonunion employer effort is, its feasibility should be examined. That is, the ingredients in the employment relationship that are essential to support a workable grievance procedure are absent in the nonunion employer. A viable grievance procedure requires these underlying characteristics:

1. *An adversary setting.* A grievance procedure must have a party (or parties) that will inherently represent or support the interests and position of the grievant. In a unionized employer, this role is filled by the unions, which provide support, assistance, and an atmosphere of protection to the employees who use the system, i.e., a representative of the grievant-employee such as the steward or other business representative; the provisions of the applicable collective bargaining agreement which provides for and enforces the procedural steps; and, perhaps of most importance, the intangible but all-pervasive environment of confrontation, whether it be subtle or distinct.

2. *Neutral third-party determination.* A fundamental characteristic of the traditional grievance procedure is the pre-existing assurance that if the matter is not settled by the parties themselves, an outside "neutral" third party will make a final, nonreviewable, nonappealable determination.* Traditionally, the neutral party is retained and paid by both the employee representative (the union) and the employer for the sole purpose of hearing the dispute and rendering a decision. He is intended to be literally independent of and without connection to either "side."

Malfunction in the Nonunion Setting

Lack of use. The fact is that the grievance procedure in the nonunion setting is, for the most part, rarely used by the employees. This is a consequence of the absence of the foregoing essential ingredients. Employees who do not have the security of a surrounding labor organization are reluctant to bring to their immediate supervisor the matters that are troubling them when the cause is that immediate supervisor's conduct. The resulting paucity of grievances deceives the employer into believing that personnel matters are in better condition than they actually are. The absence of grievances in the nonunion setting tends to signal a good environment when, in reality, it is merely a symptom of fearful employees. Another difficulty occurs when it is believed that the procedure's existence is solving problems when it is not, and such problems, without real attention, will persist. Put another way, the existence of the procedure encourages management to rely on it, and when it is not performing as intended, attention is not being given to the ongoing and recurring dissatisfactions experienced by employees. Ironically, the procedure conceals the very conditions it was designed to improve.

The problems when it is used. What, then, of the implicit suggestion that if the grievance procedure is used, the major drawback is eliminated? Or, can it be reliably observed that a used grievance procedure is necessarily better than none at all?

No. There are also significant dangers in the procedure when it is used. Assuming that there is an earnest effort to structure the procedure so that the final step will produce a fair decision by a fair-minded person, there is the ever-present risk that every decision will be viewed by some number of interested persons in an unfavorable light. Specifically, whenever the final step of the procedure results in a denial of a

---

*This does not refer to the usual civil court procedures that allow a party to challenge an award on procedural grounds, but not on merits.

grievance, observers of the system are inclined to charge that the procedure is a ruse, a "kangaroo court," a "management tool" designed to deceive employees, and so forth. That kind of charge has the ironic result of putting the employer in the position of being on the defensive for a program that was designed to produce a positive result.

Equally noteworthy are the decisions that uphold the grievances. At first or early blush, it would appear that nothing better proves the value of a grievance procedure than a grievance granted. It is submitted that the negative aspects of even this "best result" outweigh any value. Not the least of the problems is that the supervisor, and every person in the managerial hierarchy who supports his position, is undermined by the formal publicized reversal of their judgment. This challenge to the supervisor's dignity, in the open, is demoralizing to one who has among his responsibilities that of building morale. Beyond that, if the supervisor has any suspicion, justified or not, that the final decision unfairly favored the grievant, the result is a decidedly bitter supervisor.

Other disadvantages. Among the additional significant disadvantages connected with the use of the ordinary grievance procedure in the nonunion setting are these: Some procedures encourage or allow employees to be accompanied by another person, presumably to provide the environment of support discussed earlier as a function of a union. A companion helps to alleviate the notion of aloneness that an employee is ordinarily bound to feel in approaching the procedure's formal steps. The problem with this practice is that a person effective in this role may mature into a person to whom others will tend to look for similar aid or support. The characteristics of this person coincide in large measure with those of the usual employee organizer: articulate, possessed of qualities of leadership, possessed of a lively awareness of events, and with courage to confront the employer and the managerial hierarchy. The transition of such a person from a sometime representative to a more regular or even full-time representative is easy and inviting. To the extent that more than one such person emerges, this particular problem and its potential are magnified.

It was suggested earlier that the mere existence of the grievance procedure, whether or not used, will incline the management to become dependent on it as the mechanism for discovering complaints. This produces another disadvantage. Other means of solving problems will either not come into being or will atrophy. Particularly, the presence of the procedure tends to undermine any motivation of supervisors to learn about and respond to causes of employee dissatisfaction. It is gainsaid to observe that the supervisor's role is difficult enough. Understandably, he will seize on any device which would, in his view, relieve him of a responsibility.

Related to that is the similar situation with the communications to employees. That is, the supervisor has also, or should have, the responsibility to communicate to his employees the management's policies, programs, and general information. When the supervisor is relieved of the requirement to deal with employees by way of *listening* to them, it is likely that he becomes correspondingly lax in transmitting information to them. This combined development is an important drawback connected with the grievance procedure and flows from the mere existence of the procedure, whether or not it is actually used.

RECOMMENDATIONS

The first recommendation is that nonunionized employers who do not now have a formal grievance procedure study thoroughly the hidden undesirable consequences of having one. Behind the initially appealing facade are the very real incongruities that flow from trying to transfer to a nonunion setting that which was generated by and within negotiated union contracts.

What then of the employer, who remains convinced that the mere availability of such a procedure is all that is needed to make it worthwhile, outweighing any potential disadvantages? Where an employer wishes to install the procedure, or to continue an existing one, there are a number of conditions that ought to be attached:

1. To set up a bypass to allow a grievant to put a matter into the procedure without being first required to confront the offending supervisor. Such a substitute may be a person in the employment relations or personnel office, or anyone filling the role of ombudsman or other similar capacity. It may even be the supervisor's superior, although the practice of "going over someone's head" is, with good reason, offensive to both the grievant and his supervisor.

2. To make it absolutely clear that any employee who feels himself aggrieved need not resort to only the formal procedure to air a problem. Management must indeed provide other genuine outlets to whom employees may address their problems, and must see to it that employees know of their availability. These alternatives for airing employee dissatisfactions include the so-called open-door policy, if it is really so, with an ombudsman or some other member of higher management. Best of all is the practice wherein managerial persons meet regularly with all employees, in small groups, to encourage the discussion of

problems, and to follow up with private talks and solutions.

3. To study whether some of the worrisome aspects of a formal procedure should be avoided by the use of an outside neutral party as the final step of the procedure. However, the use of an outside neutral results in the important disadvantage of having an outsider make a final decision on an internal matter. In any event, the procedure should be examined as to whether and to what extent the procedure is authentic or a mere gesture. It is not suggested by this that a gesture, in itself, is bad; if the grievance procedure is only that, there is all the more reason for evaluating its effects, its dangers, and its limitations. Nevertheless, the use of an outside final judge may have the benefit of avoiding the need for a member of management or supervision to publicly reverse a lower-level decision. An outside reversal can always be grumbled about internally at the same time that the grievance is granted. In this way, the grievant is served and the supervisor's need to maintain his position is achieved. Perhaps the difficulty of this particular aspect focuses on the main problems and features of the voluntary girevance procedure and, as such, should be considered in that light.

4. To make absolutely sure that other means of communication are not abandoned or ignored and are, in fact, encouraged.

Within the last observation is the essence of this article. Ultimately, neither the goal of good personnel relations generally, nor maintenance of a nonunion condition specifically, are achieved through devices, mechanisms, or shortcuts. The business of personnel is a sometimes tedious, always burdensome, and a universally difficult undertaking. The sooner and the better management commits itself to the discovery of and response to employee dissatisfactions in an atmosphere where the employee can communicate effectively and without inhibition, the more assured is the achievement of employer goals. The grievance procedure in the nonunion setting is only one example of a wholly inadequate substitute for the real thing.

The Antiunion Grievance Ploy

Of all the techniques that managements are using in the current campaign to create a "union-free environment," probably the most important was originated by the unions. It is the establishment of a system for adjudicating a worker's complaints about his job or his boss. Increasingly, companies are installing grievance procedures, often patterned after union systems, and sometimes even including arbitration as the final determinant, for nonunion employees. But the final irony may be that this antiunion ploy itself contains the seeds of unionism.

The spread of grievance mechanisms in nonunion situations is partly attributable to employer recognition that today's workers are more independent and better-educated than ever before and partly to a very conscious effort to keep the unions at bay. A workable grievance procedure is "probably the single most important way to keep a union out of a plant," says John G. Wayman, a senior partner of the Pittsburgh law firm of Reed Smith Shaw & McClay, which represents employers on labor matters. "It's essential that an employee has some way to present his complaint, to have someone pay attention to that complaint and give him what he will consider to be a fair answer," Wayman says.

That kind of advice is typically given these days by the many consulting firms that thrive on advising companies how to avoid unions. Indeed, the ability of unions to protect employees from arbitrary actions by managers has probably been a more powerful attraction for workers than organized labor's wage-bargaining power. "Gaining justice on the job and restricting the right of management to do what it wants with the employee would not have happened without unions," says Ben Fischer, a grievance and arbitration expert who recently retired after thirty-four years on the staff of the United Steelworkers.

The USW and other old CIO unions, such as the United Auto Workers, have been the leaders in developing comprehensive grievance procedures with arbitration as the endpoint. These procedures generally provide three or four steps at which a worker's complaint is considered by union and management officials at ever higher levels, followed by a binding decision by an arbitrator, if necessary. Grievance arbitration has been especially effective in the steel and auto industries, where permanent umpires—outside arbitrators and their staffs—are maintained by union and management at each company.

Nonunion grievance systems range from the structured procedure of the typical union setting to mechanisms that are purposely kept formless so as not to present a target for union organizers. Many companies have long had an "open door" policy under which a worker theoretically can take his gripe up through management ranks and even into the chief executive's office. But this system usually promises more than it delivers and often does not alleviate a worker's fear of retribution for complaining about his boss. The existence of a more formalized structure seems to encourage employee use.

Hundreds of companies have installed such a system. For example, Tektronix Inc., of Beaverton, Oregon, a large electronics manufacturer that has no unions, provides a five-step procedure for its 20,000 employees. A worker's complaint is reviewed by successively higher layers of management. In the fifth step, the employee meets with President Earl Wantland, who has the final say. Only three or four cases have gone that far in the last three years. About 90 percent of the grievances are resolved at the first step, says Jim D. Harper, a human resources department manager. He says this is because lower-level managers "don't want to go up the chain and have a group vice-president tell them that they were wrong."

FEAR OF RETALIATION

Making a formal procedure work in a nonunion shop requires constant care and attention, and such systems often fail because they are essentially one-sided. The president of a plastics manufacturer in Connecticut says his company installed a grievance procedure about two years ago but found that "it doesn't work in a nonunion circumstance." He adds: "People are afraid of management retaliation. They don't understand it."

A formal system can also make a company ripe for unionization. "To the extent you formalize a process, you invite union representation," says the employee relations vice-president of a large Midwest manufacturer. "The union organizers tell the workers that the process is failing because the representation is wrong. They say, 'Leave the structure, we'll provide the representation.' "

The most famous example of a union capture of a nonunion grievance system occurred in the 1930s. To avoid unionization, most large steel companies had installed "employee representation plans," which enabled workers to select other employees to represent them in grievance meetings that were controlled by the company. Steel-union organizers zeroed in on those representatives, converted them to union activism in many plants, and on this foundation organized most of the industry within a few years. "As soon as the company begins formulating structures for the employee, he begins walking toward a union," says Ben Fischer. "There's a point at which the worker demands better representation, and a company union ceases to be a company union."

RETAINING CONTROL

Such a turnaround is by no means inevitable, and many companies are convinced that they can retain control of a formal procedure. Moreover, the companies seldom relinquish the final decision-making power in the grievance process. Some companies have tried to make that process more objective by appointing an ombudsman to rule on workers' complaints. McDonald's Corporation, the giant hamburger chain —which has 4,000 nonunion stores—recently created such a position. And Singer Company started the practice three years ago for its 30,000 nonunion employees. One ombudsman says the concept works fairly well but he admits that "as a member of management, I can't be completely impartial."

A relatively few companies—Northrop Corporation and Trans World Corporation, among others—take the additional step of submitting unresolved grievances to outside arbitrators. At Northrop, which is a large, nonunion aerospace company, three or four cases annually go to arbitration following a three-step appeals procedure.

TWA provides a three-member arbitration board to resolve unsettled grievances filed by its 7,500 nonunion workers, including airport agents, reservation clerks, and nonmanagement administrative employees. The system has existed since 1960, but only after it was streamlined in recent years did the arbitration procedure receive frequent use. In 1969, only twelve cases went to arbitration, compared with fifty in 1978.

If a worker is not satisfied with the handling of his job complaint at two lower-level steps, he can appeal to the board and select a co-worker to be his representative on the board. The company is represented by a manager from a rotating panel; the chairman of the board is an outside arbitrator in all discharge cases and the personnel vice-president in other cases. "The employee's representative knows the work scene very well and can explain the facts of life on the job," says Mary Jean Wolf, TWA's director of personnel. "It gives the employee a good shot at getting a fair decision." Although a majority of the three board members can decide a case, the decision is almost always unanimous, Wolf says.

ON THEIR TOES

There are some dangers in widespread use of the procedure, Wolf says. Supervisors tend to "rely on it to do their job for them," she says. At some TWA locations, a few employees have become "almost professional representatives of workers, and they're very open about their hopes of organizing a union." But TWA's awareness of the threat of unionization keeps managers on their toes. Moreover, Wolf adds, "I think if we didn't provide an outlet for grievances, the employees would find one."

There is reason to believe that more companies will turn to outside arbitrators to resolve grievance disputes in nonunion situations. An increasing number of worker grievances involve race, sex, and age discrimination, which often wind up in costly and lengthy court cases. For this reason, the American Arbitration Assn. has drawn up rules for arbitrating such issues before they get to court, and AAA President Robert Coulson thinks that eventually companies may submit all types of unresolved grievances to outside arbitration.

VII.

The Right of Participation

Employee Participation in Corporate Decision Making

Phillip I. Blumberg

American labor has traditionally concentrated on basic economic considerations rather than on achieving participation in the exercise of corporate power. To the limited extent that significant labor participation in corporate decision making exists in the United States, it arises out of the collective bargaining process, reflecting the distinctively different pattern of American labor relations. Nevertheless, there are incipient signs of change. This summary review explores the wide spectrum of employee or union activities through which influence on management decision is being exerted directly or indirectly in the United States today, as well as possible areas for increased participation in the future.

I. MANAGEMENT PARTICIPATION AS A SOLUTION TO JOB DISSATISFACTION

The attitudes of American employees toward work are a matter of increasing concern. Job alienation, widespread absenteeism, increased labor turnover, declining worker productivity, resistance to repetitive work assignments, poor morale, and hostility toward the production line are familiar features of the current American scene. Lordstown has become a familiar part of the vocabulary. As a result, there has been increasing discussion in the United States of job dissatisfaction and the importance of the work environment. Job redesign, job enrichment, improved upward communications, and improving the quality of factory and office life have become recognized public concerns.

There have been many experiments in job redesign and job enrichment in the United States, which have become increasingly well publicized. These rest on the view that worker participation in the decisions that affect the nature of their jobs coupled with an atmosphere of mutual confidence and respect between employer and employee may contribute to solution of the underlying problems. This, of course, means worker participation in decision making on the factory floor or office level. It may also seem to represent a loss of management prerogatives to the extent that workers help decide questions previously decided by management. This, however, depends on whether these programs are regarded as steps toward industrial democracy or other fulfillment of worker objectives, or as managerial techniques. In such experiments in the United States, management has encouraged worker participation because it leads to more efficient operations. What is accomplished is being done under employer leadership for the employer's benefit. Further, the fact of the matter is that with isolated exceptions, these developments involve very small numbers of employees and represent only the earliest of beginnings. Estimates of all workers in the entire country involved in such programs range from three thousand to ten thousand. Nevertheless, these projects may well be a significant portent of the future.

Thus far, the initiative has come from management, while union leadership is doubtful or suspicious, if not hostile. Job redesign is dismissed as a pretext for imposing heavier work loads or reducing the number of jobs. This represents a challenging opportunity to which American union leadership has not generally responded.

There is a substantial view that meaningful participation requires direct, rather than representative, employee participation and that the solution to worker alienation is to be achieved in the factory or the office, not through representation on the remote board of directors. One may well inquire, however, whether union participation on the factory and office level in the restructuring of work will not also ultimately lead to union pressure for board representation. Although participative management rests on personal involvement of the worker, representation on the board—if it develops—would serve union aspirations for increased power. The two possible objectives clearly fulfill different functions. Union involvement in the one may, nevertheless, lead to union pressure for the other.

II. PARTICIPATION THROUGH MEMBERSHIP ON THE BOARD OF DIRECTORS

A. Union Attitudes and Efforts

In the past, American unions have been almost entirely unconcerned with the issue of union or employee representation on the board of directors. Notwithstanding the widespread development of co-determination in Europe, the interest of such organizations as the International Confederation of Free Trade Unions and the International Labor Organization in which American unions have been active, and considerable discussion in American intellectual circles without trade union affiliations, the American labor movement has ignored the issue. Recently, however, there have been a number of developments that might herald some intensification of American union interest in representation on the board.

1. *The Providence and Worcester Railroad.* In what has been described as a "precedent-shattering labor agreement," a recent labor agreement with the United Transportation Workers provides for a union representative on the board of this tiny former fragment of the Penn Central System. This is apparently the first American labor agreement of its kind. The small number of workers affected and the Lilliputian size of the railroad, however, remove most of the significance that would otherwise attach to this development.

2. *General Tire and Rubber.* Union representation on the board of directors of General Tire and Rubber Company was publicly announced as one of the 1973 negotiating demands of the United Rubber Workers. The final agreement contained no such provision, and it does not appear that this was a serious objective. The demand arose on the local union level, and the United Rubber Workers itself has taken no official position in favor of, or in opposition to, union representation on the board.

3. *United Airlines.* United Airlines pilots affiliated with the Air Line Pilots Association conducted a 1972 campaign to elect a pilot to the board of the airline's parent, UAL, Inc. Reflecting concern over the poor operating result of the airline, the campaign had the ostensible objective of improving communications, rather than participation in decision making. The pilots hoped for support from sixteen thousand employees with voting rights under the employee pension fund, holding

approximately 1,000,000 shares out of 18,424,065 outstanding. At the annual meeting, however, only 5 percent of the shares were voted for the pilots' proposal. Although the pilots announced that they would continue their efforts, the campaign was not renewed in 1973. It may be noted that the campaign received no support from the national Air Line Pilots Association. It is also not without interest that this campaign for board representation involved highly skilled employees, earning in some cases $50,000 to $60,000 per year; ideological considerations were clearly not involved.

4. *McDonnell Douglas Corp.* In 1973, local officers of the International Association of Machinists, whose members reportedly hold more than 10 percent of the stock of McDonnell Douglas through the employee stock purchase savings plan, have announced their intention to win proxy authorization from union members to vote their shares at the 1974 annual meeting.

5. *Grumman Aircraft.* A group of Grumman Aircraft shareholders and employees calling themselves "Concerned Shareholders and Employees" announced that it would present an opposition slate of directors at the Grumman 1973 annual meeting of stockholders. As in the case of United Airlines, the proposal did not rest on ideological considerations. It reflected the concern that poor management performance and the loss of important contracts with the Department of Defense threatened contraction of operations and extensive layoffs. The program was apparently later abandoned, and the nominations were not presented to the annual meeting.

In summary, despite the isolated instances described above, there does not appear to be any significant American union interest in board representation at the present time. On the contrary, as Professor Robert Dahl points out, "Workers and trade unions may be the greatest barriers at present to any profound reconstruction of economic enterprise in this country."

B. Social Reform Efforts Through the Proxy Process

In contrast to union attitudes, employee participation in corporate decision making on the board level has attracted support from intellectual circles not affiliated with the labor movement. This has been evident in shareholder proposals under Rule 14a-8(c) of the Rules of the Securities and Exchange Commission, leading to so-called public interest proxy contests. These proposals, which have reflected a wide spectrum of contemporary concerns for social reform, have included proposals for employee representatives on the board, usually coupled with proposals for representatives from other groups, such as blacks and women or dealers and consumers, as well.

In Campaign GM Round II, for example, the Project for Corporate Responsibility supported by Ralph Nader submitted three "public interest" resolutions to the General Motors 1971 annual meeting, including a proposal that the General Motors board include a representative of employees, as well as of dealers and consumers. Irving Bluestone, vice president and director of the General Motors department of the United Automobile Workers, attended the annual meeting to express union support for the proposals. The resolution for board representation received only 1.1 percent of the votes cast. Although Mr. Bluestone has spoken extensively on worker participation in decision making, he has not pressed for board membership. Nor has the United Automobile Workers adopted the objective, although Walter Reuther had attempted for a while to interest the American labor movement in participation in management.

Shareholder proxy proposals calling for employee, black, and women directors were submitted to four major corporations in 1972. They received no significant assistance from labor groups and, as with other shareholder proposals, were overwhelmingly defeated. The greatest support was the 4.9 percent of the vote cast at the 1972 Chrysler Corporation annual meeting for a proposal to add employee, black, and women representatives to the board. A similar proposal at the Ford annual meeting received only 1 percent of the vote.

Even more important, the proposals for employee representation, unlike those for black or women members on the board, have attracted no public support. Thus, public pressures intensified by the publicity generated by such "public interest" proxy proposals have led more than eighty major corporations to elect black directors and twenty to elect women directors; a new pattern in corporate affairs has been established. With corporate acceptance of black and women directors accelerating, proposals for black or women directors or consumer directors continued to be presented to the 1973 annual meetings of major corporations; in others, management was challenged at the annual meeting about the absence of black or women directors. In contrast, there was no proposal for employee directors in 1973.

It may be premature, however, to assume that proposals for employee representation on the board will not reappear in the event unions develop interest in this objective. The Northern States Power episode involving cumulative voting may point the way. Encouraged by a 9.13 percent vote in favor of a 1972 shareholder proposal to add two public-interest advocates to the Northern States Power board, social reform groups sought to elect one director to the fourteen-member board of the company in 1973. Management responded by legal maneuvers (involving reduction of the board to twelve members, of whom four would be elected each year for three-year terms) to increase the percentage of the vote required for the election of a director through cumulative voting from 6.67 percent to 20.01 percent. In the ensuing litigation, the management proposal was held invalid by the trial court. As this is being written, the result of the election is not known.

The Northern States Power model may well be adopted by reform groups in other companies employing cumulative voting. In such event, it is not unlikely that labor groups may be inspired to follow suit. As we have seen, United Airlines was involved in just such an effort in 1972. Thus, the proxy process, particularly in those companies where cumulative voting survives, may yet prove to be a meaningful avenue for attempts to elect employee or union representatives to the board.

C. Management Efforts

In at least one recent case, an American corporation of significant size has elected local union officers to its board. Consolidated Packaging Corporation, a listed corporation with 1972 net sales of approximately $70 million and two thousand employees, elected a production worker (and union officer) from one of its problem plants to its board in 1972 to develop better communications and union credibility in management financial reports. The company subsequently reported that the contributions of the employee director (who was the president of one of the two local unions of the United Paper Workers) were "one of the factors contributing to improved operating results." The practice was repeated in 1973 with the selection for the board of another production worker from the same plant who was an officer of the other local union.

III. PARTICIPATION THROUGH COLLECTIVE BARGAINING

In the United States, the collective bargaining agreement strengthened by the employer's duty to bargain under the National Labor Relations Act ("the Act"), rather than direct governmental controls, has served as the basic legal process imposing restraints on employer power for the protection of employees. One example will illustrate. In the United States, the employer is, as a matter of law, free to discharge an employee

—not protected by contract—without severance pay or notice, for any reason whatsoever or for no reason at all (except for such matters forbidden by statute as discrimination for race, color, religion, sex, national origin, age, or union activity). Such unrestrained employer legal power is, however, limited by collective agreements, which almost invariably prohibit discharge without "just cause."

In this manner, the basis for American union or worker participation in decision making may be found in the collective bargaining process rather than in statute or administrative regulation. Thus, Professor Sturmthal notes that "to the uninitiated observer, it might appear that United States labour does not participate in management at all," but concludes that "collective bargaining as practiced by United States unions has represented an effective form of workers' participation in management, though by indirect means."

American union objectives have traditionally involved economic matters such as wages, hours, vacations and holidays, pension and insurance benefits, working conditions, safety, training, and union and job security. Participation in management has not been an objective of American labor; there has been no ideological concern with industrial democracy. Nevertheless, through the collective agreement, the interaction between union and management in its administration, and the arbitration machinery to resolve differences, unions in the United States play a role in decision making at the plant level. Further, out of concern for job security, American unions have sought participation in management decisions affecting the availability of work.

Under recent legislation in Germany, the Netherlands, and Denmark, and under the proposed draft statute for a European Company *(Societas Europaea)* in the European Economic Community, European work councils have been given a consultative role in such management decisions affecting job security as mergers, plant relocations, and shutdowns.

In the United States, the right of management to make such decisions or to act without any obligation to consult with unions or employees has been determined by the relative economic strength and priorities of management and labor in the bargaining process. American employers on the whole have been successful in insisting on a management control clause under which such matters have been expressly reserved for management decision. On the other hand, a 1969 survey of the Bureau of Labor Statistics revealed that as many as 21.5 percent of the agreements surveyed, covering nearly three million workers, contained some restriction on management's right to close or remove a plant. With such exceptions, American management is thus still generally able to make fundamental business decisions of this nature without direct labor intervention.

It should be recognized, however, that even where collective agreements do not deal directly with such matters, the arbitration process may result in limitations on managerial decision. Arbitrators may find implied obligations regulating managerial discretion in these areas and require a demonstration of "good faith" or "fair dealing" evidenced by a rational basis for the management decision relating to efficient operations and reflecting concern for employee interests and expectations.

In their effort to limit managerial power over decisions affecting job security, American unions have sought assistance from the National Labor Relations Board ("the Board"). For years, unions exerted substantial pressure on the Board to hold that management was under a duty under the Act to bargain on such decisions related to job security as the sale or relocation of the business or the subcontracting of work. The Board refused and required employers to bargain only over the provision to be made for the employees adversely affected by such decisions. In 1962, the Board changed its policy and held in *Fibreboard Products.* [1] that an employer was required under the Act to bargain over a decision to subcontract work. The Supreme Court affirmed. [2]

After its reversal of policy in the *Fibreboard Products* case, the Board ordered employers to bargain in good faith over decisions to close or relocate plants, to sell part of the business, or to transfer work between plants although valid business reasons supported the decision and no antiunion objective could be shown. [3] The Board's expanded position was not upheld by the circuit courts. In 1971, the Board retreated and held that contrary to its decisions after 1962, the Act did not require bargaining over an employer's decision to close or sell part of its business. [4] This reversal of position has restricted the use of obligations under the Act as a method of enabling unions to play a participative role in fundamental management decisions affecting job security. Unions may, of course, attempt to persuade employers to bargain over such matters, but it is no longer an unfair practice under the Act if employers refuse to do so. It should be noted, moreover, that even where an employer is under a statutory duty to bargain, there is no obligation to reach an agreement. An impasse in the negotiations may develop without violation of the Act.

Railroad workers have received greater statutory protection than workers generally. Section 5(2)(f) of the Interstate Commerce Act, for example, requires the Interstate Commerce Commission in approving railroad mergers to "require a fair and equitable arrangement to protect the interests of the railroad employees affected," for a period of four years. Similarly, the Railway Labor Act has been held to require bargaining over a management decision to eliminate railroad stations (and thereby reduce jobs).

In summary, the collective bargaining process, its day-to-day administration, and its arbitration machinery have provided American labor with important influence over managerial decision making, notwithstanding the absence of formal corporate machinery for such participation or of worker representation on the board of directors.

IV. PROFIT SHARING AND PARTICIPATIVE MANAGEMENT

Above and beyond the customary collective bargaining relationship, a number of companies have adopted programs of participative management combined with profit sharing as an inducement to worker and union acceptance of technological change. Under these programs, workers and unions participate in decisions with respect to technological improvements and the introduction of new equipment and new processes. The best known of these programs, the Scanlon Plan, provides for worker production committees under union leadership to join in such decisions, with workers receiving the major portion of the labor savings resulting from the increased plant efficiency.

The combination of profit sharing and participative management, which has also been termed "progress sharing," has received some degree of acceptance by management and labor alike. Examples include the Kaiser Steel Long Range Sharing Plan introduced in 1962 and the program at American Velvet Company which goes back to 1940. The American Velvet Company Plan involving four hundred unionized workers allocates 30 percent of total net profits (not merely profits or savings resulting from innovation) to employees. Extensive union and worker participation in decision making at the factory level has contributed to sweeping technological change, which has enabled the plant to remain competitive. The firm, which had previously been considering liquidation or relocation from Connecticut to the South, has prospered, and both the owner-management on the one hand and the union and employees on the other are enthusiastic about the results.

V. DIRECT PARTICIPATION: EXPERIMENTS IN EMPLOYEE-OWNED ENTERPRISES

There are a number of American enterprises of significant size which are employee-owned or in which employees have a substantial direct stock interest. Although the number of such enterprises is larger than generally recognized, these instances are isolated. The development is not without interest but hardly may be regarded as a likely model of future industrial organization. These include such companies as American Cast Iron Pipe Co., Champion Home Builders, Inc., Chicago & Northwestern Transportation Co., Levi Strauss & Co., Lincoln Electric, and Overnite Transportation Co. Sales to employees as a method of divestment have also achieved a certain prominence. Thus, it has been reported that employee purchases were accounting for about 5 percent of corporate divestitures.

The sale of the Chicago & Northwestern Railway to the railroad's employees has attracted considerable attention. In 1972, the Chicago & Northwestern Railway was sold by its parent, Northwest Industries, Inc., to a newly organized corporation owned by 1,000 of the railroad's 13,500 employees, including senior executives, who invested approximately $3,600,000. This appears, however, to represent more of an ingenious method for the parent to divest itself of its railroad operations yielding an inadequate return and burdened by $338,804,000 of indebtedness than a grass-roots effort by employees to establish a new industrial society. Thus, it has been reported that shares that were originally purchased by employees for $50 have been resold at prices ranging from $125 to $500.

The critical question is whether in these firms employee participation in decision making differs significantly from conventional firms. Employee stock ownership may contribute to increased motivation and higher productivity, but there is little evidence to suggest that management functions have been affected. Notwithstanding significant employee ownership, none of the companies specified above has any non-executive employee on the board. Thus, in the Chicago & Northwestern, the ICC-approved plan provides for a three-person board of directors, consisting of two senior executives and an outside director. These three men are also trustees of a ten-year voting trust with sole right to vote for directors and certain other matters.

Smaller employee-owned firms may involve genuine employee participation in management, but in view of their small size and isolated number, they have no real significance. Thus, employee stock ownership in the United States does not appear to have led to any meaningful reallocation of corporate power.

VI. PARTICIPATION THROUGH EMPLOYEE STOCK PURCHASE AND BENEFIT PLANS AND "PASS THROUGH" VOTING

Employee stock purchase plans and employee pension, profit sharing, and savings and thrift plans investing in employer stock are increasingly common features of American corporate life.[5] Substantial positions in some of the largest American corporations are held by, or for the benefit of, American workers in this manner. These holdings provide a potential instrument through which employees may influence corporate policy and participate in the decision-making process. As noted, the recent developments involving United Airlines and McDonnell Douglas are initial isolated steps in this direction.

Under most plans, the corporate stock is held in an employee trust fund and voted by the trustees, administering the fund. These trustees are almost invariably either individuals associated with the senior management of the employer or institutions, appointed and usually subject to removal by the employer, and thus, as a practical matter, under its control. It is only where the trustees "pass through" their voting power to the participants in a plan that the possibility of employee influence through the substantial concentrated holdings of employer stock held by a fund becomes realistic.

Such pass-through voting has become increasingly common. The Gilbert Brothers' Annual Survey for 1972 lists forty-seven major corporations with trust funds providing for pass-through voting. The Bankers Trust Company 1972 survey lists savings and thrift plans of 105 additional major firms with trusts utilizing pass-through voting, in whole or in part.[6] These impressive totals reflect the wise policy of the New York Stock Exchange Department of Stock List, which since 1961 has pressed corporations to authorize pass-through voting where 1 percent or more of outstanding stock was held by an employee trust fund.

Sears, Roebuck & Co. is perhaps the best-known example of this development. As of December 31, 1972, 30,735,251 shares (or approximately 20 percent of the outstanding stock) with a market value of $3.5 billion were held by the Sears Savings and Profit Sharing Pension Fund for the benefit of 224,142 employee participants, subject to pass-through voting. This is in addition to substantial shares previously distributed to employees upon retirement; for example, in 1972 alone, almost 3,200,000 shares (or approximately 2 percent of the outstanding shares) were so distributed. It should be noted that employees retiring with twenty-five to thirty years of service during 1972 received on the average a distribution of $114,832 in cash and Sears stock. It may be noted that the participants with an average stake of approximately $15,600 each in the trust fund and anticipating distributions of such magnitude upon retirement most likely regard their indirect interest in Sears as an investment rather than as a form of industrial democracy. In such event, the participant as investor will have replaced the participant as employee.

Other corporations providing for pass-through voting stock held in employee benefit or savings funds include:

Company	Number of Shares Held by Fund[7]	Number of Outstanding Shares 1972[8]	Percentage of Outstanding Shares[9]
Bendix	1,450,000	12,344,067	11.8
Broadway-Hale Stores	2,000,000	16,587,333	12.0
Burlington Industries	2,863,074	26,796,463	10.7
Caterpillar Tractor	2,581,388	57,028,955	4.5
General Dynamics	1,141,293	10,546,279	10.9
General Motors	10,231,467	285,922,900	3.6
International Harvester	1,476,517	27,469,736	5.4
McDonnell Douglas	4,237,031	37,672,397	11.2
Phillips Petroleum	5,484,091	75,386,711	7.0
TRW	1,290,586	25,375,369	5.0
Textron	2,952,322	27,284,000	10.8
United States Steel	5,953,347	54,169,462	11.0

Some of the larger holdings may possess the potential concentrated power to influence corporate policy, provided that the participants concerned are prepared to vote in concert. Although this potential power has never been exercised, the existence of such power is, however, a factor of significance. It seems not unlikely that sooner or later unions in one or more of these enterprises will endeavor to induce members to vote their shares for shareholder proposals furthering union objectives or to elect representatives to the board.[10] If such unions can successfully mobilize their member-participants, the balance of power in industrial relations in such concerns could be profoundly affected.

VII. PARTICIPATION THROUGH SHAPING THE CLIMATE OF PUBLIC OPINION

A significant recent development has been the dramatically increased concern of employees about the social, moral, or environmental implications of corporate decisions.

Corporations conducting substantial defense business, doing business in South Africa, accused of discriminatory employment policies, of unsafe products, or of adverse impact on the environment have been faced with confrontation with their own employees in addition to public opposition. Underground newspapers published by employees for employees, such as *The Stranded Oiler, The Met Lifer, The AT&T Express,* and *The GE Resistor,* the distribution of employee leaflets on company premises and other opposition to an employer's "complicity" in the war in Vietnam, and employee boycotts and picketing in opposition to corporate policies, as in the case of Polaroid and South Africa, reflect this new development. These activities have a common objective: an attempt to influence corporate decision making through the now-common confrontation techniques in which social or political protest is expressed in a manner calculated to achieve high public visibility and thereby generate public pressures.

Unauthorized disclosure of aspects of corporate behavior believed socially undesirable, or so-called whistle-blowing, is perhaps the most frequent form of employee social protest. Employees concerned with corporate behavior in areas of public policy concern have been reported to constitute an important source of disclosure about corporate conduct involving such areas as discrimination, product safety, and the environment. Jack Anderson, for example, reports: "Conscientious and concerned employees have turned over to us thousands of incriminating documents [on safety defects] from the files of General Motors, the world's largest corporate citadel."

These acts reflect a new view of responsibility on the part of employees: a view that the employee's duty as a citizen transcends his duty as employee, a view that the employee should act primarily for the good of the country—the public interest—rather than for the good of the employer. They also involve the principle that employees should play a part in the corporate decision-making process in issues of public concern involving questions of corporate social responsibility.

Such response by employees placing presumed social or moral values above traditional concepts of their duties of loyalty and confidentiality to their employer is a marked departure from the past. However undesirable it may be in particular cases, it is a reality that cannot be ignored. In view of the sensitivity of corporate management to the climate of public opinion and the increasing extent to which corporate decision making is influenced by public expectations and demands, the technique of unauthorized disclosure is influential. It should be recognized as a powerful instrument by which employee action may play an important role in the corporate decision-making process. It may well prove to be more significant in the United States than academic proposals for representation on the board.

VIII. PARTICIPATION THROUGH LEGISLATION

There has been no political interest in employee representation on the board. On the contrary, isolated state statutes that previously permitted corporations to provide in their certificate of incorporation or by-laws for election of directors by employees have been repealed.

Incipient steps for adoption of a federal incorporation act, at least for corporations of major size, may place the matter on the political agenda. If concern over the power of the major corporation in American society should lead to serious consideration of federal incorporation, the composition of the board of directors, including employee representation, will inevitably be a major area of concern. In this fortuitous manner, the possibility of legislative provision for employee representation on the board could conceivably develop in the future.

CONCLUSION

Except to the extent provided through the collective bargaining process, employee participation in corporate decision making in the United States is not a reality, and there is little indication that it will become a serious possibility in the immediate future. Until participative management and employee representation on the board are adopted as major objectives and vigorously pursued by American unions, they will remain theoretical suggestions. Nevertheless, there are powerful factors at work which in time could make these matters—entirely visionary at the present time—a more realistic possibility. Changing social values and employee attitudes, concern over the nature of the role of the major American corporations in American life, which is reflected in sharply increased public expectations with respect to so-called corporate social responsibility, and the increasing momentum of the movement for employee participation in Western Europe constitute deep-seated underlying forces that could conceivably create a social and political climate in which employee participation could emerge as a matter of realistic concern in the future.

Notes

1. 138 N.L.R.B. 550 (1962).

2. Fibreboard Paper Products. Corp v. N.L.R.B., 379 U.S. 203 (1964).

3. E.g., Ozark Trailers, Inc., 161 N.L.R.B 561 (1966); Royal Plating & Polishing Co., Inc., 160 N.L.R.B. 990 (1966), rev'd, 350 F.2d 191 (3d Cir. 1965); McLoughlin Mfg. Co., 182 N.L.R.B. No. 139 (1970); Drapery Mfg. Co., 170 N.L.R.B. No. 199 (1969), rev'd, 425 F.2d 1026 (8th Cir. 1970); Thompson Transp. Co., 165 N.L.R.B. 746 (1967), rev'd, 406 F.2d 698 (10th Cir. 1968); Transmarine Navigation Corp., 152 N.L.R.B. 998 (1965), rev'd, 380 F.2d 933 (9th Cir. 1967).

4. General Motors Corp., 191 N.L.R.B. No. 149 (1971); Summit Tooling Co., 195 N.L.R.B. No. 91 (1972). See *Annual Survey of Labor Law,* 13 B.C. Ind. & Comm. L. Rev. (1972), pp. 1347, 1408–13. It may be that cases involving union attempts to bargain over particular management decisions should be distinguished from cases involving union efforts to obtain contractual provisions controlling managerial decisions in a particular area.

5. See M. Meyer and H. Fox, *Employee Stock Purchase Plans* (New York: The Conference Board, 1967); Annual survey, "Employer Stock in Profit-Sharing Funds," *Profit Sharing* (June 1972), p. 14; Bankers Trust Co., "Study of Employee Savings and Thrift Plans" (1972). In addition to the larger concerns noted in the text, there are approximately thirty-five smaller firms that have adopted or are adopting the program devised by Louis A. Kelso of San Francisco to raise additional funds through the sale of shares of stock to qualified employee retirement trusts, with the purchase price provided by employer-guaranteed bank loans. Subsequent cash contributions by the employer to the trust fund, deductible for tax purposes up to 15 percent of aggregate compensation of participating employees, provide the sums required for repayment of the bank loans. The Kelso Plan has the attraction to the employer of providing for the financing of new capital through the use of pre-tax dollars. It contemplates the gradual shift of ownership to employees

as stock ownership is increasingly concentrated in the trust fund and its beneficiaries. L. Kelso and P. Hetter, *The Two Factor Theory: The Economics of Reality* (New York: Vintage Books, 1967). See Henderson, "Radical Capitalism," *Business Today,* Autumn 1970, p. 10; *Business Week,* November 20, 1971, p. 86; *New York Times,* January 16, 1972, Section 1, p. 29; letter dated March 21, 1973, to the author from Louis A. Kelso, on file in Boston University School of Law Library.

6. Bankers Trust Co., "Study of Employee Savings and Thrift Plans" (1972), pp. 37–254. This review found that 76 percent of the plans studied that offered company stock as an investment fund gave the employee the right to vote all shares, or at least the vested portion. It also noted a trend that where employees do not choose to vote, the trustee votes such shares, not at its own discretion, but in the same proportion as those shares voted by employees. Idem., pp. 33–34.

7. See L. Gilbert and J. Gilbert, *Twenty-Third Annual Report of Shareholder Activities at Corporate Meetings* (1972), p. 260. The Broadway-Hale Stores holding has been adjusted for a three–two stock split. Lowe's Companies, Inc. with 30 percent of its stock and McGraw-Edison with 18 percent of its stock held by employee benefit funds are examples of two corporations with very substantial concentrated stock holdings in employee funds that have not yet adopted pass-through voting. Lowe's Companies, Inc., *1972 Annual Report,* p. 34; letter dated March 13, 1973, to the author from Robert L. Strickland, Senior Vice-President, Lowe's Companies, Inc., on file in Boston University School of Law Library; statement of Chairman Raymond H. Giesecke, McGraw-Edison Co., before General Subcommittee on Labor of House Education and Labor Committee, March 8, 1973, p. 10.

8. Moody's *Handbook of Common Stocks* (second 1973 ed.). The totals for all corporations are as of December 31, 1972, except for Bendix (September 30), Broadway-Hale Stores (January 29, 1973), Burlington Industries (September 30), and International Harvester (October 31).

9. Since the number of shares held by the funds were determined as of various dates in 1972, comparison with outstanding shares as of the dates specified may not be accurate in all cases. It is not believed that the differences will be material.

10. It should be recognized that one of the major incentives for the introduction of employee stock purchase plans and benefit plans investing in employer stock may be to deter unionization. Overnite Transportation Co. is an example of a major firm with employee ownership that is nonunion in a strongly unionized industry.

Worker Participation and Employee Rights: Some Necessary Links

Paul Bernstein

Obviously, if employees are to decide on issues extending beyond their immediate tasks, they need information on those more distant areas. Technical information that heretofore only the company engineers were familiar with must now be available to them. Economic information that previously only the accounting and finance departments were concerned with must be made available as well. If such information is not forthcoming when employees feel the need for it, not only is frustration on that issue likely to result, but also employee confidence in the entire co-management system may disappear. This is what occurred in the Belgian attempt to create meaningful works councils after World War II. When the crucial component of management-level information was withheld from workers by reluctant managers, workers withdrew from further attempts at participation and the system essentially died.

To be supportive of democratization, it was found that the amount of information available to employees must be *at least* what *they* feel they need for adequate decision making. (This is why demands raised by unions such as the United Auto Workers for corporate books to be open to employees by right make sense in a strategy for democratization.) But firms committed to democratization go beyond this. Rather than passively *allowing* worker participants to find out crucial information, they actively establish mechanisms to keep all participants informed and to assist their utilization of this information. Written reports on the performance of each department and the state of the

Reprinted from the *Journal of Economic Issues* 10, no. 2 (June 1976) copyright © 1976 by special permission of the copyright holder, the Association For Evolutionary Economics. Footnotes and text citations deleted.

whole enterprise are distributed, as are written reminders on issues approaching a decision point. Also, those occupying manager positions remain available for frank questioning by other participants, not only in formal meetings set aside for that purpose but also as an accepted custom whenever chance encounters arise.

Up to this point we have been discussing the *availability* of information. Just as consequential a factor is the employees' *ability* to handle the necessary information. Obviously, in the beginning stage of democratization many employees may be, or may feel themselves to be, ill prepared for handling all the requisite data. This fact points to the need for specific training to precede, or at the least to accompany, any consciously implemented plan of democratization. Swedish unions have established such training courses as their country moves toward greater worker participation, as has Yugoslavia. Besides on-the-job training, changes within the basic educational system will probably be necessary to facilitate workplace democratization in the United States, for there is evidence that school experience deeply affects how young people later approach their jobs and careers, including how they approach authority figures at work. In addition, the experience of democratization itself can develop participants' abilities to deal intelligently with the requisite complex information. Just how well this occurs in any particular case seems to depend in part on how committed are the workers' own leaders and the firm's managers to developing all employees' business expertise and participatory skills. (Such a commitment by leadership is considered here to be part of the necessary component of consciousness, discussed below.)

Serious problems can arise in the practical implementation of the informational component. Space permits only identification and brief presentation of possible solutions to these difficulties. One problem is that of industrial secrecy, at least whenever workers' control is implemented in a market economy. In such a situation, firms may still need to prevent certain technical data and financial plans from being released to other firms if they are to retain a competitive advantage. Swedish unions and employers have designed a clever solution that allows managers to request the withholding of disputed information, but leaves ultimate release power in the hands of workers' elected representatives. By contrast, systems that allow *managers* to retain this ultimate power are likely to weaken democratization, as the German co-determination firms have found.

A second problem in the operation of the informational component is that employees may not make use of available information on issues of less than immediate, personal interest to them, that is, on issues besides wages and physical working conditions. This is a problem of citizen participation common to all democracies, societal as well as intra-organizational. One means for solution in the workplace is for managers and the workers' own elected leaders to make clear to the participants how the areas they have been ignoring do relate directly to the areas of their immediate concern. This kind of communication was observed to be effective in several of the U.S. plywood cooperatives.

A third problem in information sharing can be the reluctance of some managers to abandon their former habits of prerogative and secrecy. This is especially likely where democratization has been forced on them (as by national law) or in the early stages of democratization when old habits and fears are still governing a great deal of managers' (and others') behavior. Although much information may be circulating to participants, certain crucial bits may be imparted only vaguely or held back entirely by individual managers, and this may reduce the overall effectiveness of the participation system.

Finally, there is the problem of managers' continually greater expertise on certain issues in contrast to the managed, even when full information is provided. This is an inevitable situation flowing from the division of labor and time inherent in any complex group endeavor. Although there seems to be no neat, final solution to this problem, certain experiences in workers' control are worth noting. *Rotation* of employees into managerial posts certainly increases the expertise of the total working group, as has been observed in Israeli kibbutzim and the U.S. plywood cooperatives. In the advanced forms, where a workers' council is superior to the specialized managers, it may be sufficient that at least these council members have gained an expertise nearly equivalent to the full-time managers. So long as these council members continue to work at regular jobs in the plant (as occurs in the U.S. plywood cooperatives, for example), or are otherwise held accountable to the interests of the rank and file, the employee group as a whole may be functioning effectively with an expertise nearly matching that of the full-time specialists. A third possibility is for the employee group to engage a staff of experts of its own to advise it on matters where it recognizes the full-time managers still have greater expertise. Such a system would be analogous to the combination of democracy with expertise practiced in the U.S. Congress, where elected legislators engage specialized staffs for work on specific issues. U.S. unions already do this, hiring professional economists to work from the unions' point of view on issues in contention with employers. The same might be done in worker participation firms.

Experience shows that it is not enough for participants to possess appropriate information and an ability to use it. They also must be protected against possible reprisals for using that information to criticize existing policies or to oppose proposed policy changes. And they must be free to differ with fellow employees on issues of moment. Without such protection, open dialogue and the important upward flow of suggestions and evaluations would be unlikely to occur effectively or for very long.

A clear case in point is the American Cast Iron Pipe Company: Although worker owned, it lacks real guarantees to the employees against penalties for criticism and is controlled, as a result, by a self-selecting set of managers. If criticism is voiced at all by employees it is generally outside the company. Employee participation in this company's decision making consequently has dropped practically to nil.

Other case histories also demonstrate that, to persist, a participation system must be supported by the rights commonly associated with political democracy: freedom of speech and assembly, petition of grievances, secret balloting, due process and the right to file appeal in cases of discipline, immunity of rank-and-file representatives from dismissal or transfer while in office, and a written constitution alterable only by a majority or two-thirds vote of the collective.

Apparently the entire set of rights is necessary, not just a few, because each right depends substantially on the others for its successful operation. For example, for effective use the right to assemble and organize must be accompanied by the right to free speech. Likewise, the right to seek redress of grievances cannot be actualized significantly without the protection of workers' representatives from dismissal or transfer and the guarantee of secret balloting to elect those representatives in the first place.

A second important characteristic of this major component is that to be effective such guaranteed protection must be absolute. Scholars of these rights in the traditional societal context have long observed that the power to abridge basic freedoms is the power to destroy them. Experience bears this out in the context of workplace democratization —the reduction of employees' rights led to the emasculation of workers' control in Soviet Russia, Poland, and Algeria.

This system of rights is not only politically necessary for the employees, but also turns out to be cybernetically valuable for the company as a whole, expanding its possibilities for adaptive self-steering. For example, free speech not only protects individuals; it also furnishes the organization with a wider range of perceptions of its own performance. Criticism, complaints, and specialized information from employees at the bottom and far reaches of the organization can improve the accuracy with which decision-making organs at the center assess the state of their organization, its performance, and its environment. Free speech also makes possible an upward flow of positive proposals, actualizing the cybernetic principle of "requisite variety." This refers to the need of self-steering systems to supply themselves with several alternative views and strategies in order to cope adequately with an ever-changing environment.

A major problem that arises in the implementation of this component is the conflict between individual rights and collective rights or needs. For example, the collective need for stable administration could argue that absolute freedom of speech, organization, and so forth is simply too disruptive, that it causes delay in reaching decisions. The individualist reply would be that to limit this freedom is to risk destroying it altogether, for a limited freedom of speech means the individual may not speak up when he or she sees fit, but only when authorities allow it—which is when they find it in their own interest. The problem is complicated further by the fact that even those democratized enterprises that aim at high individual freedom sometimes produce informal but powerful group pressures against the individual. For example, the supposedly libertarian kibbutzim in Israel admit to aiming for "a complete identification of the individual with society." "Tyranny of the majority" may indeed become operative in such cases.

Solutions to these conflicts will perforce be complex and subtle. Cases of democratization stemming from anarchist movements have perhaps gone the farthest toward preserving the autonomy of the individual. In Republican Spain (1936–1939 period), for example, anarchist unions held individual autonomy to be the inviolable right and limited their community authority structures by that principle. A second strategy is to balance carefully the two principles as norms internalized within each participant of the self-managing enterprise. Of particular usefulness here is the balance between individual self-reliance and receptivity to others' needs. Still another means for satisfying the conflicting rights of the individual and the group is the auxiliary system of adjudication we have identified as an additional, major component of democratization. To that component we now turn.

Even though employees may be participating in decisions that affect them, they will not always agree that the rules so democratically arrived at are being applied accurately or fairly. In order to resolve such disputes, an independent judicial procedure within the firm is needed. This system differs from conventional "grievance machinery" in being broader in scope, more balanced in its power base, and more face-to-face in its implementation.

Specifically, adjudicative systems in democratized firms have the following three functions: (1) settlement of rule infractions in a just manner; (2) upholding the basic rights (those listed as additional components); and (3) protecting the by-laws (constitution) of the enterprise from violation by any member, whether manager or managed.

To be able to fulfill these functions, the adjudicative system must be independent of all factions within the enterprise. Various forms have evolved in practice to ensure that independence: use of outside arbitrators or labor ministry professionals to ensure neutrality; a joint tribunal consisting of workers and managers from within the firm to ensure balance; or referring the matter to the entire assembly of enterprise members (or representatives chosen from them by lot) to ensure judgment by one's peers.

Whichever form is taken, it is crucial that the impartiality of the adjudicative system be real and be perceived by the managed. Their confidence in the justness of the entire democratization system, not just this component, is at stake. For that reason, the inclusion of peers in the adjudicative system is of special value: Clearly, employees will cling more closely to the participation system if they know that they themselves, not autonomous managers, have the last word on how its rules are applied, how basic rights are upheld, and how the opportunities for participation are guaranteed.

The settlement of disputes and the upholding of rights usually takes place in two stages. First, an act is committed or a person is accused of committing an act that violates one of the organization's rules. This may be handled on the spot by a supervisor's decision that identifies the violation, decides guilt or innocence, and determines punishment or acquittal; or the matter may be sent to a special tribunal for decision —in the more democratized systems. (Democratization at this stage is still rare.) Second, there may be an appeal, which more commonly involves peers in the judgment process. The employee and accuser each present their view of the incident, and the appeals board or assembly upholds, modifies, or reverses the earlier sentence. Customarily, punishments range from reprimands and warning slips (analogous to traffic citations or demerit points), to temporary suspension of one or more privileges, to expulsion. The latter is rarely invoked, least of all in communitarian situations, such as Israeli kibbutzim or Chinese communes. But in Western enterprises (such as the plywood co-ops) it has once or twice been resorted to in a case of repeated drunkenness.

It seems that democratized enterprises have, in general, not developed this adjudicative component as far as they have developed some of the others. In particular, some of the safeguards that evolved in the societal arena to protect the individual from unjust authority are still absent in most democratized firms. Research might beneficially be applied to discover the value such societal principles could bring to the workplace. For example, in the first stage—rule violations—relevant principles that could be added include the following: (1) The accused is presumed innocent until the accuser can prove guilt; (2) proof of guilt must be established by due process involving judgment by one's peers (fellow workers); and (3) equal application of the laws—managers must be as much subject to the process as the managed.

In the second stage, the first two principles are already present, but fairness could be advanced in the appeal process by adding the principle that the review must be speedy, and its sessions must be open to all employees.

Worker Participation: Industrial Democracy or Union Power Enhancement?

Herbert R. Northrup

THE MEANING OF PARTICIPATION

According to Webster, participation is "the art . . . of sharing in common with others." There is no connotation that this sharing should be confined to any one type of organization or method. The success and strength of the German economy, however, had centered attention on its system and tended in the minds of many to make that system synonymous with participation. This has been done either despite, or in complete ignorance of, the German heritage and the characteristics of its system, which are not replicated outside of Europe, and which are even fundamentally different in other European countries.

Foremost among these differences is works council representation at the local level. This is common in Europe, but nonexistent, and probably illegal, in the United States. The works council system has a long and honorable European history, and in Germany the duties of, and obligations to, the works council are set forth in great detail by the Shop Constitution Act of 1972. In the broadest sense, participation of German workers is very great with the works council. Yet although employee works council members are usually union members, the existence of works councils as separate and distinct organizations from unions results in what to Americans seems to be a curiously divided employee representation. For along with the presence of the works council in various European countries is the absence of local unions.

Excerpted from speech delivered at the 64th National Foreign Trade Convention, November 1977, reproduced with permission of the author, Dr. Herbert R. Northrup, Professor of Industry and Director of Industrial Research Unit, The Wharton School, University of Pennsylvania.

Contracts are regionally or nationally negotiated between unions and companies, but local conditions are negotiated with the councils, or in Britain with shop stewards. Works councils and unions are in conflict in many ways. This shows up clearly in union demands for changes in participation legislation. I refer, of course, to the already successful drive of the German unions to have union appointees, rather than employee-elected personnel, on the Supervisory Board and to the Dutch union push for greater union control of works councils.

Two other basic differences, again between the German system particularly, but also European ones in general, and the United States one, are the presence of a two-tier board system in the former, and Germany's inflation and war experiences. Until now, at least, except in the coal, iron, and steel industries, and at Volkswagen, the German two-tier system has tended to separate policy making and management and keep the labor members, who were a board minority, out of management decision making. In addition, memories of the ravages of inflation and wars have led to restraint on the part of German employee and union participants and willingness to forego present demands for future needs. Those who would generalize from the German system would do well to hold themselves in check for a few years in order to see how the new rules providing for greater employee and union representation work in practice, and whether a new generation will heed the lessons of inflation and war. They might also carefully study the coal, iron, and steel experience and that of Volkswagen, both of which I shall briefly return to later.

In sum, then, the word "participation" has been transposed from its proper, basic meaning to one that connotes employee and/or union (and it is rarely made clear which or both) representation on the board of directors of a company along the lines of the German model. Moreover, this is typically done without due regard to the special characteristics of the German system, environment, and background, and with a presumption that, despite very fundamental changes in the German law of co-determination, and the coming to power of a new generation raised in prosperity and without experience in the ravages of war and inflation, past in Germany will be prologue.

PARTICIPATION IN THE UNITED STATES

It is common for writers to state that participation does not exist for employees or trade unions in the United States. Unless this refers to the German model, it is totally incorrect. Participation in the United States actually is widespread in areas in which it is the most meaningful. In the United States, as I believe in Canada, also, local unions are directly affiliated with, and subordinate in varying degrees to, national unions. Collective bargaining may be national, regional, or local, but in any case, much is left to local union-management determination.

Under United States law and practice, companies must bargain over "terms and conditions of employment," and this phrase has been most generously interpreted by the National Labor Relations Board and the courts. Thus, besides wages and fringe benefits, the employer must discuss and bargain about such matters as hours of work, starting and quitting time, shift practices, layoff and rehiring procedures, premium pay for overtime, supervisors' rights to do journeyman work, contracting out work, automation, plant relocation, partial and complete plant closings, and a host of other matters. In addition, if disputes regarding these or other matters arise during the life of the labor agreement, the issue is generally settled by binding, third-party arbitration, from which there is no appeal.

New products or processes usually involve new methods of work. Their success can be assured or thwarted by the degree of union cooperation in their installation and manufacture. The point is, of course, that the union, and employees through the union, do indeed participate in such decisions, or in some cases even have a veto over whether matters go forward. Moreover, they participate where it counts—on the shop floor or in the negotiation process, which continues throughout the life of the contract.

Nor is this all. Unions in the United States have participated in a host of decisions affecting company management in a variety of ways. Unions energetically lobby for tariffs and quotas, usually in cooperation with management; like managements, unions also seek special legislative favors in order to bolster companies' abilities to pay higher wages; they promote products through advertising or use of the union label; and they influence the demand or supply of products in numerous ways. In short, by a variety of means and activities, unions participate in management decision making.

To the employee, however, participation on the shop floor remains the most significant. This affords him protection against arbitrary action of his supervisors, sees to it that such matters of grave importance to his future as hours of work, layoffs, rehiring, upgrading, training, transfers, choice of shifts, extra compensation for difficult work or hours, protection against the risks of old age, unemployment, accident, and health, and, of course, compensation are all co-determined. This is where the action is.

The United States worker, accustomed to the co-determination of what is important to him, is likely to find European-type participation not to his liking. The six U.S. automobile workers who were sent to Sweden by the Ford Foundation with the hope that they would be living proof that socialized Sweden is a heavenly spot, undoubtedly reacted as most other United States workers would:

> The American reaction was indifferent or negative to the worker participation schemes. They observed that the works council meeting seemed more like a mixture of shareholders and general sales meeting, and that the members of the works council did not seem to be a representative sample of workers throughout the plant. The production and development group meetings seemed an adjunct of the works council meeting. There were discussions of problems with little attention directed at possible solutions. *In general, all six workers viewed the production and development groups as inadequate in handling disputes at the workplace* [emphasis added].

The official union position in the United States is no different. Despite a tongue-in-cheek suggestion at Chrysler which excited some *New York Times* reporters, and other pseudo-avant-garde types, and publicity seekers, the United Automobile Workers aimed directly at the pocketbook, rather than detouring toward the board of directors in the recent labor negotiations. If the UAW officials had exchanged some cents per hour for a place on Chrysler's board, I suspect that they would soon be among the unemployed.

Meanwhile, George Meany was electing a president of the United States, has been telling Congress what to write in labor laws, and not worrying about representation on anything as insignificant as a company board of directors. His executive assistant, Thomas R. Donahue, previously summed it all up by declaring that moves of unions to join a board of directors "offer little to American unions" on the job. "We do not want to blur in any way the distinctions between the respective roles of management and labor in the plant," he said. If unions were to become a "partner in management," he suggested that they would "be, most likely, the junior partner in success and the senior partner in failure." Unions, he noted, "currently bargain on more issues than the number we might have any impact on as members of a board of directors." . . .

"WORKER" PARTICIPATION AS A UNION POWER VEHICLE

We could go from country to country and find that participation exists in various facets of industrial relations in many ways that reflect the history and institutions of the land involved. Why then a push for the German model, such as received support in the United Kingdom from the so-called Bullock Committee, or the new Swedish law, or the inter-est generated by co-determination in Canada? Certainly, no one has been able to discern any significant rank-and-file interest, or to contend seriously that the men in the shop would be better off financially or emotionally if a designated worker sat on the company board.

The answer, of course, is that both the German model and its emulation abroad are power issues, not industrial relations issues. The Labour Party–dominated Bullock Committee in Britain recommended *union official board members,* not worker board members, with the former appointed, not elected. A brief review of the evolvement of the German systems further underscores the power element involved.

CHANGING CHARACTER OF THE GERMAN SYSTEM

Participation at the supervisory board level in Germany was designed in part to insure that unfettered managerial control of industry would not again lead to cooperation with fascism. It provided for one-third of the supervisory board members to be elected from the worker group. The system, which still applies to companies with less than two thousand employees, seems to have worked well in the German environment. In most situations, where the employee board members had no political allies on the board, it did not seemingly interfere with economic decision making and sometimes aided effective personnel management by bringing operating managements' attention to people's problems that required correcting. Of course, there was wide diversity in results from company to company.

Unions, were, however, quite dissatisfied with the results. They wanted "true" co-determination—equal supervisory board membership, control over the "labor director," and union appointment, rather than worker election, of "worker" directors. All these they had in the steel and coal industries by special legislation and at Volkswagen by de facto arrangements. They received somewhat less, but they have obtained, for companies with more than two thousand employees, some union-appointed directors and near equity between worker and shareholder supervisory board members. Where union board members are able to dominate other worker directors—and it is reasonable to expect that over time this will be increasingly the situation—the unions may force management to make many concessions in order to be able to operate the business. Control of the labor director, not mandated by the new law, is a key union objective, and it is not impossible that other members of management may decide to become beholden to the unions in order to advance their careers.

From a libertarian point of view, union control of industry must be regarded most gravely. In effect, it makes the social partners a single institution, thus negating checks and countervailing power. Like other forms of power, participation advocates talk in favor of democracy while stepping toward tyranny. The idea that workers will be in a superior position because their union leaders are also their bosses is extraordinary on its face. The United States was compelled to enact special legislation as early as 1959 because of union leadership malpractices in regard to their members. To enhance that power over employees and to term it "democratic" is to delude ourselves and to pervert the meaning of democracy. There is nothing in the union official—or any of us—that provides exemption from the dictum that power corrupts, and absolute power corrupts absolutely.

In terms of social well-being, worker participation has equally unappetizing aspects if carried toward the goal advocated by European trade unionists. Equal participation, as already noted, means that the worker board members, who may be expected to be union dominated, have a veto over managerial action. This inevitably means that key decisions are made on an internal political basis rather than on an enterprise economic basis. Previous studies of German co-determination have tended to ignore how much postwar growth and prosperity have covered up the contradiction inherent in having representatives of different constituencies on a board of directors. Now more realistic studies are appearing.

For example, little has been written about the experience of the coal and steel companies. In fact, however, Germany's largest union, Industriegewerkschaft Metall (IG Metall) exerts considerable control over these companies. Recently, the worker representatives at one major company, Stahlwerke Roechling-Burbach GmbH (SRB), persuaded the neutral chairman to vote with them to override management's decision not to make a DM 400 million investment in a new plant in the Saar. The union wanted it because of unemployment among its members; the management, noting that the company is already losing money and that the steel industry is very depressed, obviously is concerned about such an uneconomic proposition and the fact that the shareholders, not the workers, take the commercial and financial risks.

Dr. Alfred L. Thimm's careful study of the Volkswagen experience affords another preview of what can happen when unions achieve a dominant position on boards of directors. Volkswagen is 40 percent owned by the German Federal Republic and the State of Lower Saxony. Alone of major German industries, it bargains directly with IG Metall, largest and strongest of German unions. On its Supervisory Board sit representatives of these governments, the president of IG Metall, a representative of a union-controlled bank which owns Volkswagen stock, plus employee directors. Private shareholders, therefore, have only a minority representation. A review of Volkswagen's Supervisory Board decisions, including the long fight over a United States plant, show a costly political tug of war, as economic decisions were vetoed or modified by union-political control. The whole story is a somber one in terms of economic efficiency and social well-being; yet it is a likely preview of the future if we march to the tune of the German-model participation siren.

Such equal or union-controlled participation puts the entire management structure in jeopardy. A union-controlled corporation forces management personnel to form a protective organization and to bargain for their income and status. This in turn ends what individual initiative that they have left. The difference between this result and the dead hand of socialism is difficult to discern.

What Managers Think of
Participative Leadership

Larry E. Greiner

Foreword

An extroverted, sensitive leader who openly shares decisions and authority with subordinates—this is the profile that emerged when 318 executives were asked their opinions on the characteristics of participative leadership. While there is much discussion—and controversy— among educators and theorists about the concept of participative leadership, managers themselves have not yet been heard. In this study, the author found a surprising consensus among managers regarding the operational characteristics and effectiveness of participative leadership. But he also found some specific and noteworthy differences of opinion between younger and older managers concerning which managerial actions get results. After discussing the findings, he draws their implications for companies, individual managers, and management educators.

During the past decade, vast numbers of executives have been schooled in the virtues of participative leadership. Perhaps no other management concept has received so much recent attention in management literature, in company training programs, and in the general press. Educators, in particular, have consistently admonished managers to open up their decision-making activities to their subordinates. Youthful critics of big business have also added fuel to the fire, contending that industrial organizations are too closed and undemocratic.

At the same time, however, there has been considerable confusion and diversity of viewpoint among management educators and social theorists over just what is meant by such a vague concept as participative leadership. To some, it means group decision making; to others, it is mutual goal setting; and to still others, it implies listening more and talking less.

These differing interpretations are further clouded by such abstract labels as 9,9 management, Theory Y, and management by objectives. In addition, scholarly critics in the wings confuse the issue by arguing that managerial styles are idiosyncratic and are determined more by an executive's personality and early background experiences than by "charm schools" in participative leadership.

But where have the managers themselves—the targets of these participative pleas, conflicts, and slogans—been all this time? While there has been considerable talk from educators and Sunday-morning quarterbacks, very little is known about how the participative message has been absorbed at the managerial level. This is the age-old problem of hearing more from the teachers than from the learners. Consider these important questions in need of new answers:

• What concrete behavioral characteristics do managers actually associate with the vague abstraction called participative leadership?

• Do managers differ widely in their specific interpretations of participative leadership, or is there a relatively uniform understanding? (For example, do younger managers subscribe more to participative methods than do older executives?)

• Most critical, even if managers understand and agree on the practical aspects of participative leadership, do they believe that participation will lead to more effective results?

The purpose of this article is to shed light on these questions by reporting the responses of 318 executives to a questionnaire that was administered while they were attending management education programs at the Harvard Business School.

The reader will be able to compare his own understanding of participation with those reported by this sample of executives. Just as important, knowing more about managerial perceptions of leadership style can help educators assess the extent to which their participative message has found its mark.

THEORIES IN CONFLICT

Before I report the study findings, let me briefly review two basic and often opposing schools of thought about leadership style. In doing so,

I shall define leadership style quite simply as a *pattern of interacting with subordinates.*

Previous research has identified a variety of leadership patterns, such as participative, authoritarian, laissez-faire, task-oriented, and so forth. The most discussed and popular of these has been participative leadership.

Advocates of the participative style fall into what I call the "actor" school of thinking. Their key assumption is that managers are like sensitive players in a drama, relatively flexible and able to alter their behavioral styles, even in the later years of life. They see managers as able to exercise conscious, rational control over their own behavior and to adapt continuously to new cues and role demands placed on them by their organizations.

With this model of a highly receptive leader in mind, members of the actor school emphasize the use of management education to convert executives to a participative style. As a result of their influence, thousands of managers have been exposed to company and university programs stressing both the humane and the productive aspects of participative leadership. These programs, however, have varied in their particular brand of participative leadership—some have focused on team decision making; others have placed emphasis on joint goal setting; and still others have taught listening skills for two-way communication.

Opposed to the actor school is what might be called the "born leader" school. Its members take the position that a leader's style is deeply rooted in his or her personality, which in turn is a complex product of genetic inheritance and the maturation process. They see each manager's style as representing a highly individualistic, often unconscious, pattern of acting out ingrained values, conflicts, and attitudes acquired over many years. And they express strong doubts that managers can easily adopt new forms of behavior as they become older.

Stated simply, the conflict between the two groups is this:

• The actor (participative) school holds that leadership behavior can be taught and is largely determined by external cues from the environment.

• The born-leader school holds that leadership behavior is individually developed and that it is largely determined by internal personality characteristics.

Both groups, of course, cite research evidence to support their own position and refute that of the other. The born-leader proponents, for example, point to the fact that people who choose professional careers tend, in greater numbers than could be expected by chance, to be *first-born* children in their families. The participative enthusiasts, however, often refer to numerous studies of company training programs showing how managers have altered their behavior in a participative direction.

Yet both groups would agree that knowing more about a manager's assumptions concerning leadership style is vitally important. Every manager carries around in his head certain "rules of thumb" that guide his behavior in leadership situations. It is these mental guidelines that I shall attempt to uncover in this article.

Interestingly enough, the findings reported here lend credence to *both* the actor and born-leader schools. While managers have definitely been attracted to participative leadership, they also have made some unique and personalized translations of it to fit their particular career situations.

THE MANAGERIAL VIEWPOINT

As mentioned earlier, two objectives of this study were (1) to discover what managers consider to be the concrete characteristics of participative leadership and (2) to determine whether they think such a style leads to effective results. Accordingly, the 318 managers in the study were given a questionnaire containing thirty-nine leadership characteristics. Then they were divided into two groups:

The *first group* of 157 managers was told to rate each characteristic on a scale from 1 to 7, with 1 equal to low participation and 7 equal to high participation. They were asked to base their ratings on their own past experiences as managers.

The *second group* of 161 managers was told to check (a) the five characteristics that they found to be *most* effective in handling managerial situations, and (b) the five characteristics that they found to be *least* effective. They also were asked to base their judgments on past experience.

Let us now turn to an in-depth look at the responses of these two groups. (Before proceeding, however, I should note that while the questionnaire was based on extensive past research and included a wide span of behavior, the findings of this study are necessarily limited to the thirty-nine questionnaire items.)

What Is Participation?

Despite the fact that participative leadership is an abstract concept, the managers in the study reached a high level of agreement in rating specific characteristics on the 1-to-7 participation scale. Among the managers in the first group who rated the thirty-nine items only for extent of participation, the average correlation of agreement is .74 out of a perfect 1.00. Even higher is their agreement in rating items at the extreme ends of the scale. No significant differences appear between younger and older managers, among types of educational background, or among current job positions.

This high level of agreement suggests that the study managers hold a reasonably clear and uniform understanding in their concrete interpretation of participative leadership. Such unanimity is quite remarkable considering the different interpretations that educators have given the concept of participation. Even the questionnaire items, because of their limited wording, are subject to divergent interpretation. Yet the managers in this study apparently were not misled.

A more complete picture of participative leadership emerges from the listing of the ten highest-ranked characteristics of participative behavior in Exhibit I. The ultimate participative act, for example, is viewed as including one's subordinates in the decision-making process. Here the respondents move significantly away from the classical notion of the manager acting as a sole decision maker.

At the same time, however, a variety of other characteristics combine to define a prototype participative leader. It is doubtful that a manager can open up the decision-making process without including some of these other participative actions. According to the respondents, the participative leader also—

- maintains free-flowing and honest communication;
- remains easily accessible;
- stresses development for his subordinates;
- expresses consideration and support;
- is willing to change.

Here is a picture of a sensitive, extroverted, and emotive leader who actively stays in close contact with his subordinates and is attuned to their needs.

Moreover, these findings indicate that education and training in participative leadership have, indeed, had an effect. Managers in the

Exhibit I. The 10 Highest Participation Characteristics

Rank		Average scale rating*
1	Gives subordinates a share in decision making	6.08
2	Keeps subordinates informed of the true situation, good or bad, under all circumstances	5.69
3	Stays aware of the state of the organization's morale and does everything possible to make it high	5.45
4	Is easily approachable	5.38
5	Counsels, trains, and develops subordinates	5.34
6	Communicates effectively with subordinates	5.22
7	Shows thoughtfulness and consideration of others	5.19
8	Is willing to make changes in ways of doing things	4.96
9	Is willing to support subordinates even when they make mistakes	4.92
10	Expresses appreciation when a subordinate does a good job	4.80

*On the scale, 1 equals low participation and 7 equals high participation.

study, lending support to advocates of the actor (participative) school, are in relative agreement about the specific actions they would rate as being highly participative. A prototype participative style emerges (from the ten highest items) which encompasses much of what has been conveyed in the literature on this subject.

But is participative leadership also viewed by these managers as the most effective style? Or are certain *low* participation characteristics also deemed effective? These are important questions, because the actor-school advocates have long portrayed the participative leader as the man who not only is more humane but also gets the best results.

Let us now look at the leadership characteristics selected by the managers in the second group; this is the group that rated the thirty-nine questionnaire items for effectiveness but not for participation.

What Gets Results?

The executives in the second group generally picked characteristics that were rated high on participation by those in the first group. Exhibit II presents the ten items that received the most votes for being highly effective. These same items, when rated on the seven-point participation scale by the first group of executives, received an average rating of 5.03, which is decidedly toward the high-participation end of the scale. Put another way, seven of the ten top effective actions listed in Exhibit II also appear among the highest participation items in Exhibit I.

Of the entire list of leadership characteristics, the item with the highest effectiveness rating is concerned with training and developing subordinates (which challenges a common stereotype that managers are preoccupied only with daily decision making). These managers place considerably more value on the role of manager as teacher than as decision maker. One explanation for this pedagogical concern of the study managers is that they completed the questionnaire while they were involved in a management development and training program. More likely, however, is the pragmatic explanation that they realize it is in their self-interest to develop a job replacement for themselves, thus making their own promotion possible.

Once again it appears that the advocates of participative leadership can take comfort in the findings—i.e., participation is seen by the respondents as being related to more effective performance. Whether these same managers actually behave as participative leaders on the job, however, is a question for other studies to answer. Also, since the questionnaire was completed by separate groups, we cannot be sure if the managers do, in fact, make a conscious link between participation and effectiveness. Nevertheless, the link is indirectly evident in the findings, so whether the managers in the study know it or not, they place themselves in the participative camp.

SOME SIGNIFICANT EXCEPTIONS

On closer examination, the study findings reveal some distinct and important exceptions to an "across the board" consensus on participative leadership. The study managers are clearly less in agreement about the meaning of effective behavior than they are about participative behavior. In Exhibit I, there was a very high correlation of agreement in rating each item for high and low participation. Yet, in Exhibit II, only the first-ranked effectiveness item—"Counsels, trains, and develops subordinates"—was checked by more than 50 percent of the respondents. Of the remaining top ten items, six were checked by less than one-third of the respondents.

This wider variance in choice of effective behavior suggests a rather loose link between perceptions of effectiveness and of participative leadership. A manager guided exclusively by effectiveness criteria will apparently favor actions that are not included in a strict interpretation of participative leadership.

Advocates of participation, of course, might claim that this divergent view of effectiveness is caused by some uninformed managers who have not yet realized the full merits of behaving solely within a participative style.

Exhibit II. The 10 Most Effective Leadership Characteristics

Rank		Percent of managers checking item most effective	Participation scale rating from first group of managers
1	Counsels, trains, and develops subordinates	56.5%	5.34
2	Communicates effectively with subordinates	44.7	5.22
3	Lets the members of the organization know what is expected of them	37.9	4.36
4	Sets high standards of performance	35.4	3.66
5	Knows subordinates and their capabilities	28.0	4.74
6	Gives subordinates a share in decision making	27.4	6.08
7	Stays aware of the state of the organization's morale and does everything possible to make it high	26.7	5.45
8	Keeps subordinates informed of the true situation, good or bad, under all circumstances	24.3	5.69
9	Is willing to make changes in ways of doing things	21.8	4.96
10	Expresses appreciation when a subordinate does a good job	21.1	4.80

But a more positive and pragmatic explanation emerges when the ten top participation items in Exhibit I are matched with the ten top effectiveness items in Exhibit II. Significantly, the first four items on the effectiveness list are completely different from the first four items on the participation list. Moreover, the four highest-rated effectiveness characteristics in Exhibit II ranked only 5, 6, 20, and 26, respectively, in a complete ranking of the participation items by the first group of managers.

Special attention should be given to the effectiveness characteristics ranked 3 and 4 in Exhibit II. These two items, which are concerned with high performance expectations, ranked only 20 and 26 on extent of participation. Such a strong emphasis on performance reflects a noticeable exception to our earlier prototype of the participative leader who is warm, emotive, and open.

In short, keeping subordinates aware of high performance expectations seems quite important to the managers in the study, even if this means using directive action within an overall participative style. Perhaps they feel that subordinates can misread an orthodox participative leader as being more concerned for their psyches than for the fruits of their labor.

Career Influences

Further analysis of the effectiveness ratings provides support for the born-leader advocates. While the main thrust toward a meshing of participation and effectiveness remains essentially unchanged, different age groups display important variances on a few of the effectiveness ratings.

Exhibit III.   Age Differences in Effectiveness Ratings

	Percent of managers in age group rating item *most* effective		
	Under 30 years	30–40 years	Over 40 years
Displays the technical competence to perform duties	28.3%	16.4%	7.7%
Backs up subordinates in their actions	23.9	5.0	5.8
Gives subordinates a share in decision making.	10.9	45.9	19.2

Exhibit III - *Continued*

Counsels, trains, and develops subordinates	37.0	59.0	71.2
Communicates effectively with subordinates	37.0	39.3	55.8
		Percent of managers in age group rating item *least* effective	
Fails to show an appreciation for the priorities of work	60.9	41.0	36.6
Treats people in an impersonal manner.	40.7	65.6	38.5

Exhibit III highlights seven of the thirty-nine characteristics for which a statistical test revealed substantial differences according to age. These results suggest that a manager's *career stage* may influence his specific leadership orientation, even when he operates within a broader participative framework. Consider the influence on these three managerial groups:

1. Younger managers in the study tend to take what Abraham Zaleznik calls a "proactive" stance; they stress (a) work priorities, (b) proving their technical competence, and (c) backing up subordinates. This more aggressive orientation is understandable if one views younger managers as full of energy and enthusiasm yet possessing self-doubts about their own competence. In addition, these managers are usually in lower-level or specialist positions, where they must visibly demonstrate their talents while also coping with heavy work loads and intense pressure for results.

2. Managers between 30 and 40 years of age emphasize a more "mediative" approach. Most of these executives are in middle-management jobs where they must deal with eager subordinates as well as complex tasks that require numerous trade-offs. Hence, they are exceptionally favorable to (a) taking a more personalized approach to others, (b) relating to subordinates, and (c) making group decisions. Psychologically, this is a time when the middle manager is often exploring his ability to handle heavier responsibility while taking greater risks, so he understandably turns to others for consultation and support.

3. Managers in the over-40 group display a shift toward "homeostatic" or fatherly and maintenance concerns. These older executives, who are usually in top management, seem strongly preoccupied with counseling, developing, and training subordinates; partly, I surmise, because they wish to leave behind some of their own personal attributes and wisdom, as well as to keep the organization in good health. They

are also concerned with the broad issue of communications; top managers frequently feel guilty and lonely in their insulated positions, where responsibility is high for maintaining a clear flow of communications throughout a complex organization.

All the foregoing exceptions suggest that one should be cautious in prescribing a uniform participative style for leaders at all levels of an organization. The born-leader theorists would agree, contending that legitimate behavioral variations occur naturally because managers seek to satisfy different personal needs as they mature in a hierarchy of upward job moves.

Moreover, a company without several older managers worrying about the development of future managers would be seriously handicapped. It is probably too much to expect this teaching responsibility to be filled primarily by middle managers who are consumed mainly by task demands, or by younger managers who are worried about their own development. Their respective uses of participative leadership will likely be slanted to fit different psychological and organizational concerns.

These results also lead me to further question the current fad toward early retirement for older managers in order to give younger managers more responsibility sooner. Companies should learn that all three age groups contribute differently to the organization, and that this variance in contribution should be more sensitively accounted for in manpower planning and performance-assessment decisions. One cannot measure all managers on a common set of standards.

In addition, individual managers should learn to be more aware of their own developmental needs as they make the transition from one job level to the next in organizations. Younger managers, for example, will probably have to master the skills of group decision making to perform effectively at middle levels. As they become ready for senior positions, they will have to develop talents in training subordinates. Company educational programs and personnel counseling services can also aid in solving these transitional problems.

CONCLUSION

The implied message from managers in this study is: "Let's stop beating our chests over the abstract virtues of participative leadership and settle down to defining its more specific uses and limitations in actual practice." For these managers, the choice of leadership style is not between participation and directiveness, nor is it between the actor and born-leader theories. Their reaction to the organizational and psychological reality that faces them in actual practice is to include aspects of all these pulls and tugs.

If executives in this study are representative, one can state that the managerial population at large has already absorbed well the message of participative leadership. There is not only consensus on the specific characteristics that comprise a participative style, but also general agreement that certain participative leadership characteristics produce more effective results. This connection between participation and effectiveness is significant because managers are more likely to act in a participative manner if they believe their actions lead to better results.

Thus the managers in the study are decidedly ahead of those social critics who claim that business executives are a bunch of authoritarians concerned only with manipulating their "puppet" subordinates. They are also beyond those participative educators who assume that businessmen are still waiting to be convinced that participation is a good thing.

Yet these managers do not accept participation on the basis of blind ideology. Instead, they seem to be saying that participative advocates should doff their doctrinaire hats and apply themselves to the application of participative leadership in more pragmatic and more flexible terms. They are quite willing, for example, to use a few directive actions to keep high performance goals in front of subordinates. They are also willing to translate participation to fit their current career and job situations. Thus a young manager on the firing line is likely to employ participative actions differently from an older manager in a senior position.

Such personalized leadership adaptations seem to make good practical sense, for the benefit of both organization performance and a manager's mental health. For the managers whose opinions are represented here, participative leadership appears to be a sound concept, but only if presented as a general model within which individual leaders can exhibit a variety of actions to satisfy different personal and career needs.

Labor-Management Cooperation Today

William L. Batt, Jr. and Edgar Weinberg

The idea of labor-management cooperation is not new. It goes back over fifty years. In the 1920s, the Baltimore and Ohio Plan attracted wide attention. The B&O Railroad and the Machinists formed joint committees in the repair shops to screen workers' suggestions about matters outside the scope of the usual collective bargaining, such as ways to increase efficiency, reduce waste, improve working conditions, and expand business.

The most extensive experience with labor-management production committees took place during World War II, when industry was trying to increase military output in the face of shortages of labor, materials, and energy. Over 5,000 joint committees were formed, about 1,000 of which concentrated on production problems. In the opinion of many employers and union leaders, these committees improved productivity and morale and enhanced mutual understanding of the broad problems of the common enterprise. When the war ended, most of the committees were discontinued.

As the scope of collective bargaining has expanded, some unions and employers have established committees on health and safety, education and training, pensions, drug addiction, alcoholism, and pre-retirement counseling. [Irving Bluestone, vice president of the UAW] has pointed out that "in the [joint safety and health committee] programs thus far undertaken in the auto industry, literally thousands of corrective actions have resulted from the joint efforts of union-management teams at the national and the local level." Successful joint efforts in these areas have led to joint experiments on the quality of work life.

Reprinted with permission from *Harvard Business Review,* January–February 1978. Copyright © 1978 by the President and Fellows of Harvard College.

Most of the 180 active committees that we have studied were formed as a result of union and management taking the initiative at various plants. To get started, a few have drawn on the services of impartial third parties from the Federal Mediation and Conciliation Service (FMCS), from productivity and quality-of-working-life centers, or from state institutes of labor and industrial relations.

Automotive industry committees have formed at General Motors, Chrysler, Bendix, Dana, Rockwell, Kelly-Springfield, TRW, and the Harman International plant at Bolivar, Tennessee. Among the food companies with joint committees are A&P, General Foods, Giant, Heinz, Kroger, Oscar Mayer, and Safeway. Steel companies making the effort include U.S. Steel, Armco, Bethlehem, Kaiser, and Crucible. All told, 113 in-plant committees are listed in 89 companies.

Unions represented include the Machinists, the Autoworkers, the Steelworkers, the Teamsters, the Meatcutters, and the Paperworkers. They include 147 locals in these and other internationals. Also listed are forty-nine committees active in agencies in the public sector at federal, state, and local levels. Most of these are the result of pressures from citizens against increased taxes but for increased services. The unions most involved are the State, County, and Municipal Employees and the American Federation of Government Employees.

What issues do labor-management committees deal with? What do they offer that collective bargaining does not provide? Bruce Thrasher, a Steelworkers representative, reminds us that "such committees are not a substitute for or an alternative to free collective bargaining. Successful committees require a mutuality of interest and serve to complement the collective bargaining process."

In recent years, worker participation through joint labor-management committees has been gradually expanding into new and previously untested waters. These include bidding on new work and bringing in work previously subcontracted outside, organizing the layout of machinery and equipment in a new plant and reorganizing it in an old one, helping to select key supervisory personnel, and planning and overseeing quality-of-work-life programs.

Bringing in New Business

At the American Sterilizer Corporation's Amsco Equipment Company, which manufactures hospital equipment in Jamestown, New York, a labor-management committee has been active since 1972 by agreement with the International Association of Machinists. James Laughner,

Amsco's plant manager, was recently seeking new products to promote company growth and job security for its two hundred workers when the opportunity came up to bid on a new product, one that the company had previously bought outside.

Industrial engineering had been used before in a similar situation but without success. This time, the labor-management committee suggested using production workers to develop a bid. A team of four workers and an engineer was formed and instructed in the bidding process. By conferring with the workers most concerned, the team developed realistic estimates of the time required to make and assemble the components. The team came in with a bid significantly lower than the purchase price of the existing product or the previous industrial engineering estimate, and plant management was able to obtain approval from corporate headquarters for the capital investment required to produce the product. This meant a 15 percent annual increase in the plant's volume and forty more jobs.

Designing Plant Layouts

At the Rockwell Standard Division of Rockwell International at a new plant in Battle Creek, Michigan, the Rockwell-UAW joint labor-management committee helped design the plant's original layout. The people with the responsibility for running the machinery collaborated with the engineers in finding a location and designing the flow of production.

In a similar case, the Carborundum Company's thirty-seven-year-old Falconer, New York, plant, which makes castings for the glass industry, faced an acute need for streamlining plant layout to improve productivity. In addition to retaining an engineering consulting firm, the plant manager decided to involve the plant's labor-management committee, a twelve-member group that meets every two months and deals with issues of production improvement, quality control, and safety. The six union members are from the Fireman and Oilers and the Machinists unions.

Rather than mastermind ideas for redesign themselves, the committee members surveyed the employees with questions on plant layout and product flow. Ideas were solicited through small group meetings in each department and shift. The groups met on released time, and the foremen and shop stewards participated. As a result, the committee collected a total of 167 statements of problems and recommendations to solve them. In August 1977, Carborundum announced a $5.1 million expansion at the facility and based the design in large part on these recommendations.

Picking Supervisors

Increased worker participation in the selection of key supervisory people is another novel use for labor-management committees.

In 1971, the executive editor of the Minneapolis *Star and Tribune* was about to appoint two new assistant city editors for the *Tribune.* The local newspaper guild asked for veto power because of the critical effect this job has on reporters' morale. While this request was denied, management did agree to pick the new editors from the people suggested by the labor-management committee. It proposed two nominees, and management appointed them both. Since then, committees have been formally organized under the contract at both newspapers, and they meet monthly to consider common problems, including promotions to fifteen supervisory positions below the city editor level. This cooperative arrangement has worked so well that within the past few months the publisher of the *Star* has sought the cooperation of the labor members of the labor-management committee in recruiting a new editor for that paper.

Under their contracts, they have agreed to discuss "any matter affecting the relationship between the employer and the employee . . . not covered by the normal bargaining and grievance machinery." These have included the quality of the newspaper, their morale, communication, and staff size, and recently the problems caused by incoming technology.

John Carmichael, executive secretary of the Newspaper Guild of the Twin Cities, was a prime mover in these committees. As Carmichael put it:

> "The idea of being asked, "What do you think about your work?" is so strange and so seldom occurs that simply posing the question to a worker does all kinds of things in terms of raising his image of what he thinks you think about him and what he thinks about himself. In all too many cases, the attitude is, "Get over there and do the job. We don't care what you think. It's not your job to think but to do what we tell you to." That's a common attitude. If you reverse it, it's a shock.

The *Star and Tribune* and the guild are currently exploring the desirability of extending their committee with its six years of experience into a more sophisticated quality-of-work-life project. This would include other crafts as well.

Improving Work Life

Planning and overseeing just such quality-of-work-life programs is the primary function of the labor-management committee in unionized plants where both management and union usually cosponsor such projects.

In the General Motors Corporation, a company-wide committee co-chaired by George B. Morris, Jr., GM's vice president for personnel, and UAW's Bluestone oversees all joint projects. Programs are under development in most divisions of the corporation, almost all involving the UAW.

At the Fisher Body #2 Plant in Grand Rapids, the labor-management committee began a program in 1973. A key element was to get employees to think as a "business team"—that is, to think in terms of cross-functional lines instead of vertical lines from the standard organizational chart. The objective was to lower the level of decision making and to develop an atmosphere of mutual trust. The pilot project was in the cutting room, where cloth and vinyl are cut for body interiors. From this beginning, the business team concept has spread through the entire plant.

At a recent conference sponsored by the National Center for Productivity and Quality of Working Life, Richard Norton, a GM manufacturing superintendent, explained that "the business team concept actually created a smaller business which set its own goals and whose members are responsible to each other for the success of the business."

In Philipsburg, Pennsylvania, the Rushton Coal Mine has been experimenting for four years with autonomous work groups. A steering committee consists of Warren H. Hinks, Jr., Rushton's president, the mine foreman and other management executives, officers of the Mineworkers union, and several members of both the mine and the safety committees.

This committee, assisted by a research team from Pennsylvania State University and the University of Pennsylvania, planned the project and now oversees its implementation. The Department of Commerce has provided research and training funds. Autonomous work groups were first tried in a section of the mine and involved twenty-seven volunteers, nine for each of three shifts. All twenty-seven have been trained in all jobs to permit full job rotation. They have been given special training in both federal and state mine safety laws and paid the top rate. Crew foremen are primarily responsible for safety and planning; the crew itself is responsible for production. This test group was successful, particularly in improving safety, so the experiment has now been extended to the entire mine.

Mark Naylor, a member of the trial group, reported that "suddenly we felt we mattered to somebody. Somebody trusted us. . . . When a machine busts down nowadays, most of the time we don't bother to call a maintenance man. We just fix it ourselves because, like I said, we feel it's as much ours as our own car at home."

According to Hinks, "We feel that the men are coming up with better attitudes; they are finding the work more interesting. Emphasis on safety has greatly increased. Formerly the idea was that you either had to go for coal output or for doing all of the safety things that complied with the law, but not for both. When the mine inspector wasn't around, the emphasis by the foreman would be on productivity, and a lot of the safety regulations would not be carried out. But now the autonomous teams do all of the work needed to be done to comply with safety regulations."

FAMILIAR TERRITORY

The more customary uses to which committees are put include improving productivity, increasing job security, and promoting the general success of the enterprise. Another frequent use of the committees is stabilizing labor-management relations. This stabilization has often come about because of an awareness on both sides after a protracted strike that there must be a better way.

Joining in the Common Cause

Committees in the steel industry are of the job security and productivity improvement sort. They grew out of the crisis caused by competition from Japanese and German imports, which gained impetus from the shortages of domestic steel during the long 1959 strike.

Although the steel industry agreement specifically excludes matters pertaining to the collective bargaining agreement, the areas that joint committees in that industry focus on are fairly broad. They include such matters as business conditions facing the company and the industry; foreign competition; excessive absenteeism; workers' morale, safety, and health; quality of work; equipment maintenance and downtime; reduction of rejects, waste, rework, and scrap; and saving of materials and energy—in short, things that improve productivity and thus job security.

In Pascagoula, Mississippi, the Litton Industries' shipyard is second in size only to the yards at Newport News and builds half the U.S. Navy's ships. It is the largest industrial employer in the Southeast. With 23,500 employees, fourteen unions, and up to five hundred union stewards in the plant on any given day, communication is a major problem.

Its labor-management committee, which meets monthly and consists of fifty members, discusses problems that affect the greatest number of employees, reviews policy changes before implementation, explores productivity improvement, and provides an opportunity for dialogue on pressing production problems. This committee grew out of a month-long strike in 1965. It was formed with the assistance of the Federal Mediation and Conciliation Service.

The need for improved communications is also felt in smaller plants like the American Velvet Company in Stonington, Connecticut, which has 375 workers. For over thirty years, the company has held morning meetings in which managers share information and ideas with each other. In recent years, the Textile Workers local union president and a union member have joined those meetings. Members read incoming mail together and talk with the sales manager in New York on conference calls. These informal daily meetings are in response to the volatility of that industry, which experiences daily shifts in demand.

Communications are also aided by the quarterly meeting of a profit-sharing committee in which all employees can offer and discuss suggestions. When demand for velvet decreased in 1975, the committee decided to operate and shut down on alternate weeks in preference to the traditional layoffs. This was done for four months until demand picked up.

Improving labor relations is the primary function of many labor-management committees, not just a by-product. Usually these committees grow out of strikes and a determination of the parties to achieve lasting industrial peace. They deal with issues that give rise to grievances and other problems before contract negotiation time.

Layoff and recall, safety and security, equal employment opportunity, overtime distribution, and fringe benefits are typical agenda items. FMCS mediators often act as third parties, usually conducting what they call a relationship-by-objectives program and then helping to organize and provide ongoing technical assistance to the committees. This concern about grievances and other contract-related matters contrasts with joint committees in industries like steel, which ordinarily rule these matters out of consideration.

SCANLON PLANS

Labor-management committees are also used to plan and administer gains-sharing programs like the Scanlon Plan. Although they have been around since the late 1930s, these plans are of special interest because they have been widely adopted in the past few years as the pressures on managements for increasing productivity and widening worker participation have intensified.

Scanlon Plans take their name from Joe Scanlon, an innovative accountant turned open-hearth worker and local union president during the Depression. Faced with the failing fortunes of his employer, a marginal steel company in eastern Ohio in 1937, he and a labor-management group went for counsel to Clinton Golden, then the Steelworkers vice president at the Pittsburgh headquarters. What emerged from their collaboration was a three-point program.

Point one was to agree on a philosophy of cooperation, participation, and frank and open consultation among plant management, workers, and the union at both shop-floor and plant-wide levels for all kinds of production problems. Point two was to establish shop-floor production committees of three members each—the foreman plus two elected workers—and a plant-wide review committee including the plant manager and the union president. Their function: to generate and pass on workers' suggestions for improvements in methods for doing the plant's work. Point three was to base a group-bonus, or gains-sharing, plan on each month's performance and to pay it monthly.

Although arrangements vary, the bonus scheme agreed on between the Edgerton, Wisconsin, plant of the Dana Corporation and the Autoworkers is typical. At Dana Edgerton, a network of twenty-one committees generated 535 suggestions in 1976, an average of one for every two employees. Resultant bonuses averaged 14 percent of payroll in 1974, 22 percent in 1975, and 20 percent in 1976. For the average worker, these amounted to $1,221 in 1974, $2,176 in 1975, and $2,153 in 1976.

Ron Sanderson, UAW local president, reported that "our people learn to be cost conscious, aware of the fact that we have to produce quantity and quality to remain competitive in the actual market, thus providing us with job security."

Scanlon Plans appear to produce readily measurable results more quickly for more employees and to last longer than many other reforms in work organization for a number of reasons.

First, Scanlon Plans do not depend heavily for survival on the continuance on the job of a single supportive manager, management, or union official, who is subject to change. Everyone has a visible, measurable stake in its continuation, the monthly bonus check. And there are regular opportunities for everybody to contribute suggestions and for elected shop committees to take part in discussion and decision making every month.

Second, Scanlon Plans are agreed on voluntarily by both union and management outside the contract and must be accepted by a substantial majority of all employees. Acceptance is determined by two secret ballot votes, one for a year's trial period and another for final adoption based on that experience.

Third, as soon as they are adopted, Scanlon Plans reach everyone from plant managers to sweepers. Many other quality-of-work-life experiments are far more ambitious but may take years of experimentation and evaluation with a small segment of employees before the benefits spread to everyone. Philips Lamp, for example, discovered in 1973— after ten years of innovative work restructuring—that only 3.5 percent of the 100,000 employees in its thirty-nine Dutch plants were affected. "We forgot to let people participate," a company official said. Today more employees are involved.

Finally, Scanlon Plans give a continuing incentive for communications to improve in all directions—top down, bottom up, and laterally. The monthly bonus figure signals immediately how the company is doing. Lateral communications improve too because everyone soon realizes that the success of each person and group depends on the success of the entire enterprise.

SIGNIFICANT FACTORS

Whatever these joint committees do, and their activities vary widely as we have seen, they all have several points in common. They provide workers a regular, periodic opportunity to participate in decision making, especially on the shop floor, where their work is most directly affected. They help management at all levels to identify and solve problems facing the organization. They provide a learning experience for all concerned on the workings of the enterprise and the way in which each person relates to it.

While the factors that are significant in the successful operation of labor-management committees differ from case to case, practitioners highlight a few crucial points:

• One of the first lessons is that joint efforts require modification of deep-seated attitudes, and these changes do not come readily. Only a relatively few managers and union officials have been willing to recast themselves as cooperative problem solvers.

Managers often report a fear of losing prerogatives in decision making, doubts that workers can make worthwhile contributions, and concern that giving workers a voice will strengthen the union's position. Managers with labor-management committees have a receptive, experimental, and open attitude. At Rushton, Hinks said, "The average worker wants to make an intelligent and creative contribution. I know it may be difficult for some of you to believe, but miners like their work. They want to be involved in decision making that involves them."

For their part, unions and employees often equate productivity with loss of jobs and workers' effort or fear that cooperation may weaken their ability to bargain for their primary goals. Thus cooperation requires a common understanding of the link between the establishment's competitiveness and job security. Where competition is intense, this connection is readily perceived. For example, the joint production committees in the steel industry were renamed Employment Security and Productivity Committees to underscore the relationship. The president of one steel local noted that "once membership realizes that productivity is job-supporting, not job-eliminating, they begin to respond."

More fundamental in lessening employees' fears are specific measures for protecting job security and for sharing the gains. Companies with a "no layoff" or attrition policy in cases of technological change are likely to be able to reduce antagonism and achieve cooperation for improving productivity readily. Under the Scanlon Plan, participation through joint production committees is reinforced by a mechanism for measuring productivity gains and sharing them according to a pre-established formula.

For both sides, one inhibitor to action is the fear of failure. And some plans do fail. Many of these, like other human relationships dependent on mutual trust and good faith, are very fragile. The failures are hard to discover because it is not in the nature of most people to publicize their failures. Sometimes, labor-management committees suspend their activities when collective bargaining and internal political issues in management or the union become more pressing. This has taken place in the Amsco case cited earlier.

• The second lesson underscores the importance of free communication and sharing of ideas as the basis of a successful joint committee. Productive committee discussion requires, according to Clyde Caldwell, special representative of the International Brotherhood of Boilermakers at the Tennessee Valley Authority (TVA), a willingness on the part of management

> to leave its authoritative hat at the door and talk eyeball to eyeball and gut to gut across the table and hear what those people really feel. Let them lay it out to you without feeling hostile, without having elements of reprisal.
>
> On the union side, are you willing to go in there and make suggestions to improve the quality of work and reduce the inefficiency of that plant that you and your people walking around in that plant see every day? Are you willing to take the initiative in this crisis situation that this American economy finds itself in?

Furthermore, rank-and-file employees and supervisors must be kept fully informed about committee activities and involved wherever possible. Otherwise, rank-and-file members may charge union committee members with "selling out," and line supervisors may feel that the union representatives are going over their heads.

Feedback from management regarding employees' questions about operations and suggestions for improvement is indispensable if their interest is to be maintained. Management's willingness to discuss the logic of what it is doing is the heart of the process. If employees get such information, observes William Black, Jr., administrator of TVA's labor-management relations, "You can count on their being more excited about their work, much more involved in it, and much more productive. Feeding the committee maintains the interest of the participants in the process."

• A third lesson to observe is that a sense of commitment, mutual trust, and mutual respect is essential for the smooth functioning of a joint committee. Top plant management and union officers not only sanction cooperative efforts but also usually participate in committee meetings. Above all, trust is forthcoming as long as each party refrains from using the committee to undermine the collective bargaining process.

• Finally, experienced consultants can play a useful role as catalysts to bring about cooperation. In some situations, trusted outside experts help adversaries accept a problem-solving approach by exploring differences and areas of common interest. Establishing a Scanlon Plan requires the services of accountants and other specialists. Quality-of-work-life experiments often involve behavioral scientists acting in the role of educators, facilitators, or researchers. Experience suggests that the decision to employ consultants and the choice and payment of experts can be best left to the labor-management committee.

FAVORABLE INFLUENCES

Given the traditional mistrust between labor and management, however, the prospects for rapid wide-spread adoption of the cooperative approach are not favorable. Nevertheless, there is likely to be a continuing but gradual increase in the number of cases of cooperation, particularly in the Midwest and the Northeast, where most of the committees are now operating. These are the old, established industrial areas with generally older, unionized plants facing competition from newer, nonunion plants in the South and abroad.

Another factor is the efforts of communities like Jamestown and Buffalo, New York; and Muskegon, Michigan; and of states like Maryland, Massachusetts, New York, and Ohio, which encourage the formation of cooperative in-plant programs in an effort to improve their economies, save jobs, and combat unemployment.

Still other favorable influences nationwide are the long-term trends in our society to increase recognition of the individual (evident in the civil rights and the women's movements) and to use collective bargaining.

Foreign visitors over several generations have consistently found American workers to be skillful and hardworking. Cooperation through joint committees at the plant and the shop-floor level may be one of the most effective ways for management to tap the creativity and ingenuity of this resourceful labor force to improve productivity and the quality of work life.

The Case for Participatory Management

Donald K. Conover

In a Western Electric drafting organization located in Chicago, productivity had been low. Employee turnover and absenteeism were high. The manager of two hundred or so employees decided to do something to improve morale and productivity: He would introduce participatory management.

First he met with the lower-level supervisors to explain his plan, get their support, and persuade them to go to the employees with him.

The first meeting with the employees was billed as a "what's up?" conference. There was no agenda, but rather an informal discussion about how the work was going. The result was a long list of suggestions to improve the physical facilities of the office: new paint, better coffee and food-vending machines, etc. This wasn't quite what the supervisors had hoped for, but the office did need attention, and the suggestions were reasonable. The supervisors said they would try to have the work done.

When most of the improvements had been made, a second conference was scheduled, again with no formal agenda. When the meeting started, there was a lot of talk about the improvements, and it was obvious that the meetings had made the employees feel that the supervisors were really interested in listening to what they had to say.

Finally someone observed, "The real problem around here isn't the office, it's the job. Some of the things we have to do don't make sense. We never know what's coming. The supervisor gives us a job and tells us how long it should take. Someone else checks our work when it's done, and back we go to the supervisor to get another job. The way

Excerpted from Clement Bezold, ed., *Anticipatory Democracy: People in the Politics of the Future* (New York: Vintage Books, 1978). Copyright © 1978 by Donald K. Conover.

things are organized we never know what's next, and there is always someone looking over our shoulder." As the supervisors listened, the discussion began to shift from what was wrong with the job to what could be done to improve it, and the ideas began to flow.

In the next several months, the employees rearranged the flow of work, suggested several labor-saving ideas that more than paid for the earlier office improvements, and developed a new way of handling work assignments. Instead of getting one job at a time, a supervisor laid out all the jobs for the next week. Employees chose what they thought they could complete in a week. Most employees had a high opinion of their ability and tended to take more work than the managers had expected. In most cases, they completed what they said they could do.

One of the jobs involved making charts of business results for a division vice-president. About a year after the meetings had begun, a staff supervisor for the vice-president asked that someone from the drafting unit be sent up to the vice-president's conference room to receive instructions about some new charts that were needed. The young woman who went had been doing the vice-president's charts for some time. When the staff supervisor started to tell her how to draw the new charts, she stopped him. "Tell me what information you want these charts to show, and I'll decide how to draw them," she said. "That's my job."

The first reaction from the vice-president's staff was irritation. But after the charts had been delivered it was clear that the woman knew her job. Not only did the charts show what they were supposed to, they included information the staff supervisor had overlooked.

Eighteen months after the first "what's up?" conference, the drafting unit was producing more than twice the number of drawings it had been. The unit's rate of absenteeism was among the lowest at the plant, and except for two men drafted into military service, turnover was zero.

Similar experiments are taking place in factories, warehouses, airlines, coal mines, banks, and company offices all over the United States. Individuals and groups of workers are getting the opportunity to plan, schedule, execute, and control more of their own work. They are managing, and, for the most part, they like it. Managers like it too, because productivity tends to go up while personnel problems go down.

Like most ideas that excite business managers, participatory management is expected to produce practical results. It isn't the easiest way to improve results because the whole culture and tradition of business organization is contrary to the idea of enlarging the scope of work at the bottom of bureaucratic pyramids. It would be much easier if the research laboratory could come up with a machine to boost productivity. But managers have to take productivity increases where they find them, and with inflation pushing labor costs higher and higher, participatory management is one of the answers.

This may strike some readers as a mercenary way to deal with a subject that could just as easily be described as the beginning of democracy in business corporations. That general idea is where the article is headed, but I'd rather not start that way. For one thing it would be hypocritical, because I still believe that the first job of business is to produce a product or service that customers need and to make a profit doing it, not to be the architect of a Utopian society. For another, I know that changing traditions and power structure in a culture as well established as American business isn't going to be easy.

I happen to believe that the time is right for a period of substantial social innovation in business organizations and that participatory management may be one of the most important safeguards to the private-enterprise system and to freedom in society as a whole. But I also think more progress will be made if the argument for change is presented in the best light to those whose support is most important to effect the change. That means finding ways to get management, labor, and the public at large thinking on the same wavelength. Since management obviously represents a major power base, it is particularly important to convince management that its best interest will be served by supporting the change.

I recall an incident in 1975 that may illustrate the problem of different points of view. I was attending the Second General Assembly of the World Future Society in Washington, D.C. A sign on the bulletin board announced a breakfast meeting the next morning for futurists from New York City. Being a New Yorker, I decided to attend. About a dozen people showed up. They were teachers, students, and freelancers trying to make a living in future-oriented activities. After introductions we chatted about how the conference was going and tried to decide if there was anything we might do together as futurists from New York. In the middle of this discussion, someone singled me out by saying, "You work for a big corporation. What are you doing here? Aren't corporations just interested in making money? They aren't interested in the future, are they?"

I have run into this same thing many times, but it always disturbs me. The impression is that the Future (with a capital F) is to be involved with government, new technology, and new lifestyles. Business and the question of how the production of goods and services will be handled seems to be relegated to a secondary position; it is something to be worked in after the big questions of law and social values have been decided. Assuming that we are talking about a future that provides more, not less, democracy, the question of business and the private-enterprise system seems too important an issue to leave out of the main discussion.

There is nothing wrong with trying to improve the government. If we can find ways to regenerate democratic principles in the context of modern society and provide for greater individual involvement in shaping the course of government, we will strengthen important freedoms and have better government as well. But government isn't the whole story.

The cornerstone of American freedom has always been the combination of representative democracy in government and private enterprise in the economy. It is important to determine how goods and services will be produced. It is important to consider the role of private property and the contributions to liberty inherent in capitalism and free market competition. Assuming that people are going to continue having to work, it is important to think about how work will be organized and how trade-offs between organizational and individual needs will be restored. Most important of all, futurists must be interested in what motivates people to be productive, to assume responsibilities, and to take the personal risks necessary to be innovative. Stated another way, we need to take a systems approach to the development of social ideas for the future.

In terms of day-to-day impact, the business corporation probably does more than any other organized institution to shape the environment where we spend most of our time and exert the greatest personal effort seeking status and fulfillment. Policies and programs chosen by corporate management substantially influence our patterns of employment, consumption, and investment. Without a sense of personal involvement and control in shaping these economic dimensions of our lives, better government alone cannot produce a freer society.

When we begin to look at life in the modern corporation in terms of the individual, a mixed pattern is evident. Materially, the system continues to produce more, and the distribution of economic benefits has enriched almost everyone. However, the size and complexity necessary for that economic growth have been accompanied by a growing depersonalization of work and a widening gap between corporate and individual goals.

The size and complexity of the modern corporation, its practice of designing and organizing jobs around increasingly specialized tasks, and the geographic and product diversification of different divisions have made it difficult for the organization to recognize the individual, and difficult for the individual to identify with the organization. In addition to the problem of finding ways to let more employees manage their own jobs, other problems have been surfacing that also need attention.

Most companies try very hard to have policies and programs that are uniform and fair in the treatment of employees. The difficulty is that in a society of free people, individual needs are not the same. When the organization gets so big that the individual is hard to recognize, the doctrine of fairness becomes the decision to treat all employees the same. For example, fringe benefits typically provide various types of insurance, such as life, medical, and disability. In general, such insurance is more valuable to a married employee with many dependents than to a single employee with no dependents. In a society where lifestyles and family patterns are becoming more varied, business can expect increased discontent with policies and programs, designed as part of employee compensation, which are weighted in terms of personal choices not part of the corporation's business.

The issues that may need clarification include hiring, hours of work, company-paid education, job rotation, relocation, career guidance, fringe benefits, retirement, and termination. In each of these there is no question of a legitimate and important company interest. What is difficult is to balance such an array of programs in a way that satisfies both the increasingly complicated needs of the organization and the increasingly diverse needs of individual employees. As every manager knows, nothing causes more unrest and discontent than a new employee program that the employees consider tilted in favor of the company or inequitable in terms of different employee groups. Conversely, one of the most powerful motivations for effective work is the successful link between organizational needs and the personal satisfaction of workers.

One possible way to let employees decide on a better personal balance between job needs and their own preferences involves more flexibility in work hours. Various approaches are being tried: *Flexi-time* involves establishing a period in the middle of a standard workday when everyone must be at work (such as 10 A.M. to 3 P.M.), and then allowing employees to decide whether to come in early or stay late to complete a full day's work. *Staggered work hours* is a similar idea, except that employees choose a fixed work schedule, perhaps 8:30 A.M. to 4:30 P.M., instead of 9 to 5. This has been used extensively in metropolitan areas where avoiding rush-hour crowds or arranging individual commutation schedules results in significant savings to the employee, with only minor adjustments in the organization's standard hours of work. *Permanent part-time employment* requires more elaborate job planning since, as the name implies, it involves an arrangement to work regularly on less than a full-time basis.

Some experiments have shown a direct relationship between employee control of hours of work and productivity on the job. At an auto-parts plant in Tennessee, mirror polishers were able to cut three hours or more off their workday by higher efficiency. Through a worker-management committee, agreements were reached so that employees finishing the expected amount of work early could leave or attend classes (to learn higher-level job skills such as welding or to study general-interest subjects like history).

A more complex innovation is being introduced at Material Management Centers in Western Electric. The MMCs are regional warehouses where the work involves six basic functions: receiving, handling materials, putting away, selecting, packing, and shipping. Because variations in what has to be handled and fluctuation in demand have always made it difficult to introduce meaningful time standards, this type of work is generally paid on a straight-time basis, i.e., hours worked at a certain hourly wage. Now, using computers to keep track of all the variations, a system involving over twelve hundred constant time elements and over five hundred actions that vary in the time needed to complete them has been developed. This system makes it possible to compare daily output to the number of hours a person works to generate a measure of how productive he or she is. This is essential data required to introduce a system of wage incentives.

Going a step farther, the management and the union have concluded an agreement called the *Productivity Pay Plan* in which there is a base rate of pay and an incentive bonus for each percent output above a predetermined standard ("Acceptable Productivity Level") up to a maximum of 20 percent.

The typical problem with plans of this sort has been disputes between labor and management about adjusting rates of pay so that increases in productivity are incorporated into the new expected standards of work. Management would like the new rates to reflect the improvements in methods of doing the work, and the workers would like to keep getting a bonus for doing more than the accepted standard of productivity in the past. In addition to these disputes, this situation also encourages a divisive undercurrent where productivity improvements may be held back by workers to prevent the "Acceptable Productivity Level" from increasing, thereby permanently eliminating the bonus on increased productivity.

The Productivity Pay Plan solves this problem in a unique way. When productivity has been at 17 or more percent above the standard for three consecutive months, management can offer to buy an increment of productivity and raise the base productivity level at a cost of from 5 to 10 percent of the workers' annual base salary. If the employees accept the offer, the payments are made in installments over five quarters with the first installment paid immediately.

This means that workers not only have the benefit of past productivity increases, but can now receive more bonus pay. Since this past increase approached the 20 percent limit, once it is incorporated into the base productivity level they can again be paid for increases in productivity. The decision to accept or reject such a purchase offer is made by a vote of the employees in the union. Thus, all parties have a mutual interest in improving output and sharing in the decision about how such gains will be reflected in employee compensation.

An example of the Productivity Pay Plan might work in the following manner. The employees in a particular pay group have had successive monthly outputs 18, 20, and 24 percent higher than the current Acceptable Productivity Level. They are paid an incentive bonus each month, 18, 20, and 20 percent above their base rate. The company offers to purchase a 5 percent increase in the Acceptable Productivity Level for 6.5 percent of the annual base salary (the higher amount to approximate the impact of the higher standard on the Acceptable Productivity Level to be used if the offer is accepted). The employees vote to accept. The following month their output is 17 percent above the new level. Workers receive a bonus for this and would already have received the first installment of the 6.5 percent of the yearly base salary when the company offer was accepted.

The same problems of corporate size and complexity that cause difficulties in the traditional areas of employee relations also affect employee attitudes about business as a social institution. If the employee is dissatisfied with his working conditions, news of a scandal somewhere in the company can more easily lead to the assumption that the whole company lacks integrity. At the same time, employees often are treated as if they don't understand, care about, or have an interest in the corporation. Yet today's employees are better educated than any work force in history. As consumers they are more aware, and as community residents they are more concerned. Often they are stockholders in their companies. They expect more from their employers than just a job and a pension. They are concerned about honesty in advertising, manipulation in the marketplace, protection of the environment, the use of natural resources, and the impact of corporate decisions to expand or contract jobs and facilities in their communities. When management decisions are poorly explained or appear contrary to the public interest, they challenge the employee's loyalty.

Even though confidence in government leadership has also fallen, the most frequent remedy for problems of corporate abuse seems to be government regulation or control. Yet I think most people believe that private industry is more effective when it comes to getting things done. The appeal of government control seems to be a hope that through the governmental process, the direction and control of economic resources will be more responsive to public need.

I am inclined to believe that the decline of confidence in business leadership has less to do with inequities or criminality than it does with the desire of the public, and more particularly corporate employees, to have a say in deciding what policies and rules will regulate their association with business organizations and how business will touch their lives as consumers, neighbors, or stockholders. Thus even the wisest and best management cannot refuse to share some of its decision-making power without causing resentment and ultimately rebellion.

How to accomplish greater employee involvement in decisions about corporate policy and business direction is a more difficult matter than involvement in the management of the workplace. At present there seem to be two different (and opposing) approaches. One, which is attracting support in Europe, involves putting employees, or their representatives, on the board of directors so that they have a voice in top-level decision making. The other focuses on various programs to encourage stock ownership by employees so that their interest can be exercised as part owners of the business.

While I acknowledge that there are pros and cons to both approaches, I am not neutral. I strongly oppose the notion that an employee representative should be foisted on the board of directors, and I believe that a wider ownership of corporate stock is a good idea. With this bias clearly established, let us review both ideas.

The logic behind the move to require a place for employee representation on the board seems to be that since the employee is so obviously affected by corporate policy and decisions, the employee is therefore *entitled* to have a say in such matters. In support of this logic, proponents argue that it is good for business to get the employees involved, to have them feel they are part of management in all phases of the business. It is also democratic—just as citizens have representatives to guard their interests in the government, so employees should be represented in the management of the business for which they work. Granting a significant measure of truth in each of these arguments, the nub of the issue is the word *entitled.*

It must be remembered, however, that by law the board of directors represents the interest of the owners of the corporation. If someone other than the owner is *entitled* to assume ownership authority, what is the owner *entitled* to? Because the decision to walk out on strike affects the stockholders, should they be *entitled* to a seat on the union's strike committee? Should taxpayers be *entitled* to help decide how large a raise municipal employees will ask for?

The plain fact is that the *entitlement* argument destroys the principle of private property. In my opinion, mandating employee representation on the board of directors is at best an expedient to compensate for out-of-date or improperly administered laws intended to intercede in conflicts between private property rights and the public interest. At worst, it is an attempt to eliminate differences of opinion (an impossibility) or to communize the ownership of capital (a revolution). Our problem is how to make the system work while safeguarding individual freedom. The *entitlement* argument is an attempt to make the system work at the expense of such freedom.

Beyond the philosophical objection, there are practical questions about how effective an employee representative at the Board level could be. As a manager, I realize I can't know all the details or make the judgments required to do the job of skilled craftsmen who may work in an organization I am supervising. If I tried, I would have to neglect job responsibilities that I am expected to be on top of as manager. Likewise, it is difficult to imagine how an employee who is close enough to the rank and file to represent its viewpoint could also be in touch with the complexities and details of top management issues. Also, I have difficulty understanding how a few employees appointed, or even elected, to serve on the board of directors would substantially increase the personal involvement of the tens of hundreds of thousands of employees in medium to large corporations. For instance, even if Western Electric were to double the size of its board (a questionable move in itself) and have employees occupy all of the new seats, there would still not be a representative from each major factory and service organization.

The other approach to more employee involvement in top management is through expanded stock ownership. On the face of it, this approach must include solutions to economic questions of where employees are going to get wealth to buy stock in any significant amount and how to make stock ownership more meaningful in the management of today's business corporations. Both are major problems. The most powerful argument that this is the place to look for answers is the fact that only by making employees owners in the traditional way can we sustain and strengthen individual rights to private property. In other words, the problems of implementation may be great, but there is a philosophical consistency that makes the effort worthwhile.

One approach that some companies are experimenting with is called ESOP, Employee Stock Ownership Plan. The basic idea is to pay part of every employee's compensation in the form of stock in the company. The tax and capitalization issues are beyond the scope of this article, but the concept is simple enough. If employees are stockholders, they have both the legal right to exercise an owner's influence and an owner's interest in the welfare of the business.

The problem of providing stockholder involvement with decisions affecting the direction or social impact of a large corporation has already been acknowledged. However, if the larger goal is the enhancement of individual involvement in decisions, it is a lot more appealing and probably more effective to search for solutions in the improvement of institutions that have already been established. This argues that the way to improve individual input to the executive suite is by expanding communication and involvement with a company's stockholders.

In companies where ESOPs have been introduced, there have been some spectacular results. The most striking example is the South Bend Lathe Company. On the verge of being liquidated, SBL got federal support for an ESOP, and the employees raised $10 million and became the new owners. After operating at a loss in 1975, productivity has increased by 25 percent and pre-tax profits were at 9 percent. ESOPs have also been introduced at such companies as the Bell System, Gamble-Skogmo of Minneapolis, Hallmark Cards, Zapata in Houston, and E-Systems, an electronics and aerospace company in Dallas. Connections between improved performance or higher employee morale and increased employee stock ownership are hard to prove. But when the employees begin to feel like owners, some of the problems of depersonalization or alienation are obviously affected for the better.

Participatory management—more employee involvement in deciding how work will be done, in deciding the policies and rules for balancing organizational and personal needs, and in deciding about the direction business may take with regard to its social impact—seems inevitable. However, there are one or two reservations before the great day arrives, and these reservations constitute the other side of the argument. They are the problems of leadership and responsibility. In presenting them I am speaking as a manager with some experience in the difference between how I might like people to act and how it is reasonable to expect they will act.

Once when I was trying to get funding for a series of television programs about the future for use within the corporation, the not-sofacetious comment of an associate highlighted this difference. We had made a pilot program dealing with problems of the city. I was taking it around the company, showing it to groups of managers and asking them to comment about its value, when another manager unexpectedly hit me with a question, "How do you want us to answer, as a manager or as a human being?"

The question reveals a lot about management. On one hand, managers acknowledge the same feelings anyone might have. However, their position as manager also entails values that may be in opposition to those relevant for dealing with certain social problems.

One of the terms managers use most frequently to describe their responsibility is *stewardship*, a term that recognizes both the private property aspect of a publicly held corporation and the balanced objectives a business must have to survive. Although today's stockholder is likely to be remote from the internal affairs of any particular corporation, the economic system and the law still regard the stock as private property. There are few circumstances where the stock is likely to be held for any other reason than the expectation of a profit. Unless we were to do away with such private property and profit seeking, everyone who exercises managerial authority is expected to have the stockholders' interest in mind when making business decisions.

Stewardship also involves questions of short- and long-term goals. Profit maximizing is often thought to be the corporation's dominant goal. Yet even if the market supported a high price today, that might not be the best way to hold a customer you hope will be back in the future. Spending money to improve quality or to develop better products or service may take something of today's profit to build a market for tomorrow. Responding to employee needs, paying a competitive wage, and offering opportunities for upward mobility have always been important in attracting, retaining, and motivating a competent work force. The net effect is that while managers may philosophically be committed to maximizing profits, time and pressure of marketplace competition force them to consider a range of short- and long-term objectives.

In addition to stewardship, management provides leadership, and in a complex world there is no way to plan, organize resources, and carry out complex tasks without leadership. Elections and committees can be very successful in assuring that different views are presented. Without a system of open communication, leadership can become remote, out of touch, and elitist. Clearly, there are ways to improve leadership, make it more responsive, provide better checks and balances; but no way has been found to dispense with it altogether. People want more opportunity to decide how to do their own jobs. They want the satisfaction and pride of responsibility for their own labor. In the contract between the employer and employee, workers want a voice in the rules and programs defining their involvement in the organization's goals and their share of the organization's success. As employee-citizens they have a wider interest in corporate objectives and the choices that affect the impact of business on the whole of society. These are the desires shaping the trend to participatory management.

However, the more important issue is what the concept itself means to business and to a free society. Participatory management promises to re-establish the personal significance of the private-enterprise system. Finding ways to enhance individual participation in management can help eliminate the feelings of depersonalization and alienation common in an advanced industrial society. It can restore both individual incentive to make the business productive and individual responsibility about the role of business in a free society.

Teaching an Old Dog Food New Tricks

Richard E. Walton

Part One: Seven Years of Work Innovations at Topeka

General Foods' radically innovative dry dog-food plant in Topeka was conceived in 1968 and started up in January 1971. In designing the new plant, the original project team, led by GF managers Lyman Ketchum and Ed Dulworth, was determined to avoid the negative worker attitudes in the existing pet-food facilities in Illinois. They were inspired by the possibility of engaging unusual human involvement in the new plant.

Self-managing teams assumed responsibility for large segments of the production process. The teams were composed of from seven to fourteen members, large enough to embrace a set of interrelated tasks and small enough to permit face-to-face meetings for making decisions and for coordination. Activities usually performed by separate units—maintenance, quality control, custodianship, industrial engineering, and personnel—were built into the responsibilities of each team. For example, team members screened job applicants for replacements on their own team.

An attempt was made to design every set of team tasks to include both manual skills and mental functions such as diagnosing mechanical problems and planning. The aim was to make all sets of team tasks equally challenging, although each set would require unique demands.

Consistent with this aim was a *single job classification* for all operators. Pay increases depended on the mastery of an increasing number

Reprinted with permission from "The Topeka Story: Teaching an Old Dog Food New Tricks" by Richard E. Walton, *Wharton Magazine* 2, no. 2, copyright © 1978 by The Wharton School of the University of Pennsylvania. Adapted by special permission from "Work Innovations at Topeka: After Six Years," by Richard E. Walton, *Journal of Applied Behavioral Science* 13, no. 3 (1977): 422–33, NTL Institute for Applied Behavioral Science.

of jobs. Since there were no limits on how many members of a team could qualify for higher pay brackets, employees were encouraged to teach each other their skills.

In lieu of the "foreman," a "team leader" position was created. Operators were provided with the data and guidelines that enabled them to make production decisions ordinarily made by higher level supervisors. The team leader had the responsibility for facilitating the team's decision making. As for plant rules, management refrained from specifying any in advance. Rules evolved over time from collective experience.

The technology and architecture were designed to facilitate rather than discourage informal gatherings of team members during working hours. Status symbols were minimized—for example, a single entrance leads into both the administrative office and the plant.

The new work system achieved highly positive results in both human and economic terms. A study by Robert Schrank of the Ford Foundation conducted in 1973 found high levels of worker participation in decisions, freedom to communicate, expressions of warmth among the workers, a minimum of status distinction, a strong sense of human dignity, commitment to the job, and individual self-esteem. Schrank gave less credit for this to certain new design features than I do, arguing, for example, that the self-managing team structure, the challenging job contrast, and the skill-based pay system were much less important than the fact that employees had the freedom to move around and socialize during working hours.

Another study of the plant was conducted in June 1974. It used the survey methodology of the University of Michigan and confirmed the Topeka work force's positive attitudes. According to Edward Lawler of the Institute for Social Research, "Our data . . . show high levels of satisfaction and involvement in all parts of the organization. In fact they show the highest levels we have found in any organization we have sampled. I specifically compared it with other small organizations and still found it superior."

Furthermore, there is no doubt about the economic superiority of the plant. Recent studies by corporate analysts outside Topeka have indicated that the savings attributable to the work innovations in the dog-food plant were in the neighborhood of a million dollars annually, a significant figure in a plant with about one hundred personnel and involving a capital investment in the range of $10–15 million.

Other pertinent statistics: The plant started up and went three years and eight months (1.3 million manhours) without a lost-time accident. Absenteeism ranged from .8 percent to 1.4 percent during 1971–74.

Turnover was reported at 10 percent per year; both the rate and nature of the turnover is regarded by Topeka employees as healthy. The impressive benefits led to a corporate policy favoring similar innovative approaches in other plants where conditions were suitable. The actual diffusion of these ideas to other General Foods plants has been slow, but for reasons other than doubt about their efficacy in Topeka. Ironically, Topeka's dramatic success and its attendant publicity created a sense of rivalry and some resentment among other GF plant managers and discouraged rather than encouraged them from taking a similar approach in their own plant.

In order to understand some of the innovations at Topeka, here is a chronology of key developments.

Phase I (1968–1970)—Pre-Start-Up

Long before start-up, team leaders were hired and included in the planning, training, and team building. Lead time was allowed for new concepts to be articulated, debated, and translated into work procedures and structures. Managers had time to develop insights into human behavior and to coalesce as a group. Team leaders screened operators, drawing 63 from more than 600 applicants to form a relatively talented and receptive work force.

Certain events helped establish the new work culture. The screening process used to select team leaders included role playing and group discussion—providing a unique, involving, and even anxiety-provoking initiation. According to one observer, this initial experience created a sense of hardiness, uniqueness, and elitism. The team leaders in turn utilized similar methods in screening workers, thereby transmitting these same feelings to the work force.

While healthy skepticism about the project existed within the new work force, these initial experiences created a readiness to give the innovations a fair trial.

Phase II (1971)—Technical and Social Start-Up

The first year of operation was marked by a variety of minor "tests" of the system, and by the development of potent group phenomena. In the first few weeks some cash was taken from an open change box. The universal response by workers and managers was to dig into their own pockets to replace the missing cash and continue the open cash box which was used for vending machines in the cafeteria. These gestures were symbolically important in confirming support for a system that could be built on the premise of trustworthiness.

After a number of weeks, the operators felt they were ready for their first pay increase, based on mastery of their first job. Management, however, did not anticipate this event. Their initial disagreement both reinforced the doubt of the skeptics and weakened the confidence of the believers. When management ultimately agreed to review the qualifications of operators for increases, they also reaffirmed the responsiveness of the system.

Soon after, a railroad strike tested the teams' capacities to solve new work problems, which the teams did effectively. Also, by interrupting regular production, the strike tested management's commitment to provide secure employment. Plant management tried to prevent corporate pressures from forcing them to make layoffs. The occasion once again crystallized fears and hopes about the system. As it happened, the strike ended before a definitive answer to the question was arrived at.

Developments within each of the six work teams largely determined how a person viewed the work system. At times team leaders provided too much structure, seeming to contradict the stated philosophy. At other times, they provided too little structure and seemed to dramatize the impracticality of worker participation. Nevertheless, sooner or later the groups coalesced. They became the most potent factor in forming and enforcing the system's norms about cooperation, openness, involvement, and responsibility.

In brief, 1971 was a period of building technical and social skills and of testing the credibility of the system. Those who were initially receptive had their commitment strengthened and, except for a small minority, many of those who were negative or skeptical decided to "buy in."

Phase III (1972)—Pushing the Technology

In 1972, the *social capital* (skills, knowledge, attitudes, and relationships) was put to work in a demanding way. Demand for production volume, resisted during 1971, now had to be met.

The maximum production effort had several important side effects: First, quality sometimes suffered, undermining one source of pride. Second, with the plant now "humming" there was less immediate need for group problem solving and less opportunity for meetings. This reduced the amount of ongoing social maintenance within groups. Third, teams often yielded to the temptation to improve their own performance at the expense of the next shift.

A management change at a higher level also troubled Topeka managers. The man who had initiated the innovations and who had held an umbrella over the fledgling system during the past year was replaced by a person who was seen as philosophically unsympathetic to Topeka. This change raised doubts about the General Foods hierarchy's understanding or commitment to the Topeka innovation.

Still, the plant was performing well, reaching capacity output with about 70 people (compared with the 110 originally estimated on the basis of standard industrial engineering principles). Substantial savings from lower overhead, fewer quality rejects, and other factors were attributed to the innovative human organization. Participants were proud.

The plant had become perhaps the most publicized U.S. example of a solution to what the media called the "blue-collar blues." A journalist's account of his visit to the plant had been featured on the front page of the *New York Times*. Along with work innovations at Volvo and ATT, it was the subject of NBC's "First Tuesday" program—sixty minutes of prime TV time. An article analyzing this "prototype" plant and its initial successes reached over 100,000 readers of the *Harvard Business Review*.

All things considered, I judge this was a period of leveling off. Comparing the production year of 1972 with the start-up year of 1971, "participation" and "openness" generally went down. However, the impressive production results increased "optimism" that the system would survive.

Phase IV (1973)—Turmoil, Decline, and Reversal

During my visit in October 1973, I found a consensus that a trough had been reached during the summer in various indexes of the system's health. This trough was followed by a steady improvement during the fall.

During the first half of 1973, the emphasis on production volume continued, along with long hours, few team meetings, and inter-shift rivalry. The negative effects were cumulative, depleting the social capital to a point that started to weaken basic commitments. Without meetings, trust and openness were declining.

The prolonged push for maximum production also deferred the movement of workers from one team to another, a movement that could occur after an operator had earned "team rate." This delay in opportunity to learn jobs on other teams postponed the date at which an employee could earn "plant rate." The delay tended to undermine commitment.

When inter-team movement was finally okayed, a large number of transfers occurred between packaging and processing. At about the same time, thirteen team members and two team leaders chose to form the nucleus for a newly constructed canned-food plant. The wholesale movement alleviated some problems but created others. The original teams often had identified closely with their team leaders, whose personal styles varied widely. Now team leaders were faced with new teams and vice versa.

Team leaders who were now trying to build a team for the second time often could not muster the same enthusiasm for the task. They felt unfairly resisted by the new teams, and often were faced with contradictory bids from two subgroups, one asking for more direction, the other for less. Perhaps to avoid these crosscurrents, team leaders held fewer team meetings and became more absorbed in plant-wide projects.

The absence of team meetings now had a dramatically negative effect. Members needed to cooperate hourly in their tasks and weekly in learning exchanges, but had not developed the necessary mutual confidence. Moreover, the recently hired employees were not learning about their rights and obligations in the system, and many were not developing commitment during the critical first few months.

Also, the new canned-food plant helped generate negativism in the dry-food plant. Many members felt they had been "deserted" by those who opted to go to a "more advanced rival." They also opposed the can plant's practices regarding pay and job design because a moratorium was placed on job rotation during the start-up phase and pay increases were tied to more traditional criteria.

By summer of 1973, the site manager, previously preoccupied with his strained relations in the corporation, started attending to the issues that troubled the Topeka organization. People became aware that they had neglected the acculturation of new members and the development of the newly formed teams; they resolved to rebuild the social capital. Openness, trust, and commitment were definitely trending up in the fall of 1973.

Another indication of strength was the fact that managers were working themselves out of their jobs by fostering the development of subordinates. The manufacturing manager of the dry-food plant asked to be pulled out of the line, eliminating one level of the hierarchy. He became a consultant to other parts of the corporation and to the Topeka plants. Also, there was growing interest in eliminating or reducing the number of team leader positions.

Notwithstanding the restored commitment and other favorable developments reported above, I detected some weaknesses during my visit in October 1973.

First, the system had not developed problem-solving mechanisms for the whole plant that were nearly as effective as those in the face-to-face teams. The problem was illustrated by two plant-wide issues in the fall of 1973: (1) differences of opinion about the selection criteria for a spare-parts coordinator and (2) whether or not the pay system for office employees could be revised along lines different from the factory pay schemes.

Representatives on the plant committees dealing with these issues were given only limited confidence. As a result, the committee actions were not truly accepted by the larger work force. Representatives were suspected of being co-opted by management. Moreover, committee members didn't support solutions shaped by problem-solving groups in which they had not been directly involved. This reflected a strong preference for "participatory democracy" over a "representative" form of self-government.

Second, although there was unusual frankness, there was also concern whether the openness and objectivity were adequate, given the stringent requirements of the plant design. For the system to work, an individual had to be candid in contributing to problem solving, conscientious in judging an idea on its merits, not its source, and objective in evaluating the qualifications of peers for higher pay rates.

I observed a strong desire by participants to increase these attributes, especially in pay decisions. When peer evaluations are "not honest," they said, there are three consequences: Pay increases are given that are not justified (creating inequities); individuals are assumed to have qualifications they do not possess (forcing others to do the work); and a basic tenet of the system is violated.

Objective criticism was muted when a person feared he would be ostracized by a clique because influence is vested more in lateral than in hierarchical relations, which makes an operator more concerned about the judgment of peers than superiors. Furthermore, there is no quantifiable, stable, automatic basis for a person's security, such as seniority. One worker explained that the tenuous basis of his security makes him continuously concerned about his relations with many people who could help or hurt him in the future. Another worker said, "The match in the gasoline is pay," explaining that decisions about the worth and pay of members are starkly real.

The result was a moderate tendency to ease up on standards, e.g., shrinking from hard, exacting evaluation of a worker's mastery of all tasks in the plant before awarding him the plant rate. Thus, reciprocation tended toward each giving the other the benefit of the doubt.

More impressive to me than the moderate gap betwen ideal and actual behavior were the high ideals themselves. The system had idealized influence based on *expertise* (information and skills), rather than either *positional power* (based on formal authority, rules, and procedures) or *political power* (e.g., cliques). The managers and workers felt guilty whenever they did not live up to the ideals of openness and objectivity. I found myself wondering at the time whether these people were expecting too much of themselves.

Third, among the team leaders there was a striking gap between ideals of high mutual support and trust and their actual behavior. Also, team leaders had a norm of self-sacrifice—most would concern themselves with improving work life for team members but not seek needed changes in their own situations. As one team leader said, "I never did think the 'Topeka system' applied to team leaders themselves." Team leaders were expected to engage in dialogue with operators and some were frequently exhausted. It had not been made legitimate for team leaders to put limits on their own accessibility.

Phase V (1974–1976)—Steady State with Traces of Erosion

When I returned in November 1976, after three years, a number of elements in the positive work culture had declined—not a steep decline, but rather a moderate erosion.

By general agreement it was still a very productive plant and a superior place to work, but the "quality of work life" had slipped. And while the majority still supported—by their own behavior—the unique strengths of the "Topeka work system," an increasing minority did not. Slippage occurred across a broad front of attributes: openness and candor, helping among team members, identification with plant management, confidence in General Foods, perceived upward influence, effective leadership within teams, and cooperation between shifts. In addition, there continued to be serious doubt about the ability of teams to make objective judgments about members' qualifications for pay increases.

Two major changes since 1973 had occurred: Team members now accepted the fact-of-life of subjectivity and other imperfections, and the clique behavior was more pronounced.

Following my visit in 1973 a concerted effort had been made to improve relations among team leaders and to increase their influence

over matters affecting them. Also their number was reduced from six
to three. However, by 1976, the team leader position was again ambiguous and unsatisfying. They were discouraged about their prospects for
advancement, a feeling sharpened by two facts: Their plant-wide project
assignments had broadened their abilities and raised their aspirations,
and team members provided them with more grief than satisfaction.
Team leaders, not unlike foremen in other plants, felt neither a part of
the work force nor of management. They complained that they were not
backed by management. As a result, the position failed to attract the
most talented team members.

Three factors had had depressing effects on the dry-plant work system during this period.

First, during 1973–1976, three of the four managers most responsible
for the Topeka system had left General Foods and the fourth had
moved from the dry-food plant to the can plant. Many perceived that
the managers who left GF had been treated unfairly by the company;
indeed, the managers themselves considered their pioneering work a
loss rather than a gain in their GF careers. These original managers had
a commitment to the philosophy and a will to "go to bat" to protect
the system, but the workers could not assume that their successors
would develop the same commitment. Also, one of the earlier managers
had played an especially strong role in the organization's development.
His contribution was missed.

Some people, however, held a contrasting view. They believed the
departing managers had been too aggressive vis-à-vis the corporate
hierarchy, thereby contributing to the strained external relations, isolating the Topeka innovation, and hurting their own GF careers and
the career opportunities of other Topeka managers.

Second, the neighboring can plant had lived under a cloud of uncertainty for three years—it would gear up for a national launching of a
new dog-food product only to have the plan cancelled when the product
did not prove out in market tests. Two layoffs had occurred in the can
plant in 1975. However, beginning in the summer of 1976 the product
took off in the market and the plant began a highly accelerated start-up,
moving quickly to three shifts and six-day schedules. In order to get the
plant on stream in the shortest possible time, management deferred the
introduction of many aspects of the new work structure from the dry
plant. This was interpreted by dry-plant members as weakened management commitment to the new philosophy.

Third, there were no new challenges of significance in the dry plant
during 1973–1976. A major expansion had been planned but did not
occur. New products requiring significant process changes were con-

templated but had not yet been introduced. So some complacency developed.

These three factors help explain the negative drift of the work culture. However, more significant for me was the absence of potent corrective devices, of a capacity for self-renewal.

As noted earlier, the work system has not dealt effectively with plant-wide issues. Committees that cut across units and levels of the plant have treated a few specific issues, but seldom, if ever, have they gained the full confidence of the employees. Moreover, there have been no regular plant-wide forums in which issues can be discussed.

In the absence of a plant-wide mechanism to which management could respond, management would have had to take the initiative to assess the health of the system, to diagnose problems, to identify opportunities, to review the adequacy of existing procedures and roles, to set goals for organizational development, and to propose innovative solutions. They have done little of this since 1973 except in relation to a proposed bonus scheme.

Equally important, though, the plant community sometimes lost its appreciation of the idea that the work system would need to evolve continually. Such evolution could only be derived from experience, with a widely shared responsibility for promoting this evolution. Within the work force there is a widely shared and deeply felt responsibility to *protect,* to preserve the work system. While this is an enormous asset, it could be an even greater asset if the commitment were less defensively oriented and initiatives were taken.

One major possibility for evolving the system—establishing a plant-wide productivity bonus—has been under consideration for several years but could not be acted on in the absence of corporate-level approval. This would be an appropriate development in many respects: Equity would be served by further sharing the fruits of this productive human system; the total plant community could be drawn together as it never has before; individuals who are topping out in the pay scheme would have another way to increase their income. In the most general sense, the plant-wide bonus could provide the work system with a timely "second wind."

The bonus has been delayed by other corporate considerations: there is no immediate motivational or productivity problem to solve by such a measure; some people question whether sufficient potential remains in the system for productivity increases to make significant bonuses possible; a bonus would create a complicating precedent for other GF plants; and, finally, the bonus design at Topeka itself becomes more complex with the addition of the can plant.

Perhaps the inability to implement this particular change, despite the attention it has been given, may inadvertently have taught the workers that they cannot innovate further.

Why Is the Work Culture So Robust?

Despite the slippage, the very positive culture has proven to be extremely robust. Earlier, there was a distinct pattern marking development/depletion/redevelopment and in recent years a pattern of moderate decline. But never has the climate truly soured or even become neutral and indifferent, although in my opinion this will happen unless concerted effort is made to evolve the organization further. It is amazing to me how much momentum has been sustained, given the modest level of social maintenance and renewal activities over the past three years.

The following explanations of the plant's robustness are offered tentatively and without any pretense of being exhaustive.

First, the original design concepts have proven sound in this situation. None have been abandoned, although, of course, some design ideals have been achieved only in relative terms.

Second, the implementation of the pre-start-up and the start-up stages was handled especially skillfully, a judgment I can now make after observing the start-ups of several similar work innovations.

Third, the system was enduring because the underlying philosophy itself was more important than personalities. Although each manager in the dry plant was respected, none aspired to become a charismatic leader. The commitment to certain philosophical principles was reinforced by the publicity given the "Topeka system." I found that many workers wanted to live up to their external image.

Fourth, pay clearly has been a pivotal element of the work system. One important factor is that it pays for skills acquired and there are no quotas to limit an individual's advancement.

Another important factor is the heavy role that peer evaluation plays in the administration of pay. On the one hand, this participative feature enhances commitment: Workers feel a serious responsibility to make both the pay scheme and the larger organization succeed; workers are keenly aware of their additional interdependence with each other; and self-management of the formal reward scheme symbolizes their relatively low dependence on hierarchical authority, which is a source of pride.

On the other hand, peer evaluation assumes that people can maintain high standards and levels of objectivity and, therefore, equity among people. These assumptions can only be valid by degree. The gap between an ideal and the actual can be demoralizing.

After assessing the pluses and minuses of this feature, I tend to believe there has been a net gain in Topeka. Still, I remain very cautious in recommending peer evaluation as an initial feature of the pay scheme in other plants.

Since my last visit to the plant a year ago, Topeka management has been addressing many of these issues and concerns. Bill Bevans, the GF organization development consultant who has been working there, reports that the new can plant is under control and operating well. Self-confidence has been enhanced at all levels of the plant community and management is able to attend to longer-term issues. The dry plant has a new manager and there has been positive response to a few issues initiated by the employees. Finally, the success and visibility within GF of similar projects in a few other plants has taken the "limelight" pressure off Topeka, freeing management from the caution that tended to immobilize it and prevent it from planning change or renewal. Although, to my knowledge, these developments have not changed anything at the shop-floor level, I find them encouraging.

VIII.
The Right to Information

Voluntary Disclosure

A. W. Clausen

Reform is no stranger to American life. Neither is the corruption that invites it. Our national scandals—and the resulting waves of reform—have been as recurrently predictable as the rise and fall of interest rates, politicians, or for that matter, stars of rock and roll.

Too often in America's past, some of the secret dollars that paid for illegal or ethically reprehensible activity have come from corporate coffers. And they did again in what former Securities and Exchange Commission Chairman Ray Garrett has called "by far the bigger half of Watergate."

Now, I'm not here to moralize. You know, as I do, that the vast majority of American business people, large and small, behave prudently and ethically. But because of Watergate and the findings of other recent investigations, every one of us in this room tonight is a member of a business community which has suffered a form of disgrace. If we're not shocked by our situation, we should be.

There is a difference between the scandals of history and those of the recent past. It's important to recognize that the difference is not just one of scale—though beyond question, the ethical blindness that emerged from recent investigations is on a scale unmatched in all the episodes of our past. What's important isn't the scale but the pervasiveness of a rationale for misconduct, the do-it-as-usual attitude that runs through so much of the testimony on the subject. Many of this nation's bluest of blue chip corporations are perceived as operating on the assumption that payoffs, bribes, influence peddling, book-juggling, falsification of records, and miscellaneous other hanky-panky are somehow a normal part and cost of doing business.

Excerpted from a speech delivered in San Francisco, January 15, 1976. Used with permission.

If we're not concerned, then we're just not sensitive to the reality of the problem or today's world. Integrity is not some impractical notion dreamed up by naïve do-gooders. Our integrity is the foundation for, the very basis of, our ability to do business. If the market economy ever goes under, our favorite villains—socialist economies and government regulators—won't be to blame. We will.

Let's stipulate as an unassailable and documented fact that there has been a massive erosion of public confidence in the integrity of business, and further, that this decline in confidence is related directly to revelations of scandalous behavior. It's our job to restore that confidence. As of this moment, the public is rightly skeptical of our practices and our preachings. To reverse this skepticism we ourselves must initiate strong and specific measures, measures that clearly show we're serious about our own integrity and the way we put it to work in our daily transactions. This is the next stage of corporate evolution. I consider it an ethical imperative, and believe it will be a key future direction for American business. IBM, Caterpillar Tractor, and Celanese, by publishing substantive ethical codes for multinational corporations, exemplify the growing awareness of this new thrust, and that it's possible to deal with it constructively.

BankAmerica Corporation, like a great many other companies, is in the process of formalizing its own code of business conduct. We will spell out our ethical standards and convictions, as well as the precise behavior we expect of all our employees, domestic and world-wide. This doesn't involve any departure for us—it's really just codification of our existing, but not previously publicized, bank standards. It is explicit affirmation of our implicit and well-established norms.

We believe it is necessary for corporate enterprise to go beyond a code of conduct, and we think banks should lead the way. There are good reasons for us to take the initiative.

Watergate is not the only trauma the nation suffered of late. Financial institutions are under special scrutiny in the wake of recent loan losses, dividend cuts, and the failures of Franklin National, U.S. National, and a number of smaller banks. These events are—in part—responsible for the new wave of disclosure demands coming at financial institutions from a host of legislative and regulatory sources. Some items have been on the SEC agenda since the late sixties but now have a new momentum.

The banking industry has an intrinsic concern here. For bankers, confidentiality, by long tradition, is a matter of professional pride as well as ethic. But now the climate is changing. At Bank of America, a good many hallowed traditions have fallen by the wayside in the evolutionary process of growing from a large regional bank to a major international institution. We recognize that candor and openness is an advantage rather than an impediment in the conduct of *our* business. That does not extend to information about the banking affairs of our customers—not at least without due process of law. Privacy of private individuals remains an important concept in any truly free society.

We have been pondering these matters at Bank of America, and we have concluded that it is time for us to generate a little "sunshine" program of our own. To implement that decision, I have this week appointed five of our senior executives to a Task Force that will be charged with developing a model Disclosure Code for Bank of America, its affiliates and its subsidiaries. No one in this audience will underestimate the complexity or the difficulty of this task. I'll talk more about our hopes and our concerns for this project in just a moment. First, it's helpful to briefly review the background.

Public disclosure of corporate information is relatively new to banks and bankers. As you know, an exemption written into the original securities laws left banks free from the SEC's registration and reporting requirements. Since the development of bank holding companies in the late 1960s, however, banks that became part of these holding companies have been subject to the traditional SEC disclosure rules. This is because the exemption for banks does not extend to bank holding companies. Thus the subsidiary banks are now subject to all the SEC regulations that have applied to industrial and other issuers for the past forty years.

As bank holding company managements, we are slowly—and sometimes reluctantly—getting used to the SEC's ever-increasing demands for fuller disclosure. As bankers, we are beginning to realize that our regulation (or, as we sometimes feel, our overregulation) is no longer handled only by the traditional bank regulatory agencies. Now I think it's time to take the next step; time to accept the best of these changes and, indeed, to go beyond. We've left leadership to the regulators for too long. Now we are ready to move into the vanguard with voluntary disclosure of relevant and appropriate matters of business practices, problems, and policies.

In matters of financial disclosure, our goals today are much the same as the goals enunciated in the original Securities Acts in 1933 and 1934. Those "Truth in Securities" laws, hammered out in the wake of the Wall Street crash and enacted in the midst of the Great Depression, grew out of the public belief that it was time:

- to eliminate fraud in the sale of securities through full and fair disclosure by the issuers,

- to restore an open and honest marketplace for the trading in securities, and,

- in the sale of securities, to change the old rule of "caveat emptor" (let the buyer beware) to a new rule of "caveat venditor" (let the *seller* beware).

We're still after the same thing, but on a broader scale. The limited areas addressed in the original Securities Acts no longer achieve these objectives. The world was less complex in the 1930s. Contemporary realities—environmental and consumer concerns among them—raise new issues. Therefore our model code will represent the more expansive, contemporary, perception of corporate responsibility. For example: We believe that corporate social performance reflects one aspect of the overall quality of management and thus, in the long run, affects the ability to attract capital and improve earnings. Thus we think appropriate guidelines for disclosure should go beyond the traditional securities-related areas addressed in the original enactments.

In the intervening forty-two years, the American public has learned a good deal about the securities markets. Not least, investors have had ample opportunity to observe that honest and forthright management is the only route to viable capital markets. We know we need these markets to sustain strong economic growth and development. And we've learned that they serve our funding needs only when the increasingly sophisticated securities community is assured that it is getting from management full and fair and adequate and honest reporting of material events. Thus, in a more perfect world, market forces and our own self-interest would eventually lead to these developments. By that I mean that the demands of our customers—our borrowers, lenders, and investors—in time would compel greater disclosure.

I want to be careful not to mislead you. Disclosure is not an end in itself, and it is not a cure-all. Voluntary disclosure can't—and won't—magically bridge the business community's very real credibility gap, nor will it instantly restore business prestige in a skeptical world. But it's an important step toward a more rational world, one in which we work cooperatively with our regulators toward our common goal: a marketplace that operates fairly and efficiently because buyers and sellers are fully informed, and investors have enough information to judge management performance for themselves.

Providing enough data to permit intelligent decision-making is a classic premise of the market economy, and critical to its efficient functioning. Regulation, on the other hand, is viewed as an inhibitor. Thus one who believes in a market economy—as I do—must conclude that voluntary disclosure is a more desirable road to travel than disclosure which has been mandated by legislation or regulation.

There are larger societal factors operating here, too. America is entering its third century as a free market democracy with a number of old burdens:

• the psychological hangover from a lengthy and unpopular involvement in a costly war,

• disappointing results from expensive—if promising—social experiments,

• the pervasive economic malaise of persistent inflation in the face of a less-than-vigorous recovery, and

• the continuing anti-business sentiment fueled by Watergate and other recent disclosures.

This nation's economy depends critically on healthy corporate enterprise. Our system provides no other vehicle for growth, jobs, and income. Overall corporate good health is obviously a matter of vital national interest, as I noted earlier. But financial institutions have a unique and special responsibility in a country where monetary policy is used to affect economic performance. The public interest has always required that the nation's banking institutions be sound, flexible, responsive, and stable. Today, financial institutions share with other members of the corporate community the additional obligation of restoring credibility in the two areas of significant public concern I identified earlier: integrity, and responsible involvement in the well-being of our local and world communities.

In that latter concern, as voters as well as financial officers, it is long past time for us to subject city and state issues to the same careful scrutiny we apply to other investment decisions. This is more than self-interest. As tax-exempt yields rise in response to psychological, if not actual, threats of default, unsophisticated investors may be tempted by increasingly risky issues. Financial executives can perform a public service by endorsing the rigorous disclosure program developed by the Municipal Finance Officers Association last year. In the absence of voluntary compliance, legislation is sure to come. I hope you will agree that states and municipalities should not be exempt from the stringent registration procedures required of corporations. New York's near-default certainly highlighted the inadequacy of financial reporting and auditing practices for municipal securities.

The need for greater disclosure is clearly not confined to corporate institutions. Disclosure issues cut a wide path through the public and private sector.

• On the federal level, Freedom of Information legislation has opened vast public files to concerned citizens, and we have been treated to some very dirty public linen as a result.

• The proposed "Sunshine" laws—nicknamed in reference to Justice Brandeis' well-known aphorism that sunlight is the best of all disinfectants—would expose the procedures and deliberations of regulatory agencies to public view.

• New SEC procedures call for corporate disclosure of environmental impact.

• At the Federal Trade Commission, there's a renewed push to scrutinize interlocking directorates.

• Proposed federal legislation asks banks to disclose credit allocations for "national priority" items—such things as capital investment, and loans to small businesses and the housing industry.

• The SEC wants to know more about loan loss experience in the recent recession.

• The Federal Election Commission is enforcing hard-nosed disclosure rules for political candidates and campaigns.

On the state level, legislatures are asking for detailed disclosure of bank pricing information, and written explanations of loan denials. In California, a Uniform Credit Code is under consideration for all financial institutions, and a new law requiring disclosure of mortgage loans by census tract is on the books for state-chartered savings and loan companies.

Shareowners are pressing for disclosure of the criteria used in selecting company directors, and for the itemization of company expenditures for lobbying.

I could go on with this catalog, but in the interest of not losing my audience to fatigue and boredom, I will forgo recitation of the rest of the disclosure laundry list. Most of us have a friendly familiarity with this subject, and considerable respect for its importance.

I'm sure you share my conviction that voluntary disclosure, while no road map to Utopia, is an important step in the right direction. Which is why so many corporations are cramming new data into their annual reports this year. A substantial majority of annual reports now include information on sales and earnings by product line, and on effective income tax rates. More than a third show foreign sales and earnings, and currency gains and losses. More than three-quarters offer comparative financial data going back ten years, and a good many offer share-holders a copy of their 10-K, EEO, and other government reports. Indeed, one firm slapped a blue cover on its 10-K and sent it out in place of an annual report last year!

Here we have a new aspect of the disclosure problem. Industry after industry is offering more and more material. We may be on the verge of an information overload—a conscientious shareowner could spend more time on our annual report this year than on his income tax return!

Why, if companies are already providing this mountain of data—and the various state and federal agencies are on the verge of demanding more—why is Bank of America about to make a major investment of time and energy in the development of guidelines for still *more* disclosure?

That's *precisely* why. We want to determine exactly what kind of information our various constituencies really want and need—our shareowners, our customers, our employees, our suppliers, and—not least—the taxpaying members of the general public. When we know that, we can develop guidelines for a thoughtful and comprehensive disclosure program.

Now, we recognize the temporal nature of this effort. No guidelines can perfectly anticipate all future circumstances, nor serve every need. But they can present a cohesive statement of principle, and articulate our commitment to candor and openness in the conduct of our business. We believe this is a proper—indeed, essential—management function in the post-Watergate era.

This won't be an easy task. The problems don't lie with disclosure *per se,* but with the ad hoc nature of the requests for information. Some overlap. Many otherwise reasonable requests present technical problems. Some are clearly illegal—for example, we cannot violate the confidentiality of customer records we're required to protect. Some are plainly impossible—computer programs haven't been developed that can produce the data. Some don't go far enough—the data that is asked for could be misleading without additional, often highly complex, information.

The fundamental problem of how to measure financial performance is complex, difficult, and endlessly debated by accounting professionals. All the major firms and associations, as well as the members of this and other groups of financial executives, have spent many weary hours in an effort to determine a uniformly acceptable definition of profit, for example, or trying to reach a consensus on the overall objectives of financial statements—so far, to little avail. These are matters the accounting professionals will have to resolve. Our Task Force, while recognizing their importance, has a different assignment. Financial disclosure is one element of the overall problem, but the "how-to-do-it" aspects are some way down the pike. *What* to do comes first.

The need here is to sort out the true public policy objectives, and then to weigh our obligations to our several constituencies. Where there are competing obligations, we must resolve the conflict. Where we operate on implicit assumptions, we must reexamine our criteria and make certain they're explicit.

So the first step is identification of information that contributes to our overall objective. The second is reexamination of the criteria we apply in determining what information to collect and disseminate. And the third is codification and publication of the results of these deliberations. This is the task I have assigned to the Bank of America Task Force, and the end product of its labors will become our Disclosure Code. . . .

. . . I have given them five underlying principles to bear in mind throughout their deliberations:

• The first is usefulness. We already gather a lot of information for a lot of people, and we must be highly selective in adding to that burden. If the material won't make it easier for people to understand how our company works, we should skip it. I see no point in gathering and disseminating information for the sake of gathering and disseminating information. It must have intrinsic value to someone—either the five primary constituencies I listed earlier, or the media, academia, or some other bona fide group with a legitimate need for information.

• The second principle is confidentiality. I've already noted our obligation to protect customer privacy. In addition, we have an obligation to protect proprietary data whose release would impair our competitive position. This again is a function of our stewardship of shareowner resources. But I have cautioned the Task Force on this point. We may be guarding a lot of barn doors whose horses would best be let out. A public interchange with our competitors may add new vitality to our own way of doing business. Someone has to jump into the icy water first.

• The third principle involves misinterpretation. Man does not live by numbers alone. The bottom line seldom tells you what's really going on —which is why we live in a rising flood of footnotes. I don't like footnotes, and I don't think anyone else does either. So, in addition to determining *what* information we can usefully disclose, I want our Task Force to determine *how* we can disclose it better. Our goal is to simplify. We can't make the intricate financial operations of a major multinational corporation comprehensible to every Sally and Sam, but we should be able to present the important information about our corporation in a form that can be easily understood by the general investing public, as well as by professionals. Our financial statements should permit any serious reader to make valid comparisons among competing institutions. I trust this group will not be astonished to learn that the absence of uniform standards impedes such comparisons. So I repeat, someone has to jump into the icy water first.

• The fourth principle involves speculation. At the risk of restating the obvious, I have reminded the Task Force that we cannot disclose information that would lend itself to speculative activity in our stock. This precludes our disclosure of future earnings estimates, and other data relating to anticipated profit or loss.

• The fifth and last general principle is cost. The days of green eyeshades are behind us. Contemporary bookkeeping involves computer programs, on-going data collection, and systems for the storage and retrieval of information. The costs are high, and the value of the information collected must be correspondingly high. Corporate resources are, after all, shareowners' resources, and we're going to tell our shareowners what it costs their company to provide information. . . .

Meaningful disclosure can help us identify a whole range of corporate behavior patterns. I am convinced that most of my corporate colleagues are doing their honest best and, because of that conviction, I am convinced that unified commitment to greater disclosure will do more for corporate reputations than all the public interest advertising and public relations campaigns we could mount.

No one can do the job for us. It's time to take the plunge.

The BankAmerica
Disclosure Code

A diversified financial organization generates an almost limitless volume of data and information. Much of it is filed with government agencies or disclosed, as a matter of policy, to inform customers, investors, employees, and the public of details of the corporation's activities.

The disclosure principles set forth here reflect BankAmerica's commitment to provide these constituencies with easy access to *all* material facts about its activities, subject only to specific constraints imposed by law or recognized by management.

Much of the information BankAmerica provides to government, for example, is of keen interest to its other constituencies. By law, certain parts of this information cannot be disclosed to the public, but the balance of it can. Past practice has tended to treat regulatory filings as totally confidential, however, and elevated secrecy to the first level of priority.

BankAmerica's disclosure principles reverse this priority, making the "right to know" paramount and imposing limits only where it is clearly appropriate. So far as the law and necessary constraints on management allow, BankAmerica now makes available to the public all information it files with government agencies.

Here, then, are the basic principles under which BankAmerica's disclosure decisions are made:

Disclosure Principles

1. Customers for deposit services of BankAmerica are entitled to the information necessary to understand and evaluate the terms, conditions, availability and safety of these services.

2. Borrowers are entitled to know the standards for credit eligibility and all information necessary to evaluate the credit extended, including all charges, the methods by which they are calculated and the conditions and obligations involved.

3. Investors in the securities of BankAmerica Corporation and its

subsidiaries are entitled to the information necessary to judge the quality of their investments, the adequacy of management and the value of their holdings.

4. Those whose funds BankAmerica manages in a fiduciary or agency capacity are entitled to the information necessary to judge the quality, costs, and results of the services it renders.

5. Customers for the specialized financial services provided by Bank-America are entitled to the information needed to evaluate the terms and conditions and the quality of the services offered.

6. Employees of all BankAmerica companies are entitled to the information necessary to make informed decisions about their pursuit of personal objectives within the organization.

7. The vendors, suppliers and other businesses with which Bank-America deals are entitled to information necessary to make sound business contracts with the corporation. This includes information about policies on agreements and transactions, competitive practices, nondiscrimination practices, and standards of fairness.

8. The public is entitled to the information necessary to judge the value and adequacy of BankAmerica's contributions to economic and social well-being and its adherence to legal and ethical standards.

Items of Disclosure

By applying its basic disclosure principles to each area of its activity, BankAmerica seeks to provide the items of information its various constituencies need to judge the adequacy of BankAmerica's performance of its ultimate function as a profit-making institution—satisfying the needs of those it serves.

Since this code is intended as a guide for those who seek information and for those within the corporation who are responsible for providing it, the specific items are catalogued according to the services and activities they describe. These services and activities, in turn, are grouped under the three principal functions which BankAmerica performs: acting as a financial intermediary, providing trust and money market services, and managing the corporate enterprise. . . .

BANKAMERICA AS A CORPORATE ENTERPRISE

In addition to its banking and financial service activities, BankAmerica performs the functions common to diversified corporate enterprises generally, including the management of corporate and subsidiary affairs; personnel administration; and the purchase of goods and services, premises and equipment. In addition, several departments have responsibility for conducting and supervising its activities as a corporate citizen.

Subsidiaries and Affiliates

As a bank holding company, BankAmerica conducts its activities through a network of interrelated companies all over the world. The ownership structure and legal relationships are complex. However, the management structure, although decentralized, is organized functionally, with well-defined areas of authority and responsibility.

Information about the management structure and the senior officers of various BankAmerica companies is necessary for understanding and evaluating the corporation's activities. BankAmerica discloses:

36. Charts showing the organization structure of BankAmerica Corporation, its subsidiaries and affiliates, and the functional and legal relationships between them.

37. Membership of all board and management committees. A description of their functions and objectives.

38. Biographies of senior management of BankAmerica Corporation and its major controlled subsidiaries.

39. Shareholder statistics of BankAmerica Corporation, showing the number of shareholders and shares held, by type and by domicile of shareholder, and by size of holding.

40. Names and locations of all subsidiaries and affiliates in which BankAmerica has an investment of $1 million or more (including equity and loans), describing:
a. The type of business in which each subsidiary or affiliate engages.
b. Its total assets.
c. The amount BankAmerica has invested in or loaned to it.
d. The percentage ownership by BankAmerica parent companies.
e. BankAmerica's aggregate investment in all its subsidiaries and affiliates.
f. Policies on intragroup pricing.

The subsidiaries form a functional whole, and their performance is generally treated as an element of BankAmerica's overall performance. Because of the interest investors and the public have shown in the activities of its subsidiaries, however, BankAmerica discloses:

41. Individual financial statements of separately-reporting foreign and domestic subsidiaries. A tabulation of assets and other pertinent data of consolidated subsidiaries, by functional group.

42. Policy controlling the allocation of corporate funds, including expenditures for research and development of new and existing services.

Management of the Corporation

Because ultimate responsibility for a corporation's activities lies with its board of directors, investors and the public wish information about this group. BankAmerica discloses:

43. The criteria and procedures for selecting outside members for boards of directors. The other corporate affiliations of directors.

44. A description of the functions and duties of the boards of directors of BankAmerica Corporation and Bank of America NT&SA.

45. Annual retainers paid to directors and the fees they receive for attendance at board meetings. Retainers and fees paid for service on board committees. Deferred compensation plans for directors.

46. The average aggregate total of loans made to members of boards of directors and the companies with which they are primarily affiliated. Policies and procedures designed to prevent self-dealing and conflicts of interest.

47. Policy on BankAmerica employees serving on the boards of other organizations.

BankAmerica's employees need information about the corporation's administration of its compensation policies. The corporation discloses:

48. Criteria used in setting salary structures. Information on the salary grade system and salary ranges within grades.

49. Information on salary surveys, and policy on the competitiveness of salaries.

50. Special compensation benefits and other programs available to employees. How employee benefit plans are funded.

51. Compensation and benefit plans extended to U.S. employees stationed abroad. The number of overseas employees, including expatriates, third-country nationals and local employees.

52. Policy on extending credit to employees.

Because BankAmerica's employment policies are significant not only for employees but also for the communities in which its companies operate, the corporation discloses:

53. Its consolidated EEO-1 report. An explanation of Bank of America's Affirmative Action programs.

BankAmerica recognizes vendors' and suppliers' needs for information about its practices as a large-volume purchaser of goods and services. It discloses:

54. Policies regarding the purchase of goods and services, including competitive bidding practices.

55. The number of bids solicited from minority vendors, and the number of orders placed with them. Dollar amounts paid to minority vendors and suppliers for architectural and construction services, office equipment and supplies.

Because BankAmerica has more than 1,000 branches in California and hundreds of offices elsewhere in the United States and overseas, its selection and acquisition of premises is a major real estate operation that has effects on many communities. BankAmerica discloses:

56. Policies and procedures for selecting sites for branches.

Given its extensive involvement with real estate as a lender and trustee, there is a possibility of conflict between the interests of customers and BankAmerica's own requirements. The corporation discloses:

57. Policies and procedures to avoid possible conflicts of interest in real estate transactions.

One of the primary tenets of banking is the protection of customers' rights to privacy in their financial affairs. But banks must also comply with legal process and legislation that require disclosure of customer records. Banks also receive many requests for information, usually at a customer's own direction, from other creditors or credit reporting agencies.

Recognizing that customers are entitled to know the extent to which confidential data may be made available under such circumstances, BankAmerica discloses:

58. Policies and practices for providing customer information to federal and state agencies under court order and administrative subpoena, and to creditors, credit reporting agencies and other third parties.

Constituencies also are concerned about the information stored in bank files, the length of time such records are retained and the possibility of inadvertent or unauthorized access to this information. BankAmerica discloses:

59. Policies and procedures for retaining records and safeguarding the confidentiality of customer information.

Corporate Responsibility

BankAmerica is firmly committed to an active and effective program of corporate responsibility. It has integrated its responsibilities as a corporate citizen into its business activities, and it also carries out this role through a number of special programs. BankAmerica discloses:

60. Details of its social policy programs and activities.

To ensure that its relations with customers and the public are conducted within a well-defined framework of fairness, the corporation discloses:

61. Policies regulating advertising practices.

62. Procedures for pursuing customer complaints to satisfactory resolution within the bank or through the appropriate regulatory agency.

As a practical necessity, BankAmerica must be alert to legislative and regulatory developments that may affect its operations. To communicate its interests effectively, BankAmerica supports both ballot measures and candidates for state and local office, in conformity with local laws. Although it may legally do so, BankAmerica does not maintain or sponsor any political funds for which it solicits employee contributions.

Shareholders and the public have the right to know the extent of the corporation's political activities and its support of candidates and ballot measures. BankAmerica discloses:

63. Policies regulating solicitation of political campaign funds or other partisan activity on corporate premises, and any breach of these policies that may occur.

64. Contributions for state and local candidates and for ballot measures.

The criteria for supporting such candidates or measures in California, and in other states (where permitted) through corporate subsidiaries.

65. Positions publicly taken on governmental issues, including written communications to members of federal, state and local legislative bodies and executive agencies expressing the corporation's position on legislative and rule-making matters.

66. The names and functions of employees whose principal responsi-

bility is to develop and present corporate positions on federal, state and local legislative and regulatory matters.

67. The direct dollar expenses of BankAmerica's government relations program at the federal, state and local levels, including costs of all participation in industry or trade associations.

Corporate dealings with foreign governments and their officials are a subject of widespread public concern. The corporation discloses:

68. Policies on political contributions and activities involving foreign governments and their officials, and any breach of these policies that may occur.

BankAmerica Foundation was established as a separate entity to be the conduit for major philanthropic contributions. It chooses and supports activities in health, social services, education, culture, civic life, and international development.

Because corporate philanthropy has an impact on society's well-being, the public, and especially charitable organizations, should be informed about funds allocated for charitable contributions and grants. The corporation discloses:

69. BankAmerica Foundation's criteria for selecting recipients of charitable contributions and grants.
The total amount of funds allocated.
The amount of each contribution or grant that is made by the foundation.
The name of each recipient.
The purpose for which the funds are given.

70. The aggregate amount of contributions or grants made by BankAmerica Foundation.

The Bank of America's
Rocky Road to Responsibility

Milton R. Moskowitz

Just because it is the world's largest commercial bank, the Bank of America has had to grapple more than most companies with the issues raised by corporate social responsibility. Ever since the 1960s it has been a target—and a highly visible one at that—for groups which have taken it as a symbol of everything wrong with United States business. In 1970, for example, a Bank of America branch near the University of California campus at Santa Barbara was burned to the ground by demonstrators agitated over what they called the "capitalist establishment."

During the past decade, the bank has been confronted with a broad range of challenges—from charges of discrimination in employment, to accusations of redlining, to demands that it halt all loans to governments run by fascist dictatorships. Very early on, though, the bank recognized that the social protest was not a fad or an aberration. Its response to the 1970 firebombing, expressed by Louis B. Lundborg, then chairman of the board, was: "The violence must be rejected, but the dissent and protest must not be."

The goal that the Bank of America set for itself was to accept the protests as legitimate aspirations. To do that, it devised internal functions designed to make social responsibility concerns regular factors in day-to-day decision-making. More important, it established "social policy as a management function."

The trouble with this kind of scenario, of course, is that deeds do not always conform to rhetoric; actions sometimes belie the words. That problem came home to haunt the bank last year when it went on the air in California with a series of television commercials promoting automobile loans. Viewers were told:

> Our rates are very competitive. You get your money at low bank rates. . . . So if you're thinking about a new car, think about Bank of America car loans.

The commercials were no different than advertisements run by a lot of banks. Exaggeration (or at least lack of precision) is an accepted mode of expression in the advertising world. In this case, however, the claim could be tested—and it simply didn't hold up. Far from being competitive, the Bank of America car-loan rates were among the highest in the state, in some cases more than three percentage points higher than rates offered by other banks. San Francisco Consumer Action proved this and turned its evidence over to the San Francisco district attorney's office, which filed a complaint against the bank. In January 1977, the Bank of America settled the case out of court. It agreed to pay the city a fine of $100,000, and it put up a fund of $175,000 for rebates to consumers who took out car loans with the bank during the time the commercials were running.

It was a humbling experience for the bank, which had invested considerable time and energies to demonstrate to employees, shareholders, and detractors that at the Bank of America there was a social policy apparatus that would foil irresponsible actions.

A short time before these commercials were aired, the bank had emphasized in public statements that its commitment to social responsibility "is simply the exercise of good business judgment," adding, "Every effort is made to implement social policy in a businesslike way —we set priorities, establish goals, assign responsibilities, establish accountability and measure results."

The incident served to illustrate once again that a major difficulty with corporate social responsibility is implementation down the line. The social policy messages enunciated by the management had somehow failed to reach the advertising department, which was conducting "business as usual." And while these ads were approved by the bank's legal department, they had not been cleared with the social policy department, which might have had the good sense to flag the egregious claim of competitive rates.

WHAT THE BANK OF AMERICA HAS DONE

Unfortunately, the problem of implementation of social policy is not a new one at the Bank of America—or, for that matter, at any other corporation which has tried to do it. In 1968, the Bank of America announced a $100 million loan program for low-income housing in the state. It was widely publicized, both inside and outside the bank. G. Robert Truex, Jr., who was then Bank of America's head loan officer in Southern California, remembers that after all the hullabaloo, the funds allocated for this purpose were not being disbursed. So he called a few loan officers in branch offices and quickly discovered the reason. They didn't believe the bank was really serious about lending that money; they figured it was just another public relations ploy.

Four years later, in 1972, Bob Truex was promoted to executive vice-president and was placed in charge of social policy. No other corporation, then or since, has assigned such a high-ranking officer to full-time duty in the social responsibility area. It was a sign that the board of directors and the president, A. W. (Tom) Clausen, were serious about the bank's social commitment. As Clausen told Truex when he assigned him to this post: "I want you to put the bank where my mouth is." There thus was recognition, at the top level, that there was a gap between what the company said and what it did.

Has the Bank of America been able to close that gap? Not completely, as last year's advertising lapse shows. But at least it's working on it, having installed what is probably the most elaborate machinery in the corporate world to make good on the promises delivered from on high. Bob Truex no longer supervises this effort. He left in 1974 to become chief executive officer of the second largest bank in the state of Washington, The National Bank of Commerce, whose name he promptly changed to Rainier National Bank. Heading up the social effort at the Bank of America today is senior vice-president James F. Langton, who came up from the public relations ranks and has played a key role in the articulation of Bank of America philosophy.

At Bank of America, social policy is brought into the structure of the bank through the following units:

• A public policy committee of the board of directors. Composed mostly of outside directors, it meets monthly to review the bank's performance in social, political, and environmental areas. Not every organization with a commitment to social responsibility has such a committee. And of those committees which have been formed at some thirty-five companies, hardly any meet monthly; the norm is more like four times a year. Among the members of the Bank of America's committee are: Franklin D. Murphy, chairman of the Times Mirror Company; Peter O'Malley, president of the Los Angeles Dodgers; and Walter A. Hass, Jr., chairman of Levi Strauss & Company.

• A social policy committee consisting of nine senior executive officers of the bank. It is charged with "identifying problems and issues and changing bank policy and practice where appropriate."

• A social policy department, directed by Langton and charged with "coordinating, administering, and monitoring socially-oriented programs throughout the bank." It functions, in effect, as staff to the social policy committee. Operations include urban affairs departments for Northern and Southern California, eight regional urban development offices, the bank's minority business loan program, and community relations activities.

The Bank of America's commitment and social policy structure have not been without consequences. In 1964, when the bank was first challenged as a discriminatory employer, minorities represented 13 percent of staff; today, they account for 28 percent of total employment. In 1964, members of minority groups held only 2 percent of positions classified as "officers and managers"; today, they hold 14 percent of those positions. Women, who always have accounted for the great bulk of Bank of America employees, are no longer relegated exclusively to low-level jobs as tellers and clerks and secretaries; they now hold 35 percent of positions classified as "officers and managers." In addition, loans to minority-owned businesses have quintupled since 1970.

To demonstrate to its staff that it means what it says, the bank announced in 1976 that it would no longer reimburse executives for memberships in private clubs which discriminate.

To demonstrate to other companies that it means what it says, the bank's trust department last year voted ninety-three times against management-backed proposals of sixty-three companies and voted forty-four times for antimanagement proposals presented to thirty-nine companies.

To demonstrate that it is concerned about the communities it serves, BankAmerica Corporation, the holding company for the Bank of America, formed a new, nonprofit subsidiary, BA City Improvement and Restoration Corporation, in January 1977. This unit will buy about thirty abandoned homes in East Oakland, rehabilitate them, and place them on the market for middle-income families. No profit will be sought on the operation. This is the first bank holding company subsidiary of its kind approved by the Federal Reserve Board. If the idea works in Oakland, BankAmerica plans to duplicate it in other California cities.

In June 1977, the bank broadened its employee gift-matching program to include contributions to cultural groups. Many United States corporations will match an employee's contribution to a college or university, and some will match donations to certain charities. However, only a handful will do the same in the cultural area, and most of these programs are limited in scope or geography. The Bank of America will match any employee contribution (from $25 up to $7,500) to museums, dance companies, symphony orchestras, historical societies, libraries, and public television stations (including memberships).

FINANCIAL DISCLOSURE

Perhaps the sharpest indication of social change at the Bank of America is in the area of disclosure. The quantity of information made available to shareholders and the public has been expanded tremendously, and so has the quality. A cursory check of annual reports, year by year, will attest to this change. The 1976 annual report breaks down the business of the bank in details that would have been considered astonishing only a few years ago—in fact, the bank itself would have been astonished if anyone had had the temerity to ask for such details! Disclosure also covers social policy activities. These are detailed in an annual report, "The Community and the Bank," which is mailed to each employee's home.

Some of the moves toward greater disclosure have been mandated by regulatory agencies, with the result that all banks have been lifting the curtains. But there's no question that the Bank of America seized the initiative in this area. In a speech delivered in January 1976, Tom Clausen announced that he had appointed a task force of five senior executives to develop a voluntary disclosure code for the bank. Clausen said he was doing this because he was sure that "greater disclosure will do more for corporate reputations than all the public interest advertising and public relations campaigns we could mount." Ten months later the code was a reality. And it did break new ground, covering seventy different categories of information about bank activities that will be made available to the public. Outsiders now have more access to information about the Bank of America than they do to any other company.

To cite just a few examples, anyone can now get from the Bank of America the following information: how much it contributed to political campaigns; the name of each recipient of a charitable grant; the fees paid to board members; the number of bids solicited from minority vendors and the number of orders placed with them; the number of times the bank's trust department voted for and against management of companies whose shares it holds; a breakdown of earnings by profit centers; a breakdown of foreign loans by geographic areas; and a list of the bank's ten largest holdings of municipal bonds and notes.

The significance of the code is not so much that it resulted in the immediate issuing of fresh information about the Bank of America as that the code is now structured as a permanent mechanism in the bank. This does not mean that all the books are open. For example, the breakdown of foreign loans is by broad geographic areas—not by countries. And loans to specific countries have created concern among observers of the banking scene.

It's an openness that may, at times, lead to some embarrassing moments for the Bank of America. But the bank seems willing to take that risk in order to show that it is trying to narrow the gap between rhetoric and performance. And, in general, the new policy on disclosure demonstrates the direction in which Bank of America is headed. No other bank—and few other corporations of any kind—have proceeded as far down that road.

Bibliography

General Works on Individual Rights in the Corporate Setting

"Big Crusade of the '80s: More Rights for Workers." *U.S. News & World Report,* March 26, 1979, pp. 85–88.

Christiansen, Jon P. "A Remedy for the Discharge of Professional Employees Who Refuse to Perform Unethical or Illegal Acts." *Vanderbilt Law Review* 28 (1975): 805–41.

"Corporate Governance in America." Speech before the 54th American Assembly, April 13–16, 1978. New York: The American Assembly, Columbia University.

"Corporate Rights and Responsibilities." Hearings before the Committee on Commerce, U.S. Senate, 94th Cong., 2nd Sess. June 15–17 and 21–23, 1976, serial no. 94–95. Washington, D.C.: U.S. Government Printing Office.

Cunniff, John. "Assails Rights Gap in U.S. Biz." *New York Post,* August 1, 1977, p. 40.

Elliot, P. "Politics of White-Collar Unionisation." *Political Quarterly* 44 (July 1973): 294–303.

"Employee Bill of Rights," *Wall Street Journal,* June 24, 1977, p. 8. ("Business pushes to blunt labor's drive for law changes.")

Ewing, David W. "Civil Liberties in the Corporation." *New York State Bar Journal* 50 (April 1978): 188–91.

———. "Freedom inside the Organization." *Society* 16, no. 2 (January–February 1979): 87–90.

———. "Winning Freedom on the Job: From Assembly Line to Executive Suite." In "Freedom inside the Organization: Bringing Civil Liberties to the Workplace," *Civil Liberties Review* 4, no. 2 (July–August 1977).

"Expected Continued Employment as a Protected Property Right." *Loyola Law Review* 22 (Summer 1976): 884–92.

Hoerr, John. "A Warning that Worker Discontent Is Rising." *Business Week,* June 4, 1979, pp. 152–53.

"Is Corporate Social Responsibility a Dead Issue?" Symposium in *Business & Society Review* 25 (Spring 1978): 4–20.

Johnson, M. Bruce, ed. *The Attack on Corporate America: The Corporate Issues Sourcebook.* New York: McGraw-Hill, 1978.

Kanter, Rosabeth Moss. "Work in a New America." *Daedalus* 107 no. 1 (1978).

Kay, Emanuel. *The Crisis in Middle Management.* New York: Amacon, American Management Association, 1974.

Lekachman, Robert. "Giving Big Business the Business." *New York Times Book Review,* December 26, 1978, p. 5.

Lynd, Staughton. *Labor Law for the Rank and Filer.* San Pedro, Calif.: Singlejack Books, 1978.

Maccoby, Michael. *The Gamesman: Winning and Losing the Career Game.* New York: Bantam Books, 1976.

May, W. F. "Executive and Employee Relations," *Vital Speeches* 41 (March 1, 1975): 310–12.

Mee, J. F. "Understanding the Attitudes of Today's Employees." *Nation's Business* 64 (August 1976): 22–24.

Miller, Arthur S. *The Modern Corporate State: Private Governments and the American Constitution.* Westport: Greenwood Press, 1976.

Nader, Ralph and Green, Mark J. *Corporate Power in America.* New York: Grossman, 1973.

Nader, R.; Green, M.; and Seligman, J. *Taming the Giant Corporation.* New York: Norton, 1976.

Sennett, Richard. "The Boss's New Clothes." *New York Review,* February 22, 1979, pp. 43–46.

Shapiro, J. Peter and Tune, James F. "Implied Contract Rights to Job Security." *Stanford Law Review* 26 (January 1974): pp. 335–369.

Stein, B. "Management Rights and Productivity." *Arbitration Journal* 32 (December 1977): 270–78.

Terkel, Studs. *Working.* New York: Pantheon, 1974. "Time to End Bosses; Power to Fire." *Rights* 24 (March–June 1978): 3.

Ways, Max. "Myth of the Oppressive Corporation." *Fortune,* October 1977, p. 149.

Westin, Alan F. "Good Marks but Some Areas of Doubt." *Business Week,* May 14, 1979, pp. 14–16.

———. "A New Move toward Employee Rights." *New York Times,* April 23, 1978, sec. F, p. 18.

New Modes of Worker and Management Participation

"A Day's Work." *Wall Street Journal,* December 7, 1972, p. 1. (Gene Cafiero labors to enhance the quality of assembly-line life; Chrysler executive's plans to "involve" auto workers raise eyebrows in Detroit.)

Alexander, Kenneth O. "On Work and Authority: Issues in Job Enlargement, Job Enrichment, Worker Participation, and Shared Authority." *American Journal of Economics and Sociology* 34 (January 1975): 43–54.

Berg, Ivar. "Employee Discontent in a Business Society." *Society Magazine* 14, no. 3 (March–April 1977): 51–56.

Bernstein, Paul. "Workplace Democratization: Its Internal Dynamics." Kent, Ohio: *Kent State University Press,* 1976.

Blackburn, John D. *Worker Participation on Corporate Directorates: Is America Ready for Industrial Democracy?* Working Paper Ser. WPS 78-65. Columbus: College of Administrative Science, Ohio State University, July 1978.

"Can Unions and Management Cooperate in Joint Projects?" *Management Review* 66, no. 10 (October 1977): 67.

Carroll, Bonnie. *Job Satisfaction: A Review of the Literature.* Key Issues Series, no. 3. Ithaca, N.Y.: Cornell University, New York State School of Industrial and Labor Relations, 1973.

Chamot, Dennis. "Professional Employees Turn to Unions." *Harvard Business Review* May–June 1976: 119–20.

Conover, Donald K. "The Case for Participatory Management." In *Anticipatory Democracy,* ed. Clement Bezold. New York: Vintage Books, 1978.

Derber, Milton. "The American Idea of Industrial Democracy, 1865–1965." Urbana: University of Illinois Press, 1970.

Dickson, Paul. *The Future of the Workplace.* New York: Weybright & Talley, 1975.

Directory of Productivity and Quality of Working Life Centers. Washington, D.C.: National Center for Productivity and Quality of Working Life, Fall 1978. (Description, goals, financing, and programs at twenty-eight centers in the United States devoted to studies of productivity and quality of working life issues.)

"Drive to Make Dull Jobs Interesting." *U.S. News & World Report,* July 17, 1972, pp. 50–54.

Fowler, Elizabeth M. "Management: Workers in Management." *New York Times,* October 1, 1976, sec. 4, p. 5.

Foy, Nancy. "Pathways to Participation." *Management Today,* January 1974, p. 95.

———. "Worker Participation: Contrasts in Three Countries: Sweden, Great Britain, and the U.S." *Harvard Business Review* 54, no. 3 (May/June 1976): 71–83.

Furlong, James. *Labor in the Boardroom: The Peaceful Revolution.* Princeton, N.J.: Dow Jones Books, 1977.

Gold, Charlotte. *Employer-Employee Committees and Worker Participation.* Key Issue Series, no. 20. Ithaca, N.Y.: New York State School of Industrial and Labor Relations, Cornell University, 1976.

Greenberg, Edward S. "The Consequences of Worker Participation: A Clarification of the Theoretical Literature." *Social Science Quarterly* 56 (September 1975): 191–209.

Greiner, Larry E. "What Managers Think of Participative Leadership." *Harvard Business Review* 51, no. 2 (March–April 1973): 111–117.

Hackman, Richard J. "Is Job Enrichment Just a Fad?" *Harvard Business Review* 53, no. 5 (September–October 1975): 129–39.

Harris, Sara and Allen, Robert F. *The Quiet Revolution.* New York: Rawson Associates, 1978.

Henke, P. and Strauss, G. "Worker Dissatisfaction: A Look at the Economic Effects." *Monthly Labor Review* (February 1974): 58–59.

"How to Promote Productivity." *Business Week,* July 24, 1978, p. 146.

"The Human Resources Development Act of 1977." Hearings before the Subcommittee on Economic Stabilization of the Committee on Banking, Finance, and Urban Affairs. House of Representatives, 95th Cong., 1st Sess., March 24, 31, and April 5, 1977.

"Humanizing Work: Industrial Society's Next Task." *Atlas World Press Review* (June 1977): 31–39.

Jackson, C. C. "Alternative to Unionization and the Wholly Unorganized Shop: A Legal Basis for Sanctioning Joint Employer-Employee Committees and Increasing Employee Free Choice." *Syracuse Law Review* 28 (Fall 1977): 809–45.

Jenkins, David. "Democracy in the Factory." *Atlantic* 231 (April 1973): 78–83.

———. *Job Power: Blue and White Collar Democracy.* Garden City, N.Y.: Doubleday, 1973.

"Job Monotony Becomes Critical." *Business Week,* September 9, 1972, p. 108.

Kandell, Jonathan. "Workers' Management Role on Bumpy Course in Europe." *New York Times,* July 26, 1978, sec. A, p. 2.

Katzell, Raymond A. and Yankelovich, Daniel. *Work, Productivity, and Job Satisfaction: An Evaluation of Policy-Related Research.* New York: Psychological Corp., 1975).

Kerppola, Klaus. "Participatory Administration and Teamwork in Labor-Management Cooperation." *American Journal of Economics and Sociology* 33 (January 1974): 19–31.

Kuper, G. H. "Developments in the Quality of Working Life." *Labor Law Journal* 28 (December 1977): 152–62.

"Labor/Management Projects Aimed at Ending Distrust." *New York Times,* March 31, 1978, p. 27.

Leidecker, Joel K. and Hall, James L. "A New Justification for Participative Management." *Human Resource Management* 13 (Spring 1974): 28–31.

Lesieur, Fred G. and Puckett, Elbridge S. "The Scanlon Plan Has Proved Itself in Good Times as Well as Bad; The Plan Has Created More Employee Interest in Change, More Improvements, More Production Efficiency." *Harvard Business Review* 47 (September–October 1969): 109–18. (Examines the principles of an employee participation management incentives system conceived in the 1930s by Joseph Scanlon and others, focusing on three companies practicing the plan.)

Mainelli, Vincent P. "Democracy in the Workplace." *America* 136 (January 15, 1977): 28–30.

Mandry, W. J. "Participative Management: The CIL Experience." *Business Quarterly* 36, no. 4 (Winter 1971): 73–87.

Miles, Raymond E. and Ritchie, J. B. "Participative Management: Quality vs. Quantity." *California Management Review* (Summer 1971): 48–56.

Mills, Ted. "Europe's Industrial Democracy: An American Response; U.S. Focus Is Turning to Quality of Work Life Efforts, Where the Approach Is Voluntary." *Harvard Business Review* 56 (November/December 1978): 143–52.

————. "Human Resources—Why the New Concern?" *Harvard Business Review* 53 (March 1975): 120–34.

————. *Quality of Work Life: What's in a Name?* Detroit: General Motors Corporation, 1978.

Mossberg, Walter. "A Day's Work: Gene Cafiero Labors to Enhance the Quality of Assembly-Line Life." *Wall Street Journal,* December 12, 1972, p. 1.

Murphy, Michael E. "Workers on the Board: Borrowing a European Idea." *Labor Law Journal* 27 (December 1976): 751–62.

Nielsen, Richard P. "The Problem-Solving Model for Cooperative Labor Relations." *Labor Law Journal* 29 (April 1978): 236–40.

Norton, Steven D. "Employee Centered Management Participation in Decision-Making and Satisfaction with Work Itself." *Psychological Reports* 38, no. 2 (April 1976): 391–98.

Pakhen, Martin. *Participation, Achievement, and Involvement on the Job.* Englewood Cliffs, N.J.: Prentice-Hall, 1970.

Peterson, B. "On Making Work Meaningful." *Progressive* 40 (November 1976): 30–31.

"Quality of Work Life." *Wall Street Journal,* February 3, 1976, p. 1. (Companies should publish data about the "kind of life they provide their employees," Ed W. Lawler, social scientist at University of Michigan, proposed.)

Raskin, A. H. "The Heresy of Worker Participation," *Psychology Today,* February 1977, pp. 111–12.

———. "Is Worker Participation Coming to the U.S.?" *New York Times,* May 14, 1976, sec. D, p. 1.

———. "The Labor Scene: Unions and a Voice in Management." *New York Times,* November 15, 1976, p. 47.

———. "A Move for Job Enrichment and Humanization of Work." *New York Times,* March 30, 1979, sec. 4, p. 1.

Roche, John M. "Workers Participation: New Voices in Management." Report No. 594. New York: The Conference Board, 1973.

Roche, William J. and MacKinnon, Neil L. "Motivating People with Meaningful Work." *Harvard Business Review* 48 (May 1970): 97–110.

Rosow, J. M. "Quality of Working Life and Productivity." *Vital Speeches* 43 (June 1, 1977): 496–98.

Sherwin, D. S. "Strategy for Winning Employee Commitment." *Harvard Business Review* 50 (May 1972): 37–47.

Sirota, David and Wolfson, Alan D. "Pragmatic Approach to People Problems." *Harvard Business Review* 51, no. 1 (January–February 1973): 120–28.

Sterne, Michael. "Plant's Employees Help in Remodeling." *New York Times,* August 21, 1977, p. 48.

Stetson, Damon. "Ways to Improve Job Conditions Outlined by Corporate Psychologist." *New York Times,* October 24, 1976, p. 42.

Susman, G. I. "Why Millions Hate Their Jobs and What's Afoot to Help." *U.S. News & World Report* 81 (September 27, 1976): 87–88.

Teller, Ludwig. "Worker Participation in Business Management—Committee on Education and Labor." House of Representatives, 87th Cong., 1st Sess. Washington, D.C.: U.S. Government Printing Office, 1961.

Tornquist, David. "Workers' Management: The Intrinsic Issues." In *Workers' Control.* Edited by Gerry Hunnis, G. David Garson, and John Case. New York: Vintage Books, 1973.

Walton, Richard E. "The Diffusion of New York Structures: Explaining Why Success Didn't Take." *Organizational Dynamics* 3, no. 3 (Winter 1975): 2–22.

———. "Improving the Quality of Work Life." *Harvard Business Review* 52 (May–June 1974): 12.

———. "1977 Perspectives on Work Restructuring." *Draft,* June 21, 1977.

———. "Quality of Work Life: What Is It?" *Sloan Management Review* 15, no. 1 (Fall 1973): 11–22.

Walton, Richard E. and Warwick, Donald P. "The Ethics of Organization Development." *Journal of Applied Behavioral Science* 9, no. 6 (November–December 1973): 681–98.

Ways, Max. "The American Kind of Worker Participation: Growth, Change and Complexity—These Three Characteristics of the U.S. Economy Will Continue to Expand the Scope and Authority of Employees at Every Level." *Fortune* 94 (October 1976): 168–71.

Weaver, C. and Horn, J. "Happy Laborers and the Sad Professionals." *Psychology Today* 11, no. 6 (November 1977): 30.

Weinburg, Edgar and Batt, William L., Jr. "Labor-Management Cooperation Today." *Harvard Business Review* 56, no. 1 (January–February 1978): 96–104.

"When Workers Help Call the Tune in Management." 80:83 *U.S. News & World Report,* May 10, 1976, p. 83.

"Where Being Nice to Workers Didn't Work at Non-Linear Systems, Inc." *Business Week,* January 20, 1973, p. 98.

Wimpfheimer, Jacques D. "Team Spirit in Industry: The Vital Factor in Britain's Recovery." Address delivered at 35th Summer Conference, St. Hugh's College, Oxford, July 9 and 11, 1965.

Windmuller, John P. "Industrial Democracy and Industrial Relations." *Annals of the American Academy of Political and Social Science* 431 (May 1977): 22–31.

Wolcman, Jonathan. "Democracy on the Job Emerges as Trend." *Record* (Bergen County, N.J.), August 29, 1978, sec. A, p. 17.

Work in America: Report of a Special Task Force to the Secretary of Health, Education and Welfare. Cambridge, Mass.: MIT Press, 1974.

"Worker Representation in Management Decision-Making Growing Throughout World, Conference Board Reports." *Management Advisor,* September–October 1973, pp. 12–13.

"Workers on Boards." *Time,* January 7, 1974, p. 74.

"Worker's Woes: Report by the Upjohn Institute." *Newsweek,* January 1, 1973, p. 47.

Zwerdling, Daniel. *Democracy at Work: Guide to Workplace Ownership, Participation and Self-Management Experiments in the United States and Europe.* Washington, D.C.: Association for Self-Management, 1978.

———. "When Workers Manage." *Progressive* 38 (July 1974): 29–31.

Employee Privacy

Balog, Roger P. "Employment Testing and Proof of Job-Relatedness: A Tale of Unreasonable Constraints." *Notre Dame Lawyer* 52 (October 1976): 95–108.

Bayh, Birch. "Employers' Lie Detectors vs. Citizens' Privacy." *New York Times,* August 30, 1977, p. 28.

"Bitter Beercot: A Dispute Over Privacy Rights." *Time,* December 26, 1977, p. 15.

Block, Eugene B. *Lie Detectors: Their History and Use.* New York: McKay, 1977.

"Breathalyser Test to Detect Drinking among Traincrew Members Protested by United Transportation Union." *Wall Street Journal,* July 27, 1976, p. 1.

"Campus Concern: Student Job Referrals by Teachers Hit Snag Due to Privacy Law; Buckley Amendment Spurs Glowing Written Ratings at Discreet Use of Phones." *Wall Street Journal,* January 14, 1977, p. 1.

"Can a Company Be Hit for Damages Because of Errors in Personnel Records?" *White Collar Management,* issue 1214 (December 15, 1974).

"Can the Company Be Sued for Recording an Error in an Employee's Personnel File?" *White Collar Management,* issue 1144 (January 15, 1972).

"Can You Safely Show Your Staff Members Bad Reports in an Employee's File?" *White Collar Management,* issue 1261 (December 1, 1976).

"Companies Using Handwriting Analysis in Hiring." *Wall Street Journal,* June 20, 1974, p. 1.

"Corporate Lie Detectors Come under Fire." *Business Week,* January 13, 1973, p. 88.

"Discrimination: Can an Employee Be Fired for Belonging to a Hate Group?" *The Businessman and the Law.* New York: Man and Manager, July 1, 1974. (Court case: *Bellamy* v. *Mason Stores, Inc.,* 368 F.S. Upp. 1025)

"Drug and Alcohol Usage by Job Applicants Is a Proper Subject for Employer Inquiries, Nat'l. Assn. of Manufacturers Said." *Wall Street Journal,* December 13, 1974, p. 1.

Editorial on decision by New York State Division of Human Rights to see that no employer asks questions that could damage applicant's chances of being hired. *Wall Street Journal,* February 8, 1977, p. 20.

Elliot, John. "Controversy in Medicine: Access to Employee Health Records." *Journal of the American Medical Association* 241, no. 8 (February 23, 1979): 777–80.

"Employee Performance: Evaluation and Control." *Personnel Policies Forum Survey No. 108.* Washington, D.C.: Bureau of National Affairs, February 1975.

"Employees Struggle to Make Personnel Screening More Job Related, Avoid Bias." *Wall Street Journal,* October 3, 1972, p. 1.

Ewing, David W. "Right to Be Let Alone." *Across the Board* 14 (1977): 62–70.

Faucher, Mary D. and McCulloch, Kenneth J. "Sexual Harassment in the Workplace—What Should the Employer Do?" *EEO Today* 5, no. 1 (Spring 1978): 38.

Fowler, Elizabeth M. "Management Challenges for Corporate Appraisals." *New York Times,* October 21, 1977, sec. D, p. 5.

Goodman, Jill Laurie. "Sexual Demands on the Job." *Civil Liberties Review* 4, no. 6 (March/April 1978): 55–58.

Gorlin, Harriet. *Privacy in the Workplace.* Information Bulletin no. 27. New York: The Conference Board, September 1977.

"Has a Worker a Right to See What a Supervisor Has Written about Him?" *White Collar Management,* issue 504 (December 1977).

Hayden, Trudy. "How Much Does the Boss Need to Know?" *Civil Liberties Review* 3, no. 3 (1976).

Leonard, John W. "Discipline for Off-the-Job Activities." *Monthly Labor Review* 91, no. 10 (October 1968): 5–11.

————. "Dismissal for Off-the-Job Criminal Behavior." *Monthly Labor Review* 90, no. 11 (November 1967): 21–26.

"Let Industry Beware: A Survey of Privacy Legislation and Its Potential Impact on Business," no. 1 *Tulsa Law Journal* 11 (1975): 68–84.

"Lie Detectors Get More Use in Personnel Work Despite Laws Barring Them." *Wall Street Journal,* July 22, 1975, p. 1.

Mayer, A. J. "Butting Out: IBM's Personnel Records Policy." *Newsweek,* November 10, 1975, pp. 95–96.

McClain, Wallis E., Jr., ed. "Access Reports." *Privacy* 1, no. 1 (August 4, 1978).

McCormack, Patricia. "Can Your Medical Records Be Sold?" *Miami Herald,* February 11, 1979.

Miller, Donald B. "Privacy: A Key Issue between Employees and Managers," *University of Michigan Business Review* 28 (January 1976): 7–12.

Minter, R. L. "Human Rights Laws and Pre-Employment Inquiries," *Personnel Journal* 51 (June 1972): 431–33.

Mironi, Mordechai, "The Confidentiality of Personal Records: A Legal and Ethical View." *Labor Law Journal* 25, no. 5 (May 1974): 270–292.

"Must You Tell an Employee the Name of the Person Who Denounced Her in a Letter?" *White Collar Management,* issue 1292 (March 15, 1978).

"New York State Assembly Approves Bill Prohibiting Use of Psychological Stress Evaluators on Employees." *New York Times,* February 14, 1978, p. 69.

"No Office Calls: To Cut Down Absences a Mass. Firm Insisted Mgmt. Personnel Would Check and Decide Whether Workers Were Really Ill; Plan Abandoned When Unionist Claimed Violation Of Law; Firm Was Practicing Medicine without a License." *Wall Street Journal,* November 6, 1973, p. 1.

Perham, John. "New Push for Employee Privacy." *Dun's Review* 112 (March 1979): 114.

"Personal Lives of Employees Can't Be Regulated by the Boss, a Ruling Says." *Wall Street Journal,* November 22, 1977, p. 1.

"Personnel Files Would Be Open to Michigan Employees under a Pending Law." *Wall Street Journal,* December 20, 1977, p. 1.

Phillips, Leslie. "For Women, Sexual Harassment Is an Occupational Hazard." Boston *Globe,* August 9, 1977, p. 10.

"Polygraph Tests for Job Applicants Termed Unconstitutional Invasion of Privacy." *Access Reports* 3, no. 23 (November 29, 1977): 5.

"Predicting Potential: Selection Procedures." *Personnel Journal* 51 (April 1972): 283.

"Previous Medical History Can Hamper an Employee's Chances for a Job." *Wall Street Journal,* August 6, 1974, p. 1.

"Privacy: The Polygraph in Employment." *Arkansas Law Review* 30 (Spring 1976): 35–48.

Privacy Protection Study Commission. "The Employment Relationship." In *Personal Privacy in an Information Society.* Washington, D.C.: Privacy Protection Study Commission, 1977. (Pages 223–75.)

"Privacy Protection Study Commission Recommended that Companies Remove Many Restrictions that Prevent Employees and Consumers from Seeing Records and Files Kept about Them." *Wall Street Journal,* March 25, 1977, p. 12.

"Psychological Aptitude Tests and the Duty to Supply Information." *Harvard Law Review* 91 (February, 1978): 869–78.

"Psychological Tests Given to Employees Must Be Disclosed to Their Unions, N.L.R.B. Ruled." *Wall Street Journal,* July 15, 1975, p. 1.

Punke, Harold H. "The Relevance and Broadening Use of Personnel Testing." *Labor Law Journal* 25, no. 3 (March 1974): 173–87.

Pyron, H. Charles. "The Use and Misuse of Previous Employer References in Hiring." *Management of Personnel Quarterly* 9 (Summer 1970): 15–22.

Quindlen, Anna. "Polygraph Tests for Jobs: Truth and Consequences." *New York Times,* August 19, 1977, p. B1.

Rice, John D. "Privacy Legislation: Its Effect on Pre-Employment Reference Checking." *Personnel Administrator* 23 (February 1978): 46–57.

"S. Ct. Limited the Right of an Employer to Interrogate an Employee without a Union Representative Present." *Wall Street Journal,* February 20, 1975, p. 12.

Schaffer, David R.; Mays, Pamela V.; and Etheridge, Karen. "Who Shall Be Hired: A Biasing Effect of the Buckley Amendment on Employment Practices." *Journal of Applied Psychology* 61 (October 1976): 571–75.

Schein, Virginia E. "Individual Privacy and Personnel Psychology: The Need for a Broader Perspective." *Journal of Social Issues* 33, no. 3 (1977): 154–68.

Schonberger, Richard J. "Private Lives versus Job Demands." *Human Resource Management* 14 (Summer 1975): 27.

Schwartz, L. S. "Bayh Bill Would Prohibit Use of Lie Detectors by Employers." *Electronic News* 22 (August 8, 1977): 44.

"Selection Procedures and Personnel Records." *Personnel Policies Forum Survey No. 114.* Washington, D.C.: Bureau of National Affairs, September 1976.

"Should Government Protect Your Job File from Prying?" *U.S. News & World Report,* January 10, 1977, p. 56.

"Should You Tell Lower Echelon Employees Why You Fired a Co-Worker?" *White Collar Management,* issue 1238 (December 15, 1975).

Singel, John B., Jr., and Gupton, Bruce O., Jr. "Privacy Regulations Are Coming: While the Privacy Act of 1974 Primarily Affects Federal Government Agencies, It May Well Be the Model for Legislation Regulating the Private Sector." *Price Waterhouse Review* 21 (November 1, 1976): 10–18.

"Singles Complain They Can't Bring Partners Along on Sales Incentive Trips for Xerox." *Wall Street Journal,* February 3, 1976, p. 1.

———. *Privacy: How to Protect What's Left of It.* Garden City, N.Y.: Doubleday Anchor, 1979.

Sussman, Arthur M. "Work Discipline versus Private Life: An Analysis of Arbitration Cases." *I.L.R. Research* 10, no. 1 (January 1964): 3.

Taylor, R. N. "Preferences of Industrial Managers for Information Sources in Making Promotion Decisions." *Journal of Applied Psychology* 60 (April 1975): 269–72.

Wallace, E. C. "Privacy Commission Plumps for Voluntary Guideline on Personnel Records." *Banking* 69 (October 1977): 24.

Wardell, Nancy N. "The Corporation." *Daedalus* 107, no. 1 (Winter 1978): 97–110.

Westin, Alan F. "Message to CEO's—About Employee Privacy: The Time for Boilerplate Is Over." *Across the Board* 16, no. 6 (June 1979): 8–13.

———. "Privacy and Personnel Records: A Look at Employee Attitudes." *Civil Liberties Review* 4, no. 5 (January/February 1978): p. 28.

———. "The Problem of Employee Privacy Still Troubles Management." *Fortune,* June 4, 1979, pp. 120–25.

"When Not to Use Lie Detectors." *New York Times,* September 6, 1977, p. 38.

White, Jane S. "Sexual Harassment: A Pivotal Issue." *Washington Post,* August 15, 1978, p. E10.

White, Shelby. "The Office Pass." *Across the Board* 14, no. 4 (April 1977): 17–20.

———. "The Office Pass—Continued." *Across the Board* 15, no. 3 (March 1978): 48–51.

"Will the Privacy Issue Hit Industry?" *Industry Week* 185 (May 5, 1975): 40–43.

Willy, F. J. "Right to Privacy in Personal Medical Information." *Medical Trial Technique Quarterly* 24 (Fall 1977): 164–83.

Fair Procedure Mechanisms

"AAA Designs Arbitration System for EEO Disputes." *Daily Labor Report No. 51.* Washington, D.C.: Bureau of National Affairs, March 15, 1978.

Aikin, O. "Trends in Unfair Dismissal." *Personnel Manager* 5 (February 1973): 44.

"The Anti-Union Grievance Ploy." *Business Week,* February 12, 1979, pp. 117–18.

Baer, Walter E. *Discipline and Discharge under the Labor Agreement.* New York: American Management Association, 1972.

Blackburn, John D. *Restricted Employee Discharge Rights: A Changing Concept of Employment at Will.* Working Paper Ser. WPS 78–46. Columbus: College of Administrative Science, Ohio State University, May 1978.

Blumrosen, Alfred W. "Strangers No More: All Workers Are Entitled to 'Just Cause' Protection under Title VII." *Industrial Relations Law Journal* 2, no. 4 (Winter 1978): 519–66.

Clark, G. de N. "Remedies for Unfair Dismissal." *International and Comparative Law Quarterly,* 4th ser. 20 (July 1971): 397–432. (A European comparison.)

Cohen, Hyman. "The Search for Innovative Procedures in Labor Arbitration." *Arbitration Journal* 29 (June 1974): 104–14.

"Constitutional Rights Can't Be Cited by an Employee Fired for Stealing Company Products, an Arbitrator Ruled." *Wall Street Journal,* May 10, 1977, p. 1.

"Corporate Lie Detectors Come under Fire: Is This the Way to Screen Job Applicants? A New Test Could Quiet Opponents!" *Business Week,* January 13, 1973, p. 88.

Coulson, Robert. "Anchor Motor Freight, Another Booby Trap for Grievance Arbitration." *New York Law Journal,* June 7, 1976.

————. *Labor Arbitration: What You Need to Know.* 2nd ed. New York: American Arbitration Association, 1978.

Dennis, Barbara D. and Somers, Gerald G. *Arbitration: 1977 Proceedings of the Thirtieth Annual Meeting National Academy of Arbitrators.* Washington, D.C.: Bureau of National Affairs, 1978.

"Disgruntled Employees at Burlington N. RR Can Lodge Gripes Directly with Top Corporate Chiefs under a New Dial a Boss Program." *Wall Street Journal,* May 30, 1972, p. 1.

Dolnick, D. "Settlement of Grievances and the Job Conscious Theory." *Labor Law Journal* 21 (April 1970): 240.

Elkouri, Frank and Elkouri, Edna A. *How Arbitration Works.* Washington, D.C.: Bureau of National Affairs, 1973.

"Employee Communications." *Personnel Policies Forum Survey No. 110.* Washington, D.C.: Bureau of National Affairs, July 1975.

"Employee Conduct and Discipline." *Personnel Policies Forum Survey No. 102.* Washington, D.C.: Bureau of National Affairs, August 1973.

Evan, William M. "An Ombudsman for Executives?" *New York Times,* August 26, 1973, pp. 110–11. (Cite I: The Idea Is to Avert Corporate Injustice. Cite II: General: Ombudsman Best Way to Protect Executives, Absent Union.)

————. "Organization Man and Due Process of Law." *Organization Theory,* New York: Wiley-Interscience, 1976.

Fisher, Robert W. "Arbitration of Discharges for Marginal Reasons." *Monthly Labor Review* 91 (October 1968): 1–5.

————. "When Workers Are Discharged—An Overview." *Monthly Labor Review* 96 (June 1973): 4–17.

Foegen, J. H. "An Ombudsman as Complement to the Grievance Procedure." *Labor Law Journal* 23 (May 1972): 289.

Fowler, Elizabeth M. "Management—Arbitrating Job-Bias Cases." *New York Times,* July 7, 1978, sec. D, p. 12.

Foy, Nancy. *The Sun Never Sets on IBM.* New York: Morrow, 1974. (Careful and elaborate procedures for dismissal of employees; IBM also has a "Bill of Rights.")

Getman, Julius G. "Labor Arbitration and Dispute Resolution." *Yale Law Journal* 88 (1979): 916–49.

Getschow, George. "Aggrieved over Grievances—Revised Complaint System Raises Tension in Coal Mines, Will Be Issue in 1977 Talks." *Wall Street Journal,* March 4, 1977, p. 30.

Harriman, Bruce. "Up and Down the Communications Ladder." *Harvard Business Review* 52, no. 5 (September–October 1974): 143. (New England Telephone "Private Lines" company encourages employees to ask management about any matter that might concern them.)

Hess, Lee. "Scanlon Plan and Productivity: A People Oriented Company (Dana Corp.)." *Vital Speeches* 43 (December 15, 1976): 141–43.

"How the Xerox Ombudsman Helps Xerox." *Business Week,* May 12, 1973, p. 188.

Hughes, Charles L. "Making Unions Unnecessary: The Open-Door Policy." *Hughes Report,* sample issue, 1978, pp. 2–5.

Jennings, Kenneth. "Arbitrators and Drugs." *Personnel Journal* 55, no. 10 (October 1976): 498–502.

Keefe, W. F. "How to Keep Your Workers Happy: Listen to Them and Communicate." *Pulp & Paper* 44 (January 1970): 139–41.

Leonard, John W. "Discipline for Off-the-Job Activities." *Monthly Labor Review* 91, no. 10 (1968): 5–11.

———. "Reinstatement of Employee Despite Offensive Conduct." *Supervision* 39, no. 11 (November 1977): 13–16.

Louviere, U. "Where Any Employee Is Heard at the Top." *Nation's Business* 62 (June 1974): 40.

Michael, Stephen P. "Due Process in Non-Union Grievance Systems." *Employee Relations Law Journal* 3, no. 4 (Spring 1978): 516.

Nelson, W. B. "Union Representation during Management Investigation of Alleged Rule Infraction." *Labor Law Journal* 26 (January 1975): 37–43.

Pettefer, J. C. "Effective Grievance Administration." *California Management Review* 12 (Winter 1970).

Polhemus, C. E. "Due Process and Pregnancies." *Monthly Labor Review* 99 (January 1976): 64–65.

"Polygraph Control and Civil Liberties Protection Act." Hearings before the Subcommittee on the Constitution of the Committee on the Judiciary, U.S. Senate, 95th Cong., on S.1845, November 15 and 16, 1977. Washington, D.C.: U.S. Government Printing Office, 1978.

"Problem Solving Program for Employees Attracts Growing Corporate Attention." *Wall Street Journal,* June 2, 1977, p. 1.

Rabin, Robert L. "Job Security and Due Process: Monitoring Administrative Discretion through a Reasons Requirement." *University of Chicago Law Review* 44, no. 1 (Fall 1976): 60.

"Rough Going: More Office Workers Battle Being Fired by Suing Their Boss; Often on Charges of Bias." *Wall Street Journal,* June 18, 1975, p. 1.

Shemaria-Weber, Victoria R. "A Remedy for Malicious Discharge of the At-Will Employee: *Monge v. Beebe Rubber Co.,* 114 N.H. 130 A.Zd 549 (1974)." *Connecticut Law Review* 7 (1975): 758.

Stanton, Erwin S. "The Discharged Employee and the EEO Laws." *Personnel Journal* 55, no. 3 (March 1976): 128–9.

Stessin, Lawrence. "Management Tunes In on Employee Gripes." *New York Times,* October 16, 1977, sec. F, p. 2.

Stieber, Jack. "Protection against Unfair Dismissal." *Michigan State University School of Labor and Industrial Relations Newsletter,* Fall 1978, pp. 4–6.

Stone, Morris. *Employee Discipline and Arbitration: Case Stories in Private and Public Employment with Suggested Questions for Discussion.* New York: American Arbitration Association, 1977.

Stone, Morris and Baderschneider, Earl R., eds. *Arbitration of Discrimination: A Case Book.* New York: American Arbitration Association, 1974.

Sullivan, D. M. "Employee Discipline: Beware the Company Position." *Personnel Journal* 53 (September 1974): 692–95.

Thomson, A. W. J. "The Grievance Procedure in the Private Sector." Ithaca: New York State School of Industrial and Labor Relations, Cornell University, 1974.

Trotta, Maurice S. and Gudenberg, Harry R. "Resolving Personnel Problems in Non-Union Plants." *Personnel* 53 (May–June 1976): 55.

"Union Presence During Investigations." *Monthly Labor Review* 98 (March 1975): 62–63.

"Unions Hail S.Ct. Decision Limiting Employer's Right to Interrogate Employee without a Union Representative Present." *Wall Street Journal,* March 18, 1975, p. 1.

Winter, Ralph E. "More Office Workers Battle Being Fired by Suing Their Bosses." Reprint from the *Wall Street Journal,* in *Personnel Administrator* 20, no. 5 (September 1975): p. 27.

Woodward, Susan L. "The Freedom of the People Is in Its Private Life: The Unrevolutionary Implications of Industrial Democracy." *American Behavioral Scientist* 20, no. 4 (March–April 1977): 579–96.

Wortman, M. S. "Arbitration Enforcement and Individual Rights." *Labor Law Journal* 25 (February 1974): 74–84.

Youngdahl, J. E. "Arbitration of Discrimination Grievances." *Arbitration Journal* 31 (May 1976): 145–63.

Rights of Expression and Dissent

Blumberg, Phillip I. "Loyalty, Obedience and the Role of the Employee." *Oklahoma Law Review* 24, no. 3 (August 1971): 279.

"Dissenters, Corporate Underground News Papers." *Newsweek,* November 8, 1971, pp. 97–98.

"Employees' Right to Speak Defended." *The Docket,* November 1977, p. 8.

Ewing, David W. "Employee Rights: Taking the Gag Off." *Civil Liberties Review* 1 (Fall 1974): 54.

Fleeson, Lucinda. "The Job Was Important, but This Came First." *Bergen Record,* March 29, 1979.

Ingram, T. H. "Corporate Underground." *Nation* 213 (September 13, 1971): 206–12.

"Individual Liability of Agents for Corporate Crimes under the Proposed Federal Criminal Code." *Vanderbilt Law Review* 31 (May 1978): 965–1016.

Kugel, Yerachmiel and Gruenberg, Gladys W. "Criteria and Guidelines for Decision Making: The Special Case of International Payoffs." *Columbia Journal of World Business* 12 (Fall 1977): 113–23. ("It is the individual executive, with given standards and moral convictions, who finally determines whether international payoffs will or will not be made.")

Nader, Ralph; Green, Mark; and Seligman, Joel, eds., *Whistle Blowing: A Report of the Conference on Professional Responsibility.* New York: Grossman, 1972.

Nelson, Sarah. "Karen Silkwood and the Nuclear Industry." *Rights* 24, no. 2–3 (March–June 1978): 5–6.

Nelson, Wallace B. "Creating Dissension or Exercising a Statutory Right?" *Labor Law Journal* 28 (September 1977): 593–96.

Palmer, David C. "Free Speech and Arbitration: Implications for the Future." *Labor Law Journal* 27, no. 5 (May 1976): 287–300.

"Remedy for the Discharge of Professional Employees Who Refuse to Perform Unethical or Illegal Acts: A Proposal in Aid of Professional Ethics." *Vanderbilt Law Review* 28 (May 1975): 805–41.

Stevens, Charles W. "The Whistle Blower Chooses Hard Path, Utility Story Shows." *Wall Street Journal,* November 8, 1978, pp. 1, 35.

"Underground Papers Needle the Bosses." *Business Week,* October 9, 1971, p. 86.

Uris, Auren. *Executive Dissent.* New York: Amacon, American Management Association, 1978.

Walters, Kenneth D. "Your Employees' Right to Blow the Whistle." *Harvard Business Review* 53, no. 4 (July/August 1975): p. 26.

Westin, Alan F. and Salisbury, Stephan, eds. *Individual Rights Sourcebook.* 2 vols.: New York: First National Seminar on Individual Rights in the Corporation, 1978.

"When Must a Lawyer Blow the Whistle?" *Business Week,* May 21, 1978, p. 117.

"Whistle Blowers; Question of Revealing Corporate Misdeeds." *Time,* April 17, 1972, pp. 85–86.

Whitten, L. "Whistle Blowers: Nader and the New Employee Ethic." *Harper's Bazaar* 105 (September 1972): 168–69.

The Editors

ALAN F. WESTIN is professor of public law and government at Columbia University and an authority on privacy, a field to which he has contributed numerous books and articles. He has been editor of the *Civil Liberties Review* and is president of The Educational Fund for Individual Rights, Inc.

STEPHAN SALISBURY is a poet and writer. He was a staff member of the *Civil Liberties Review* and is now a reporter for the *Philadelphia Inquirer.*

The Contributors

WILLIAM L. BATT, JR. is program manager for labor-management cooperation at the National Center for Productivity and Quality of Working Life in Washington, D.C. He has held several government positions and has published numerous articles in the field of labor management.

PAUL BERNSTEIN is an assistant professor of political and social science at the University of California, Irvine. He received his Ph.D. from Stanford University in 1974, and specializes in comparative politics.

KATE BLACKWELL is an associate of Ralph Nader and co-author with him of *You and Your Pension.*

LAWRENCE E. BLADES received his J.D. at the University of Michigan. He taught law at the University of Kansas, and later served as dean at the University of Iowa's College of Law. He is currently practicing law with the firm of Simmons, Pervine, Albright and Elwood in Cedar Rapids, Iowa.

PHILLIP I. BLUMBERG, a graduate of Harvard Law School, is dean of the University of Connecticut School of Law. He is the author of many books and articles, including *Corporate Responsibility in a Changing*

Society and *The Megacorporation in American Society: The Scope of Corporate Power.*

FRANK T. CARY is chairman of the board and chief executive officer of the International Business Machines Corporation. He is a director or trustee of several prominent organizations.

A. W. CLAUSEN is president of BankAmerica Corporation.

G. H. COLLINGS, JR. is corporate medical director at the New York Bell Telephone Company. He has a master's degree in public health, and has written many articles in his special field of occupational medicine.

DONALD K. CONOVER is director of corporate education in Personnel and Labor Relations Division of the Western Electric Company. He is also chairman of the Organization Development Council and has presented papers at numerous conferences and universities.

FREDERICA H. DUNN is dean of women at the Community College of the Finger Lakes. Prior to this appointment, she was the first ombudsman for the Aircraft Engine Group of the General Electric Company.

JOHN E. DUNSFORD is a professor at the St. Louis School of Law. He has held numerous positions with the National Academy of Arbitrators, and was appointed its vice-president in 1976.

RICHARD L. EPSTEIN was formerly with the Chicago law firm of Sonnenshein, Carlin, Nath and Rosenthal. He is now vice-president of the American Hospital Association.

DAVID W. EWING is a professor at the Harvard Business School and executive editor for planning of the *Harvard Business Review.* He is the author of numerous articles and books, including *Freedom Inside the Organization: Bringing Civil Liberties to the Workplace* and *The Managerial Mind.*

LIN FARLEY's course at Cornell University, Women and Work, served as the basis for her recent book, *Sexual Shakedown: The Sexual Harassment of Women on the Job.* She is active in the effort to make public the sexual pressures encountered by women in the workplace.

LUCINDA FLEESON is a staff writer for the *Bergen Record.*

DAN GELLERT, an Eastern Airlines pilot, was grounded for reporting a serious defect in the new Lockheed 1011 aircraft to the National Transportation Safety Board. He sued Eastern, was awarded $1.6 million, and now is flying again for Eastern.

JULIUS G. GETMAN is a professor of law at Yale University, specializing in labor law, and has been an arbitrator since 1963. He is the author of *Law Practice and Policy* and *Union Representatives Elections: Law and Reality.*

IRA GLASSER, formerly the head of the New York Civil Liberties Union, is now executive director of the American Civil Liberties Union. He is the author of numerous books and articles, including *Doing Good: The Limits of Benevolence* (joint authorship).

HARRIET GORLIN has been employed by the Conference Board since 1973, currently as a research associate. She researches and publishes predominantly in the area of employee services.

LARRY E. GREINER is assistant professor at the Harvard Business School and a frequent contributor to the *Harvard Business Review.* He specializes in the field of organizational behavior.

HARRY R. GUDENBERG is director of labor relations at the International Telephone and Telegraph Corporation. He has served on the labor law committees of numerous bar associations and has lectured extensively on labor relations.

ANDREW HACKER is professor of political science at Queens College of the City University of New York and has written extensively on corporate matters. He is the author of a widely used high school textbook, *Free Enterprise in America.*

TRUDY HAYDEN has been associated with the American Civil Liberties Union since 1967 and was the author of the monthly *Privacy Report* of the ACLU's project on privacy and data collection. She recently left the ACLU to work for the city government of New York.

CHARLES L. HUGHES received his Ph.D. in industrial psychology from the University of Houston. He has been director of personnel and organizational development for Texas Instruments since 1972.

KENNETH JENNINGS is an assistant professor of management and labor relations at the University of North Florida, Jacksonville.

ROSABETH MOSS KANTER is professor of sociology at Yale University and a partner in the organizational consulting firm Goodmeasures. She is a member of the board of directors at the American Center for the Quality of Worklife, and a widely published author.

ALLAN H. KNAUTZ is vice-president of general management systems at Equifax Services, Inc., with which he has been affiliated since 1957. He is also a member of Sales and Marketing Executives, Inc., Atlanta.

STAUGHTON LYND is a historian and labor attorney. He was chairman of the first march against the Vietnam war in Washington, D.C., in 1965 and director of the freedom schools during the Mississippi Summer Project of 1964.

DONALD L. MARTIN is professor of economics at the University of Miami School of Law. He specializes in the fields of labor and industrial organizations.

ANTHONY MAZZOCCHI is a vice-president and has been citizen legislative director of the Oil, Chemical and Atomic Workers International Union.

ARTHUR SELWYN MILLER is professor of law at George Washington University, where he has taught since 1961. He also serves as a consultant to the General Accounting Office in Washington, D.C. The author of several books and countless scholarly articles, he served as editor for the *Journal of Public Law* from 1953 to 1961.

MILTON R. MOSKOWITZ is senior editor of *Business and Society Review.*

RALPH NADER is the noted consumer advocate.

HERBERT R. NORTHRUP received his Ph. D. from Harvard University and is teaching at the University of Pennsylvania's Wharton School. His specialties include union policies and international labor relations.

DAVID C. PALMER is an attorney at Kilpatrick & Cody in Atlanta, where he specializes in labor law.

PETER PETKAS is an associate of Ralph Nader.

ROBERT ELLIS SMITH is the publisher of the Washington newsletter *Privacy Journal* and the author of *Privacy: How to Protect What's Left of It.*

JACK STIEBER is director of the School of Labor and Industrial Relations and professor of economics at Michigan State University. He has served as an impartial arbitrator in both public and private employment, and has written several books and numerous articles in the fields of collective bargaining, arbitration, and manpower.

CLYDE W. SUMMERS has taught law since 1942 and spent the years 1956–1975 at Yale University. Since 1960 he has served as a hearing examiner for the Connecticut Commission on Civil Rights. He is the author of *Labor Cases and Materials.*

ADRIENNE TOMKINS was a victim of sexual harassment on the job. She sued, won an appeal in a federal court, and accepted an out-of-court settlement for $20,000. The company agreed to publicize procedures for remedying similar situations in the future.

MAURICE S. TROTTA is professor emeritus of industrial relations and management at New York University. He has been an arbitrator for over twenty-five years and is the author of several books, including *Arbitration of Labor Management Disputes.*

AUREN URIS has been on the staff of the Research Institute of America since 1947, and is currently serving there as a consulting editor. He is also a newspaper columnist and a member of the operating management of the Celanese Corporation of America.

KENNETH D. WALTERS is a graduate of Stanford University School of Law and the Graduate School of the University of California, Berkeley. He is an assistant professor at the School of Business Administration at the University of Washington. Several of his articles on employee rights have been published.

RICHARD E. WALTON is professor of business administration at the Harvard Business School. He has written extensively on conflict resolution and the quality of working life.

MAX WAYS began as a reporter for the *Baltimore Sun* and the *Philadelphia Record* and eventually made his way to the board of editors of *Fortune* magazine, a position from which he recently retired. He has served in various editorial capacities for *Fortune* and continues to write for the magazine.

EDGAR WEINBERG is assistant director of the National Center for Productivity and the Quality of Working Life and heads its human resources program. He previously served as deputy assistant commissioner of the Office of Productivity and Technology in the Bureau of Labor Statistics.

Index

Aaron, Benjamin, 172
abuse of process, 48
abusive discharge, *see* discharge
academic community, 146, 257, 304; tenure, 55, 59, 81, 151, 258. *See also* school teachers
access to information, xv–xvi, 6, 68; business plans, 223–4; consumer reports, 193–9; costs of implementing, 275–8; on employer policies, 239–40; exempt data, 257–8; insurance records, 264–4, 266–8, 271–2; investigative reports, 260–2; legislation on, 236–8, 255–6; medical records, 195, 200–4, 262–3, 266–7, 270–1; of nonunion employees, 258, 259; and participatory management, 351–2; personnel files, 68, 188, 221, 222–4, 233–8, 255–60, 265; Privacy Protection Study Commission recommendations on, 257–74; references, 257–8; unions and, 258. *See also* confidentiality; disclosure; privacy legislation; privacy policies; privacy and privacy issues
accountants, 77
Across the Board, 85–90
Adcock v. *Board of Education,* 98–99
advancement opportunity, 8, 137, 257, 312
Advise and Dissent: Scientists in the Political Arena (Primak and Von Hipple), 92, 104
Aeromotive Metal Products, 293–4
Aetna Life & Casualty, 184, 246, 251
affirmative-action programs, 4, 8, 146, 228
AFL-CIO, 153. *See also* unions
AFTRA (American Federation of Television and Radio Artists), 168
age and age discrimination, 137–8, 341

agency law, 146
Air Line Pilots Association, 107, 337–8
airline industry, 89, 140, 142, 143, 144, 337–8, 345; whistle blowing in, 106–10
Alabama, 12; employee-rights cases, 51, 54
Alaska: *Watts* v. *Seward School Board,* 100–1
ALCOA, 184
Alexander v. *Gardner-Denver,* 170
Algeria, 354
alienation, 6, 7. *See also* job satisfaction
Amalgamated Food Employees Union v. *Logan Valley Plaza, Inc.,* 12, 13, 14
American Arbitration Association, 332
American Association for the Comparative Study of Law, Inc., 335–50
American Association of University Professors (AAUP), 151
American Bar Association, 150
American Cast Iron Pipe Company, 344, 354
American Chemical Society (ACS), 102, 152
American Civil Liberties Union, 33, 206
American Federation of Government Employees, 378
American Federation of State, County and Municipal Employees (AFSCME), 122–31, 154, 378; Women's Committee, 124–7
American law: abusive use of a right, 53; corporate malice concept, 132–4; employee protections, xi, 21; employer prerogatives, xi–xii, 21, 29, 32–37; on labor relations, 360; right to discharge, 59, 140, 141, 142–3; rights of employment, 102; tort liability, 47–54; whistle-blowing cases, 94–101; wrongful procurement, 50. *See*

also common law; Constitution of the United States; federal legislation; state courts; state legislation; Supreme Court *and* names of cases
American Metal Climax, Inc., 147
American Society of Civil Engineers, 151
American Society of Planning Officials (ASPO), 152–3
American Sterilizer Corporation, 378–9
American Telephone & Telegraph, 184, 251, 398, 405
American Velvet Company, 343, 383
Amsco Equipment Company, 378–9, 386
anarchist movements, 355
Anderson, Jack, 347
Anticipatory Democracy: People in the Politics of the Future (Bezold, ed.), 389–400
A&P, 378
appellate courts: *Holodnak* v. *Avco Corporation and UAW Local 1010,* 157–8, 159, 160, 167, 169; *Stillman* v. *Ford,* 133, 134; *See also* circuit courts; state courts; Supreme Court
aptitude tests, 219. *See also* employment testing
arbitration and arbitration system, 141, 142, 143, 151, 156, 258, 329, 341, 342; advisory vs. binding, 305; basic substantive rights, 283–5; church support for, 306–7; on drug use, 291–301; enforceability of, 156; on free-speech issues, 156–60, 163–7; judicial deference to, 167; in participatory management, 356–7; procedural rights, 282–3, 288–9; public policy questions, 156, 166–9; Supreme Court as model for, 281–90; on unjust dismissals, 56–58. *See also* due process; fair procedure
Arbitration 1976, 281–90
Armco Steel, 378
arrest records, 249. *See also* criminal convictions
Association for Computer Machinery, 190
Atlantic Richfield Oil, 184, 247, 251
Atomic Energy Commission, 89
AT&T Express, The, 347
Attack on Corporate America, The (Johnson, ed.), 15–20
authority, 86, 87. *See also* corporate decision-making; management; supervisors
Automobile Dealer Franchise Act of 1956, 46–47, 51–52
automobile industry, 46–47, 51–52, 89, 101, 137; labor-management cooperation in, 377, 378, 379, 381, 385; unions, 153. *See*

also United Auto Workers *and* names of companies
automobile workers, 140, 361. *See also* United Auto Workers
Avco Corporation, 157–8

Baltimore and Ohio Plan, 377
Bank of America, xvii, 415–36; code of business conduct, 416–17; as corporate enterprise, 425–30; disclosure code, 417–36; job application procedure, 226–9; Open Line, 231–2; personnel files, 226–9, 231, 232–43; privacy standards and programs, 226–43, 246, 247
Bankers Trust Company, 345
banks, 186; ethical standards, 416–17. *See also* Bank of America; Bankers Trust
Barr, Roy, 123–4, 125, 130
Batt, William L., Jr., 377–88
Belgium, 351
Bell, Bill, 109
Bell Aerospace decision, 74
Bell System, *see* American Telephone and Telegraph
Bellow, Saul, 29
Bendix Corporation, 378
benefits and benefit plans, 239, 240, 257, 393; participatory management and, 345–7; pensions, 152, 345; profit-sharing, 343, 345
Bergen Record, 111–16
Bernstein, Paul, 351–7
Bethlehem Steel, 378
Bezold, Clement, 389n
Bill of Rights, xviii, 16, 17, 68–69, 179, 180. *See also* Constitution of the United States; constitutionalization movement
Black, William, Jr., 387
blacklisting, 68
black people, 11, 13, 339; Bill of Rights extended to, 68–69
Blackwell, Kate, 91, 92, 104, 150–5
Blades, Lawrence E., 33–34, 45–54, 102, 141–2
Block, Howard, 292
Blowing the Whistle: Dissent in the Public Interest (Peters and Branch), 92
Bluestone, Irving, 339, 377, 381
Blumberg, Phillip I., 101, 140–9, 335–50
Blumrosen, Alfred W., 142
board of directors, 361; employee membership on, 337–40, 396–7
Borman, Frank, 107, 108–9
Branch, Taylor, 92, 93, 95, 104
Brandeis, Louis D., 179–80, 420

Brecht, Robert, 288
Brown and Williamson Tobacco
  Corporation, 296
Buckley v. *American Federation of Radio
  Artists,* 168
Bunting, Robert, 16
Bureau of Labor Statistics, 341
Burton v. *Wilmington Parking Authority,*
  159
Business Week, 329–32
Buttion, Tim, 109

Caldwell, Clyde, 387
California, 13, 182, 239; *Adcock* v. *Board of
  Education,* 98–99; Bank of American in,
  431, 432; privacy legislation, 236, 237,
  239, 241, 248–9, 257; Roberti Bill, 182;
  Uniform Credit Code, 420
California Processors, Inc., 285
Canada, 360, 362
Canon Law Society of America, 307
capitalism, 392
Carborundum Company, 379–80
Carmichael, John, 380
Carter, James Earl (Jimmy), 5, 41
Cary, Frank T., xix, 184, 214–25, 247
Caterpillar Tractor, 184, 191, 416
Celanese Corporation, 416
Cenco, 37
Champion Home Builders, Inc., 344
Chapman, Brian M., 132–3
Chicago & Northwestern Transportation
  Company, 344
Chicago Police Department, 96
child labor laws, 49
Chinese communes, 356
Chrysler Corporation, 339, 361, 378
CIO, 73, 329. *See also* AFL–CIO; unions
circuit courts: *Buckley* v. *American
  Federation of Radio Artists,* 168; *Linscott*
  v. *Miller Falls Co.,* 168; *Mushroom
  Transportation Company* v. *NLRB,* 162–3;
  NLRB v. *Kearney and Trecker Corp.,* 161;
  NLRB v. *Nu-Car Carriers,* 162; *NLRB* v.
  *Peter Callier Kohler Swiss Chocolate Co.,
  Inc.,* 162. *See also* appellate courts;
  district courts; state courts
Civil Liberties Review, The, 106–10, 117–21,
  193–9
civil rights, 88
Civil Rights Act of 1964, 4, 13, 170, 181
Civil Rights Cases (1883), 11, 13
Civil Rights and Fair Employment Practices
  Commission, 46

civil service systems, xx, 55, 59. *See also*
  public sector
Clark, Ramsey, 78
Clausen, A. W., xvii–xviii, 239, 415–23, 433,
  435
Cleveland, 154, 206
client-professional relationship, 150
closed-shop agreements, 13
clothing and grooming, 29–31; dress codes,
  230, 242
Coal Mine Safety Act, 102–3
collection agencies, 196
collective bargaining, 6, 21, 55, 59, 63, 140,
  141, 147, 257; on access to records, 259;
  for civil liberties, 74–75; on employee
  privacy, 177; grievance procedures, 322–3;
  "just cause" clauses, 56, 59, 101, 140, 141,
  142; for nonunion employees, 74; and
  participatory management, 340, 382; on
  unauthorized disclosure, 147–8; union
  shop provisions, 168. *See also* just cause;
  unions
college students, 5
Collings, G. H., Jr., 209–13
Columbia Law Review, 45–54
Columbia University, 180
Comerford v. *International Harvester Co.,* 51
common law, 53, 59, 140; employment
  relationship in, 53, 54; privacy in, 179–80;
  rights of the employee, 147. *See also*
  American law
Communist Party, 141
company image, 32, 294
complaint procedures, *see* grievance
  procedures
computers and computer systems, 178, 238,
  247, 394, 421
Concept of the Corporation, The (Drucker),
  136
Conference Board, Inc., The, 177–92
Conference of Human Resource Systems
  Users, 189
confidentiality, 68, 200, 257, 348; banking,
  416–17, 422; medical, 209–13, 245; of
  personnel files, 232–4; and whistle
  blowing, 100. *See also* access to
  information; disclosure; loyalty; personnel
  records; privacy and privacy issues; whistle
  blowing and whistle blowers
Congress of the United States, 13, 112, 353.
  See also federal legislation; Senate
Connecticut, 330, 383; Board of Mediation
  and Arbitration, 57; State Labor
  Department, 37

Conover, Donald K., 389–400
conscientious objection, 71
Consolidated Packaging Corporation, 340
Constitution of the United States, 18; and
  arbitration, 281–90; Bill of Rights, xviii,
  16, 17, 68–69, 179, 180; proposed
  employee rights amendment, 69, 81. See
  also constitutionalization movement; due
  process; First Amendment; free speech;
  privacy and privacy issues
constitutionalization movement, 15–20,
  67–82; costs factor, 18–19, 22, 39–40;
  Ewing proposal, 67–82; perceived merits
  of, 40; "state action" problem, 158–60,
  167–9; stockholders and, 22, 39–40;
  Supreme Court decisions on, 11–14; survey
  of management views, 21–42; and unions,
  73–75
consumer reporting agencies, 193–9; Privacy
  Study Commission on, 260–2, 265
consumerism, 242
contract law, 47, 51, 156, 285
Control Data Corporation, 251
Cooley, T., 52
cooperative loan exchanges, 196
corporate decision-making, 369, 396;
  affecting job security, 341–3; public
  opinion and, 347–8; on technological
  improvements, 343. See also management;
  participatory management
corporate employees, see employees
corporate ethics, see ethics
corporate leaks, 144–6. See also disclosure;
  whistle blowing and whistle blowers
corporate malice, 132–4
corporate person, 11
corporate power, 345
corporate state, 10
corporations: board of directors, 337–40,
  361, 396–7; privacy policies, 29, 178, 184,
  210–25, 238–40, 246, 247–52; as public
  institutions, 144; scandals, 22, 415;
  self-disclosure, xvii, 415–36; social
  responsibility of, 103, 144, 347–8, 418,
  419. See also constitutionalization
  movement; employer prerogatives;
  management
costs: of constitutionalization, 18–19; of
  converting personnel records, 188–90; of
  information-access programs, 275–8; of
  privacy policies, 188–90, 241–2, 275–8; of
  voluntary disclosure, 423
Coulson, Robert, 332
courts: blacklisting and, 68; damage actions,
  45–54, 132–4; inadequacy of, 56. See also

appellate courts; circuit courts; district
  courts; state courts; Supreme Court
CPC International, 251
Cranz, Galen, 198
credit, 240
credit agencies, 186
credit records, 194
criminal convictions, 227, 229, 292–3
criminal investigations, 234
criminal law, 281–90
Cross, Robert D., 146
Crucible Steel, 378
Cummins Engine, 184, 189, 246, 251
Cuyahoga River, 154

Daedalus, 3–9
Dahl, Robert, 338
Dallas, 398
damage actions, 45–54, 132–4; British
  system, 61–62
Dana Corporation, 378, 384
Daugherty, Carroll, 282
decision-making process, see corporate
  decision-making
defamation of character, 292
defense contracts and contractors, 157–8,
  159, 338
democratization, see industrial democracy;
  participatory management
Dendor v. Board of Fire and Police
  Commissioners, 99
Denmark, 341
Department of Commerce, 381
Depression, see Great Depression
desks, 68, 78, 225
discharge: arbitration on, 163–5; British law
  on, 59–63; for criminal conviction, 292;
  damage action for, 45–54, 132–4; for drug
  use, 291–301; as employer's prerogative,
  33–34, 45–64, 81, 140–9, 340–1; for
  insubordination, disobedience, or
  disloyalty, 141; public opinion and, 144–6;
  reasons for, 68; for refusal to participate in
  illegal, immoral, or unprofessional acts,
  147; tort liability for, 47–51. See also just
  cause
disclosure: internal, 268–72; legislation on,
  420; of personnel information, 188;
  unauthorized, 143–6; voluntary, 415–36.
  See also confidentiality; loyalty; privacy
  and privacy issues; whistle blowing
discrimination, 137–8, 341, 347; racial, 7,
  11–13, 81, 228. See also equal employment
  opportunity; sex discrimination; women

disloyalty, *see* loyalty

dissent, *see* expression and dissent; free speech; whistle blowing and whistle blowers

Dissent and Independent Initiative in Planning Offices (Finkler), 152–3

district courts: *Burton* v. *Wilmington Parking Authority,* 159; *Dendor* v. *Board of Fire and Police Commissioners,* 99; *Downs* v. *Conway School District,* 96, 99; *Geary* v. *U.S. Steel Corp.,* 42; *McIntire* v. *DuPont,* 5, 42. *See also* circuit courts; state courts

Domestic Council Committee on the Right of Privacy, 183

Donahue, Thomas R., 361

Donnelly Mirror Corporation, 39

Downs v. *Conway School District,* 96, 99

dress codes, 230, 242. *See also* clothing and grooming

Drucker, Peter: *The Concept of the Corporation,* 136

drug industry, 88–89; whistle blowing in, 111–16

drug use, 291–301; entrapment, 297, 299–301; evidence and proof of, 297–9; record of, 293–5; seriousness of, 291–3; type of, 295–7

due process, 6, 10–14, 15, 16, 17–20, 22, 24, 68, 71–72, 200; in arbitration system, 282; methods of, 40; Supreme Court on, 11–13. *See also* arbitration and arbitration system; fair procedure; grievance procedures

Dulworth, Ed, 401

Dunn, Frederica H., 311–14

DuPont de Nemours, 152, 184, 251

Durham, Henry, 37

E-Systems, 398

Eastern Airlines, 106–10, 140, 142, 143, 144

Educational Fund for Individual Rights, Inc., The, v

Eighteenth Amendment, 80–81

Eisenhower Era, 85–87

Ellsberg, Daniel, 77

Elvidge, Richard, 62

Emerson, Thomas I., 101

employee bill of rights, *see* constitutionalization movement

employee boycotts, 347

employee privacy, *see* access to information; personnel records; privacy and privacy issues

employee records, *see* medical records; personnel records; privacy and privacy issues

Employee Relations Law Journal, 322–8

employee rights: choice of employer, 49–50; college students' views, 5; conflicting, 7; constitutional amendment for, 68–69; costs of extending, 39–40; custom and legal precedent on, 21, 32–37; enforcement, 24; entitlement view, 5; history of, 72–73; vs. management efficiency, 140–2; management views, 21–42; public policy on, 3–4; social science view, 5–8; three major positions on, xviii–xx; trends in movement for, xvi–xviii; union views, 5, 8, 19. *See also* access to information; constitutionalization movement; due process; expression and dissent; free speech; off-duty conduct of employees; participatory management; privacy and privacy issues

Employee Stock Ownership Plan, 398

employees: as board members, 337–40, 396–7; changing profile of, 85–90; educated elite, 7–8; needs, 3, 315; nonunion, 56–64, 74, 258, 259, 302–10, 322–8, 329–32; off-duty conduct of, 230, 291–301; professional and scientific, 102, 150–4; public-sector, 73, 94–101, 158–9, 171–2; retired, 5, 152; as stockholders, 337–40, 344–6, 395, 396, 397–8; underground newspapers of, 347; union members, 6. *See also* unions

employer prerogatives, xi–xii, 21, 43–64, 236; limits on, 341–2; on medical data, 203–4; in participatory system, 386; right to discharge employees, 33–34, 45–64, 81, 140–9, 340–1; whistle blowing and, 102–3. *See also* employment relationship

employment applications, *see* job applicants

Employment Protection Act of Great Britain, 59–60

employment relationship, 17, 18, 49–50, 93, 132, 140, 141–2, 150, 286; common law protection of, 53, 54; and employee rights, 47, 49, 167; free speech and, 159–60, 164, 165–7; Supreme Court on, 157

employment testing, 67, 219–20, 252, 253–4, 257

engineers, 151–2

England, *see* Great Britain

entitlement view, 397; psychology of, 5. *See also* right to employment

environmental abuse, 60, 143, 144–5, 154, 347; voluntary disclosure on, 420
Epstein, Richard L., 322–8
equal employment opportunity, 4, 8, 81, 189, 231, 239, 247–8; Supreme Court on, 156, 171
Equal Employment Opportunity Commission (EEOC), 119–21, 146; guidelines for personnel records, 181
Equal Rights Amendment, 4
Equitable Life Assurance Society, 184; privacy principles, 244
Equity Funding, 37
Ervin, Sam, 178, 206
ethics, 67, 154, 217; professional, 150–1
Europe, 112; employee rights, 5–6; participatory management, 337, 341, 352, 358–9, 361, 362–4, 396
European Company (Societas Europaea), 341
European Economic Community, 341
Ewing, David, xviii, 21–42, 67–69; criticism of, 70–75
Executive Dissent, 135–9
expression and dissent, xiii–xiv, 83–174; Ewing's view, 67, 70, 77–78; management views, 22, 24, 26–28; in participatory systems, 354; productive, 135–9; professional societies and, 152–3; retaliation for, 24–25; by retired employees, 152. See also free speech; whistle blowing and whistle blowers
Exxon, 184

factory system, 72
Fair Credit Reporting Act (FCRA), 181, 193–9, 229, 240n; Privacy Study Commission on, 260–2, 265
fair hearings, 68, 71, 153, 160
fair procedure, xiv–xv, 78; conflict analysis and the decisional process, 302–5; for nonunion employees, 302–10; ombudsman's role, 311–14. See also arbitration and arbitration system; due process; grievance procedures
Farley, Lin, 122–31
Federal Bureau of Investigation, 108, 109, 146, 229
federal contracts, 13
federal courts, see appellate courts; circuit courts; district courts; Supreme Court
Federal Deposit Insurance Corporation, 227
Federal Election Commission, 420
federal employees, see public sector
Federal Highway Safety Bureau, 145

federal legislation: Automobile Dealer Franchise Act, 46–47, 51–52; Civil Rights Act, 4, 13, 170, 181; Coal Mine Safety Act, 102–3; on discrimination, 137; on electronic eavesdropping, 206; on employee rights, 4; Fair Credit Reporting Act, 181, 193–9, 229, 240n, 260–2, 265; Freedom of Information Act, 181, 420; General Education Provisions Act, 181; H.R. 1984, 180, 181–2, 183, 185, 238, 241, 248, 249; Interstate Commerce Act, 342; Labor-Management Reporting and Disclosure Act, 161; minimum wage laws, 19; National Labor Relations Act, 73, 74, 81, 141, 143, 149, 161–3, 168, 340; Occupational Safety and Health Act, 147; Privacy Act, 29, 178, 180, 181, 182, 183, 197, 201–2, 237, 238, 248, 265–6; Railway Labor Act, 168, 343; Securities Acts, 417–18; Selective Service Act, 56, 71; Taft-Hartley Act, 17; Wagner Act, 17; Water Pollution Control Act, 146–7; workmen's compensation acts, 52, 213
Federal Mediation and Conciliation Service (FMCS), 378, 383
Federal Reserve Board, 435
Federal Trade Commission, 186, 197, 420
Federation of American Scientists, 102
Fibreboard Paper Products Corp. v. NLRB, 342
Fifth Amendment, 141, 289
files, 68, 71, 78, 225
Financial Executive, 178
fingerprinting, 227, 229
Finkler, Earl, 152–3
fire departments, 99
First Amendment, 70, 73, 77, 157–8; in arbitration, 156–71, 283–5; whistle blowing and, 94–103. See also Constitution of the United States; constitutionalization movement; free speech
First National Seminar on Individual Rights in the Corporation, 251
"First Tuesday," 405
Fischer, Ben, 329, 331
Fisher Body, 148, 381
Fitzgerald, A. Ernest, 24–25, 37; The High Priests of Waste, 92, 104
Fleeson, Lucinda, 111–16
Florida, 100
Food and Drug Administration, 112, 113, 114
food industry, 245
Ford, Gerald, 183

Ford Motor, 184, 361, 402
Forrester, Jay W., 103
Fortune, 79–82, 85, 145, 245–52
Fortune "500," 38, 250
Fox, H., 349
France, 7, 53
Frankfurter, Felix, 12
Franklin National Bank, 416
free association, 169
free speech, 6, 78, 80; arbitration on, 156–60, 163–7; court cases, 157–8, 283–4; disclosure of confidential information as, 143, 144–6; employer's, 17; and employment relationship, 160, 164, 165–7; individual vs. representative, 161–3; in NLRA, 161–3; public controversy, 143, 154–5; of public employees, 73, 94–101, 158–9, 171–2; value of, 354–5; whistle blowing as, 94–103; in the workplace, 70–71, 73. *See also* confidentiality; expression and dissent; First Amendment; loyalty; whistle blowing and whistle blowers
Freedom of Information Act, 181, 420
Freedom Inside the Organization (Ewing), 67–69, 79; critiques of, 70–82
freedom of religion, 12
futurism, 391–2

Gamble-Skogmo, 398
Garrett, Ray, 415
GE Resistor, The, 347
General Accounting Office, 89
General Education Provisions Act, 181
General Electric Corporation, 184, 190, 311–14
General Foods, 378; participatory management at, 401–12
General Motors Corporation, 92, 101, 147, 148, 184, 378; information policies, 185; participatory management, 339, 381; whistle blowing at, 347
General Tire and Rubber, 337
Georgia, 180
Germany, 341, 352; worker participation system, 358–9, 362–4
Getman, Julius G., 281–90
Grumman Aircraft, 338
Giesecke, Raymond H., 350
Gilbert Brothers' Annual Survey, 345
Gilbert, J., 350
Gilbert, L., 350
Glasser, Ira, 76–78
Golden, Clinton, 384

Goldstein, Robert C., 189
Goldwater, Barry, Jr., 180, 238, 248
Gorlin, Harriet, 177–92
Gottschall, Kenneth L., 192
government agencies, 186; consumer reports and, 197; requests for information from, 221
government regulation, 396; vs. voluntary disclosure, 419. *See also* federal legislation
Grainger v. *Hill,* 48, 53
Great Britain, 53, 359; Advisory Conciliation and Arbitration Service (ACAS), 60–61; Bullock Committee, 362; Employment Appeal Tribunal, 60; Employment Protection Act, 59–63; nonunion employees in, 59–64; Policy Studies Institute (PSI), 63
Great Depression, 86, 384, 417
Great Lakes Steel Company, 283
Gregory, Edward A., 101, 153
Greiner, Larry E., 365–76
grievance procedures, 74, 78, 124, 153, 258, 303, 355; action review, 308–10; collective bargaining on, 322–3; fear of retaliation for, 330–1; IBM, 39, 222–3; key elements of, 307–8, 316–17, 322–3, 324–5; malfunction, 325–7; management control of, 331–2; management view, 25–26; nonunion, 305–10, 322–8, 329–32; ombudsman role, 311–14; open-door policy, 315–21; and participatory management, 383; purpose of, 324; unions and, 322–3, 324–5, 329–32; whistle blowing and, 96–98, 103. *See also* fair procedure
Gudenberg, Harry R., 302–10
Gulf Oil Corporation, 147

H.R. 1984, 180, 181–2, 183, 185, 238, 241, 248, 249
Hacker, Andrew, 45, 51, 85–90
Hague v. *CIO,* 73n
Hall, Floyd, 107
Hallmark Cards, 398
Hand, Learned, 81, 162
handicapped, 229
Harman Industries, 5
Harman International, 378
Harper, Jim D., 330
Harris, Louis, & Associates, 246
Harvard Business Review, xviii, 91–102, 184, 189, 214–15, 365–76, 377–88, 405; survey of management attitudes, 21–42

Harvard Business School, 189; participation survey, 366–76

Harvard Law Review, 179

Hass, Walter A., Jr., 434

Hayden, Trudy, 193–9

Health, Education and Welfare Department (HEW), 97; fair information practices, 181, 185, 238

health insurance, 248

Hetter, P., 350

Heyns, Roger W., 273

Higgenbottom, Samuel, 107

High Priests of Waste, The (Fitzgerald), 92, 104

Hinks, Warren H., Jr., 381, 382, 386

Holdsworth, W., 53

Holodnak, Mike, 157–8, 161, 162

Holodnak v. *Avco Corporation and UAW Local 1010,* 157–8, 159, 160, 167, 169

homosexuals, 230

Honeywell, Inc., 147, 184

Hoover, J. Edgar, 88

hours, 74, 393–4

Houston, 398

Howard, Thomas M., 37

Howmet Corporation, 298

Hughes, Charles L., xix, 315–21

Hughes Report, 315–21

Hurd v. *Hodge,* 168

IBM, xix, 80, 184, 238, 416; grievance procedures, 39, 222–3; privacy policies and programs, 29, 178, 184, 214–25, 246, 247–8, 251; stockholders, 221–2

IG Metall, 363

Illinois, 401

immoral instructions, 33, 34. *See also* ethics

Indiana: Governor's Commission on Individual Privacy, 183, 189

individualism: vs. social stability, 22, 40, 41

industrial democracy, 15–20, 73, 336, 341, 346. *See also* constitutionalization movement; employee rights; participatory management

Industrial Revolution, 72

industrial secrecy, 352

Inland Steel Container Company, 184, 190, 297

Institute for Social Research, 5, 402; Survey of Working Conditions, 8

insurance and insurance companies, 186, 234, 261, 393; company-run, 29; credit reports, 194–6

insurance records: correcting, 266; internal disclosure of, 271–2; Privacy Study Commission on, 263–4, 266–8, 271–2

Internal Revenue Service, 190

International Association of Machinists, 338, 377, 378–9

International Brotherhood of Boilermakers, 387

International Confederation of Free Trade Unions, 337

International Labor Organization, 337

Interstate Commerce Act, 13, 342

Interstate Commerce Commission, 342, 344

investigative reports, 260–2. *See also* consumer reporting agencies

Iowa University Law School, 33

Israeli kibbutzim, 353, 355, 356

Jackson v. *Metropolitan Edison Co.,* 14

Jehovah's Witnesses, 73

Jennings, Kenneth, 291–301

job applicants: access to information, 261; personal information on, 218; privacy of, 193–9, 218–20, 226–9, 245, 247–8, 261; racial information, 228

job satisfaction, 8, 335–6

job security, 341, 342; participatory management and, 407

John Pirre v. *Printing Developments, Inc.,* 132–4

Johnson, M. Bruce, 15n

Johnson & Johnson, 113

Jones and Laughlin Steel Corporation, 154

Journal of Economic Issues, 351–7

just cause, 56–57, 59, 140–1, 142, 143, 144, 147, 281, 283, 341; in arbitration, 287–9; language of, 285; nonunion statute, 56–58

justice, 81–82

Kadish, Sanford H., 289, 290

Kaiser Steel, 343, 378

Kansas, 13

Kanter, Rosabeth Moss, xvi, 3–9

Karrh, Bruce, 273, 274

Kelly v. *Florida Judicial Qualifications Commission,* 100

Kelso, Louis A., 349–50

Kelso Plan, 349–50

Kennecott Copper Corporation, 147

Kennedy, Richard, 123, 130

Kerr, Clark, 93, 104

Ketchum, Lyman, 401

Knautz, Allen H., xix, 275–8

Koch, Edward, 180, 182, 238, 248

Koven, Adolph, 285, 294

labor disputes: state mediation services, 57.
  See also arbitration and arbitration system
labor force, *see* employees
Labor Law Journal, 156–74
labor-management cooperation, 377–88. *See
  also* participatory management
labor market, 19; monopsonistic, 16, 17
labor unions, *see* unions
Langton, James F., 433
Laughner, James, 378
law, *see* American law; common law;
  contract law; federal legislation; state
  legislation
Lawler, Edward, 402
Lawrence, Paul R., 93, 104
lawyers, 77, 150–1
leadership and leadership style, 366–76,
  398–400. *See also* management
Leavitt, Harold J., 93, 104
legislation: for participatory management,
  348; professional lobbies for, 151–2. *See
  also* American law; federal legislation;
  state legislation
Levi Strauss & Co., 344, 434
libel, 70, 179, 180, 292
lie detectors, 78, 205, 245. *See also*
  polygraphs
Lincoln Electric, 344
Linowes, David, 178, 185–6
Linscott v. *Miller Falls Co.,* 168
Litton Industries, 383
lockers, 68, 78
Lockheed Corporation, 37; 1011 aircraft,
  106–10
loperamide, 111–16
Lordstown, 7, 335
loyalty, 85–90, 92–93, 140–9, 163, 170–1,
  348, 396; and public interest, 144–6. *See
  also* confidentiality; whistle blowing and
  whistle blowers
Lundborg, Louis B., 431
Luther, Martin, 93
Lynd, Staughton, xviii, 70–75

Macy's, 206–7
mailing lists, 233
Maine, 182; privacy law, 255–6, 257
Mallozzi, Robert 37
management, 68, 71–72; age differences,
  373–5; bank, 418; dissent policies of,
  135–9; regional differences in, 28; response
  to privacy questionnaire, 184–92; as
  stewardship, 399; view of worker

participation, 365–76. *See also*
  corporations; employer prerogatives;
  employment relationship; participatory
  management
management educators, 365–6, 367
management prerogatives, *see* employer
  prerogatives
Manufacturers Hanover Trust Company, 184
marijuana, *see* drug use
Marsh v. *Alabama,* 12, 13, 14, 17, 73
Martin, Donald L., xix, 15–20
Martin, Richard, 92, 104
Maryland, 388
Massachusetts, 7, 388
Mayer, Jean, 273
Mazzocchi, Anthony, 203–4
McDonald's Corporation, 331
McDonnell Douglas Corporation, 338, 345
McGovern, George, 87
McIntire, Louis V., 36–37; *Scientists and
  Engineers: The Professionals Who Are Not,*
  92, 104
McIntire, M. B., 104
McIntire v. *E. I. DuPont de Nemours & Co.,*
  5, 42
Meany, George, 361
mediation agents, 57–58
medical ethics, 111
medical records, 182, 195, 236, 257;
  confidentiality principles, 187–8, 209–13,
  245; correcting, 266; defined, 263;
  "information" vs. "conclusions or
  judgments," 211–12, 213; internal
  disclosure of, 270–1; job applicant's, 226,
  227; Privacy Study Commission on, 262–3,
  266–7, 270–1; for worker-health
  surveillance, 200–2
Meltzer, B., 171
mental hospitals, 95–96
Met Lifer, The, 347
Meyer, M., 349
Michigan, 379, 388; privacy legislation,
  249–50, 252
Michigan State University, 122–31; School of
  Labor and Industrial Relations *Newsletter,*
  59–64
Miller, Arthur Selwyn, xviii, 10–14, 94
Miller v. *Credit Bureau, Inc.,* 198
Millstone v. *O'Hanlon Reports, Inc.,* 197–8
minimum income, 5
Minneapolis, 398
Minneapolis *Star and Tribune,* 380
Mississippi, 383

Mobil Oil, 184
Modern Corporate State, The (Miller), 10–14
Monge v. *Beebe Rubber Co.,* 102
monopsonistic labor markets, 16, 17
morality, 147
Morris, George B., Jr., 381
Moskowitz, Milton R., 431–6
Muller v. *Conlisk,* 96
Munger, Guy, 130–1
Municipal Finance Officers Association, 419
Murphy, Franklin D., 434
Mushroom Transportation Company v.
 NLRB, 162–3

Nabisco, 184
Nader, Ralph, xviii, 89, 91, 92, 104, 145,
 149, 150–5, 339
National Bureau of Standards, 188
National Center for Health Statistics, 201
National Center for Productivity and Quality
 of Working Life, 381
National Floor Products Company, 292
national health insurance, 201
National Labor Relations Act, 73, 74, 81,
 141, 143, 149, 340; free speech and, 161–3;
 on union shop provisions, 168
National Labor Relations Board, 46, 71, 342,
 360; *Fibreboard Paper Products* v., 342; v.
 Kearney and Trecker Corp., 161; v. *Local
 Union No. 1229,* 140–1; v. *Magnavox Co.,*
 161; v. *Nu-Car Carriers,* 162; v. *Peter
 Callier Kohler Swiss Chocolate Co., Inc.,*
 162; *Republic Aviation Corp.* v., 73
National Quality of Work Center, 6
National Society of Professional Engineers,
 151–2
National Transportation Safety Board
 (NTSB), 89, 107–8
National Women's Political Caucus, 5
Naylor, Mark, 382
NBC, 405
Negroes, *see* black people; race
 discrimination
Nelson, Joan, 127–8
Netherlands, 341, 359
Neumann, Gerhard, 311
New Deal, 73
New Hampshire, 102
New Jersey: common law, 115; medical
 research case, 111–16; sexual harassment
 case, 117–21
New Jersey Bell Telephone Company,
 299–300
New York (city), 97; near-default, 419

New York (state), 378–9, 388; corporate
 malice case, 132–4; futurists, 391;
 mediation board, 57; privacy legislation,
 253–6; whistle-blowing cases, 97–98
New York Stock Exchange, 345
New York Times, 87, 145, 311–14, 361, 405
New York Times v. *Sullivan,* 159, 172
Newspaper Guild of the Twin Cities, 380
newspaper writers, 165
Nixon, Richard, 87, 93, 183. *See also*
 Vietnam War; Watergate
Nolan, Richard L., 189
nonunion employees, 74, 148; access to
 records, 258, 259; British, 59–64; fair
 procedure for, 302–10; grievance
 procedures for, 305–10, 322–8, 329–32;
 "just cause" statute for, 56–58
North Carolina, 57; *Grainger* v. *Hill,* 48, 53
Northern States Power, 339–40
Northrop Corporation, 331
Northrup, Herbert R., xix, 358–64
Northwest Industries, Inc., 344
Norton, Richard, 381
nuclear power plants, 89

obedience, 140–9
occupational health surveillance, 200–2,
 209–13
occupational prestige, 8
Occupational Safety and Health
 Administration, 190, 201
O'Connor, Rochelle, 192
off-duty conduct of employees, 67, 230, 292;
 drug use, 291–301
office design, 218
Ohio, 384, 388
Ohio Bell Telephone Company, 206
Oklahoma Law Review, 140–9
Olesen, Robert, 182
O'Malley, Peter, 434
ombudsman, 311–14, 331
oral contraceptives, 112, 114
Oregon, 330
Organization Man, The (Whyte), 85
Ortho Pharmaceutical Corporation, 111–16
Orwell, George, 180
Oscar Mayer, 378
outside activities, *see* off-duty conduct of
 employees; privacy and privacy issues
Overnite Transportation Co., 344, 350

Palmer, David C., 156–74
participatory management, xv, 5, 7, 335–412;
 adjudicative systems, 356–7; benefit plans

and pass-through voting as, 345–7; board membership as, 337–40, 361, 396–7; chronology for, 403–11; collective bargaining as, 340, 382; defining characteristics, 358–9, 369–70, 385–8; dissent and, 354; effectiveness ratings, 371–3; European, 337, 341, 352, 358–9, 361, 362–4, 396; expertise issue, 353, 397; favorable influences, 388; futurism and, 391–2; for improving labor relations, 383; individual vs. collective rights in, 254–5; and industrial secrecy, 352; information sharing in, 351–4; labor-management committees, 377–88; leadership and responsibility in, 398–400; through legislation, 348; management view, 27, 28, 365–76; new business and, 378–9; outside consultants, 387–8; pay decisions, 407; picking supervisors, 380; plant design, 379–80; practical results, 389–400, 401–3, 405; and productivity, 389–95, 398, 400; public opinion factor, 347–8; quality-of-work-life programs, 381–2; Scanlon Plans, 384–5, 386, 387; social-science view, 5–6; as solution to job dissatisfaction, 335–6; stock ownership as, 395, 396, 397–8; training for, 352, 367–8, 369; unions and, 336–8, 339–43, 349, 359–64; workplace issues, 393–5
Pasquale, Sam, 113, 115
pass-through voting, 345
paternalism, 75
payroll, *see* salary
Penn Central System, 337
Penney, J. C., 184
Pennsylvania, 381; Compulsory Arbitration Act, 58; employee-rights cases, 33, 36
Pennsylvania State University, 381
pensions and pension rights, 152, 345. *See also* benefits and benefit plans
Pentagon, 24–25
Pentagon Papers, 77
performance evaluations, 186–7, 220, 235–6, 258–9, 312
personality tests, 67, 219. *See also* employment testing
Personnel, 302–10
personnel administration, xii, 14
Personnel Administrator, 275–8
personnel files, *see* personnel records
Personnel Journal, 291–301
personnel records, 177, 178; access to, 68, 188, 221, 222–4, 233–8, 255–60, 265; Bank of America, 226–9, 231, 232–43; contents

of, 178; conversion costs, 188–90; corrections to, 179, 264–8; destruction of, 238–9; EEOC guidelines, 181; evaluations of potential, 258–9; federal requirements, 248; IBM, 218–21; internal disclosures, 232–3, 268, 270–1; job-related information, 220; legal content, 239; medical data, 182, 187–8, 195, 200–4, 209–13, 245, 262–3, 266–7, 270–1; ownership of, 257; performance appraisals, 186–7, 200, 235–6, 258–9; photocopying, 239; physical security of, 234; references, 187, 219, 229, 257–8; salary and promotion recommendations, 186; security records, 259; sex discrimination and, 231; third-party access to, 188, 221, 233–4, 265. *See also* access to information; privacy legislation; privacy policies; privacy and privacy issues
Petermann v. *International Brotherhood of Teamsters,* 102
Peters, Charles, 92, 93, 95, 104
Petkas, Peter J., 91, 92, 104, 150–5
Pettis, Charles, 151
Phelps Dodge Corporation, 147
Philadelphia, 58
Philips Lamp, 385
Pickering v. *Board of Education,* 73, 94–95, 97, 98, 101, 143, 158
Pierce, A. Grace, 111
Pittsburgh, 329
plant layout, 379–80
Platt, Harry, 288
plywood co-ops, 356
PoKempner, Stanley J., 192
Poland, 354
Polaroid Corporation, 140, 142, 347
Policy Studies Institute (PSI) of Great Britain, 63
pollution, *see* environmental abuse
polygraphs, 67, 219, 249, 252. *See also* lie detectors
power, 7–8
pregnancy, 231
Presthus, Robert, 93, 104
Primack, Joel, 92, 104
Privacy Act, 29, 178, 180, 181, 182, 183, 197, 201–2, 237, 238, 248, 265–6. *See also* privacy legislation
Privacy and the Employment Relationship: A Study of Computer Use in Personnel Administration, 226–43
privacy legislation, 177, 182, 240–1, 248–9; compliance costs, 188–90; corporate view,

183–91; federal, 29, 178, 180–2, 183–6, 193–9, 201–2, 229, 237, 238, 240, 248, 265–6; state, 182–3, 249–50, 252–6, 257. *See also* federal legislation; National Labor Relations Act; privacy policies; privacy and privacy issues; Privacy Protection Study Commission

privacy policies, 179, 258; Bank of America, 238–40, 246, 247; basic principles, 251; Equitable Life Assurance Society, 244; IBM, 29, 178, 184, 214–25, 246, 247–8, 251; legislated vs. voluntary, 249–52. *See also* privacy legislation; privacy and privacy issues; Privacy Protection Study Commission

privacy and privacy issues, xiv, 21, 67–68, 175–278, 284–5; after-hours phone calls, 207; appearances, 29–31, 230, 232; collective bargaining on, 177; in common law, 179–80; computers and, 247; consumer reports, 193–9; costs of, 188–90, 241–2, 275–8; defined, 178; desks and files, 68, 71, 78, 225; disclosure of personal information, 205–6; employer efficiency and, 18–19; exempt data, 186–8; hearings and study groups on, 183, 189, 251; of job applicants, 193–9, 218–20, 226–9, 245, 247–8; Harris Poll on, 246; of management, 186–8; and occupational health surveillance, 200–2, 209–13; off-duty conduct, 67, 224, 225, 230, 291–301; physical, 207, 218; private-sector views, 183–6; surveillance, 67, 78, 206–7, 224; survey of management views, 22, 28–31. *See also* access to information; confidentiality; medical records; personnel records; privacy legislation; privacy policies; Privacy Protection Study Commission

Privacy Protection Study Commission, xvii, xix, 29, 41, 178, 182, 183, 184–92, 203–4, 248, 249; business view of, 275–8; recommendations, 249, 250; Report of, 249, 250, 257–74

private detectives, 196

product safety, *see* environmental abuse; safety; whistle blowing and whistle blowers

productivity: and participatory management, 389–95, 398, 400; pay plans, 394–5

professional autonomy, 154

professional societies, 150–4; ethical codes, 150–1; independent appeal procedures, 151; lobbying efforts, 151–2; pension

funds, 152; unions and, 153–4. *See also* employees: professional and scientific

professionalism, 86, 87, 88

profit sharing, 343, 345. *See also* benefits and benefit plans

Project for Corporate Responsibility, 339

promotion, *see* advancement opportunity

Prosser, William L., 52

Providence and Worcester Railroad, 337

Proxmire, William, 24–25, 38

proxy contests, 338–40

Prudential Insurance, 247, 251

Psychological Stress Evaluators, 252, 253–4

psychological tests, 257. *See also* employment testing

public controversy, 143, 154–5. *See also* free speech; off-duty conduct of employees; whistle blowing and whistle blowers

public employees, *see* public sector

public interest, 158–9, 347–8

public-interest groups, 239

public-interest clearing house, 142, 144–6, 147

public opinion, 347–8

public sector, 29, 51; access to records in, 197; free speech in, 73, 94–101, 158–9, 171–2; labor-management committees, 378; management, 38, 59; whistle blowing in, 94–101

Public Service Electric and Gas Company, 117–21

Pugliese, Gilbert, 154–5

race discrimination, 7, 81, 341; on job applications, 228; Supreme Court decisions on, 11–13

Rafferty v. *Philadelphia Psychiatric Center*, 95–96, 99

railroad industry: participatory management in, 337, 342–3, 344–5, 377

railroad workers, 342–3

Railway Employees Department v. *Hanson*, 168

Railway Labor Act, 168, 343

Rainier National Bank, 433

Reed, Smith, Shaw & McClay, 329

references, 187, 219, 229, 257–8; access to, 257–8. *See also* personnel records

reinstatement, 60–62

Republic Aviation Corp. v. *NLRB*, 73

Retail Clerks Advocate, 205–8

Retail Clerks Union, 205

Retail Credit Company, 198, 229

retirement, 5, 152

Reuther, Walter, 339
right to discharge, *see* discharge; employer prerogatives
right to employment, 5, 21, 46, 51, 87. *See also* entitlement view
Roberts, Norbert, 274
Roche, James, 89–90, 92–93
Rockefeller, Nelson, 183
Rockwell International, 182, 184, 378, 379
Roman Catholic Church, 306–7
Royall, Thad, 108
Ruff, Harold C., Jr., 192
Rushton Coal Mine, 381–2, 386
Rutgers Law School, 120

Saab-Scania (Sweden), 8
saccharin, 112
safety, 34–36, 70, 74, 89, 153, 154, 347; airline, 106–10; drug research, 111–16. *See also* environmental abuse; whistle blowing and whistle blowers
Safeway Stores, 378
salary, 74, 221, 240, 257, 258; lined to productivity, 394–5
sales practices, 154
San Francisco, 206
San Francisco Consumer Action, 432
Sanderson, Ron, 384
savings and thrift plans, 345
Scanlon, Joe, 384
Scanlon Plans, 343, 384–5, 386, 387
Schacht, Henry, 189
Schaeffer, Ruth G., 192
Schein, Virginia E., 192
school records, 181. *See also* personnel records
school teachers, 94–95, 96, 97, 100–1, 142, 158; *Downs* v. *Conway School District,* 96, 99; *Pickering* case, 73, 94–95, 97, 98, 101, 143, 158; *Watts* v. *Seward School Board,* 100–1. *See also* academic community
Schrank, Robert, 402
Scientists and Engineers: The Professionals Who Are Not (McIntire), 92, 104
Sears, Roebuck & Co., 345
Secrist, Ronald H., 37
Securities Acts, 417
Securities and Exchange Commission, 338, 415, 416, 417, 420
securities markets, 418
security records, 259; internal disclosure, 269–70
Seeman, Melvin, 7
Selective Service Act, 56, 71

Selznick, Philip, 4
Senate, 89; Labor Committee hearings, 6. *See also* Congress of the United States
seniority system, 7, 257, 258, 407
Sentry Insurance, 246
sex discrimination, 7, 81, 341. *See also* sexual harassment; women; women's rights movement
sexual behavior, 285. *See also* off-duty conduct of employees
sexual harassment, 117–31; defined, 127; union investigation of, 122–31
Sexual Shakedown: The Sexual Harassment of Women on the Job (Farley), 122–31
Singer Company, 331
Sixth Amendment, 73
slander, 179, 180
slavery, 49; factory labor as, 72
Smith, Robert Ellis, 205–8
Smith v. *Allwright,* 12
social and economic order, 22, 40, 41
Social Policy, 76–78
social reform: and participatory management, 338–40, 347–8, 391–2. *See also* social responsibility
social responsibility, 103, 144, 347–8, 418, 419; and disclosure codes, 429–36
social science: "displacement of frustration" hypothesis, 7; and employee rights, 5–8
Social Security Administration, 190; disability program, 201
social security numbers, 222, 238; deletion of, 185, 190–1
South Africa, 347
South Bend Lathe Company, 398
Southwestern Bell Telephone Company, 295
Soviet Russia, 354
Spain, 355
Stahlwerke Roechling-Burbach GmbH (SRB), 363
Standard Oil (Indiana), 251
state action concept, 12–13, 14, 158–60, 167–9
state courts, 13; on abuse of process, 48, 53, 54; corporate malice concept, 132–4; employee-rights decisions, 33, 35–37, 51, 54; privacy decisions, 180; whistle blowing and, 97–99, 100–102. *See also* appellate courts; circuit courts; district courts; names of states
State Farm Insurance, 198
state legislation, 12; antidiscriminatory, 4, 7; on employee access to personnel files, 236–7; "just cause" proposal, 56–58; on

privacy, 182–3, 249–50, 252, 253–6, 257.
    See also American law; federal legislation;
    legislation
steel companies: labor-management
    cooperation, 378, 382–3, 384, 386
steelworkers, *see* United Steelworkers of
    America
Steelworkers Trilogy, 156, 167
Steinbach, Sheldon Elliot, 273
Stieber, Jack, 59–64
Stillman v. *Ford*, 133, 134
stock purchase plans, 345
stockholders, 399; and constitutionalization
    movement, 22, 39, 40; disclosure demands,
    420, 421; employees as, 337–40, 344–6,
    395, 396, 397–8; privacy of, 221–2; proxy
    process, 338–40
Stollman, Israel, 153
Stranded Oiler, The, 347
Strickland, Robert L., 350
strikes, 404
Summers, Clyde W., 55–58
"Sunshine" laws, 420
supervisors, 8, 72; participatory selection of,
    380; sexual harassment by, 117–31. *See
    also* management
Supreme Court: *Alexander* v.
    Gardner-Denver, 170; *Amalgamated Food
    Employees Union* v. *Logan Valley Plaza,
    Inc.*, 12, 13, 14; as arbitration model,
    281–90; *Bell Aerospace* decision, 74; *Civil
    Rights Cases* (1883), 11, 13; *Fibreboard
    Paper Products* v. *NLRB*, 342; *Hague* v.
    CIO, 73n; *Hurd* v. *Hodge*, 168; *Jackson*
    v. *Metropolitan Edison Co.*, 14; *Marsh* v.
    Alabama, 12, 13, 14, 17, 73; *New York
    Times* v. *Sullivan*, 159, 172; *NLRB* v.
    Local Union No. 1229, 140–1; *NLRB* v.
    Maganavox Co., 161; *Pickering* v. *Board
    of Education*, 73, 94–95, 97, 98, 101, 143,
    158; *Railway Employees Department* v.
    Hanson, 168; *Republic Aviation Corp.* v.
    NLRB, 73; on retroactive seniority, 7;
    Smith v. *Allwright*, 12; *Spielberg* and
    Collyer doctrines, 156; on "state action,"
    159; *Steelworkers* trilogy, 156, 167; *Terry*
    v. *Adams*, 12; *Thomas* v. *Collins*, 73n;
    Thornhill v. *Alabama*, 73n; *Tinker* v. *Des
    Moines School* District, 285; on workplace
    free speech, 71, 73
surveillance, 206–7; recording conversations,
    67, 224; video, 67, 78; wiretapping, 206
Swarthmore College, 146
Sweden, 352, 361, 362

Taft-Hartley Act of 1947, 17
tax law, 77
Taylor, Frederick Winslow, 26
Teamsters, 378
Tektronix Inc., 330
television, 140–1
Tennessee, 378, 394
Tennessee Valley Authority (TVA), 387
tenure, 55, 59, 81, 151, 258
Tepedino v. *Dumpson*, 97
Teple, Edwin R., 171
Terkel, Studs: *Working*, 28
Terry v. *Adams*, 12
test scores, *see* employment testing
Tether, C. Gordon, 62
Textile Workers, 383
Thimm, Alfred L., 364
Thomas v. *Collins*, 73n
Thornhill v. *Alabama*, 73n
Thrasher, Bruce, 378
Times Mirror Company, 434
Tinker v. *Des Moines School District*, 285
Tomkins, Adrienne, 117–21
tort liability, 47–54; abuse of process, 48;
    third-party interference and, 48–50;
    wrongful motives, 47–48, 49
Trans World Corporation, 331
Trotta, Maurice S., 302–10
trucking, 245
Truex, G. Robert, Jr., 433
"Truth in Securities" laws, 417–18
TRW Inc., 251, 378
TWA, 331–2
Tyger, Frank, 37

unemployment, 22
unemployment compensation, 33
union activity, 46, 81, 161, 231, 341
unions, 13, 21, 71, 78, 144, 150, 315; access
    to records, 258; British vs. American
    membership, 63; and constitutionalization,
    73–75; on drug use, 292, 294–5, 296, 299,
    300; on employee privacy, 205, 206;
    employee-rights views, 5, 8, 19; European,
    358–9, 362–4; joint programs with
    management, 377–88; leadership
    malpractices, 5, 74, 363; legally protected
    status of, 49; and participatory
    management, 336–8, 339–43, 349, 359–64;
    and professional societies, 153–4; and
    sexual harassment, 122–31; and whistle
    blowing, 101–2, 153–5. *See also* collective
    bargaining; names of unions
United Airlines, 337–8, 345

United Auto Workers, 5, 153, 157, 329, 339, 351, 361, 377, 381, 385
United Fund, 206
United Mineworkers, 381
United Paper Workers, 340, 378
United Rubber Workers, 337
United States v. Seeger, 71
United States Fidelity & Guarantee Co. v. Millonas, 48–49
U.S. Civil Service Commission, 197
U.S. National Bank, 416
U.S. Steel, 378
United Steelworkers of America, 75, 154–5, 329, 331, 378, 384
United Torch Services, 206
United Transportation Workers, 337
university communities, see academic community
University of Michigan, 402
University of Pennsylvania, 381
Uris, Auren, xix, 135–9

video surveillance, 67, 78. See also surveillance
Vietnam War, 22, 71, 88, 347
Virginia Law Review, 55–58
Volkswagen, 359, 362, 364
voluntary disclosure, 415–36; vs. government regulation, 419. See also access to information; disclosure
Volvo, 405
von Hippel, Frank, 92, 104
Volcan Materials, 293

wages, see salary
Wagner Act, 17
Walker, Mary, 124–7
Wall Street Journal, 91–92, 137
Walters, Kenneth D., 91–105
Walton, Richard E., 401–12
Wantland, Earl, 330
Warren, Samuel D., 179–80
Washington, 433
Washington, D.C., 198
Washington Monthly, 92
Water Pollution Control Act, 146–7
Watergate, 22, 183, 275, 415, 416, 419, 421
Watson, Thomas J., Jr., 215, 224
Watson, Thomas J., Sr., 215
Watts v. Seward School Board, 100–1
Wayman, John G., 329
Ways, Max, xix, 79–82
Weinberg, Edgar, 377–88
West Virginia, 294
Western Electric, 389–90, 397; Material

Management Centers, 394
Westin, Alan F., 180, 188, 200–202, 215, 245–52; Privacy and the Employment Relationship, 226–43
Wharton Magazine, 401–12
Whistle Blowing (Nader, Petkas, and Blackwell), 91–92, 150–5
whistle blowing and whistle blowers, 21, 39–40, 85–90, 91, 347; airplane safety, 106–10; confidentiality issue, 100; discretion issue, 99–100; drug research industry, 111–16; economic effects of, 89–90; Ewing's view, 70, 76–77; grievance procedures and, 96–98, 103; legal view, 94–103; management view, 92–93; motive, 95–96; and organizational friction, 98–99; in private organizations, 101–3; professional societies and, 151–2; in public organizations, 94–101; reducing need for, 103–4; for sexual harassment, 117–31; steel industry, 154–5; survey of management views, 22, 37–39; unions and, 101–2, 153–5. See also disclosure; expression and dissent
white-collar crimes, 18
Whyte, William H., 46, 51; The Organization Man, 85
wiretapping, 206. See also surveillance
Wisconsin, 384
Wolf, Mary Jean, 332
woman suffrage, 69
women, 88, 339; personnel files, 231; post–World War II, 86; sexual harassment of, 117–31; in union affairs, 122, 124–31
Women's Rights Litigation Clinic, 120
women's rights movement, 4, 5, 6
Work in America Institute, 6
work hours, see hours
Working (Terkel), 28
workmen's compensation acts, 52, 213
workmen's compensation boards, 201
workplace civil liberties, see constitutionalization movement; employee rights
works council system, 358
World Future Society, 391
World War II, 86, 377
wrongful procurement, 50

Yale Law Journal, 60–75
Yugoslavia, 352

Zaleznik, Abraham, 374
Zinman, Shirley, 33

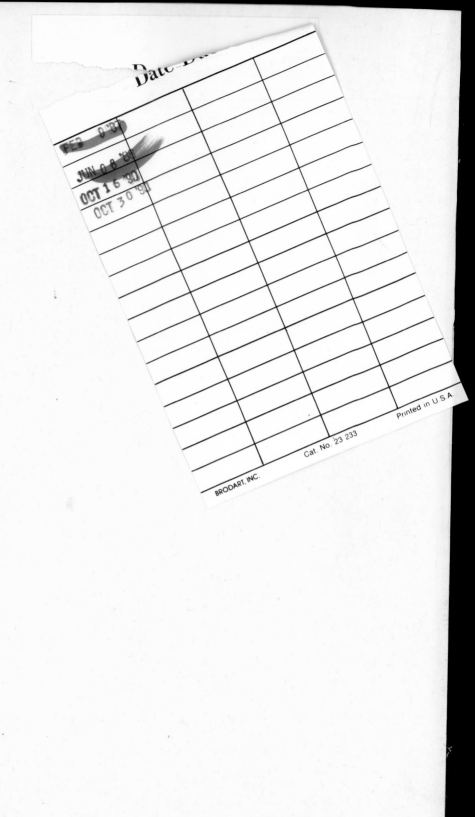

Date-Due

FEB 0 8 '8?

JUN 0 8 '8?

OCT 1 6 '90

OCT 3 0 '90

BRODART, INC.

Cat. No. 23 233

Printed in U.S.A.